WTO, Globalization and China's Health Care System

WTO, Globalization and China's Health Care System

Mei-ling Wang, Shuo Zhang and Xiao-wan Wang

palgrave
macmillan

First published 2007 by
PALGRAVE MACMILLAN
Houndmills, Basingstoke, Hampshire RG21 6XS and
175 Fifth Avenue, New York, N.Y. 10010
Companies and representatives throughout the world

PALGRAVE MACMILLAN is the global academic imprint of the Palgrave Macmillan division of St. Martin's Press, LLC and of Palgrave Macmillan Ltd. Macmillan® is a registered trademark in the United States, United Kingdom and other countries. Palgrave is a registered trademark in the European Union and other countries.

ISBN 13: 978–1–4039–4326–2
ISBN 10: 1–4039–4326–5

This book is printed on paper suitable for recycling and made from fully managed and sustained forest sources.

A catalogue record for this book is available from the British Library.

Library of Congress Cataloging-in-Publication Data
Wang, Mei-ling, 1960–
WTO, globalization, and China's health care system / Mei-ling Wang, Shuo Zhang, and Xiao-wan Wang.
p. cm.
Includes bibliographical references and index.
ISBN-13: 978–1–4039–4326–2
ISBN 10: 1–4039–4326–5
1. Medical care–China. 2. Globalization–Health aspects–China. 3. World Trade Organization–China. I. Zhang, Shuo. II. Wang, Xiao-wan. III. Title.
RA395.C53W36 2007
361.10951–dc22 2006050502

10 9 8 7 6 5 4 3 2 1
16 15 14 13 12 11 10 09 08 07

Printed and bound in Great Britain by
Antony Rowe Ltd, Chippenham and Eastbourne

For my dearest grandmother, Yang Zong,
who taught me to be honest and truthful;
never to flinch in the face of injustice and unfairness;
and to be brave and fight for the right cause and for the excluded

Contents

Acknowledgements

On completion of this book I would like to pay tribute to Dr Michael Reich, Professor at the Harvard School of Public Health, because the book was developed from a paper I wrote for his 'International Health' class, in which he inspired me to take a truly global view of public health issues. Part of this writing was also published in the *Harvard Journal of Health Policy Review*. I would also like to thank Dr Shuo Zhang for her participation in this project, and for tolerating my endless nagging about deadlines. Thanks also go to my co-author, Xiao-wan Wang, whose insights on China's health provision were useful in the completion of Chapter 5. I am also very grateful to Dr Zhang Wei for providing me with some first-hand information and insights for some of the discussions of health care provision in China.

I would like to thank the Harvard School of Public Health for teaching me the importance of considering social epidemiology in analysing a health system. The education at Harvard gave me the impetus to synthesize my ten years of research on various dimensions of social exclusion and create my conceptual framework in social exclusion in global health. This framework has expanded the perspectives and depth of this book. Some of my work in this area was later used to support the discussions of the Commission of Social Determinants of Health of the World Health Organization.

Special thanks go to the staff of the World Trade Organization, the World Health Organization, and the Chinese Embassy in Washington, DC; the China AIDS Foundation; Beijing University; Professor Lee Dzih-yuen at the University of the Sciences in Philadelphia; and Dr Howard Perlmutter, a leading global development scholar at the Wharton School of Business at the University of Pennsylvania, for providing me with relevant information and constant encouragement. The book was written in the challenging context of globalization. I will always be grateful for Dr Perlmutter's moral support.

In addition, my everlasting gratitude goes to my loved ones, especially my parents, who always give me the courage, strength and fighting spirit to proceed when the challenges seem overwhelming and the task impossible. My mother taught me always to believe in myself.

Lastly, my thanks go to my editors, Jacky Kippenberger and Mirabelle Boateng, at Palgrave Macmillan for their patience and understanding about my expanding the scope of the project to accommodate updated information.

Mei-Ling Wang

1

China's Health Care System at a Crossroads in the World Trade Organization Framework

Mei-ling Wang

After fifteen years of negotiations, China finally became the 143rd member of the World Trade Organization (WTO) in December 2001 in the WTO's fourth round of ministerial meetings in Doha, Qatar. It was a historical moment that China had awaited anxiously since it submitted its application to be a General Agreement on Tariffs and Trade (GATT) observer in September 1982.

Since 1982, China has made a circuitous journey to join the WTO. On 11 July 1986, China applied to become a GATT member. On 29 September 1992, GATT announced that China's application would precede that of Taiwan, which was crucial in gaining the endorsement of China's political apparatus for the WTO application. On 17 December 1994, China was not included as one of the founding members of the WTO because of its inability to reach agreement with other member nations, but on 1 July 1995, the WTO accepted China as an observer state. On 17 June 1998, President Jiang Zemin announced China's intention to apply for WTO membership with developing country status. The application to GATT encountered many obstacles and no understanding was reached until China had concluded five rounds of negotiations with the USA, on 15 November 1999, when China and the USA signed a bilateral agreement supporting China's WTO membership. On 19 May 2000, China and the European Union (EU) signed a bilateral agreement supporting China's WTO membership. After concluding a bilateral agreement with Mexico, China finally completed the process of bilateral negotiations with WTO members. On 17 September 2001, the WTO approved all the legal documents submitted by China. In retrospect, China's WTO membership was a worthwhile result for China and for most WTO members. China is believed to have made positive contributions to the global community, as the WTO recognized in its 2006 report, despite some concerns about issues such as intellectual property rights and dumping. These issues will continue to be debated in WTO meetings. Overall, the Chinese government's efforts to comply with WTO regulations has been highly rated.

WTO membership has brought enormous opportunities and challenges to Chinese society as well as to the global community. The major challenges are that China is required to 'have an impartial judiciary, neutral regulatory body, transparent legal prosecution system and regularity in the administration of law' (*Siyuan*, 2002, p. 4). It was noted that, to prepare for its entry, the Chinese government had to change 2,300 laws and regulations, including the abolition of 830 outdated laws. In addition, the Chinese government has instituted another 325 laws to meet WTO regulatory requirements. In this new framework, the major changes to Chinese governance to be: regulating the new economic order, improving the legal and regulatory capacity, and addressing the social and political consequences of the economic changes, including the widening gap in access to health care (see *World Journal*, 2001).

Gaining admission to the WTO framework indicates that the global community has gradually come to recognize the pulse and momentum of China's economic development because of the economic potential of the 1.3 billion population. By March 2006, China was ranked as the third-largest trading nation in the world; at the time of writing, China's GDP is growing at a rate of about 10 per cent per annum; China's exports grew by 28 per cent in 2005 compared to 2004; and China's exports in 2005 increased by 18 per cent over 2004 WTO, 2006). China's health care system is an inseparable feature of this growth and has generated opportunities and challenges to the global community.

Before we begin to analyse China's health care system, some basic facts about China are necessary to gain a deeper understanding of the major issues under discussion. China is the third-largest country in the world, with a land area of more than 9.6 million square kilometers (see the related discussions in the *Columbia Encyclopedia*, 2001–5). In terms of climate, China extends through tropical, subtropical, warm-temperature, temperate and cold-temperature zones. The country has five time zones. Most of the Chinese territory has a warm climate and distinctive seasons, characterized by a monsoon climate in most provinces. The northern and western part of China's land is characterized by steep mountains and desert, which creates harsh living conditions in the inland provinces. China is one of the most ancient civilizations in the world, with humans being recorded there some two million years ago, in the Old Stone Age (*Columbia Encyclopedia*, 2001–5). It is generally agreed that the Chinese civilization started from the Yellow River and the Yangtze River around 4,500 years ago or even earlier, when China established a monarchical system. In 221 BC the Qin Dynasty unified the feudal states and produced the first centralized dynasty in Chinese history. Since then, the centralized monarchial system that lasted for more than 2,000 years controlled every aspect of Chinese society. The monarchy ended in 1912, when Dr Sun Yat-sen, a physician educated in Hawaii, became the first president of the newly formed Republic of China.

On 1 October 1949, the People's Republic of China was founded by Mao Zedong to establish a socialist rule. Between 1949 and 1978, the Chinese political system was based on the communist ideology advocated by Karl Marx, Engels, and Joseph Stalin. From 1978 onwards, China under Deng Xiao-ping initiated market reforms to improve China's economy, which he labelled as 'socialism with unique Chinese characteristics'. This market reform was the driving force of China's social development today but, politically, the Chinese Communist Party and its ideology still provides the leadership in legislative, executive and judicial branches of the government.

Chinese culture has influenced most of its Asian neighbours and, in a span of more than 2,000 years' interaction with them, China has gradually incorporated the cultural practices of adjacent minority territories into its own. Prior to the nineteenth century, China had made significant scientific advances, resulting in the invention of the compass, papermaking, gunpowder and printing. In addition, the Chinese ethnomedical system, characterized by its comprehensive and non-intrusive nature, has provided major care for the Chinese people for the past 5,000 years. Some of these ancient medical practices still continue today in most Asian countries and territories, and their therapeutic effectiveness is currently being researched in Western biomedical institutions. In Japan, Korea, Taiwan, Hong Kong and Singapore, Chinese medicine is not 'alternative medicine'; it is as legitimate as biomedicine. Sometimes, it is used in conjunction with the Western biomedicine in hospitals. In Southeast Asian countries, it is also widely practised, especially among those who cannot afford biomedicine.

A discussion of China's health care system cannot be separated from a review of China's economy (a more detailed discussion of this will be presented in Chapter 5). China's economic reform since 1978 has had an enormous impact on its population and on the whole world. It is now a major driver of global growth and an important source of revenue for many of the top 500 Fortune companies. China's economy started out among the ranks of low-income developing countries in the 1980s and early 1990s. Its exports was just US$26 million in 1978 but by the fourth quarter of 2005 was US$109 billion. China's GDP had risen from US$147.3 billion (Rmb362.4 billion) in 1978 to 1.6494 trillion US dollars in 2004. In 2006, China was the fifth-largest economy in the world. By 2020, China aims to achieve a GDP of US$4 trillion and its GNP per capita will be between US$1,200 and US$3,000. Foreign trade accounts for 70 per cent of GDP. By October 2005, China imported goods valued at US$300.9 billion from Asia, and by 2011, it will become the largest exporter in the world. US–China relations are considered to be of great importance these days. The volume of US–China trade was worth US$2.5 billion in 1978, but by October 2005 it was worth US$170 billion. US exports to China in 2005, had grown by 81 per cent since 2001, and the USA has become China's second-largest trading partner, with 40,000 US investment projects in the country. In terms of financial performance, by 2003, the state-controlled companies had a rate of return of 10.2 per cent, while private companies had a rate of return of 15.0 per cent. The economic activities are mainly decentralized. Most life insurance, trusts, investments and securities are controlled by local government. China's economy was believed to be conducive to poverty reduction, and China has claimed to have decreased the number of population living under conditions of poverty by 200 million (Zheng, 2005).

China's position in the global economy is improving, but the country is still facing many challenges. In October 2005, the North had 55 per cent of gross domestic product (GDP) and Asia 26 per cent of GDP, but by 2030, Asia is expected to have a 50 per cent share of GDP. By 2030, the USA, China and India will between them have a 60 per cent share of GDP; China's share will increase from 13 per cent to 34 per cent of real world GDP, owning 30 per cent of US tradable securities by 2009, an increase from 8.5 per cent in 2005. By 2005, China had foreign currency reserves of US$790 billion and currently holds US$248 billion Treasury International Capital (TIC). China is also facing increasing global scrutiny of its commercial practices. For example, by October 2005, 24,000 trade infringement suits were filed against China; 167 million pirated copies of music were confiscated; 24 illegal CD production lines were closed; and 260,000 IPR (Intellectual Property Rights) infringement cases were heard (Zheng, 2005).

The Chinese government is confident that it has executed market reform successfully in overhauling the banking and regulatory systems; reducing the high level of non-performing loans (by large government injections); and the modernization of banks and the risk management and accounting system. Banks are free of obligations to extend policy loans, and move open to foreign investment (OECD, 2005). China is in the process of planning reforms in several areas: reorganizing banking and restoring financial solvency; improving the governance of banks; reducing concentration of ownership increasing non-state participation; broadening the financial market; developing equity and bond markets; liberalizing the initial public offering system; increasing the tradable portion of SOE (state-owned enterprises); improving the access of financial institutions to securities markets; fully integrating the government bond market; and preparing regulations to permit the development of institutional investors as the leading force in the capital market (OECD, 2005). In the face of seemingly successful market reform, China recognizes that the country:

- needs more balanced development outcomes: meeting the need of energy, resources, and use of talents;
- addresses the gap in development between coastal and inland provinces;

- examines the gap between city and rural villages, especially the issue of migrant workers;
- promotes sustainable development. Environmental pollution is the greatest threat to sustainable living; and
- enhances a harmonious society. Disputes over an imbalance of resources between the haves and the have-nots have led to serious social dislocation and conflict.

These issues have had a direct impact on health care in Chinese society (Zheng, 2005).

Health care has never occupied as much of the public's attention and that of the Chinese government as it does at present, the Chinese population's need for a more comprehensive health care system has never been more urgent. This need is accentuated further by the Chinese involvement in the global trading system, as evidenced in its accession to the World Trade Organization (WTO) in 2001.

Today, within China, there are still divergent views as to which party should be responsible for health care. As in other countries, Chinese society has struggled with two different ideologies of health care since the early 1900s. Some believe that health care is a public good shared by all in the society; but others see it as a commodity subject to the regulating force of the market. The Chinese communist revolution, led by Mao Zedong, claimed a victory for the former view; that is, that health care is a fundamental obligation of good government.

Globalization, as fostered by the omnipresence of the WTO, has sharpened the conflict between these two views. China's entry to the WTO is a litmus test of its ability to sustain the success of its socioeconomic reforms and to upgrade its national status by improving overall population health. The crux of this test is its ability to build a health care safety net for the largest population on earth. As a result of the free trade principle stipulated by the WTO, the stakeholders in the Chinese system will be affected differently. The factors that determine the access, quality and equality of care are intermingled with other external or internal systemic variables, such as the government's determination and political leadership, geographic location and multi-sector collaboration. The purpose of this chapter is to provide an overall background to Chinese socioeconomic reform; a synopsis of the history, policy objectives, structure and current framework of China's health care system; China's commitments to WTO and their possible impact on the health care system in general and on China's health care system in particular; critical problems and main challenges facing the health care system and health policy-making; how current policies meet the health care needs of different populations, the stakeholders in China's health care system; and a brief overview of the following chapters in this book.

History

Pre-1949

In the years between the mid-1800s and 1949, Chinese society was challenged severely by major political, economic and social upheavals. The Ch'ing Dynasty, which preceded the Republic of China (established in 1912), relinquished most of its sovereign control to imperialistic powers after several major international conflicts, the most important being the Opium War. The Opium War led to a degeneration in China's social and population health. As a result, the Chinese came to be called, 'the sickest in Asia'. China, between 1912 and 1949, was divided and ruled mainly by feudal lords or foreign colonialists. Most of the Chinese were peasants and extremely poor, whose mode of living was by subsistence agriculture, and whose livelihoods were seriously affected by the relentless threats of floods, famines, and social and political turmoil. There was no institutional health care system prior to 1949. The morbidity and mortality status was one of the lowest in Asia (*Columbia Encyclopedia*, 2001–5).

In this context, the Chinese population relied mainly on traditional medicine for health care in the early 1900s. In an attempt to improve the population's health, Chinese Nationalists attempted to eliminate traditional Chinese health care and adopt fully Western biomedical practices, such as vaccination, sanitation and antibiotics. Most of the population, however, still practised traditional health care because biomedicine was beyond the reach of most individuals. This is still true today.

1949–78

After the communist takeover in 1949, the communists, led by Chairman Mao Zedong, were determined to reduce inequalities in wealth by engaging in massive wealth redistribution. Under Mao, the state controlled all means of production to ensure equitable access to and universal availability of economic resources, such as access to food, education, housing, jobs and health care. Social and economic stability was regained in the early years of the communist government. It contributed directly to an immediate decline in mortality and to declines in fertility after 1950. From 1952 to 1982, infant mortality fell from 200 per 1,000 to 34 per 1,000 live births and life expectancy increased from 35 to 68 years (Blumenthal and Hsiao, 2005).

Chairman Mao attempted to improve the health of the population by establishing a Western-style scientific medical system. However, Mao restored traditional Chinese medicine as the primary health care system, not for ideological reasons but out of concern that the expensive Western-style health care systems might be a major burden for China's fragile economy. Mao engaged in a major effort to integrate the teaching of traditional medical literature in medical schools, and created a system of health care that aimed to provide health care to all at low or no cost. Instead of creating a national health insurance system, this system was incorporated within China's industrial and agricultural systems organized in 'work units'. In 1961, Mao created a co-operative health care system in rural villages, the Co-operative Medical System (CMS). The two major goals were universal participation and convenient access. The coverage was effective because, under Mao, every Chinese belonged to a work unit (see Dong, 2001; Blumenthal and Hsiao, 2005). It was estimated that more than 90 per cent of work units were covered by co-operative health care. In addition to 510,000 formally trained physicians, there were 1.46 million 'barefoot doctors' and 2.36 million health workers. With an average investment of US$5 for each Chinese, this was lauded by the World Bank and the World Health Organization as the most efficient system in the world. Life expectancy reached 68 years (Lo *et al.*, 2004). In this system, all individuals paid a fixed amount of user fees, commensurate with their pay scales. For those who could not afford it, the mutual support fund in their work unit helped to pay for it. This system reimbursed 80–100 per cent of the cost of prescription medicine.

The major policy directive for establishing China's public health for all was issued by Chairman Mao on 26 June 1965, in which he mandated the importance of building up rural public health infrastructure by deploying public health professionals in the villages. He also mandated an increase in hospital beds in rural areas. It was estimated that, between 1965 to 1980, about 40 per cent to 60 per cent of hospital beds were in rural areas.

During this period, China's health care system was characterized by four major principles:

1. Medicine was at the service of the people;
2. Prevention played a key role in public health;
3. Health education was carried out through mass campaigns; and
4. There was close integration of both biomedicine and Chinese medicine (Rosenthal, 1987).

Special attention was also paid to women's health, and there was a female health worker in every work unit. There were special health policies that protected women's health; for example, that pregnant women were prohibited from engaging in hazardous work. The government was the source of finance for China's health care system. This subject will be discussed in more detail in Chapter 4.

The rural health system was different from that in urban areas. China's progress in rural health between 1950 and 1979 was widely recognized across the world, and there has been a great improvement in major health indicators. The rural health system was a five-tier system, in which the use of a large number of basic-care health workers, the so-called 'barefoot doctors' from 1965 has resulted in major benefits (Dong, 2001). Beyond the primary care by barefoot doctors, there were practitioners that provided more advanced care at hospitals at different levels. The urban health care system has a more sophisticated structure, including clinics for primary care, local hospitals and provincial/municipal hospitals.

Health care reform after 1978

Health care reform in the 1980s was directly related to the market reform after 1978. The Chinese government has reduced its role in universal health care provision and let the private sector shoulder some of the burden of health provision and financing. A major reform by the Chinese State Council in 1985 included aiming to decentralize health provision and management, improve productivity and efficiency, and encourage privatization. The rapid progress in privatization and the positive economic outlook have led to increasing participation by the private sector, including by the multinationals, in China's health system. This well-intentioned reform and transition has caused many unanticipated complications in China's health system. These complications have become major social and political concerns, which will be discussed further in Chapter 5.

Gains and losses

Overall, the gains resulting from this new health care reform have been in several areas. First, it was able to contain health care costs; and second, the coverage was extended to more uninsured or underinsured people.

The health financing reform gave rise to a new set of problems, however. Government-sponsored health care decreased from 69 per cent in 1980 to less than 20 per cent in 1983, and 5 per cent in 1986. (Lo *et al.*, 2004). Health clinics or units become the private clinics of the providers. The reduced health services contributed to an increasing prevalence of tuberculosis (TB), hookworms and so on in the rural areas.

In the urban areas, fees for insurance increased dramatically as a result of the increase in the number of beneficiaries, an increase in chronic diseases, and an increase in input prices and health service prices; for example, in pharmaceuticals, new technology, or tests or treatments. A co-payments increase was a related phenomenon. The other phenomenon was the retreat of the government from financing the health care sector. It was pointed out that, in 1993, more than half of the Chinese population was not covered by any form of health insurance in urban areas. The Government Insurance Programme (GIP) and the Labour Insurance Programme (LIP) covered about 9 per cent and 40 per cent of the urban populations, (or 2.5 per cent and 11.7 per cent of the total population), respectively (Hsiao, 1995; see also Song, 1991).

It was noted that rural populations initially faced a major disadvantage in this reform. Under Mao, about 90 per cent of the rural population had access to basic health care, but in contrast during the 1980s, an e[illegible] 90 per cent of rural dwellers lacked medical coverage (Beach, 2001[illegible] reduction of health care resources from the public sector made people [illegible] to private clinics, where fees were charged for care, but the fees were ofte[illegible] beyond the means of rural populations. It was estimated that a single medical visit might cost US$20 or more, or about 15 per cent of an average farm worker's annual cash income. Yet most rural populations could not access the health care services even when they were available, as the services were mainly concentrated in urban areas. It turned out that about 60 per cent of total public spending on health was consumed by 15 per cent of the population – primarily those living in urban areas in coastal provinces. There will be more discussions on this subject in Chapter 5 (ibid.).

Because of the lack of data, the immediate effects of the retreat of the public sector from health care were not known. Yet, the most immediate effect was believed to be increasing infant mortality and maternal mortality, and the disease burden on rural populations, including increases in the prevalence of TB, hepatitis, and other infectious diseases, because of decreases in immunization rates. It was noted that, in 1999, the rural areas had a much higher infant mortality rate, of 37 per 1,000, than that in urban areas, around 11 per 1,000. In 2002, the mortality rate among children under five was also much higher at 39 per 1,000, than in urban areas: 14 per 1,000. The disparity was also noted in maternal mortality rates: the rural areas were much higher: 54 per 100,000 compared to urban areas' 72 per 100,000 (Blumenthal and Hsiao, 2005). It was estimated that, during the 1980s, childhood immunization coverage had reached 98 per cent in many areas. By 1990, at least 97 per cent of all children had received the bacillus Calmette-Guérin vaccine (BCG) against TB as well as the DPT vaccine against diphtheria, pertussis and tetanus; the polio vaccine; and the MCV vaccine against measles. By 1999, immunization rates for these diseases had begun to decline. In one estimate by the World Health Organization (WHO), BCG coverage in the population had dropped to 77 per cent and polio 3 to 79 per cent by 2001 (Riley, 2004). The disparity between Chinese and minorities regions was also pronounced. It was noted that the life expectancy in Tibet, Qinghai and Xinjiang were below the national average by 6–9 years, with higher infant and maternal mortality. ('Attention urged to people's health in Western areas, China Internet Information Centre (CIIC, 12 March 2001).

China's health care system in the twenty-first century: socioeconomic transitions and changes in health care policies

Overall, the Chinese health care system is moving towards a new era. Although Chinese life expectancy has reached 71.8 years, the beginning of

tury has witnessed major health events that directly
health care system. The exponential growth of the
IDS; the outbreaks of SARS and avian flu; the recur-
ctions in rural areas, and the rapid increase of cases of
nt a strong signal about the necessity to improve
lic health infrastructure and health care system.
rapidly upgrading its bureaucratic structure to tackle emergent challenges in the twenty-first century. The Ministry of Health retains control over the regulation of health care and provides technical supervision through an interconnecting chain of agencies reaching down to the village level (Chen, 1989). New initiatives are being proposed and piloted to address emerging issues at both regional and local levels.

Health care policy

China's health care policy is changing rapidly. The current framework is based on the Decision on Health Care Reform and Development made by the Chinese Central Committee and the State Council in 1997, which was later elaborated by the State Council. The major goal is to change the scheme of health care financing, as stated in Urban Employees' Basic Health Care Insurance Schemes. Under this new scheme, individuals are required to take on a larger burden of health care. The goals outlined are: (i) to establish a cost-sharing system to contain the escalation of health care expenditure and protect urban workers' basic health care; (ii) to allow more patient choice among providers by promoting competition and a related improvement in quality and efficiency; and (iii) to discourage monopolies in pharmaceutical research, production, marketing, consumption and increasing the quality control of drugs, and reducing costs.

The Chinese government has speeded up improvements in policy capacity in the wake of the SARS crisis. In January 2004, the government established a National Infectious Diseases and Sudden Public Health Emergencies Direct Reporting Network. This network issues regular reports to the public about major outbreaks and infectious diseases. With a total investment of US$1.5 billion, this system covers more than 3,000 hospitals, including 93.21 per cent of county hospitals and clinics, and 42.77 per cent of borough and township clinics. In 2005, an additional US$50 million was provided from central government (*People's Daily*, 15 May 2005). On containing the spread of HIV/AIDS, the Chinese government issued its 'Four-Frees' policy (1. free HIV screening; 2. free ARVs (anti-retrovirals) for HIV infected people in the rural areas; 3. free education for the HIV infected and affected orphans; 4. free counselling, blood screening, and ARV treatment for pregnant women). In addition, the government provides welfare assistance for those infected and affected by HIV. Regarding other public health threats, the government supports twelve vaccines for children, including smallpox, hepatitis B, TB, measles, and so on. New measures were taken so that 95 per cent of the population was covered by TB treatment. The early detection rate was 64 per cent. This policy was said to have increased the recovery rate from TB to 91 per cent. Blood worm treatment in villages has also contributed to reducing the infection rate by 34.6 per cent (*People's Daily*, 15 May 2005).

Several major policy directives were mandated from central government: Central Government, State Department Decisions on Strengthening Public Health Work in Rural Areas; Opinion on Establishing New Co-operative Health Insurance; and Guidelines for Bettering the Co-operative Health Insurance. These policies were designed to subsidize the new insurance system. It was mandated that, with the new system, central government will subsidize by US$1.25; local governments will subsidize by US$1.25; the registration fee is US$1.25; and user fees are US$3.75 per person annually. Central government also mandated the selection of certain cities, autonomous regions and provinces in which to pilot the project. The goal is to build a social security system against major catastrophic diseases. The major principles are: voluntary participation; central government being the overseers; government sponsorship, guidance, monitoring and organization; and achieving the dual goal of integrating poverty-prevention in health insurance and supporting the health insurance of the poor (Lo *et al.*, 2004).

Health care provision

The government remains the major provider of health care for state-affiliated enterprise employees, and these are mainly in urban areas. In the urban areas, government and private enterprises are the health care providers. The Labour Insurance Programme (LIP) and Government Insurance Programme (GIP) are the mechanisms through which health care is provided. This caused serious problems for those state enterprises that had a large percentage of older workers or retirees, who were more likely to utilize medical care than individuals in other demographic categories. Firms doing poorly financially often encountered difficulty in meeting payments. In the early 2000s, the LIP covered about 156 million people – around 43 per cent of the total urban population. In contrast, employees in government sectors have been covered through the GIP and managed by the Ministry of Finance since 1952. The GIP also covers university students and retired officials, representing approximately 24 million beneficiaries, or 7 per cent of the total urban population. In the rural areas, health care for the 900 million population is mainly via the government's public health system: disease monitoring and surveillance stations at the county level, health clinics at the township level, and health units at the village level, respectively (ibid.). These establishments are responsible for the prevention of infectious diseases, vaccination, women's and children's health, health education and so on.

Results of health reform

Despite many criticisms, the cost-saving measures in reforming health provision are believed to have achieved the following results:

- Improved efficiency. There has been an intense effort to reduce excess care among the urban population. It also asks those insured to take on greater responsibilities by increasing co-payments and user fees.
- Establishment of an independent insurance system separate from the employment-based health insurance. This has been one of the largest challenges facing the Chinese government but it is believed that some improvements have been made. This system will support employees and retirees whose health-care coverage was affected by their insolvent employers.
- The opening-up of resources to the public: state-affiliated clinics and hospitals are now accepting all clients, not just state employees.
- An increase in competition among all providers, which helps to improve the quality of services.

Major issues and challenges

China's health care system is facing very complex challenges, which will be discussed further in Chapter 5. These challenges are closely related to the changing environment of its development goals.

In the 2000 World Health Organization Report, China was ranked at 144 out of 191 countries in terms of health improvement, government responsibility and equity. It was reported that, in 2000, infant mortality was 32 per 1,000, compared to 42 per 1,000 in 1980; and life expectancy was 70 years compared to 67 in 1980. About 10 per cent of the Chinese population was infected by hepatitis A, compared to 1 per cent in the USA and Japan. There were more than 5 million Chinese affected by resistant-strain TB the second highest level in the world. The prevalence of typhoid fever and hepatitis B among infants was also one of the highest in the world. By 2010, those infected by HIV in China are likely to reach 10 million. According to the 1997 World Bank Report, the health expenditure per capita for urban residents was four times more than that for rural residents, and more than 700 million rural residents had to pay for their own health care. Adding to the burden on the Chinese health care system, the population will be ageing rapidly by 2025 (World Bank, 1997).

In this environment, overall major policy challenges are: the reaffirmation of the leadership of the government in health care and multi-sector participation; efficiency and quality of care; investing in the poor population; addressing the social determinants of health, such as education, employment and so on; ensuring basic care, vaccination and the prevention of infectious diseases; fundamental mandatory care: family planning, women's and children's health, prenatal and postnatal care, targeting infectious disease intervention (such as against TB); prioritizing health care financing; protection of health consumers; investment in diversifying health care provision; long-term monitoring (disease surveillance, monitoring major health indicators, measuring and assessing the effectiveness and efficiency in the health care system and public health); establishing regulations and legislation; health information and education, food and drug safety; health financing from both public and private sectors; and participation in the global health market. Other related issues are: central–local co-ordination of health reform; health disparity between coastal and inland provinces; eliminating provincialism; effective allocation and use of local resources; capacity building (using charities and NGOs, civil societies); and the care of socially excluded or mobile populations.

Keenly aware of the gravity of these issues, the Chinese government has actively engaged in infrastructure reconstruction since the SARS crisis. For example:

- In 2004, there were 2,425 projects for disease prevention and control, with total funding of US$150 million. These included major infrastructure building, improving emergent care, infectious disease centres and so on.
- In 2004, under the policies of PRC Infectious Disease Regulations, and Emergent Public Health Response Regulations, the central government established Rapid Response Guidelines for National Public Health Emergency Cases and Emergency Care Guidelines for Sudden National Public Events. The government also established emergent infectious disease co-ordination centres in charge of emergency care, surveillance and rapid response.
- In January 2004, the Disease Reporting and Information Network surveying 80 per cent of cities and 50 per cent of counties (including thirty-one provinces, most autonomous regions and major cities) came into operation, with guiding principles of timeliness, accuracy and predicable power.
- In 2004, China's Ministry of Health established ten national emergency care teams to respond to sudden, catastrophic events. These teams provided an effective response to an outbreak of SARS in Beijing and the Anhui Province in China, plague in Qinghai province, and to tsunami relief for the December 2004 earthquake.
- In 2005, National Guidelines on SARS Prevention and Intervention were put in place.
- Guidelines on Reinforcing AIDS Prevention and Intervention. The government invested US$100 million to develop a pilot implementation in 300 locations to reinforce the Four-Free policy, as mentioned earlier: procurement and distribution of ARVs, comprehensive HIV prevention

and intervention, surveillance and monitoring, and strengthening prevention (China Internet Information Centre, 11 May 2005).

The central government also selected several areas of high HIV prevalence, including Henan, Yunnan and Xinjiang provinces, for HIV-related health education (ibid.). In May 2005, in a special press conference, the Chinese government released its report on the progress of HIV prevention and intervention. Related tasks are: special health campaigns aimed at young people, rural populations, and high-risk populations; TB prevention, and intervention programmes. Since 2004, central government has increased its spending on high-prevalence, emergent catastrophic diseases by US$190 million, with matching promises of US$180 million from public and private donors (Wang, Y. D., 2005). There are specific issues deserving special attention, and these will be discussed further in other chapters. We provide only a sketch of these issues in the following section.

Rural health

It is already obvious to all that the most intractable task facing Chinese society in health care is how it provides different solutions for different regions, especially between rural and urban areas. Rural health care is a more urgent issue than that in urban areas, and rural areas are faced with health challenges that are different from those in urban areas. These include: extreme poverty, lack of access to socioeconomic opportunities, lack of health financing, lack of access to health care facilities, hazardous working conditions, lack of preventive care, widespread parasitic problems and other infectious diseases, food poisoning, malnutrition, and environmental pollution (Phoenix TV News, 2003).

The Chinese government had begun to address rural development issues in the late 1990s and this effort was intensified further in 2005. In the late 1990s, the Ministry of Public Health responded to the problem of the gap in health care by launching the 'Health for All by 2000' campaign, a collectively-funded (including funding from the World Health Organization) rural medical service designed to cover all farmers. In this programme, each village is mandated to contribute a set amount to the local clinic each year. Villagers would be treated free of charge or have part of their medical expenses reimbursed (interviews with Lee Shuan, official of China's Ministry of Health, 17 March 2002, Cambridge, Mass.). Between 2000 and 2006, the government has experimented further with different rural health insurance schemes. In 2005 and 2006, government has rolled out a number of ambitious, large-scale restructuring plans aimed towards addressing the social determinants of health.

Rural health is difficult to reform, however, despite these efforts. In one example, where central government was the major party endorsing an experimental scheme, rural residents were reluctant to join the rural co-operative health care insurance for several reasons:

(i) The coverage was limited and user fees and co-payments were high;
(ii) There was an imbalance in demographic participation for any form of universal health care. The young and healthy, who considered themselves to be invincible to health risks, feared that their contributions to the system were simply a waste of money; while the retirees could not wait to take advantage of any universal health care programmes that provided them with better coverage. In most cases, retirees accounted for the majority of enrollees. This creates an immediate burden on the health insurance scheme;
(iii) There was a fear of corruption by the health care providers, especially in the use of prescriptions. Some were afraid that health providers would prescribe better medicine for their families and friends, or for those who could afford higher fees, while prescribing less effective medicine for the majority of villagers;
(iv) There was mistrust of the lack of quality care in rural health care system; and
(v) Difficulties in financing the scheme limited its effectiveness. The source of financing in rural cooperative health care insurance is still central government, whose annual expenditure was US$62,500 with matching funding from local governments. In other words, public investment in this insurance is US$0.015 for every rural resident. This was tantamount to a drop in the ocean compared to what is needed to improve the situation. (Lo *et al.*, 2004).

Among these problems, the major issue remains that the majority of rural residents, especially in the central and western provinces of China, cannot afford to pay for emergent and intractable diseases. Some of these dilemmas were addressed by central government after the SARS crisis in the strengthening of new co-operative health insurance system, as mentioned earlier. Yet the government's effort had only partially addressed some of those concerns:

(i) it only provides some support for the health care of acute catastrophic diseases, not routine health maintenance. Preventive care is left to individuals;
(ii) the reimbursement system is still affected by individual factors. Decisions could be arbitrary and show favouritism. Individuals who do not receive immediate direct benefits from the system do not want to join;
(iii) user fees and co-payments are unreasonable;
(iv) there remains mistrust that health administrators might misappropriated the fund; and

(v) the low reimbursement rate. Less than 50 per cent of medical expenses were reimbursed. In most cases, the reimbursement rate was 20–30 per cent. The decision to reimburse was often affected by favouritism.

Systemic limitation

The other issue is intrinsic restrictions within the exisiting system. China's current health care programme developed from a dual-track system in regional governments: health service provision is supervised by local medical units, while financing and administration is overseen by local and central government. This limits the development of health infrastructure. Administrative officials and staff account for a larger number of employees in local health clinics and consume a large portion of revenues, especially in poor townships and villages. Local government officials often put their relatives and friends on the payroll. In the end, resources have been diverted to personnel, instead being used for medicine, equipment or facilities (Lo *et al.*, 2004; see also Wang and Chen, 2005). The health care providers lack the autonomy to make financing and resource allocation decisions.

A shortage of public health professionals and their uneven quality

China is experiencing a major shortage among public health professionals who can provide leadership in infectious disease control, community health support, testing and screening, health policy and management. A comparison with the USA is instructive here. In the health agencies in the US government, public health professionals accounted for 10 per cent to 20 per cent of all health professionals. And among health policy-makers, 50 per cent to 60 per cent are equipped with an MPH (Master of Public Health) degree. In comparison, in the health agencies in the Chinese government, less than 1 per cent of public health professionals have a Master's degree in a health-related field. After the SARS epidemic, the Chinese government intensified its public health training by supporting twenty two universities to offer MPH degrees (*Sina Finance News*, 10 May 2003).Yet more needs to be done to train health professionals to cover the vast rural areas. The other issue is that, even if providers have increased in numbers, their quality and ethical standards are questionable. Economic reform since the 1980s has encouraged increasing numbers of private clinics and hospitals but the quality of care is uneven, and increases in malpractice and patient complaints have worsened the problem (Henderson *et al.*, 1994; Hsiao, 1995).

Decreasing health financing and investment from the public sector

It was noted widely by many that the nationwide policy goal of increasing gross domestic product (GDP) was often carried out at the expense of other goals, such as public health investment (see Zheng, 2005). The reinforcement of a market-driven economy was an effective strategy to reduce the government's fiscal burden, yet it places the public health burden unfairly on those who cannot afford it. It was reported that the public carry more than 60 per cent of health care burden; in contrast, in most developed countries, governments support 60 per cent of expenditure on public health (Lo *et al.*, 2004). Health care in the government's total budget decreased from 36 per cent in early 1980s to 14.6 per cent in 2000, and government-sponsored health insurance decreased from 44 per cent to 24.5 per cent of the total social health insurance cost (Three propositions to the government to improve public health infrastructure, *Southern City News*, 2004). In contrast, individual health-care spending increased from 23 per cent in 1980 to 60.6 per cent in 2000. This rate has increased further between 2001 and 2005, and far exceeds the 27 per cent mark for most developing countries. The percentage of China's total health spending in total GDP was 0.8 per cent in 2000, and about 2 per cent in 2005, comparing to the 5–7 per cent for developing countries and 13 per cent for the USA (ibid.).

In the past, the government subsidized a substantial amount of health care even for the uninsured, thus basic health care was affordable for most of the uninsured population. Now subsidies have been reduced and service providers have been asked to shoulder a larger proportion of their budget. The service providers responded by raising their fees and charges, and, as a result, overall health care costs have been escalating at an annual rate of 20 per cent in recent years (Yuen, 1996). It was estimated that, in Shanghai, the largest city in China, the annual health care cost increase in the early 1990s was 25 per cent higher than the rate prior to 1978. The increase was in hospital-based care, drug prices, consultations, surgical operations, high-tech and therapeutic treatments (World Bank, 1989; Hsiao, 1995). It has been pointed out that the rapidly increasing health care costs, aggravated by the low coverage and poor risk-pooling capacity under GIP and LIP, have also created a major health care issue for state enterprises (Liu and Hsiao, 1995). Decreased financing also leads to low pay-rates for rural health care professionals and this further decreases the willingness of medical school graduates to serve the rural poor. The vicious cycle of reduced financing and poor efficiency, heightened pressure to make profits on the part of health providers, and the increasing prevalence of disease and illness have further burdened the health system.

Health insurance

Whether or not health insurance can be part of the solution remains to be seen. There are difficult issues that need to be resolved. First, health insurance in most cases has limited health coverage, and does not cover expensive treatment or acute diseases. Even when it covers some difficult diseases, the coverage is not sufficient. Second, the issue of the uninsured is the most difficult challenge facing Chinese society. Most Chinese do not have health insurance to begin with. And the trend toward employment-based insurance only increases uninsured populations. Under Mao, affiliation with a work unit was enough to be included in an expanded safety net. Work units provided all kinds of benefits, including accommodation, food, child care, retirement benefits, and health care support, but such benefits have been cut drastically under the new reform policy. Now private enterprises fulfil the social responsibility of providing for health care. But the new jobs created were not sufficient to cover the employment need, and the issue of floating migrants from the villages is especially problematic. Since the government relaxed its migration control policy, China's rural population has migrated in large numbers to urban settings for better employment opportunities. In one estimate, China's urban population doubled between 1978 and 1988. In Shanghai alone, by 2001, one-tenth of the population were migrant workers (Wang *et al.*, 2001).

Limited action

The Chinese government has begun to respond to the insurance needs of the urban population in recent years, but questions remain. The major issues are that health care reform in the urban setting still focuses on the employed population; and whether this scheme is sufficient to address unexpected, emergent conditions is also questionable. For example, a health insurance reform for the urban employed population was initiated in 1994. The new medical insurance system was designed to cover all of the 150 million urban employees. In this system, medical expenses were to be shared between employers and employees. Employers were asked to contribute 10 per cent of the entire staff's salaries for social medical care insurance: 5 per cent went to employees' personal medical care accounts, and the remaining 5 per cent was deposited in the 'Social Overall Medical Funds.' Employees were asked to pay 1 per cent of their monthly salaries into their personal medical care accounts. However, this rate was changed in 1999. In the 1999 scheme, the employees were asked to pay 2 per cent of their salaries to their own accounts, and employers were to contribute 6 per cent of the entire staff's salaries for social insurance. The percentage of money to be deposited in the employees' accounts was to be determined by the local government. This rate was standardized at city and county levels in 1999 (interviews with Liu Shuan, 2002, Boston, Mass.).

The major issue in health insurance is that this kind of programme is not adequate to address the needs of the chronically ill. When medical costs for an individual are less than 5 per cent of the patient's annual income, the money will be taken from the individual's medical care accounts. The Social Overall Medical Funds pay 80–90 per cent of medical expenses when those expenses exceed 5 per cent of a person's average annual income, but less than 5,000 yuan (about US$600). It was estimated that the country's average annual income for an urban employee was 6,470 yuan (US$780) in 1997. The Social Overall Medical Funds would pay 90–92 per cent of medical expenses, if the expenses exceed 5,000 yuan but less than 10,000 yuan (about US$600 to US$1,200); and it would pay 98 per cent if the expenses exceed 10,000 yuan (US$1,200). However, the Funds will not pay the bill if the expenses exceed four times the individual's annual income in cases of serious illness. The individual will have to pay out of his/her own pocket or turn to commercial medical insurance to cover the rest of the medical expenses.

Health disparity

Health disparity is the most serious social issue facing China today. It occurs mainly between the coastal provinces and inland provinces; between rural and urban residents; and between those having stable employment and those who do not, in three major areas: government health spending, health insurance and individual health spending, and access to employment or residence-related benefits (*Southern City News*, 2004). It was estimated that the rural residents, accounting for 85 per cent of the total population, access less than a third of health-care resources. A large number of health professionals, who often have to travel across difficult terrain with an emergency kit to reach the sick in villages, were often not paid for the services they provided (Lo *et al.*, 2004). It was estimated that China's rural-urban health disparity was ranked at 188 out of 191 countries. For example, government spending in rural areas was 34.9 per cent in 1993, 24.9 per cent in 1998, 22.5 per cent in 2000, a more than 10 per cent decrease in seven years (ibid.).

In 1998, the Chinese government spent 15.9 per cent of revenues in total health spending in rural areas. This was a decrease of 12 per cent compared with the previous year. In 2003, government expenditure in medical services for urban residents was US$16 per capita but only US$1.25 per capita for rural residents. The distribution pattern was also inequitable. In 2000, about 7,000 urban units (including cities and urban towns) – some 6 per cent of the population – consumed US$1,670 per capita of health insurance resources while most of the rural residents did not have any forms of health insurance. Putting this figure in context, the gap is even larger when taking into account other free health resources or fringe benefits. In 2001, the disposable income of urban residents was 2.9 times that of the rural residents. The health care resources available to urban residents – about US$81.5 per capita annually were 3.55 times more than those available to rural residents. In terms of health provision, the Chinese government has mandated that there should be between 4.5 and 9 health professionals for disease surveillance for a town of 30,000 individuals. By 2000, the reality was that each rural township usually had fewer than one surveillance professional (*Southern City News*, 2004).

In terms of the gap in public financing of health care; in 1998, the disparity in financing was ten times as much for haves' as for 'have nots'. The highest amount – US$12.5 per capita per annum – invested by the government was in Shanghai. In contrast, the lowest amount of investment was in the northern province of Henan, where US$1 was invested for each individual ('Three propositions to the government to improve public health infrastructure', 2004). This gap has widened since 1998. The lack of investment has led to an erosion in health capacity. For example, in the Dzechiao township clinic, a budget of US$2,750 supports the health care of twenty-seven villages, with a total population of 42,368. The clinic is characterized by a single room, a medicine cabinet, an emergency kit and a table, which is a typical setup for local health clinics. In terms of hospital beds, numbers decreased from 60 per cent for rural residents in 1982 to 34.2 per cent in 2001 and continues to decrease at the time of writing. In 2001, there were 6.28 beds per 1,000 population in Beijing while, in contrast, there were only 1.51 beds per 1,000 for the residents in Guelin Province, one of the poorest, in south-west China.

The increasingly inequitable access to health care has become noticeable since the 1978 reforms. The increase in health care costs has had a serious impact, particularly on populations with the lowest socioeconomic status, and the socially excluded (the unemployed, retirees, non-public-sector employees, and migrants). As mentioned earlier, both rural and urban residents felt the burden of health care. Those who benefited from the economic reforms can afford expensive, hi-tech medical treatment while the majority of the population, mainly those in the rural areas but also the unemployed in urban areas, cannot afford even basic care. It was noted that the health care equipment and facilities in some Chinese hospitals have reached the levels of those in mega-cities such as New York and London in developed countries, while the rural health clinics resemble those in the poorest of the developing countries, such as Bangladesh or Botswana (Lo *et al.*, 2004).

The disparity issue is difficult to resolve in view of the Chinese government's financial position. The government is determined to increase national health expenditure to 5 per cent of GDP by 2010, and possibly 7 per cent of GDP by 2030. Yet, given the fact that the Chinese government also has other pressing issues in hand such as rural development reform, it is doubtful whether the allocations to health care are fully on target. In a report to the National Assembly of the People in 2002, China was already showing a budgetary deficit of 19 per cent (*Le Monde*, 8 March, 2002; see also Chen, 1989).

In a nutshell, the public health infrastructure established in the early 1950s that was capable of meeting the basic health care needs of Chinese society is no longer adequate to meet the major health challenges of the twenty-first century. The prevalence of sudden outbreaks of disease (such as

SARS or avian flu), infectious diseases (such as TB, hepatitis, HIV/AIDS and STDs), or the emergence of chronic diseases (such as diabetes, cardiac disease and cancer), have become a major burden for its public health system. In the early 1990s, it was found that 23.7 per cent of the Chinese in urban settings were affected by one or more types of chronic disease, and 10.5 per cent per thousand persons fall ill in every two weeks (Huang, 1994). Changes in demographic patterns have brought some benefits to China's population health, but have also added unexpected problems to its health care system. The one-child policy that started after the 1978 economic reform and the rise in the ageing population play an increasingly important role in influencing the future of China's health care system. The disappearance of China's traditional family structure, where family members take on the major responsibility of the care of sick members, shifts the burden of health care on to society at large. The growing share of the elderly in China's total demographic structure also entails an increase in the need for health care. Effective solutions to these issues in China's health care system have not yet been found. Therefore, the major challenges to China's health care system are: fairness, equity, efficiency, resource allocation and financing. The health providers need to focus on supportive policies, financing and more equitable resource allocation in the following areas:

Providing preventive care for all demographic sectors, such as vaccinations and routine health checks, health education; addressing social determinants of health, such as education, poverty/nutrition, and access to socioeconomic opportunities; improving maternal child health care, especially prenatal care and vaccinations; increasing infectious disease monitoring, surveillance and prevention, such as for TB, HIV/AIDS, hepatitis. The surveillance system, including self-reporting and routine detection, needs to be improved; increasing infrastructure and capacity building in all geographic areas and sectors; strengthening policy and ethical capacity building; improving pharmaceutical access; and the training of health care professionals.

China's membership of the World Trade Organization

WTO membership has obviously brought some tangible benefits for China, but whether similar gains in health care are transferable are questionable. Some understanding of the WTO is in order before we examine the link between China's health care system and the WTO.

The World Trade Organization

The World Trade Organization, established in 1995, has a similar structure to the International Monetary Fund (IMF) and World Bank (Blackhurst, 1998). As of 1997, the WTO had 131 members, with applications from another twenty-eight governments, including China, Taiwan, the Russian Federation, Saudi Arabia and Vietnam, being considered (ibid.). By the end of 2001, both Taiwan and China were granted membership. A major obligation WTO membership entails is that each member state is required to have a free-market economy in which the private sector plays a major role (Yin, 1999). In short, the WTO, evolved from the General Agreement on Tariffs and Trade (GATT), is a legal and institutional foundation of a multilateral trading system. Unlike the GATT, which operated through bilateral trade agreements between nations, the WTO has a much more effective mechanism, mainly through the decisions made by dispute settlement procedures. When necessary, it can evoke trade sanctions on members that violate the WTO rules.

The WTO provides the framework for the international flow of goods and services, to secure stability in international economic relations (Blackhurst, 1998). According to Article 3 of the WTO, its major goals are:

1. Enforcing multilateral and pluri-lateral trade agreements that make up WTO;
2. Serving as a forum for multilateral trade negotiations;
3. Organizing arrangements for the settlement of disputes;
4. Reviewing national trade policies; and
5. Establishing coherence in global economic policies through working with the IMF and World Bank.

Its major concern is with the negotiation and enforcement of explicit global rules on international trade. The legal mechanism is central to the WTO. In other words, the WTO draws on international law principles in conducting its operations. WTO's key concern is how one government treats services produced in other states in relation to those within its own state (Vines, 1998).

The major principles involved in WTO's trade regulation are *reciprocity, non-discrimination* and *transparency*. The major assumption underlying these principles is that states must make trade concessions in order to get better results from bilateral trade. The mechanisms through which these principles are enforced are: the most-favoured-nation (MFN) treatment (Article 1); the national border treatment obligation (Article 9); the principle that only government contracting parties are restrained, but not private-sector actors; the no-process-measure principle; and that all trade protection must be obvious and quantifiable. So far, WTO has established rules of open trade in manufacturing, services and agriculture, and intellectual property.

However, the way that the WTO operates is not without controversy. WTO as a supernational organization is already facing many challenges. It is likely to be overburdened because of the wide range of issues it is facing (Vines, 1998). Jackson (1998) pointed out that the WTO has to work out a way to tackle the harmonization of domestic policies across countries, environmental concerns, and concerns for workers' rights. The concern about inappropriate incursions on sovereignty is a serious issue. The fact that WTO rules are legally binding and are capable of passing judgment on domestic laws, regulations, and on the practices of each individual country, has led to much debate in the United States Congress (Wachtel, 1998). In addition, the conflict between trade policy and social objectives remains to be resolved. There is also concern about conflict between environmental protection and liberal trade principles, and another problem centres on developing coherence in global trade policy-making. At the micro-level, many technical issues remain unclear. For example, there is much definitional confusion in efforts made to delineate what are considered to be governmental subsidies or measures simply reflecting a given government's priority setting in economic planning, such as through the investment in research and development (R&D) in biomedicine. What is also at issue is how one can distinguish 'restricting market access' from 'measures by individual governments to enforce national standards to protect the health of the people', such as food safety standards (see a related discussion in Vines, 1998). China had repeatedly protested at European countries' 'nit-picking' because the European Union (EU) refused to import certain Chinese products because of China having a reportedly higher pesticide residue in its agricultural products. These issues revolving around the conflict between global commercial harmonization, domestic politicking and protectionism remain to be resolved.

China and the WTO

China was one of the twenty-three original signatories of the General Agreement on Tariffs and Trade (GATT) in 1948. After China's revolution in 1949, the government in Taiwan, which was recognized as a legal representative of China, announced that China would leave the GATT system. Although the government in Beijing has never recognized this withdrawal decision, almost forty years later, in 1986, China notified the GATT that it would resume its status as a GATT contracting party. Initially, China's status of a Working Party was established under GATT in 1987, which concerned only China's trade regime for goods. In 1995, China was converted into a WTO Working Party to include trade in services, new rules on non-tariff measures, and rules relating to intellectual property rights. China became a member on 11 December 2001, after an accession process involving fifteen years of bilateral negotiations between China and WTO members, and other meetings concerning either informal or formal sessions of the Working Party (WTO Press Release, 2001).

Before its entry to the WTO, China was already a formidable trading partner in the world. In 2000, China was the seventh leading exporter and eighth largest importer of merchandise trade – exports: US$ 249.2 billion

(3.9 per cent share); imports: US$ 225.1 billion (3.4 per cent share). For commercial services, China was the twelfth leading exporter and the tenth largest importer – exports: US$ 29.7 billion (2.1 per cent share); imports: US$ 34.8 billion (2.5 per cent share) (WTO Press Release, 2001).

The entry of China into the WTO had already aroused concern among WTO members before 2001. Many believed that the WTO would not have any legitimacy if a fifth of the population was excluded from participating in its activities (Blackhurst, 1998). Most importantly, the WTO would force China to stop engaging in trade practices that had created problems for the international system of trade. However, the fact that China did not fit into any economic model also complicated the issue. Several facts were reported. Prior to China's accession, China's GDP was relatively low, approximately at the level of developing countries, but it had a very large and growing export trade surplus. That China was not a true market economy and economic planning was still decided by the central government made China's application an unusual case for WTO members (Groombridge and Barfield, 1999).

Domestically, there were many dissenting voices on China's WTO membership. The major concern was that it might entail many daunting challenges to China's nascent reform. It was believed that China had more at stake in being a WTO member than any other nation. Certainly, there are some potential benefits for China being a WTO member, the most important of which is that it can grant China more stable access to foreign markets as a result of the non-discrimination principle, and that it can prevent insulation from unilateral trade sanctions (Cheng, 1999; Groombridge and Barfield, 1999). However, as a result of WTO membership, China will have to restructure its state-owned industries. The structural changes resulting from entry to the WTO may generate a multi-layered shock to the country's system. The most serious cost of restructuring is the increase in unemployment, which is already a problem threatening Chinese society. The reform has also brought about a significant reduction in government-sponsored welfare and health benefits. All considered, China would be severely challenged by the WTO framework. Before July 2001, some believed that China still had time to consider its option of delaying entry into the WTO, but by mid-July 2001, China already made major concessions that would lead to an immediate entry (see Yin, 1999, for related discussions).

Initial reports on China's WTO membership indicated positive evaluations, but concerns were voiced by some WTO members. According to the Chinese government's own estimates, in 2002, the combined volume of imports and exports reached US$620.8 billion, an increase of 21.8 per cent (22 per cent increase for exports and 21 per cent for imports). This was a surprising result, when compared to other major economies such as the United States, Japan and the EU in a context of global recession. It was noted that China's economic output was expected to triple over the following 15 years, exceeding Japan's in 2015 and the USA by 2039. The active participation by major multinationals in China's economy after WTO membership was also encouraging to China's position. For example, Wal-Mart imported US$18 billion-worth of goods from China after 2001. Of Wal-Mart's 6,000 suppliers, 80 per cent were in China (*Newsweek*, 9 May 2005).

WTO and health care in China: a brief review

Given China's internal issues in economic development in general, and in health care specifically, WTO membership is likely to have an impact on China's health system in many areas. These include: the provision of health services; distribution of pharmaceutical products; health insurance; and other related social, cultural and economic practices. The way the WTO affects these issues is through China's compliance with its requirements.

China's commitments to the WTO are:

- China will provide non-discriminatory treatment to all WTO members. All foreign individuals and enterprises, including those not invested or registered in China, will be accorded the same treatment as accorded to enterprises in China with respect to the right to trade.
- Anti-dumping: China will eliminate dual pricing practices as well as differences in treatment between goods produced for sale in China and those produced for export.
- Price controls will not be used to protect domestic industries or service providers.
- China will harmonize its domestic laws and regulations to comply with the WTO Agreement.
- Within three years of accession, all enterprises will have the right to import and export all goods throughout the customs territory, with limited exceptions.
- China will not maintain or introduce export subsidies on agricultural products (WTO Press Release, 2001).
- Most of the trade restrictions facing foreign companies are to be eliminated apart from in selected areas, such as cereals, tobacco, fuels and minerals, and in transportation and distribution of goods inside the country, which would gradually be phased out. Regarding the protection of intellectual property rights, China has fully complied with the TRIPS (Trade-Related Aspects of Intellectual Property Rights) Agreement since its accession.
- The Transitional Safeguard Mechanism: during a 12-year period starting from the date of accession, there will be a special Transitional Safeguard

Mechanism in cases where imports of products of Chinese origin cause or threaten to cause market disruption to the domestic producers of other WTO members (WTO Press Release, 2001).

- Transparency-related commitments: China agreed to publicize all WTO-related law, and apply the law in a uniform and neutral manner. China also allows for a judicial review of the status of its implementation, such as through reviews of WTO-related administrative decisions or annual transitional reviews of its compliance with WTO-related obligations, for eight years following accession.

China made specific commitments in the following areas.

Goods

China will gradually eliminate trade barriers and expand market access to goods from foreign countries. After implementing all the commitments made, China's average bound tariff level will decrease to 15 per cent for agricultural products, whereas the existing range is from 0 per cent to 65 per cent, with the higher rates being applied to cereals. For industrial goods, whose existing range is from 0 per cent to 47 per cent, the average bound tariff level will go down to 8.9 per cent, with the highest rates applied to photographic film, automobiles and related products. China committed to eliminating some tariffs and reduce others by 2004, but in most cases tariffs are to be eliminated no later than 2010 (WTO Press Release, 2001).

Textiles

China followed the rules applied to all WTO members to end quotas on textiles by 31 December 2004, but a safeguard mechanism will be in place until the end of 2008 permitting other WTO member governments to take measures to deal with domestic market consequences resulting from competition with Chinese textile products (ibid.).

Agriculture

China had agreed to limit, (but not to eliminate) its subsidies for agricultural production to 8.5 per cent of the value of farm output (as per Article 6.4 of the Agriculture Agreement) and has agreed to apply the same limit to subsidies covered by Article 6.2 of the Agriculture Agreement (ibid.).

Services

China has agreed to comply with WTO rules in several sectors. On telecoms, China agreed that foreign service suppliers will be permitted to establish joint venture enterprises, without quantitative restrictions, and provide services in several cities. The cap for foreign investment in the joint venture is no more than 25 per cent. By December 2002, China allowed foreign business to expand to include services in other cities but the ceiling for foreign investment was set at 35 per cent. Within three years of accession, the maximum amount of foreign investment was to be no more than 49 per cent. Within five years of accession, China would completely eliminate geographic restrictions (ibid.).

Banking

China would permit foreign financial institutions to provide services in China without client restrictions for foreign currency business. For local currency business, by 2004, foreign financial institutions were permitted to provide services to Chinese enterprises and in 2006, foreign financial institutions will be permitted to provide services to all Chinese clients.

Insurance

China would permit foreign non-life insurers to establish a branch or a joint venture with 51 per cent foreign ownership. Within two years of China's accession, in 2003, China would allow foreign non-life insurers to be established as wholly-owned subsidiaries. At the time of accession, foreign life insurers were already permitted 50 per cent foreign ownership in a joint venture with any chosen partners. For large-scale commercial risks, reinsurance and international marine, aviation and transport insurance and reinsurance, China permitted, at the time of accession, the establishment of joint ventures with less than 50 per cent of foreign equity. By 2004, the foreign equity share was increased to 51 per cent and, by 2006, wholly foreign-owned subsidiaries will be permitted. More details will be provided in Chapter 2.

China had also agreed to some overarching principles underlying WTO operations. These are non-discrimination and market access.

Non-discrimination

China has committed to reviewing its framework of laws and regulations governing trade in goods and services that discriminate against multinationals in certain sectors at both central and local levels. For example, most-favoured-nation treatment is extended to government procurement or services. In the past, China has charged a higher tariff for imported products in certain sectors, such as in pharmaceuticals, chemicals, some liquor products, and some commercial services. In the first year of China's WTO membership, China made required tariff reductions, mainly for information technology products, chemicals, motor vehicles and parts, wood and paper products, and many agricultural goods, including beef, dairy products and citrus products, among others (United States Trade Representative, 2002, p. 3). China has reviewed more than 2,500 trade-related laws and regulations for WTO consistency. By mid-2002, it had reportedly repealed 830 of these laws and regulations and amended 325 more (ibid.). China has devoted considerable effort to restructuring related government ministries and agencies. In addition, the country has engaged in a major educational effort in training central and local government officials and state-owned enterprise managers regarding both the requirements and the benefits of WTO membership.

Market access

China has increased market access for foreign service suppliers in the sectors of financial services, telecommunications, audio-visual services, tourism and travel-related services, construction and engineering services, educational services and environmental services (ibid.).

Trade in services

Among all sectors, the WTO regulations on trade in services has serious implications for health care. The trade in services is regulated mainly through the GATS (General Agreement on Trade in Services). National treatment in the GATS requires that 'each member shall accord to services and service suppliers of any other Member, in respect of all measures affecting the supply of services, treatment no less favorable than it accords its own like services and services suppliers' (Article 17:1) (quoted in Snape, 1998). For the present, services are categorized into 161 sectors, such as legal, R&D on natural sciences, real estate, postal, and rail transport.

Trade in services takes up a considerable share of domestic economies in most industrialized countries as well as in international trade in goods and services. According to the WTO, by 1994, world trade in commercial services had reached US$1.1 trillion and was growing at an average annual rate of 8 per cent (Krueger, 1998, quoting WTO, 1995). Trade in services are subject to the least restricting regulations in the existing WTO framework because, first, the range of services is very broad and might vary from one country to another in terms of content, quantification and types. Second, services tend to be location-specific in their production or consumption. Not all services are easy to regulate. The barriers to trade in services depend on the nature of the services (see Krueger, 1998). Some service categories can easily be subjected to regulation, such as banking and telecommunications, while others, such as health services, are difficult to regulate. Third, services are sometimes subject to cultural tastes. Since health care involves different social, cultural and individual preferences, the WTO principle of non-discrimination and no subsidy would be difficult to apply. In addition, the definition of health services is ambiguous. In all countries, the public sector provides subsidies to health care, and most governments impose strict regulations in terms of foreign providers' entry to the health care market. If health care services were defined as commercial goods, individual governments would have to give up their control over the sector, which can become a major political landmine in virtually all societies. Lastly, it would be hard to 'harmonize' the conflict if trade in services were to be intersected with other political issues, such as immigration. For example, under the free trade principle, should Nation B allow migration of health care workers to Nation A without inhibition if Nation B can supply the labour force at a lower cost? Theoretically, free trade implies some freedom of movement of labour; however, in reality, free movement of labour is difficult to tackle in the existing framework.

A general concern voiced by the health care community about the WTO's expanding influence over health services focuses on the commercialization of all health services. According to Eaton (2000), Article 6.4 of the GATS is being strengthened so that it is likely to lead to a more restrictive practice of trade policies in the health sector. Under this conceptual framework, the possible legal tests would include outlawing the use of non-market mechanisms. In health care, for example, these mechanisms include cross-subsidization, universal risk pooling, solidarity, and public accountability in the design, public funding and delivery of services. If these mechanisms are seen as being restrictive to trade, the domestic policies of national governments would have to conform to the WTO definition and outlaw these practices in their service provision. If not, those governments are likely to be subject to trade sanctions under the WTO dispute panel process. Despite the objection from most health policy planners to this idea, many believe that the WTO is moving towards imposing the market reform obligations on all health-related services and processes (Eaton, 2000). In this scheme, the role of market forces has become an increasingly important determinant in this debate. Eaton (ibid.) pointed out that the service industries account for two-thirds of the EU's total exports, and half of all foreign investment from the EU to other parts of the world. The EU reportedly manoeuvred the delay of China's WTO membership because China failed to approve a licence to a European health insurer to operate its business in China. European insurers were said to be waiting to capitalize on the potential market presented by China's cutting of government welfare benefits and the consequent increase in health care and pension costs for workers.

Can health services be excluded from the current WTO regulations? The answer to this question is complex. According to GATS Article 1.3(b), services are defined as 'service except services supplied in the exercise of governmental authority'. If this article is interpreted narrowly, health services cannot escape the WTO framework of liberalization and deregulation, since health services have the potential to include a large commercial component. This trend bodes ill for all developing countries, including China. For now, the voluntary nature of GATS allows countries to retain national sovereignty over public services and to devise their own domestic regulations in the pursuit of public policy objectives, such as universal health care, public safety, and enhanced quality of service. However, the Working Party on Domestic Regulation members have constantly reviewed related suggestions, and are moving towards a tighter regulatory framework (ibid.). China, for example, was forced to open up its health services sector by the end of 2003 because of the WTO requirement. The dispute over the privatization of water since 2001 has been another litmus test on divergent views of liberalizing the service sector in the WTO framework.

The impact of the WTO on China's health care system

How is GATS going to affect China's health services? Applying the GATS rule, the WTO can demand that China privatizes and deregulates its health sector. For decades prior to the reforms, enterprises in China had functioned as a social safety net for much of the citizenry. Many large, state-owned companies maintained day-care centres, kindergartens, elementary and middle schools, universities, stores, post offices and local police stations (Groombridge and Barfield, 1999). But this system has been experiencing a lot of strain since the reforms started in the late 1970s. Many state-owned companies have declared bankruptcy because of the government's insistence on enforcing a merit-based performance system. If the position of the state-owned companies continues to be aggravated, the safety net is also likely to be downsized. When the government retreats from its position of providing affordable health services to all, employees would have to buy the services from private insurers at a higher cost. For a society used to receiving subsidized health care, the consequences may be dramatic. This change is likely to have both measurable and immeasurable impacts on Chinese society. This will be discussed in later chapters of the book.

Major actors in China's health care system

The possible reduction of the government's role in the provision of health services is likely to change the dynamic of the major players in the health care sector. China's entry to the WTO provides a golden opportunity for private health providers, especially foreign insurers, to gain a foothold in the large health services market. The potential of the Chinese market is the major incentive for these foreign players. Chinese citizens spent about US$20–30 per capita on health care annually prior to the year 2000 and, as we shall discussed later, this amount is increasing rapidly; in comparison, Americans spent more than US$3,600. And many expect that this expenditure will increase substantially when China's proposed health-care coverage extends to the majority of the population (Chao and Tyson, 1997). In addition, the state project entitled 'Health Care for Every Rural Resident by 2000', initiated by the Ministry of Health, instituted a three-level network of care by hospitals and health centres. Together, they provide much more extensive health care than the previous services for the 70 per cent of China's rural population. According to the calculations of some foreign businesses, the volume of health care provision in China has much room for expansion, and at the time of writing, China does not have the capacity to meet the demand for this expansion. It was estimated that the number of health-care institutions and personnel, relatively small on a per capita basis by US standards, can expand to a larger capacity with approximately 60,000 hospitals, 2 million doctors, 600 medical colleges and research institutes, and 800,000 other medical service facilities (ibid.). Also, since the biomedical hospitals are now under a great deal of market pressure to be profit-orientated, the need for high-tech medical products and treatment procedures is rising at a significant pace, despite the fact that this trend is going to benefit only a minority of the population. These changes will continue to have an impact on the dynamic of the major actors in the system. A number of actors, detailed below, will decide the volume of supply and demand in the health sector.

Multinationals

Multinational health care businesses are likely to be the largest beneficiaries if the WTO imposes a more rigid regulatory framework for the GATS article. If these businesses can gain entrance to China's health market, they are likely to be strong competitors in China. As mentioned earlier, the Chinese government is in the early stages of reforming its health care system, and the growth potential in this market is virtually unlimited. Related questions are then: Which part of the health services market would be open? Would multinationals be able to compete with local producers? How about the health education or training institutions? If the health insurance and related services are forced to be open, the difficulty lies in whether or not WTO members would be able to reciprocate in their own domestic markets to accommodate the Chinese. Among the majority of WTO members, the government plays a significant role in regulating health care provision in its domestic market and, in many cases, the government is the dominant player in the health care system. Given the WTO's general non-subsidizing principle in trade, opening the health sector is tantamount to asking most governments to withdraw their authority in health provision. If they cannot enforce this principle themselves, how can they demand that the Chinese government does so? Again, this would trigger a much more complex philosophical debate on many issues, such as the nature of health care, the primacy of national sovereignty over the power of a supernational organization, and so on. If China is forced to open up its health services market to the multinationals, would the Chinese government have the political leverage to demand that other nations open up their market to Chinese medicine, acupuncture or alternative treatment services? The advancement of the multinationals in China's health services market is predictable, but there remains the question of how far they can go. And the question also remains as to what benefit the presence of multinationals has to Chinese society besides the obvious profit motivation? Which part of the population would benefit from the improved quality of the health services provided by the multinationals? These issues will be explored in later chapters.

The government

The socialist orientation of the Chinese system makes it difficult to carry out a risky experiment in health care that would leave a large number of unattended underprivileged citizens. Achievements in public health in China have earned the government solid support from its political base – the rural and urban working populations, but a drastic reform moving in the direction of reducing subsidized benefits is likely to erode this support, and ignoring the needs of the underprivileged population might lead to social unrest. The government will need to engage in a political 'cost–benefit' analysis before it decides which sectors should be opened to private providers, if they have the power to determine this at all in the current WTO framework.

The urban population

The urban population is expected to benefit from the opening of the health care market because it is obvious that foreign health businesses have targeted them as their primary customers. The fact that the size of Chinese urban middle class is larger than the total US population offers a large market potential for foreign health providers, and there is added advantage from increasing income levels, and openness and exposure to Western lifestyles among urban residents. The urban populations of Shanghai, Beijing and Shenzhen enjoy a standard of living comparable to that of Hong Kong, Singapore or Taiwan. Given their buying power, they are more likely to use the health services or high-tech treatment for major health problems. The opening of the market would provide more quality services to meet their needs. Another reason that explains the concentration of health services in urban centres is that it is easier for the multinational health insurance businesses or service providers to build their business networks on the basis of the marketing and information infrastructure already in place in these cities. However, a major problem, as mentioned earlier, is that there is also a widening gap between the haves and have-nots within the urban population (information from a talk given on 29 June 2001 by Dr Wenkang Zhang, Minister of Health for China). And have-nots in cities face similar dilemmas to those in rural areas. Given their mobility and close physical contact with other at-risk populations in the city, they are more vulnerable to infectious diseases, such as HIV, TB, and hepatitis B, C and D.

The urban poor can become the greatest threat to public health if their health needs are ignored.

The rural population

The rural population – the core supporters of the communist revolution and the focus of Chairman Mao's zeal – need the most attention from policy-makers once China opens its health care market. There is also market potential for domestic and foreign stakeholders. Given the wide range of income gradients within this population, the majority of peasants will need major subsidies from the government for their health care needs, while a small percentage of 'rich farmers' will benefit from the opportunity to access quality health care provided by the market. Yet it is important to note that this latter small percentage might be by no means small when judged by Western standards. Overall, the most important issue facing rural health care is its cost. At the time of writing, health care is already too costly for most Chinese (Chen, 1989). If the foreign health care businesses are allowed to enter China, prices are only going to increase, because of the capital cost of high quality medicine, services, marketing and so on. If the government removes all free basic care services, or charges an unreasonable level of user fees, it will be a total disaster to this population, who deserve the most attention in health care reform. However, the challenge also offers opportunities. Policy-makers might be able to develop a model of health provision for this population that meets the criteria of universality, equality and affordability if they reform the current provision and put a larger emphasis on prevention. The introduction of market forces by allowing multinationals to enter this framework might be one way of improving access and quality of care for the rural population.

The medical technology/pharmaceutical industry

The foreign pharmaceutical/medical technology industry, especially from the USA, is faced with a number of opportunities after China's entry to the WTO. Several facts are relevant here. In terms of medical equipment, according to an estimate by the US Department of State (2001), China offered the second-largest medical-device market in Asia (after Japan), totalling more than US$4 billion for 1999. It is now the third-largest in the world for high-technology equipment like CT (computed tomography), nuclear medicine, MRI (magnetic resonance imaging) and ultrasound equipment. Imports of such equipment accounted for 40–50 per cent of market share, with the USA being the largest importer (with a market share of 37–39 per cent of the total imports), followed by Japan and Germany. The growth rate in this area is expected to continue at a rate of around 10 per cent. By 2005, the Chinese market was already the largest for the USA and other Western stakeholders in this area. The growth rate is likely to double by 2008 (KPMG, 19 January 2005).

This foreign presence in the high-tech sector of health care in China can have complex consequences. On the one hand, it might spur the development of the indigenous hi-tech industry, as in biopharmaceuticals, for example. It is estimated that the Chinese biopharmaceutical industry will grow at 12 per cent, or even higher, annually for a some years. On the other hand, this trend might stymie China's fledgling biopharmaceutical industry. It would bring about realignment and integration, as has already occurred at a rapid pace since the start of the 2000s. What has already occurred is that the domestic companies have sought an alliance with domestic or international partners, and many have been phased out of the market because of lack of competitiveness.

Overall, foreign multinationals have already been major beneficiaries since China's economic reform. According to one estimate (US State Department, 2001), from 1990–9, the Western pharmaceuticals market grew by almost 20 per cent annually in China, and China was ranked as a top market by multinationals by 2005. Western pharmaceutical companies have made major inroads into the Chinese market and have consolidated their sales. For example, joint-venture drugs account for more than 60 per cent of the drugs market. However, despite the large profit margins they enjoy, the foreign companies still complain about the many obstacles they face that prevent them from taking an even larger market share. For example, some argue that recent reforms, aimed at containing health care and pharmaceutical costs, have led to a reduction in their comparative advantage.

The health care reform the Chinese government has embarked on since the 1990s was designed to reduce health care costs for both the government and the Chinese public. In late 1996, China's State Development and Planning Commission (SDPC) proposed price/profit controls on drugs to regulate the pharmaceutical market, and these controls came into force on 1 December 1998. The reform measures included the government's publication of a National Essential Drug Bulletin, which lists all drugs that are available for state reimbursement. Other related reform measures were: larger individual contributions for health insurance coverage, the prospect of individual choice for hospital services and healthcare products, and new retail outlets for medicines.

The price-control measures raised strong objections from the USA, the European Commission (DG-I), and Switzerland, that the new pricing regime had violated the WTO's 'National Treatment' principle. The US State Department pointed out that this practice unfairly promotes domestic companies by listing only those foreign drugs that did not have a domestic substitute, and that the reimbursement system was also said to favour domestic medicines. PhRMA, the representative of US pharmaceutical interests, also voiced a strong complaint. Citing what had happened in Guangdong, it was concerned that this cost-cutting policy was likely to spread to all regions in China (US State Department, 2001). (In Guangdong, the local government had limited increases in sales of medicines by Chinese 'medical units' to a maximum of 15 per cent annually. It further directed 'medical units' to limit their purchases of imported and foreign joint-venture pharmaceuticals to no more than 30 per cent of total purchases. This measure was said to have led to a sharp fall in sales of imported and foreign medicines.)

In all, the PhRMA in the late 1990s accused China of violating WTO rules in: (i) the 'national treatment' principle; and (ii) GATT Article III: 4, the WTO Agreement on Trade-Related Investment Measures (TRIMs). The proposed Chinese regulations were said to (a) promote 'import substitution'; (b) establish different and less favourable pricing schemes for imported pharmaceuticals; and (c) to provide preferential treatment for certain Chinese-made products. In addition, it protested that the proposed regulations violate the transparency requirement of the WTO. The PhRMA took the position that the price and profit control regulations place research-based US pharmaceuticals in a severely disadvantaged position in China's rapidly expanding market.

Foreign companies have also complained about the inefficiency of the drug distribution system, which increases costs to retailers. The new tendering system in the procurement of drugs that is being implemented in some regions is said to have had an unfavourable impact on imported and joint-venture drugs. Yet, these claims should be placed in the framework of the juxtaposition between multinationals and domestic players, because domestic manufacturers have also complained about unfair competition from multinationals because, in order to gain higher profit margins, hospital staff and physicians were recommending the more expensive foreign brands to patients.

Because of these developments, the US pharmaceutical industry and its European counterparts would prefer China to be an active and constructive player rather than a distracting force. Many believed that WTO accession had forced China to open up its distribution system to enable private and foreign firms to operate there.

Despite these complaints, however, the foreign pharmaceutical companies were in fact the beneficiaries of a legal reform. A new law passed by the Chinese National People's Congress on 28 February 2001, has standardized the pharmaceutical drug procurement and distribution system, to further encourage open market competition in the industry and to deter drug counterfeiting. The new law, a reaction against the government's recent decentralization initiatives that have put pharmaceutical regulation under the control of provincial government agencies, was designed to provide stricter controls on price management, manufacturing registration, import inspections, and law enforcement. This new law has moved China closer to the standards of the WTO. It will give foreign companies a competitive advantage over Chinese producers through their expertise, better product quality, and marketing knowledge. Other regulatory improvements in the pharmaceutical sector since 2001 will also improve the positions of both the multinationals and the domestic producers in good standing; this will be discussed in Chapter 3. In the light of this, China's WTO membership has no doubt benefited the foreign pharmaceutical companies. As long as multinationals capitalize on their strengths in R&D in biomedicine, and their know-how in distribution and marketing, it will be some time before domestic players are strong competitors in those areas. This will be discussed further in Chapter 3.

The Chinese indigenous health care industry

On the domestic side, the Chinese pharmaceutical industry is experiencing large-scale changes that may threaten its survival. These challenges had been obviously daunting after the WTO opening. In 1999, their gross domestic output value was US$23 billion, increasing by 21 per cent over the previous year, but many companies have also experienced losses and overproduction. By 2005, it was obvious that domestic players were finding it increasingly difficult to maintain their profit margins. The structural reform in which the government is engaging in more than 6,000 pharmaceutical companies was designed to correct this problem by improving their efficiency and competitiveness. The comparative advantage of the domestic industry is in non-branded generic production and Chinese herbal medicines, while the major disadvantage has been the lack of quality control on counterfeit medicine. It is uncertain whether Chinese domestic industries can cope with the competition after the WTO framework becomes stronger in China. The domestic industries are likely to lose the biomedicine market to the foreigners; however, if they adhere to their strongholds, such as the traditional Chinese medicine market and integrated care, they are likely to gain in the long run because of the two-tier medical system in China, which gives traditional Chinese medicine an equally prominent role in health care.

It is premature to dismiss completely Chinese potential for R&D in health care development, however. In 2004, Chinese scientists developed an AIDS vaccine that entered Phase I clinical trials. At the same time, they also developed the SARS vaccine, the first in the world, which began Phase I clinical trials. By March 2006, the Chinese government had approved some ground-breaking cancer drugs, based on advanced biomedical technology.

Besides the obvious challenges in legal, commercial and trade issues in health service provision, health insurance and pharmaceuticals, there are many other social, cultural and ethical issues that will have to be addressed when the WTO rules begin to affect the Chinese health care market. For example, how can the Chinese government balance public health objectives with the business model of health care operations? How can Chinese government utilize the market mechanisms to improve China's health care system without increasing health inequity? How can the government tackle the growing gap between the 'haves' and 'have-nots' in health care provision? The rapid improvements in living standards in the major cities already deters health professionals from working with the poor in rural areas. How can the government channel health care services and resources to rural areas to prevent the gap from widening further? What is the potential risk to China's public health system of a large, uninsured population? What are the political ramifications of having such a large uninsured population? How would China be able to negotiate compulsory licensing or parallel imports in the WTO framework for the HIV infected populations, or other subpopulations affected by incurable or chronic illnesses who cannot afford medication? How would the emphasis on profit-making affect medical practice? For example, since the economic reform began, some hospitals were said to be refusing to service patients who could not afford to pay. How would the availability of advanced medical technology affect society in some already controversial issues? For example, is the availability of sex-selection screening likely to further disrupt the sex ratio in the population, since most families prefer male children over female? And for the insured population in urban settings, will they abuse the system because of easy access and affordable fees? Or will there be an oversupply of services for this population? Would the convenient availability of biomedicine change the health maintenance behaviour of the Chinese culture which, for thousands of years, has subscribed to the idea of 'prevention over intervention'? These emerging issues demonstrate that the social, cultural and political challenges to the Chinese society resulting from the overhaul of its health care system in the wake of the Chinese entry to the World Trade Organization have the potential to be enormous.

Overall, China's entry to the World Health Organization is likely to affect is health care system in a significant and unprecedented manner. The benefits of improving quality in the biomedical sector of health care for some subpopulations will be measured against potential losses in other areas. The foreign pharmaceutical companies are likely to gain because of their financial clout, superior biomedicine products, and expertise in the distribution of the products. Some urban populations might benefit from the change, because of rising income levels and easier access to biomedical facilities in the cities, but what would be the major losses to the victims? Given the possibility that the major beneficiaries in China's health care system are likely to be the foreign health providers and some urban populations, what impact would this trend have on Chinese society and on the policy-makers? The government will have to address the health care issues of the vast rural population who do not have the financial capacity to meet the rising user fees but who need the subsidized health care most. Most important of all, China's entry to the WTO raises a fundamental question about how we define health care in relation to other commercial services as well as to social and cultural needs in the policy-making process. It also forces us to address the philosophical issue about how health care as a public good should be safeguarded in the conceptual framework of free trade. If health services are subject to the prevailing WTO framework, how can the government enforce its authority to ensure the widely honoured principles of universal and equal access for all in the health care system? How does a given government resolve the contradiction of improved quality in health care resulting from WTO membership and the widening gap between the rich and poor? And most importantly, how the market opportunities afforded by WTO membership are used in the most positive manner to address these contradictions and dilemmas in the current system? A thorough analysis of these issues in the WTO framework will be offered in the following chapters.

In summary, the ensuing chapters aim to provide a comprehensive overview of China's existing health care system and to offer specific discussions of the sectors of health insurance, pharmaceutical access, and health care provision in the WTO framework. Chinese WTO membership presents an excellent opportunity for policy-makers, health practitioners, economists, global business operatives, communities and social critics to examine the force of globalization in shaping social, political, economic and cultural practices, and the way in which these practices affect health care. The challenges to the existing Chinese health care system are not unique to the Chinese society; they are also relevant to other developing countries who are facing similar concerns. In discussing the possible impact of these challenges on Chinese society, this book aims to encourage an innovative conceptual framework that aims to provide ingenious solutions for the policy-makers and those practitioners who operate within the WTO framework. I hope it will also disentangle the puzzles and conflict brought about by the negative impact of globalization.

Chapter 2 is entitled 'The WTO and China's Health Insurance Sector'. The goal of this chapter is to present an overview of China's health insurance sector, its advantages and disadvantages, and how WTO rules affect the legal and regulatory framework of the health insurance market; the dynamics of the domestic insurance market in terms of the leverage of domestic insurance companies *vis-à-vis* that of the foreign companies; the rural–urban gap in access to health insurance; and public versus private funding mechanisms. Detailed analyses are provided on the operational framework of the health insurance market, the comparative advantages of different players, and the impact of changing market conditions on Chinese populations under WTO rules.

Chapter 3 is entitled 'The Global Pharmaceutical Industry and China's Position'. The purpose of this chapter is to examine the prospects for the global pharmaceutical industry, China's pharmaceutical industry and its position in the global market, and major advantages and challenges facing China's pharmaceutical sector.

Chapter 4 is entitled 'The WTO and the Present and Future of China's Pharmaceutical Industry'. This chapter examines WTO and TRIPS rules relating to the pharmaceutical industry as a whole; WTO's challenges to regulatory and legal systems in China (especially surrounding the patents issue), pharmaceutical quality control, price control, and the potential of Chinese herbal medicines; and the WTO's overall impact on the development of indigenous pharmaceutical and bio-tech industries.

Chapter 5, entitled 'WTO, Hospital Reform and Health Service Provision in China', discusses the ways in which the WTO affects health service provision in China. It provides information on the current health needs of the Chinese population, trends in health care spending, the distribution of public and private health services in the urban and rural populations, legal and regulatory stipulations on health service provisions, and monitoring mechanisms on malpractice and quality control. It examines current legal and policy changes in investment in hospitals and assesses the positions of foreign ventures *vis-à-vis* local investors in their arrival in the health care provision market under WTO rules.

Finally, Chapter 6 is entitled 'The WTO and Challenges and Opportunities for China's Health Care System'. This chapter provides a long-term assessment of China's health care system within the WTO framework, and addresses the following issues: (i) the status of China's WTO membership and its macroeconomic and development outlooks; (ii) the capacity of the current health care system to meet the changing health needs of the population; (iii) capacity building in improving the quality and quantity of health care provision; (iv) an assessment of the initial impact of China's WTO membership on its health care sector; and (v) China's potential to participate in the global health care market.

2

The World Trade Organization and China's Health Insurance Sector

Shuo Zhang and Mei-ling Wang

The WTO and health insurance in China

It has been widely recognized that both opportunities and threats exist for developing countries in the globalization of health goods and health services in the WTO framework, yet the positives of opening up the insurance sector as a whole are likely to outweigh the negatives. This is particularly true for health insurance reform in China, for several reasons:

(i) The socioeconomic reform has given rise to an increase in income and the need for an improved safety net, such as protection for health, unemployment, unexpected disasters, pensions and so on. The need for health insurance has never previously been felt so acutely across all segments of Chinese population;
(ii) Improved health insurance programmes are beneficial to all stakeholders, including the government, multinationals, domestic actors and, most important of all, the Chinese people themselves;
(iii) Health insurance has a social purpose that is deeply rooted in the Chinese cultural psyche and socialist ideology, and most important of all, it is vitally linked to China's social stability; and
(iv) Health insurance is deemed to be an important policy objective and is likely to affect the Chinese government's political capital.

The recent announcement of the entry of American International Group, Inc., into the Chinese market has intensified the interest of global insurance stakeholders in the vast potential of the Chinese insurance market in general, and in health insurance area in particular. It is predicted that health insurance will be the core business for most insurance companies. The AIG, founded in Shanghai in 1919, was the first foreign insurer to embrace the Chinese market during Deng Xiao-ping's economic reform after 1979. It is the only company that controls 100 per cent of its Chinese subsidiaries. By 2002, it had licences for eight cities, offering mainly life and property/casualty insurance, and another four cities offering only life insurance. It operated through the American International Assurance Company and the American International Underwriters Insurance Company. Having the bulk of its business in life insurance, the AIG is the largest insurer in the world, with revenues of US$108,905 million, profits of US$10477 million and assets of US$853,370 million by 29 May 2006. It averages about 12.4 per cent returns to investors. AIG's entry into China will be a formidable challenge to other large insurers, such as Berkshire Hathaway, AllState, Hartford Financial Services, St Paul, Travelers', and Nationwide. For the present, AIG is permitted to issue group contracts for life insurance, personal accident and health insurance, and other products (see ABC News, 2006).

China's WTO commitments

On its accession to the WTO, the Chinese government made several commitments in health insurance sector. These include:

(i) Foreign non-life insurers can establish branches or joint ventures in China. In a joint venture, foreign equity was allowed to control 51 per cent of the business. Since 2003, wholly foreign-owned subsidiaries of life insurers have been permitted to establish their operations without a Chinese partner. Foreign life insurers are allowed to establish joint ventures in China, but their equity should be no more than 50 per cent.

(ii) Geographical restrictions will be relaxed. Foreign enterprises are permitted to provide services in other cities. When China first joined the WTO in 2001, foreign life and non-life insurers were only permitted to provide services in Shanghai, Guangzhou, Dalian, Shenzhen and Foshan, but from 2003, those companies that are already providing such services are allowed to expand into another ten cities. In addition [in 2001 the Chinese government decided that, starting in 2004,] foreign non-life insurers were permitted to provide identified services in specified areas, but this limitation was abolished after 2 years. Before 2003, foreign life insurers were only allowed to provide individual insurance, but from 2004 they were allowed to provide health insurance, group insurance and pension/annuities insurance, to both foreigners and Chinese. Business licences have been issued to foreign insurers with no quantitative limits since 2001.

(iii) Qualifications (the prudential criteria) for entry are stipulated. Foreign insurance companies have to originate from a WTO member nation and have to have more than thirty years' experience. They should have established a representative office for at least two consecutive years in China. A company's annual assets value should be more than

US$5 billion prior to its application to enter China. In addition, the home countries of insurers are required to have a sound financial regulatory and supervision system (*People's Daily*, 23 November 2001).

(iv) The Chinese government will lift restrictions on other insurance products. For example, the China Insurance Regulatory Commission worked towards removing remaining barriers to foreign insurers, such as the right to offer motor vehicle third party liability insurance by 2005. Foreign companies are now allowed to establish wholly-owned foreign life insurance businesses ('Insurance market to keep WTO promise', China Organization Net, *China Daily*, 24 May 2005).

China's insurance market

China's insurance market offers a major potential for growth. Estimates vary depending on the source, but the rate of growth has averaged about 10–15 per cent in revenues since early 2000 and is likely to grow at a faster pace. Compared to the gross value of US$77.4 million in 1980 and US$19.2 million by 2000, the total value of premiums reached more than US$33.82 billion in 2005, about 2.3 per cent of GDP value (*China Insurance Almanac*, 1999). China's insurance market, according to an estimate by Swiss Reinsurance, is likely to expand to more than US$200 billion ('China's risk revolution', *Radio Free Asia*, 29 May 2006). Mass layoffs boost insurance industry. Growth in life insurance, property-liability insurance and health insurance is widely anticipated.

China's potential in insurance market in general is unlimited. While most of the savings pool of US$1.3 trillion in China was on pensions, education, medical care and accident provision, only a small percentage was for insurance. The insurance penetration was 3.34 per cent by 2004, which was low by global standards, and the premium per capita by 2005 (density) was US$27.78, compared to the world average of US$360. In addition, the insurance industry accounts for only 2 per cent of its economy, compared with 11 per cent in Japan and 8 per cent in the USA. Less than 5 per cent of Chinese households have home insurance; most vehicle coverage is just 30 per cent; and about 65–85 per cent of the population do not have health insurance (ibid.).

Both domestic and multinational insurers are likely to benefit from the opening up of the insurance sector. For now, the multinationals share less than 3 per cent of the insurance market. By 2005, there were about thirty-seven foreign insurers in the Chinese market, the major multinationals being the German Gerling-Kohzern Allegemeine Versicherungs AG and Allianz; Swedish Surrch Insurance Company; CNP from France; Transamerica Occidental Life from the USA; the Commercial Union Assurance Co. PLC, and the Royal & Sun Alliance Insurance Group PLC, from the UK; and Shanghai-based JV with French AXA ('China unveils WTO details on opening insurance market', *People's Daily*, 23 November 2001). Most of the multinationals have averaged more than 30 per cent annual growth over more than twenty years. This growth has been rapid, especially in the affluent coastal areas. For example, AIG has grossed more than 30 per cent in life insurance premiums. By 2005, the multinationals' business accounted for about 2.5 per cent of the insurance market share and it is estimated that, by 2010, they will have gained about the 10 per cent of the market share. The Chinese government has encouraged the entry of multinationals into the less affluent inland areas (*China Daily*, 2005). By 2005, there were sixty-nine insurance companies, five insurance groups and holding companies, four insurance asset management companies, and 1,317 professional insurance intermediaries in China. It was noted that, among Fortune 500 companies, forty-six were insurance companies, and among these, twenty-seven had a presence in China. As mentioned earlier, AIG was the first and only foreign company to be approved to sell life and property insurance in China. ING Insurance, a division of Netherlands ING, opened its first representative office and received its JV life insurance permit in 2000. The potential of Chinese domestic insurers cannot be underestimated either. These include: PICC, China Life Insurance and China Reinsurance (the dominant three), the Life Insurance Department of the Central Trust of China, Taiwan Life Insurance Co. Ltd, the Prudential Life Assurance Company Ltd, Cathay Life Insurance Co. Ltd, Nan Shan Life Insurance Co. Ltd, Kuo Hua Life Insurance Co. Ltd, Shin Kong Life Insurance Co. Ltd, Fubon Life Assurance Co. Ltd, Global Life Insurance Co., Ltd, Mass Mutual Mercuries Life Insurance Co. Ltd, Shinung Life Insurance Co. Ltd, and the Far Glory Life Insurance Co. Ltd (*Economy Watch*, 2001).

China's health insurance system – past and present

Although the insurance industry is still in its infancy in China at the time of writing, the concept of insurance is not new in China (D'Arcy and Xia, 2005). China saw its first insurance company, Canton Insurance Society, established by British and Indian businessmen in South China in 1805. In 1865 the first Chinese-owned insurance company, Yi He Insurance Company, began operating in Shanghai; and the Chinese-owned Commercial Bureau of Insurance, formed in 1875, had some influence on China's insurance scene. By 1914, about nine Chinese insurers and 148 foreign insurance companies, who controlled some 80 per cent of the business, were operating in the Chinese market. The First and Second World Wars generated a boom in China's insurance industry: by 1948, there were 241 insurance companies operating in China, including 178 Chinese insurers and 63 foreign companies (ibid.). Between 1949 and the 1980s, Chinese PICC (under the People's Bank of China) monopolized China's insurance industry and it was not until 1988 that the monopoly was broken, when Ping An Insurance Company established a shareholding company (ibid.).

The economic reforms of 1978 gave a major impetus to the growth of the Chinese insurance business. By early 2002, China had granted twenty-two licences to companies from eleven countries, five branches licences for AIG, and two for the UK's Royal & Sun Alliance and France's AXA, among which seven were for property and sickness/accident, and fifteen for life insurance (including the five American insurers: Chubb Insurance, John Hancock Mutual Life, Transamerica (ARGEON), New York Life and MetLife). By the time China was granted WTO membership in 2001, there were thirty-one insurance companies operating in China, including seventeen foreign and fourteen domestic insurers (ibid.).

In retrospect, the founding of the People's Republic of China in 1949 gave birth to a comprehensive health care system, which include state ownership of the insurance industry. Under the socialist regime, the Chinese government played a dominant role in the provision of health care. Most hospitals or health care institutions were owned and financed by the government. The charges made by the health service were much lower than the full cost, and controlled by the government.

In 1952, two health insurance systems were launched in urban areas. The first, 'public insurance' (PI), covers government employees those employed by public institutions, and college students. Almost all the health services received by the insurees are free of charge or can be reimbursed. The second insurance plan is the 'enterprise worker health insurance' (EWHI). Most enterprises have their own health facilities, which vary in size, and provide health care services for their employees. The operating costs of these health facilities are factored into the enterprises' total production cost. The health insurance of enterprise workers is mainly tied to the enterprise's production performance. These two insurance plans once covered the majority of the urban population before the 1980s.

In rural areas, where 70–80 per cent of China's population live, a co-operative medical insurance system (CMS) was set up almost overnight through its strong promotion by the communist government at the end of the 1950s. The CMS was largely financed by collective funding, along with a small portion from farmers' contributions. In the 1970s, its golden age, CMS covered over 90 per cent of villages. The administrative management system in rural China was on three levels: village, township and county, and the rural health care system was based on this. Each village, the most basic unit of rural society, was to have a clinic, at least one village doctor, a midwife and a nursing assistant. The housing, equipment and salaries of the health workers were all financed by the CMS.

Since the 1980s, when China was switching from a centrally planned economy into a market economy, China's government reformed the health system. On the supply side, the government is no longer able to finance the thousands of nationwide health facilities. It has been estimated that central government decreased its share of health spending from 32 per cent in 1978 to 15 per cent in 1999, and some responsibility for health care was transferred to local authorities (Blumenthal and Hsiao, 2005). Market financing has now over taken government subsidy as the main resource of hospital revenue. The government has also loosened its control over prices. However, the freed-up prices still do not reflect the market value of the services, which results in distorted behaviour among health service providers, such as financing hospitals by prescribing more drugs and more physical tests, especially tests with high-tech equipment.

As for the demand side, the lack of containment of consumption has turned the state insurance plans into a major financial burden for the government. At the same time, because of the increasing bankruptcy of state-owned enterprises and the growth of self-employment and private enterprises, more and more workers are losing their EWHI coverage. So, starting in the early 1990s, the government conducted experiments in two medium-sized cities, Jiujiang and Zhenjiang, attempting to integrate two urban insurance systems into one universal urban safety net, covering government employees, state-owned enterprise workers and employees of private enterprises. In 2000, the government required all cities to introduce this new insurance system to their populations following the form of the pilot model used in the two cities. However, according to Zhang Zuoji, the Minister of Labour and Social Security: '33% of China's cities are yet to submit a plan on reforming health insurance for their residents, while 58% of cities are yet to implement such a plan' (*Chinaonline*, 2001). Overall, at the time of writing, about 50–60 per cent of the urban population is covered by health insurance. In a nutshell, as mentioned in Chapter 1, the Chinese government has attempted to insure the urban population by requiring employers to provide insurance for disasters and individual medical savings accounts, the latter requiring a deduction of some 10 per cent of individuals' annual wages. After individuals have exhausted their funding from their savings account, the remaining expenses are largely paid by the disaster insurance (Blumenthal and Hsiao, 2005). This scheme is not without its problems, however. For example, the employers might refuse to pay, or find legal loopholes to avoid fulfilling their obligations; the floating population is usually not covered; and coverage is not extended to family members (see ibid.).

In rural areas, alongside the land reform that started in 1978 and began China's twenty years of economic reform, the collective economy collapsed, and the CMS. Although the government and international organizations have been trying to restore the system to some extent in rural areas, the coverage has dropped to some 10–15 per cent today. When agriculture was privatized, more than 900 million poor villagers lost their health insurance (ibid.). The government has tried various experiments to support the health insurance of the villagers and its efforts deserve a mention. For example, in 2002, a universal plan was attempted. In this plan, the government paid US$2.50 per rural villager for basic care, with each individual making a contribution of US$1.25 per year. These plans provide a very crude form of inpatient care, without covering primary care or medicines. This insurance plan is under revision and modification to include both insurance and services through public and private financing (ibid.).

Obviously, there is a remarkable disparity between urban and rural areas in terms of the health resource distribution. Eighty per cent of all the health resources and 60 per cent of the total public health resources are located in cities. Only 20 per cent of the total health resources are allocated to rural areas, where 70–80 per cent of the population live. (China Ministry of Health, July 2000) As discussed earlier, the disparity is also reflected in major health indicators.

Regulatory capacity

The Chinese leader Deng Xiao-ping's economic reform in 1978 invited the return of private health insurers to the Chinese market. The Chinese regulatory authorities have also made changes to accommodate the reforms. The relevant regulations for insurance are: 1983 Regulations on Contracts for Property Insurance and 1985 Provisional Regulations on the Administration of Insurance Enterprises mainly regulated domestic stakeholders; the 1992 Provisional Measures on the Administration of Foreign Investment was to address issues for foreign insurers (D'Arcy and Xia, 2005). In 1982, the PICC (People's Insurance Company of China) was established and had a monopoly position in the Chinese market. In 1998, this was reorganized into 3 PICC companies: China Life Insurance, China Property Insurance (PICC), and China Reinsurance. In 1992, AIG was granted a permit to offer life insurance and property insurance in Shanghai. Another sixteen large insurers were allowed to enter the Chinese market. On 1 October 1995, China's insurance law was effective to regulate China's insurance industry, which also covers foreign insurers. In November 1998, China's State Council established the China Insurance Regulatory Commission as the official overseers of insurance business. The policy environment has been developed in such a way that it is conducive to the operation of multinationals.

Overall, the guiding principles of the Chinese Insurance Regulatory Commission are promoting development and regulation, and preventing risks. It has embarked on several important activities:

(i) it has consolidated the reform and explored various ways of improving effectiveness;
(ii) it has improved the ownership and governance structure, and spearheaded privatization by restructuring and reorganization;
(iii) it has updated means of capital accumulation by floating on domestic and overseas stock markets. In doing so, it has allowed the flexible use

of various financial instruments, such as stocks, and has expanded the means of using insurance funds;

(iv) it has improved the efficiency of the utilization and management of insurance funds by establishing insurance asset management companies and employing professional management and a centralized system of operating the funds;

(v) since 1998 it has strengthened the regulatory capacity of the Administrative Licensing Law by reinforcing the Measures for the Implementation of Administrative Licensing and improving examination and approval procedures;

(vi) it has reinforced the legal capacity to monitor and assess insurance operations;

(vii) it has attempted to improve the risk management system; for example, it has strengthened the five lines of defence of risks, including 'the corporate governance as the basis, the regulation of solvency as the core, on-site inspections as an important means, the regulation of funds utilization as a key function and insurance guarantee funds as protection' (Wu, 2006, p. 8); and

(viii) it aims to establish a comprehensive framework that contains an internal risk management system; a solvency reporting system; a financial analysis and monitoring system; a regulatory intervention system; and a follow-up remediation system.

Overall, guided by a framework of solvency, corporate governance and market behaviour, China's Insurance Regulatory Commission aims to transform itself from being a business-scale, regulation-orientated organization into a risk-based, dynamic regulatory body; from being a reactive regulatory body to being a pro-active regulatory agency focusing on the risk management needs of business; from 'the ex post result-oriented regulation to the ex ante process-oriented regulation' (ibid., p. 5). In this framework, the core businesses identified are enterprise annuity, agriculture insurance, health insurance and liability insurance.

The status of health insurance

With its 1.3 billion population and rapidly expanding economy, China today is the largest potential insurance market in the world. China has experienced a steady economic growth since the 1980s. The average annual increase in GDP is 9 per cent and the yearly increase in per capita consumption around 7 per cent. Individual wealth is also growing. The total amount of private bank savings has reached 10,000 billion Chinese yuan (US$1,250 billion) (National Bureau of Statistics of China, 2005). This exceeds the amount owned by the government. While personal income has increased, the insurance market in China still remains underdeveloped, evidenced by its low insurance density and penetration (D'Arcy and Xia, 2005). For 1998, the share of all premiums in GDP was only 1.49 per cent for China, whereas it was 4.38 per cent for Hong Kong and 13.87 per cent for South Korea (Swiss Re/Sigma, 2001). As mentioned earlier, by 2005, the share was still only about 2 per cent. Only about 10 per cent of the rural population and half of the urban population are currently covered by certain kinds of health insurance. The majority of the huge population has no coverage. The government-sponsored health insurances still dominate the market, while the role of commercial insurance companies is still trivial. They usually operate locally and offer insurance packages to targeted groups (Wu, 1997).

The impact of globalization and the WTO framework

In this already crowded market place, what will be the major impact of global trade liberalization in the Chinese health service system?

First, increased foreign investment will increase access to new technologies and enhance information and knowledge exchange among health professionals. This will also update Chinese management methodologies and expertise, which will eventually improve the quality of health care.

Second, foreign investment and increasing privatization in the health services will help to improve the efficiency and productivity of health facilities through intensified competition and the likely merger or purchase of unsuccessful facilities. This will increase the range and diversity of products offered to consumers.

Third, increased foreign investment could create employment opportunities. Yet joint ventures or direct foreign investment will bring stiff competition to domestic suppliers as the state insurance gives more freedom to insurees in their choice of hospital. Some local hospitals will find it hard to survive.

Fourth, international experience has shown that top doctors and skilled health professionals often switch to commercial providers to gain a better working environment and higher salaries (Business Coalition for US–China Trade, 2001). 'A terrific deal for American Coalition for US–China Trade'. And 'the for-profit providers tend to avoid unprofitable services and unprofitable patients' (Kuttner, 1996). The public sector will have to accept whatever is left. The increase in health expenditure is likely to accelerate as the growing foreign investment implies more use of high-tech equipment, advanced technology and expensive imported medicine.

Prospects

As mentioned earlier, after China's entry to the WTO, China's large market is open to foreign insurers. Geographical restrictions on operations are being lifted, and the scale and scope of insurance that the foreign insurance companies are allowed to offer will be expanded (*Chinaonline*, 'US, China conclude WTO negotiations', accessed 26 June 2001). The foreign insurers will be able to offer commercial-risk policies worth US$50,000 or more, down from at least US$120,000 currently. Starting in 2005, the foreign insurers will not be required to cede 20 per cent of all commercial-risk re-insurance policy premiums to state-appointed reinsurers (Ahmad, 2000). In the longer term, multinational insurers will be allowed into 'group, health and pension lines of insurance, representing 85 per cent of total premiums. Licences will be awarded without economic needs testing or limits on number of licences (Kuttner, 1996). Additional regulatory relaxations are also on the way in the years to come. China's effort at opening up the health insurance sector has been widely recognized despite the remaining technical and operational issues.

The accelerated entry and perhaps fast growth of foreign insurance companies in the Chinese market is being anticipated. China now has almost all the elements that are of interest to foreign investors: a large population, a low proportion of which is covered by private insurance; increasing wealth but a small percentage of GDP spent on health insurance; a growing upper/middle class; and accelerated privatization. Moreover, the accession to the WTO is also bringing in multinational corporations who are seeking health insurance for their China-based employees. In fact, some big insurance companies have already positioned themselves well for the upcoming huge market. For example, according to the *Chinese Medical News* (*Chinaonline*, 2001, an independent website providing business information about China), the CIGNA Corporation has helped to set up health insurance testing centres in Beijing, Shanghai and Nanjing. According to the report, officials from China's Ministry of Labour and Social Security told the media that 'the testing system will provide opportunities for understanding the development of the medical and health insurance system, as well as provide a reference for building up China's qualification testing system for medical insurance professionals' (*Chinaonline*, 'CIGNA Corp. helps set up health insurance test centre in China').

As the majority of the Chinese population does not have any insurance for their health expenses, the introduction of additional insurance would be welcome, especially for certain groups, such as multinational companies, the upper-class population and private enterprises. Higher-income populations have reportedly shown resistance to joining the new urban Health Insurance Plan that has been promoted by the government, as they wanted to have higher-level benefits – for example, the coverage of health services overseas. Foreign commercial insurance might be able to meet the needs of these people. However, as was found in Dr Stocker's study about American insurance penetration in Latin America, for-profit insurance is likely to attract healthier, younger and wealthier patients, and skim out the sicker and older patients to the public sector (Stocker *et al.*, 1999). Also, since most of the uninsured population are farmers and urban unemployed who cannot afford private health premiums, it is unlikely that foreign commercial insurance will make contribution to increasing the coverage of these insolvent populations.

In addition, health insurance is part of a larger reform programme in health care, and this reform is likely to contribute, in a major way, to a more efficient health system. The Chinese government has adopted a series of measures to tackle problems in the health system. It has turned its 60,000+ public hospitals into three different types: government not-for-profit hospitals, non-government not-for-profit hospitals, and private for-profit hospitals, and set up different subsidy, taxation and price control policies for each type. The government not-for-profit hospitals now take responsibility for providing basic health care for the vulnerable population (*Chinaonline*, 26 June, 2001). The government has also proposed to correct the distorted health service pricing system to correct the distorted behaviour of health care providers. The Chinese government has stated its objectives of controlling drug sale discounts provided to hospitals, clinics and other end users. Pharmaceutical enterprises are not permitted to offer discounts higher than 5 per cent (China Ministry of Health, July 2000). The government is on the way to enforcing the financial separation of pharmacies and hospitals, and the effects of these policies are yet to be examined. In this scenario, an improved health insurance programme that offers a strong third-party payment system is likely to help the government correct these issues.

The opening up of health insurance should have a constructive impact on the effectiveness of China's own domestic health insurance sector. The entry of commercial insurance will certainly bring much-needed management and risk adjustment experience into China, where the insurance markets are still underdeveloped and insurance professionals relatively inexperienced. It was noted that, in China's insurance market, there has been a lack of creative products; there is an imperfect product structure; there needs to be major improvement in the management framework and mechanisms; an open flow of information is lacking, quality and effectiveness needs to be enhanced; the governance structure of insurance companies needs to be improved, especially in transparency and accountability; and the risk assessment system needs to be modernized. Accordingly, increased spending on administrative costs and return to the investors are also expected, as has been seen in other developing countries (Wu, 2006).

Overall, the prospects for China's health insurance market are largely positive for one very important reason: the supportive policy, social and cultural environment. The new stipulation by President Hu Jintao to build a harmonious society pays particular attention to the building of a safety net, in which health insurance is an important element. With this political thinking, Hu's government aims to build 'a society defined by democracy, the rule of law, equity, justice, sincerity, amity, vitality, stability, orderliness and the harmonious coexistence of man and nature' (ibid., p. 3). Historically and culturally, the Chinese government is expected to shoulder the responsibility of providing a universal safety net for the Chinese people, long espoused in the philosophies of Taoism and Confucianism, the mainstay of Chinese cultural thinking. Since the 1978 reform, concerns about the rising costs of health care have been major social and political issues in China. The government has made intense efforts to address these problems, and has acknowledged its inadequacy in this. The arrival of private health insurance is likely to provide much-needed help for the Chinese government and society in tackling the issues of access and equity in health care.

Overall, the challenges can be summarized as: (i) the need for an improved legal and policy environment; (ii) the need for managerial capacity; (iii) the need to increase health care penetration among excluded populations and remote geographical areas; (iv) the need for a diverse range of products; (v) the need for public–private partnership; (vi) the need for synergy between domestic actors and multinationals, especially in complementing each other in financing and distribution; and (vii) the need to establish an insurance culture in China (see D'Arcy and Xia, 2005, for some of the discussions).

Recommendations

In an era of globalization, China has no option but to take up the challenge of reforming its health sector, including health insurance. The government can do several things to minimize the possible negative effects of WTO entry and enhance the efficiency and effectiveness of health insurance provision. The macroeconomic and macro-social factors are intricately linked in complex ways.

The government's role in the new era

The Chinese government will continue to play an important role in health services and insurance in different ways. The government has not only provided finance for health facilities, but has also been involved in the micro-management of those facilities, setting the prices for the services, controlling the purchase of equipment and even overseeing the appointment and removal of personnel. Now, in a changing economic and political environment, it is time for the government to adjust its role from being in charge of everything to become an effective macro-manager. Since the late 1980s, the government has been trying to cut back financial subsidies and escape the huge financial burden it assumed decades before. In this era of globalization, the privatization of the health services in China is unlikely to stop. The government should focus more on building a competitive environment by formulating and enforcing the legislation, regulations and economic incentives. The health facilities and institutions should be allowed the autonomy to function and progress in this environment as long as they comply with the law and regulations.

Equally important, the government should stick to its obligation to provide health insurance for the underprivileged, especially the poor, to enable them to gain access to health services. With the private sector taking over more financial responsibility, the government will be able to focus more of its resources on the most important areas, such as public health, prevention of disease, basic medical services, and the alleviation of poverty. The most important issue for the government is how to assure the equity and quality of health care and ensure access to health care for vulnerable populations. This will be discussed further in Chapter 5. After all, 'governments have a fundamental responsibility to ensure universal access to good quality health care according to people's needs, and not according to their ability to pay' (Ahmad, 2000).

Resolution of the main problems in the health market by building a strong, competitive, efficient and effective health insurance sector

As discussed above, the distorted behaviour of health providers, such as the overuse of medication and high-tech diagnostic devices, is a major challenge for the government. According to the SDPC, 30 per cent of total drug use is unnecessary (US & Foreign Commercial Service and US Department of State, 1998–9). Since pharmaceuticals account for 50 per cent of total health care costs, unnecessary prescriptions make up 15 per cent of total health care costs. This problem can only be corrected by a balance between the government's role and that of the private health insurance sector, mainly through the revision of its health care pricing policy. The Chinese government has realized this, and has launched a series of policy measures. Some are already in place; some are still on the way. While most measures are geared to eliminating incentives for drug overuse, the government has to encourage health insurance companies to play a balancing role. The insurance sector will have to play a pivotal role in health care financing.

The role of state health insurance

Although the two state health plans (PI and EWHI) only covered 15 per cent of the total population, they used two-thirds of public health expenditure. As the Chinese government is expanding the two plans into universal health insurance covering all urban areas, more population and more health resources are expected to be covered. Thus this state insurance could be an effective means of government control and management.

For example, as the biggest insurer, the government has the leverage to negotiate low wholesale drug prices that will eventually be beneficial for the people. Through its purchasing and reimbursement strategy, the government can also affect the behaviour of health service providers; promote the rational use of drugs, diagnostic devices and technology; and encourage the use of generic medication. Furthermore, the government can achieve, or at least get closer to, health care equity by subsidizing or directly providing health insurance for the vulnerable population. One of government's new reform policies is to impose a tax on for-profit hospitals. This tax income could be used to provide preventive and basic health care for the people who are most vulnerable to the anticipated rise in health care costs following WTO entry.

The cost-effectiveness and import of technology

Despite debates over trade globalization, free trade will definitely promote information exchange and technology transfer among countries. As China opens its doors to embrace the information and technology inflow, there is a need for government to be cost effective. High technology may mean an advanced diagnostic ability and better health outcomes, as well as higher costs. Technology transfer is very important for domestic R&D and the advancement of a country's science and technology; however, when it comes to large-scale application, it is also important to take into account affordability and appropriateness. Given that the annual per capita health expenditure in China is one-tenth of that in the USA, China will have to think carefully about what technology is appropriate to transfer. The Chinese government should institute a strategy that promotes research on cost-effectiveness and includes such analyses in its decision-making procedure with regard to health care technology. Public and private insurance should also take into account issues related to technology transfer and cost-effectiveness.

Systematic and psychological readiness for a new era

After entering the WTO, the legislation, the regulation, the ways that the government functions and the ways that the market operates should be adjusted in order to harmonize with the rules of globalization. This will not only affect the economic behaviour of markets and individuals, but will also have an impact on many other aspects, such as lifestyle and sociopolitical structure. Although this won't happen overnight, or in one year, it will come eventually. Are the Chinese, particularly the government, psychologically ready for the changes? The old system has been in place for decades in China. Most urban citizens are still accustomed to free or low-priced health care; hospitals are not used to competition. The adjustment and redistribution of interests and authority require the psychological preparation of society. The building of an insurance culture as part of a safety net, for example, is an important step in this psychological building process.

Overall, as China is now determined to move on to the global stage, it is time for the Chinese government to position itself, create a framework of balance among other key players in the health sector and, very importantly, to help prepare Chinese citizens for a new era of competition and commercialization. To formulate and publicize new legislation and new regulations to regulate health consumption and provision behaviour through a third-party payment system would be the priority. In this picture, the health insurance sector will be able to affect behaviour at both ends. Without a healthy and competitive health insurance sector, China will continue to be affected by those problems that have plagued its health care system for decades. The health insurance reform will benefit all stakeholders if they are ready to adjust themselves to the new framework and capitalize on their niche markets. The multinationals will probably gain in the middle-to-high-income market; the local insurers can gain in the middle-income populations in the cities and in inland remote provinces; while the government will have to increase its financing and payments for excluded populations, including the floating populations, villagers, underprivileged populations in the cities (elderly, unemployed, those affected by chronic diseases and illnesses, the disabled, and dislocated, poor women and children). Public-and-private partnership in a creative form that uses market mechanisms but addresses socialist goals of equitable access – that is, a true 'capitalist system with socialist characteristics', might offer a possible solution in insuring and assuring the health of Chinese people.

3
The Global Pharmaceutical Industry and China's Position

Mei-ling Wang

Discussions of China's pharmaceutical industry in the WTO framework cannot be separated from an analysis of the global pharmaceutical industry. The global pharmaceutical industry has never played a more important role than it does today in addressing the mortality and morbidity of global populations, given the threatening increase of global pandemics and emergent health issues, such as HIV/AIDS, avian flu, SARS, TB, hepatitis and debilitating chronic diseases (cancer, diabetes, Alzheimer's disease and so on). Global developments will inevitably have an impact on the position of the Chinese pharmaceutical industry as China is integrated into the global market by the WTO. The purpose of this chapter is to examine prospects for the global pharmaceutical industry, China's pharmaceutical industry and its position in the global market, and the major benefits and challenges facing China's pharmaceutical sector.

Potential of China's pharmaceutical market

China's potential in pharmaceutical development is widely recognized; it is expected to become the fifth-largest drug market in the world by 2010. Growth will be driven by factors such as an increasingly ageing population, the increase in life expectancy, the large market size (urban and rural), government support for restructuring the highly fragmented industry, and improved IPR policies. Beyond demographic factors, it is obvious that the market reform has led to the emergence of a large middle class (the size of the total US population). This middle class is health conscious and has an expanded range of health needs. Yet the potential of the health care market has not been fully realized. According to a global estimate in 2000, the average pharmaceutical consumption in the globe was US$50 per person: including an average of US$300 in the USA, US$400 in Japan, and US$40–50 in middle-income countries. In comparison, China in 2000 spent an average of less than US$10 per person and was therefore believed to have much room to grow. Rising incomes and fast-paced economic growth is likely to change this picture, however. It was noted that China's pharmaceutical market was worth US$19 billion in 2000 and will increase to US$60 billion by 2010, with more than US$24 billion in revenues. In 2020, China's pharmaceutical market will gross US$120 billion, above that in the USA (see *Chinapharm*, 2002, 'The development of three ventures in China in globalization framework: Series four', 6 March 2002; see also KWA Pharmaceutical Services, 2006; and an interview with Dr Wei Zhang, Beijing University, 20 January 2006). On the whole, China will remain an attractive market for foreign drug companies for many years to come, because China offers many advantages in terms of the size of its market place, its low labour cost, and its unrealized market potential.

The major impetus for China's pharmaceutical growth comes from larger contextual factors. China has made considerable progress towards macro-economic growth, which has led to improved living standards, increasing concern about health issues, more disposable income for health needs, and increasing demands for better health services. The market for high-quality, patient-orientated healthcare services is small, but growing steadily. There is no universal health care in China and most Chinese lack health insurance. Only a small fraction of the population, mainly those in major cities, can afford top-end Western medical care. Currently, there are many successful foreign and joint venture health care service providers that have been operating in China since the early 1980s. Their experiences point to growing opportunities in the pharmaceutical sector.

The global pharmaceutical industry and China's position

Global pharmaceutical production includes the discussions about raw materials, formulations, Chinese herbal medicines, Chinese herbal formulas, antibiotics, biotech productions, radioactive products, medical equipment, health care devices, and pharmaceutical production facilities and equipment, pharmaceutical packaging materials and trade marks. Overall, global pharmaceutical consumption has increased rapidly year by year. In 2000, the total was more than US$368 billion and reached more than US$550 billion by 2004. The annual growth rate was about 7 per cent in the 2000s (IMS Health, 2006; see also *Chinapharm*, 2 July 2004). 'A review of the planning of pharmaceutical sector in the Tenth Five-Year Plan'. Major global events and trends have also influenced this picture: (i) the increase in the ageing population in developed countries, which has increased pharmaceutical needs; (ii) Increasing health care costs reduce the number of days for in-patient care for which the insurers are willing to pay. The use of pharmaceuticals to relieve the burden of hospital care is useful to the industry; (iii) new diseases and epidemics provide new opportunities for pharmaceutical development; (iv) the potential of biotechnology has provided unlimited opportunities for developing testing devices, vaccines and pharmaceuticals; and (v) Increases in generics, food supplements and preventive care products also increase the room for growth.

In this environment, the global pharmaceutical business is facing both challenges and opportunities. Several facts are worth noting. First, it is estimated that the cost of developing a drug averages more than US$800 million and is increasing. Second, only three out of ten drugs are able to generate profits. Third, on average, it takes about ten years to develop a new drug. Fourth, the pharmaceutical business is not a purely commercial pursuit: it has a public health component. Fifth, the pharmaceutical market is expected to grow by some 6–9 per cent each year between 2005–9; in comparison, the biotech sector is likely to increase by 20 per cent, but with very risky prospects (Gerbino, 2006; Verret, 2006).

The developments in China's pharmaceutical sector have a two-directional interaction with the global market; that is, China's pharmaceutical market will have an impact on the growth of the global pharmaceutical industry, and similarly global pharmaceutical progress will affect China's pharmaceutical domestic supply and demand. Globally, by 2000, the top ten pharmaceutical companies held 50 per cent of market share in prescription drugs, which had decreased to 47 per cent by 2004. Several global trends are worth noting:

(i) In terms of global market competition,
   (a) smaller pharmaceutical companies have been growing at a faster pace;
   (b) pharmaceutical manufactures, especially those in China, India, Pakistan, Brazil and Indonesia are expanding;
   (c) biotechnology businesses are growing at a faster pace than conventional pharmaceutical companies – for example, the US company Amgen has grossed more than US$ 10 billion and been ranked in the top 500; and
   (d) the rate of rolling out new products is slow because of setbacks during the clinical trial stages of promising new drugs unexpected side effects of such drugs and the nearing of expiration of profitable brands.

   These trends have both direct and indirect effects on the returns of multinationals.

(ii) In terms of pricing and market share, developed countries are still the major markets, but most of the disease burden is in developing, resource-poor countries. India, China, Africa, Latin America and Eastern European countries share most of the disease burden, and they also share the greatest risk of emergent diseases. It has been noted that pharmaceutical prices have increased four times more than the global increase of GDP. Pharmaceutical production in the USA, Japan, Germany, France and the United Kingdom combined accounted for two-thirds of global production. Competition in generics is increasingly intense, but profits derive mainly from brands. In the USA, generics account for more than 50 per cent of sales. Multinationals on the whole control global pharmaceutical production and marketing. On average, the multinationals have seen their sales increase by 30 per cent in China, but a slower rate is expected in over-the-counter products (OTCs) and generics.

(iii) Research and development of new products remains the key factor for sustainable profits for all pharmaceutical manufactures (*Chinapharm*, 2005).

The future of the pharmaceutical industry is promising, but the complexity and diversity of global health issues presents many challenges to the sector. The 1990s saw major breakthroughs in pharmaceutical developments but it is questionable whether that golden age will be repeated in the twenty-first century, for several reasons: (i) decreasing R&D investment by multinationals; (ii) a distorted investment structure. For example, it was noted that only 10 per cent of investment targeted 90 per cent of the major health issues in the global community, while 90 per cent was invested in only 10 per cent of human health problems. The increasing share of marketing and advertising in pharmaceutical expenditure has also been criticized; and (iii) increasing costs in developing drugs and a high failure rate in clinical trials. The cost of developing new drugs, compounded by the increasingly rigorous standards demanded in developed countries before approving them, is making it more difficult to increase investment in new drugs. This might explain why the numbers of new compounds approved by the Food and Drugs Administration (FDA) have decreased since 2000, from thirty-eight in 2000 to twenty-three in 2004. The advancement in human genetics and biotechnology has provided a glimmer of hope for the industry, albeit under certain conditions, such as the need to lower R&D costs and provide a faster translation between upstream and downstream development. In this global environment, the collaboration between conventional pharmaceutical businesses and new biotechnology research centres, and between multinationals and pharmaceutical businesses in developing countries, is inevitable.

Overall, the major motors for growth in the global pharmaceutical industry are: innovation in biotechnology, an increase in the ageing population, and emerging geographical centres, such as China and India. These phenomena have motivated pharmaceutical companies to increase collaboration with biotech companies to share their expertise, products and operations to overcome the productivity gap and increase growth (*Business Insights*, 2005). The key issues facing global pharmaceutical industries in China in the WTO framework will be:

(i) the market entry principle: based on principles of non-discrimination and fair competition;
(ii) manufacturing principles: price, safety and efficacy;
(iii) the protection of pharmaceutical IPRs;
(iv) marketing, advertising and distribution issues;
(v) understanding the demographic needs and disease profiles of populations (see *Chinapharm*, 2001).

In a very competitive global market, the greatest threats to fully realizing sales and marketing effectiveness of all pharmaceutical businesses, including those in China, are competition and price containment. Biotech will be the focus of attention in this picture. Biotech is currently the fastest growing sector in the pharmaceutical industry globally, and is forecast to have record sales of US$ 250 billion by 2015 (20.3 per cent of the global market). Biotech in the USA grew at a rate of almost twice that of the overall drug market in the second quarter of 2004. About 91 per cent of industry executives believe pharma–biotech mergers will increase during the next ten years, and 69 per cent also believe there is likely to be increased consolidation between companies within the biotech sector (*Business Insights*, 2005, p. 131). It is believed that by 2015, the large pharmaceutical companies will synergize their R&D networks with biotechs and focus on their core competitive sales and marketing (ibid.). China has taken note of this trend and made major investments in developing biotech products. Its recent progress in cancer drugs was an important step for the growth of its biotech-related pharmaceuticals.

As mentioned earlier the global pharmaceutical market is expected to grow by 6–9 per cent between 2005–9 (Gerbino 2006; Verret 2006). At the time of writing, China accounts for about 1.5–2 per cent of the global pharmaceutical market and this market share is likely to increase to 5 per cent by 2010–15. China is expected to rank eighth in the global market, with 13 per cent to 16 per cent of annual growth (*Chinapharm*, 2005). In 2004 alone, China's pharmaceutical market was worth US$9.5 billion, a record 28 per cent growth over 2003, but this was still a small percentage compared to the global picture; for example, the USA reached US$ 248 billion, accounting for 45 per cent of global growth (IMS Health, 2006).

China's pharmaceutical industry

Despite the fact that pharmaceuticals manufacturing was not previously thought of as a pillar of Chinese economic development, the Chinese government has articulated a detailed framework for the overall development of the pharmaceutical sector in the Tenth Five-Year Plan (March 2001). The conceptual framework outlines the following guidelines for increasing the competitiveness of the pharmaceutical sector: the Chinese pharmaceutical sector will continue to support Chinese social development and focus on structural adjustment. It will be market and private-sector-orientated. China will also focus on developing its niche areas in pharmaceutical growth. It will support public health and improve the quality of health for its population through the development of preventive medicines. It will filter out high-polluting, energy-consuming and low-efficiency products. It will improve pharmaceutical informatics through digitalizing monitoring and surveillance systems, accounting systems, and population informatics. It will develop the as yet unrealized market potential in the inland region and improve pharmaceutical access there. It will upgrade the technology capacity of the sector, especially for biotech products and Chinese herbal medicines, with the ultimate goal of improving product quality and increasing China's position in global competitiveness. It will globalize its production, marketing, distribution and capital investment. The key areas selected for government support are: biotechnology, Chinese herbal medicines and niche raw materials. The substantive goals are:

(i) pharmaceutical manufacturing is expected to grow by at least 12 per cent;
(ii) value-added products in the pharmaceutical sector are expected to grow by at least 13 per cent;
(iii) the sale volume of pharmaceutical-related products is expected to grow by 9 per cent;
(iv) pharmaceutical exports are expected to grow by 6 per cent; and
(v) the profit margins for the pharmaceutical industry are expected to grow by 13 per cent (*Chinapharm*, 2004).

To reach these targets, China will engage in major structural adjustment in product composition, R&D upgrades, and improvements in capital investment and organizational structure. On product composition, China will aim to increase the share of high-end products in the market. For example, China plans to hold the patents of about ten new brands that will enter the global market place. About fifty new drugs will be at the clinical trial stages. About ten to fifteenth biotech products are expected to enter the global markets. More than twenty Good Manufacturing Practice (GMP)-certified facilities will be completed to process multiple pharmaceutical tasks. Exports of Chinese herbal medicines will grow. Chemical raw materials, such as artemisinin and Vitamin C, will increase their global market share. The percentage of formulations in total share of exports market will increase from the current 0.2 per cent to 5 per cent. On R&D upgrades, large-scale pharmaceutical businessess will establish their R&D centres and it is expected that they will increase from the current 2 per cent to 5 per cent. The biotech sector is expected to make major progress in genetic engineering, such as recombinant technology. The technology for chemical production, especially for artemisinin and Vitamin C, will be enhanced. On capital investment and organizational structure, China will focus on the establishment of large-scale pharmaceutical businesses through both vertical and horizontal integration, such as IPOs (Initial Public Offerings), mergers, joint ventures, and reorganizations. It was noted that efficiency was a major issue prior to 2004. For example, in 2003, on average, only 44–60 per cent of production capacity was realized in the pharmaceutical sector. The excessive number of small pharmaceutical companies has decreased China's global competitiveness. In contrast, the global top ten 'pharmas' accounted for 47 per cent of pharmaceutical production across the world; in India, the top twenty pharmaceutical producers accounted for 50 per cent of all revenue; in the USA, the top three wholesalers accounted for more than 90 per cent of medicines (*Chinapharm*, 2003). The opening of the financial sector will allow an increase of venture capital in pharmaceutical investment. China is determined to streamline pharmaceutical production in the areas of unrealized production capacities, unhealthy competition among small-sized producers for duplicated products, and lack of efficiency. It will strengthen its enforcement and control of pharmaceutical quality control. It is expected that the ten largest manufacturing businesses, grossing more than US$6.25 billion each, will own 30 per cent of the market share in China. China will facilitate the formation of large-scale distributors, each of which is expected to have a capital investment of more than US$2.5 billion. China will also be instrumental in the establishment of ten large retail chains, each owning more than 1,000 stores as well as smaller regional chains that are expected to own more than 100 stores each *Chinapharm* 2004).

China's pharmaceutical development has shown a large growth potential:

(i) it has been noted that its growth since in the 1980s has outpaced the increase in China's GDP. The fact that its total value accounts for 5.5 per cent of China's GDP, less than the 10–15 per cent of the total GDP share for the industrialized countries, shows that it still has much room to grow (*Chinapharm*, 2005; *see also China Pharmaceuticals*, 2002). In one estimate, in the early 1990s, the pharmaceutical sector in China was calculated to account for only 1.83 per cent of its total industrial value, and was ranked at only 22 out of 37 sectors; by 1999, the value had increased to 2.1 per cent and ranked 19; and in 1999, its value was 2.4 per cent and it was ranked 17th. In 1999, the total profits, profit return rate, cost return rate and production efficiency were ranked 7th, 5th, 4th, and 8th respectively (*Chinapharm*, 2004); and

(ii) despite some operational issues in China, the country is still the fastest-growing pharmaceuticals market in the world. Between 1978

> and 2005, the gross value of China's pharmaceutical industry increased by 17 per cent annually, one of the fastest-growing industries in China (*Chinapharm*, 2005). In another estimate, the pharmaceutical market was calculated to have increased by 28 per cent between 2000 and 2005, compared to a 7 per cent global growth. The total pharmaceutical needs were estimated to be more than US$2.7 billion (*Chinapharm*, 2005). It was predicted that, at the current growth rate, China is likely to be the fifth-largest pharmaceutical market in the world, and will exceed the market volume of Germany and France, respectively, by 2015. The major areas to have shown a large potential are Chinese herbal medicines and raw chemicals. Domestic pharmaceutical investment has also been increasing through the capital accumulated in the stock market. Most of the pharmaceutical stocks received positive ratings because of lower risks compared to other stocks. It is also hoped that the influx of venture capital to the Chinese market will encourage dynamic growth in this sector (*China Pharmaceuticals*, 2002).

The presence of multinationals in China is increasing. Since China approved the first joint venture in pharmaceuticals in May 1980, the top twenty pharmaceutical multinationals have all established their presence in China. After China's WTO entry, the multinationals could not wait to capitalize on this potential. For example, as early as 2002, the Boehringer Ingelheim International Group, the world's largest private medicine manufacturer, invested US$41 million in Asia's second-largest pharmaceutical plant, in Pudong, China (*China Health Sciences Newsletter*, 2002). The multinationals entered the Chinese market either individually or as joint ventures. It was estimated that drugs produced by joint ventures claimed 30 per cent of the market share, and imported drugs accounted for 23 per cent, by 2002 (Hong Kong Development Council, 2002). Overall, the foreign pharmas' position in China's market has changed significantly, having decreased from an average rate of 20 per cent sales growth and quick returns to a lower rate. Before the WTO accession, China's laws were more protective of domestic producers, but since WTO membership, the competition for profits has led to more domestic–foreign partnerships, such as in the form of foreign-invested enterprises (FIEs). By 2005, the value of foreign investment was about US$2 billion in the pharmaceutical sector (Gross, 1998).

A related point is that capital composition in China's pharmaceutical industry has also changed tremendously since 1978. Joint ventures accounted for 18.8 per cent in 2004, increasing from 15 per cent in 1995; private producers accounted for 33.2 per cent, rising from 12 per cent in 1995, and state-controlled businesses have decreased from 55 per cent to 36.1 per cent since 1995 (*Chinapharm*, 2004). By 2004, China already saw more than

200 retail pharmaceutical businesses controlling more than 5,000 retail pharmacies. On the whole, multinationals have the most influence on global economic development, and it has been estimated that they accounted for one-third of the world's GDP and controlled 50 per cent of world's trade, 80 per cent of patents, and 75 per cent of technology transfer by 2001. This is also true for the pharmaceutical sector. According to an estimate by Forbes, there were fourteen pharmaceutical multinationals in the top 500 Fortune companies. Each of the top three (Merck, Pfizer and Novartis) grossed more than the combined revenues of all the pharmaceutical manufacturers in China in 2000. All nations and businesses considered, multinationals accounted for the top 50 per cent of the GDP in the world. And the total revenues of Chinese pharmas was less than the sheer volume of Pfizer's in 2005 (*Chinapharm*, 2002).

To recap, the major advantages of Chinese markets are the size of its market, emerging health care issues and disease profiles, potential for R&D, human resources, the government's commitment to improving the health sector, the relatively easy access to patients available for clinical trials, and lower clinical trial costs (*Research and Markets*, 2005; *Digital Vector*, 2005, p. 360). For example, because of changing lifestyles and changing demographic needs, China's demand for cardiovascular drugs and cancer treatment have grown at a fast pace in 2004, and it was estimated that up to 2009, both production and demand will continue to grow (AMID, 2003).

China has continued to improve its international competitiveness and has changed its strategy towards the pharmaceutical market, from acquiring a market share to comprehensive competition. Biomedicine is growing steadily, with major input for research and development, and traditional Chinese medicine is being modernized but still faces major challenges (see related discussions in Okokok Research Centre, 2005). In 2004, China ranked as the seventh-largest pharmaceutical market globally, with a value of US$ 14 billion (up from US$4 billion in 1996), compared to India's US$4.5 billion (*Business India*, 2005, p. 92). Pharmaceutical imports have been growing at a rate of 20 per cent since the early 1990s and exceeded US$930 million by 2000. In 2004, China's pharmaceutical industry continued to maintain its growth momentum, achieving a stable rise in both output and sales revenues.

Looking to the future, China is expected to become the fifth-largest drug market in the world by 2015, with an estimated value of US$24 billion (*Business India*, 2005, p. 92). It is also expected to become the world's largest pharmaceutical market by 2020 (Gross, 1998). As discussed earlier, the major drivers of growth are changing demographic trends, the disease and health profile in China, and socioeconomic changes, such as economic growth and increases in incomes, population growth, an increasingly ageing population, increasing pharmaceutical consumption per capita, market size (urban and rural), government support in restructuring the highly fragmented industry, IPR policies, increasing life expectancies, HIV, lifestyle changes, and liberated sexual behaviour.

Improvements in living standards, reduced levels of poverty and strong macroeconomic growth, also affect the health care market as a whole. These developments have both positive and negative consequences for health. Many developments also mean tremendous potential for the growth of pharmaceuticals consumption among the population. For example, in 2004, pharmaceuticals consumption was less than US$10 per capita in China; in comparison, it was more than US$300 in the USA and other industrialized countries. With health care reform, both the public and private sectors will pay more for their pharmaceutical needs, and the Chinese government is determined to implement universal health care in all villages by 2008. Urbanization has also increased pharmaceutical needs. For example, about 460 million Chinese lived in cities and towns in 2000 and this trend is increasing by 2.7 per cent each year – more than 10 million population are added to the cities annually. Pharmaceuticals consumption has a ratio of 7:1 between urban and rural populations, and urbanization will also increase the size of the pharmaceuticals market. China's population grew to more than 1.3 billion by 2005. In addition, the ageing population is increasing by 3 per cent each year. The regulatory environment has also helped the pharmceuticals market, and it is estimated that retail pharmacies are increasing in number by 15 per cent each year. As mentioned earlier, the decrease of tariffs in the WTO framework will also help both domestic and multinational producers. The market for high quality and patient-orientated health services is small, but is growing steadily. Most Chinese do not have health insurance. Only a fraction of the population can afford high-end Western medical care.

Economic development and demographic trends are conducive to pharmaceutical growth, and the total volume of China's pharmaceutical industry is growing. By 2005, about 6,000 domestic pharma manufacturers controlled roughly 70 per cent of the pharmaceuticals market (*Business India*, 2005, p. 92). There are about 17,000 joint ventures with China, including all the leading pharmaceutical companies. By the end of 2004, 3,731 pharmaceutical manufacturers in China were GMP-certified (*Chinapharm*, 2005), By July 2004, China had about 3,613 pharmaceuticals-related manufacturers, in which only 423 (11.7 per cent), were considered to be large-scale producers. The majority of producers were small-scale, lacked distinct products and brand recognition, had an out-of-date, traditional management style and were loosely organized. They produced more than 15,000 kinds of pharmaceutical-related materials, totalling 430,000 tons annually (*Chinapharm*, 2004). They also produced 34 formulations and more than 4,000 kinds of drugs. The top 60 businesses accounted for 35.7 per cent market share in China while in contrast top

20 global producers accounted for 60 per cent of global market (ibid.). About 97 per cent of the products are generic. On average, each batch of raw material can make three formulations. In contrast, the multinationals can make 18–80 formulations (ibid.). By 17 February 2004, there were 7,486 pharmaceutical wholesalers, including 6,936 business owners and 551 partners. In comparison, in the USA there are ten, and in Sweden, two. The preferred global standard for retailers is that there should be less than 7 minutes' walking distance between a neighbourhood and a pharmacy. China is below this standard. China now has 15,1760 retailers, and 719 chains. In total, the total number of stores and chains that sell pharmaceutical products is 230,000 (*Sina News Taiwan*, 2004). In 5–10 years, it is believed that generics will account for 70 per cent and prescriptions 30 per cent of China's pharmaceutical market (*Chinapharm*, 2005). China's potential for pharmaceutical production and consumption was recognized in the 1990s.

China's pharmaceutical sector is experiencing a multi-directional dynamic to improve its domestic positioning. China's pharmaceutical industries are catching up to global competition by forming alliances, and employing horizontal and vertical integration. For example, in the first half of 2005, LAMP acquired New World for US$14 million; the Green Valley Group's US$6.25 million developed a strategic alliance and R&D investment with Chinese Academy Sciences; TaiGen partnered P&G Pharmaceutical to develop a novel antibiotic to address drug-resistant pathogens; and the Shanghai Pharmaceutical Group Co. Ltd (SPGC) invested US$12 million to launch a joint venture in Chongquing with a local drug firm, the Mokom Group, and SPGC plans to hold a 60 per cent stake in the new company, Shanghai Pharmaceutical Mokom. The Chongqing Mokom Group will retain 40 per cent in return for contributing its infrastructure. This will allow the SPGC to expand its sales networks into rural markets. Mokom has the third-largest chain of drug stores in Chongquing and major sales network in the rural markets of South-west China. An alliance of five major pharmaceutical holding companies aims to pool resources and share regional distribution rights and channels to increase competitiveness and cut costs. Each of the five alliance members – Shanghai Pharmaceutical Holdings Ltd; Beijing Pharmaceutical Holdings Ltd; Tienjing Pacific Group Ltd; Chongqing Pharmaceutical Holdings Ltd; and Guangzhou Pharmaceutical Group Ltd is one of the top ten revenue producers in its segment. AXM Pharma Inc., the owner of AXM Pharma Shenyang through a wholly-owned subsidiary of Werke Pharmaceuticals, Inc., reached a distribution agreement with Sinopharm Holding Guangzhou Co. Ltd, an affiliate of China National Pharmaceutical Group Corp. The agreement was for an expected US$6.5 million in sales of Elegance feminine hygiene products by December 2005, and the sales territory includes regions in Southern China (BGCG, 2005, p. 17). It was noted that feminine hygiene products have a major potential in China. This kind of dynamic is likely to help domestic producers increase their R&D and management capacity, and in return the multinationals can gain domestic distribution channels.

Creative partnerships are being generated to build competitive capacity in China. For example, TaiGen Biotechnology Co., a privately held biotech with headquarters in Taiwan and with subsidiaries in mainland China, has completed a project with Procter & Gamble Pharmaceuticals (P&G). This agreement will take advantage of TaiGen's network of clinical investigators and be responsible for the Phase IB and Phase II clinical testing of a novel, non fluorinated-quinolone antibiotic from P&G. P&G retains the right to evaluate the product given positive Phase II studies, and with TaiGen may seek another pharmaceutical company for Phase III development and commercialization. For its risk-sharing, TaiGen will be rewarded with a share of the financial rewards from the re-partnering of the Phase III-ready antibiotic and will retain the rights of this compound in China, Korea and Southeast Asia. Procter and Gamble has obtained US$133 billion market capitalization. But risks remain for both companies: for example, for P&G, anti-infectives are not a core strategic focus for its revenues, and it needs to lower development costs. It also needs access to patients for clinical trials. Partial collaboration with a focused target is also a clever strategy. For example, PharmaEngine, another Taiwan life science company focusing on cancer, immunology and infectious disease therapeutics, obtained exclusive rights to Xenova Group PLC's brain cancer treatment, TransMID, in China and South Korea. What Xenova gets is an advance payment as well as milestone and royalty payments and it will retain manufacturing rights and the exclusive supplier right of TransMID to PharmaEngine. At the time of writing, TransMID is in Phase III clinical trials for the treatment of glioblastoma multiforme (GBM). PharmaEngine's current prospects include one Phase I candidate for cancer and one Phase II candidate for both asthma and chronic obstructive pulmonary disease (COPD) (BGCG, 2005, p. 17). In April 2005, the Shanghai Institute of Materia Medica (SIMM) at the Chinese Academy of Sciences Shanghai Life Science Institute made a joint announcement with the Green Valley Group about a partnership and co-development agreement for traditional Chinese medicine (TCM). The Green Valley Group will invest US$6.25 million as start-up funding for projects in cancer and cardiovascular diseases. Green Valley specializes in marketing and selling TCM products. It has offices and subsidiaries across China and owns two state-of-the-art GMP manufacturing facilities in Shanghai and Xian, with a third being built in Shanghai (Green Valley Financial Services, 2005).

China has also become a centre of outsourcing for multinational pharmaceuticals, including R&D. To access the Chinese market and its low-cost manufacturing capabilities, the Lam Pharmaceutical Corp. of Lewiston, NY, signed an agreement in January 2005, to acquire privately-held New World Kellerton in Xinyang for US$14 million in cash and stocks. The New World's leading product is Hipreomycin, approved for treating TB in China and India. This also has the potential to be exported to other developing countries. Ciba Specialty Chemicals has opened a new US$20 million R&D centre in Shanghai. It will bridge chemical knowledge with formulation science to create new products and solutions for both Asia and the world at large. Besides the R&D centre, Ciba already has six branch offices, twelve production sites and three trading companies. Ciba's Chinese operation accounted for 7 per cent of its US$5.8 billion global sales in 2004. China is also making an effort to reach global markets. Yangzijiang Pharmacy Corp. reached an agreement with Stanford University in the USA to build a research facility in Shanghai for new drugs. This is the second R&D facility after its collaboration with Merck to build a similar centre in Beijing, where its investment totalled US$2.25 million. The Shanghai project will focus on cardiovascular medication. Yangzijiang will provide the funding facilities and testing and Stanford the intellectual expertise. Yangzijiang will have first claim to any products developed (BGCG, 2005, p. 17).

China has increased its quality control in pharmaceutical production incrementally, especially in GMP and GSP (Good Scientific Practice) certification. On average, GMP certification costs about US$2.5–3.75 million. By 2003, between 1,800 and 2,000, companies, about a third of all manufacturers in China, spent more than US$6.25 billion on becoming GMP certified (*Chinapharm*, 2003). By 2004, 60 per cent of all manufacturers (controlling 90 per cent of total production) were GMP certified. Those who did not have GMP or GSP certification, (including more than 2,000 businesses, 900 whole salers and 5,000 retailers), were told to close down their company (*Chinapharm*, 2004).

Foreign pharmaceuticals have taken note of China's need to deal with emergent diseases, and that tackling infectious diseases is at the top of China's public health agenda. Sinovac Biotech Ltd (SVA), a leading biotech company in China, has obtained encouraging results from its clinical trials of a SARS vaccine. The Chinese CDC (Centre of Disease Control) revealed that, in initial clinical trials, the SARS antibody was found in all volunteers six months after receiving the test vaccine. SVA also received Chinese marketing and sales approval for its Slit Influenza vaccine and for Bilive, a combined hepatitis A and B vaccine (BGCG, 2005, p. 17).

Yet China's pharmaceutical sector is also facing grave challenges, which will be further discussed later. However, in the WTO-regulated economy, the possible opportunities facing Chinese pharmaceutical makers can also be enormous (Access China Management Consulting Ltd, 2005, p. 39).

The competitive advantages of China's pharmaceutical sector

Overall, China's pharmaceutical sector and market has several major advantages, as mentioned earlier: mainly the size of its market, lower costs for labour, production and clinical trials, and quicker drug approvals, a talent pool, policy environment and commitment to health care improvement, and emerging health issues. As became obvious after China's entry into the WTO, the country's pharmaceutical industry is at a major turning point. China has become a multi-tasking centre for global pharmaceutical products (*World Journal*, 2003).

Specifically, China's major advantages are as follows.

A future R&D and global manufacturing centre for new drugs

It is estimated that in the USA and Europe, developing a new drug costs an average of US$800 million to US$1 billion because of the high cost of clinical trials and the high attrition rate, which means that only 15 per cent of new drugs entering development eventually reach the market (Tufts Center for the Study of Drug Development, 2002; see also Kemani, and Findlay, 2000). Finding themselves in this disadvantageous position, Western pharmaceutical companies are constantly looking for ways to cut costs, such as identifying new pathways to develop new molecular medicine and accelerating targets by using new technologies. This explains why most major pharmaceutical companies, such as Pharmacia-Upjohn, Glaxo SmithKline, Novartis and so on had established their R&D centres in China by the early 2000s. Yet, the challenge to global pharmaceutical businesses is to find innovative operational models for drug development. This new framework of thinking puts China in an advantageous position:

(i) *Cost-effectiveness*: China's research scientists are paid a fraction of the salaries of their Western counterparts, which lowers the overall cost of developing new drugs, testing drug compounds and manufacturing in a highly scalable fashion. Even compared with other developing countries, China's labour advantages cannot be underestimated. For example, China's labour costs are a third or a quarter of those in Brazil or Mexico (*Sina News*, 2006).
(ii) *A vast research talent pool*: The return of a large number of Western-trained talent in the pharmaceutical sector increases China's competitiveness (Wang, 2005). By September 2005, more than 200,000 had returned, most of them highly educated having received advanced training in the West, especially the USA.
(iii) *Increasing expertise*. In highly specialized areas, such as biopharmaceutical discovery research and clinical development.
(iv) *Increasing investment*. China's increasing investment through public and private expenditure on drugs.
(v) *An increasing share of the pharmaceutical market.*

However, for China to become a formidable player in a globally competitive environment, it needs to address the following issues: (1) it needs to improve its drug development infrastructure to comply with international regulatory standards if it wishes to become part of the fully integrated global 'virtual drug development model'. China has moved in the right direction with its mandatory implementation of Good Laboratory Practice (GLP) in September 2003, which require that all data for the safety evaluation of new drugs must come from GLP approved labs; and (ii) China needs such channels as 'the Life Sciences Bridges' to facilitate the bi-directional transfer of knowledge, technology, capital and other resources between its own tech hubs and other life science hubs in the world. China needs major information channels to absorb up-to-date biomedical scientific discoveries in the West and to transfer its own discoveries to the West to realize the full commercial value of its pharmaceutical research (BGCG, 2005, p. 14). Invitrogen's acquisition of Chinese competitor Bio Asia in December 2004 shows that life science R&D capacity in China has been noted by foreign competitors in biotech research equipment and reagents. It also shows that China has made some progress in integrating itself into the new global drug development paradigm.

Overall, (i) the traditional costly drug development paradigm is being evaluated by Western pharmas. Multinationals need to assess the cost-effectiveness of this model and final alternatives to reduce production costs; (ii) China can provide a new paradigm for drug development that 'leverages the most efficient drug development resources worldwide' (BGCG, 2005, p. 15); and (iii) China's engagement in infrastructure and capacity building to comply with global standards is a good first step to becoming a respectable partner in the global arena.

In terms of manufacturing, low-cost prescriptions and generics have multiple global markets. The role of such emerging pharmaceutical producers as China, India and Brazil are worth noting. The USA and Japan are the largest pharmaceutical exporting countries, but also the largest importing countries of pharmaceuticals. US pharmaceuticals sales accounted for 18.4 per cent in the global market place in 1976, and 52 per cent or more since 2000. EU sales total more than 26 per cent; Japanese sales grosses more than 10 per cent, but Chinese sales are about 2 per cent (*China Pharmaceuticals*, 2005). High income countries, which account for more than 15 per cent of the global population consume more than 90 per cent of the pharmaceuticals, and pharmaceutical consumption in the least developed countries has been decreasing, from 3.5 per cent in 1985 to 2.9 per cent in 1999. Pharmaceuticals sales in these countries decreased from 0.98 per cent in 1990 to 0.64 per cent in 2000. Yet, pharmaceuticals sales and consumption have been increasing in middle-income countries, including China. In terms of access, about a quarter of the global population had less than US$5 available for pharmaceutical expenses. More than half of the global population had difficulty in paying for medicines, and in China, more than 60 per cent population had problems in paying for health care. There is about a 100 times difference between high-income and low-income countries. On average, pharmaceuticals accounted for 15 per cent of total health care cost for global populations, while in China they accounted for more than 60 per cent. Pharmaceuticals are a major health care expenditure for most Chinese people (ibid.).

As well as those markets in developed countries, the potential in developing countries cannot be ignored by producers in China. These markets are not a source of profit for multinationals and are therefore not the focus of their attention. According to a 2004 WHO report, more than 2 billion people did not have access to essential medicines, including 1 billion in China. Essential medicines are exempt from tariffs in all but ten countries, but in those ten countries, imported raw materials for essential medicines are taxed at 23 per cent, while an average rate of 12 per cent is levied on finished products. Most middle-and low-income countries still purchase their medicines from other low- and middle-income countries. Like Brazil and India, China is well-positioned to enter those markets with essential medicines, low-cost generics and herbal medicines. China's largest competitor in this area will be India, whose pharmaceutical products are priced at 60 per cent less than Chinese products (ibid.).

A rapidly growing market

China has changed its position from being ranked eleventh in 1996 to seventh in 2002, and is projected to be the fifth by 2010, with estimated sales of US$24–26 billion per year. The sheer size of population and the demographic trends of the Chinese population offer a growing potential for pharmaceutical products, as mentioned earlier. In 2004, prescription sales grossed more than US$10 billion, with a rate of increase of 27 per cent over the previous year. As a whole, China's pharmaceuticals retail totalled more than US$97 billion; hospital pharmacies sales totalled US$141.4 billion; and pharmaceutical advertising totalled US$20.5 billion. Profits were US$30 billion for the pharmaceutical industries; US$11.7 billion for retail; and US$44.4 billion for hospital sales (ibid.).

Several specific demographic characteristics and trends in China are: (i) the size of population is 1.36 billion and it is increasingly conscious of its health needs; (ii) since 1998, pharmaceuticals sales have increased by at least US$500 million; (iii) the ageing population leads to increased pharmaceutical consumption. According to China's 2000 census, about 10 per cent of the Chinese population were aged over 60 years old, and this population is increasing by 3 per cent every year. For the purpose of comparison, the Japanese are the second-largest pharmaceutical market because of the high percentage of elderly people in its demographic composition; (iv) the rapid pace of urbanization in China has also increased the pharmaceutical need for OTCs in retail pharmacies, especially the need for imported medicines. Urbanization increased by 4.4 per cent between 1990 and 1995, and by 30.89 per cent between 1998 and 1999. If this trend continues, there will be plenty of room for the growth of pharmaceutical products (BGCG, 2005, p. 1). The long-term prediction is that, by the middle of the century, drug sales in China will outstrip those in every other region (see also 'Analysis of strategies and markets for multinationals', *China Pharmaceuticals*, 2002).

Cost advantages

China's low production costs are its major advantage. These include the costs of labour, facilities and equipment, raw materials, distribution, marketing and advertising. Certainly, the most conspicuous is the cost of labour, as mentioned earlier. China is known for having one of the largest, most inexpensive, and best-trained labour forces. It has been estimated that the average salary for a Ph.D.-level scientist in China was US$25,000 a year – about 10 per cent of a corresponding US compensation package. In addition, the large number of returning scientists from the West adds a further advantage to China's cost calculations. A global human resource firm, Watson Wyatt, found that the annual salary before tax for R&D professionals in China was even lower than in South America. In contrast, it was estimated that 80 per cent of total R&D costs typically pay for the salaries of research scientists in the West. This explains the increasing interest of the West in turning to Chinese scientists to conduct new drug research.

Centres of clinical trials

The cost of conducting clinical trials, including the associated hospital fees, is also much less in China than in the West. According to some conservative estimates, clinical trials costs in China are a third of those in the USA. (PriceWaterhouseCoopers, 2004). On average, for the drug development processes in China, the preclinical cost is approximately 20 per cent of that in the USA. It has been estimated that it costs about US$120 million to develop a new drug in China (*General Biologic*, 2004). It was noted that that more than 800 drugs, most of which are new drugs in Phase III of clinical trials, are tested annually in China. Usually, more than 500,000 Chinese are involved in the process (*World Journal*, 2005).

The scientific research tradition

(i) China has a long history of scientific research and has developed its talents over a twenty-year period. Scientists of Chinese origin have won four Nobel prizes in science-related fields, and the third and fourth generations of Chinese leaders were all from science backgrounds. China has a well-established universal education system, generated about 1.87 million undergraduate degree holders and 111,000 postgraduates in 2003, according to the Chinese Ministry of Education. It has a talent pool of more than 50,000 research scientists. In addition, each year, about 500–1000 Chinese who have obtained doctorate degrees from overseas institutions return to China, providing major support for large research institutions (see *Asia Pacific Biotech News*, 2005). The Chinese government also implemented a policy that encouraged collaboration between the private sector and universities, to develop patentable products. This policy has provided a major impetus for research institutes. For example, the Shanghai Institute of Materia Medica, China's leading centre for pharmaceutical research and development, is also a major target for collaboration by multinationals.

(ii) A large number of pharmaceutical researchers in US pharmas came from China, and a good percentage of them have returned to China, as mentioned earlier.

(iii) The Chinese ethnomedical system, which has been practised for more than 3,000 years, has provided many innovative ideas for drug development. It suggests great potential for future new drug developments.

(iv) There have been many successful collaborations between Chinese research institutes and multinationals since the 1978 economic reform. Their profit returns have been the major drivers for the multinationals' stay in the Chinese market (*Chinapharm*, 2001).

Government support

The Chinese government is supportive of pharmaceutical development. Since the late 1990s, government policies have encouraged foreign investment in the pharmaceutical sector in China. For example, (i) China offered special tax incentives for pharmaceutical investors, reducing the levy on their capital gains from 33 per cent to 17 per cent; (ii) there was no limit on the maximum investment that foreign investors could transfer from the gains of their previous investment into pharmaceutical investment; and (iii) the government includes such products as genetic engineering, vaccines and advanced biotechnology in the government's purchasing priorities, but Chinese herbal products remain the monopoly of local manufacturers (*see also China Pharmaceuticals*, 2002).

In 2000, the Chinese government made further endeavours to improve the policy environment to make it conducive to multinational investment, through legislation such as the People's Republic of China Joint Investment Law, People's Republic of China Joint Ventures Law, and People's Republic of China Foreign Ventures Law. On 1 December 2002, China also passed the Qualified Foreign Institutional Investor Act (QFII), which allowed foreign entry to Chinese stock markets. This made it possible for foreign capital to be an engine of growth for Chinese businesses, including the health care sector (*China Pharmaceuticals*, 2002). In January 2003, the Chinese government also abolished a wide range of limitations on foreign investments, such as the volume of stocks in which foreign parties could invest, the Chinese government's protection of multinational rights, and the amount of commission charged for pharmaceutical investment. This step was crucial to funnelling foreign funds into high-growth sectors, such as pharmaceuticals.

In this environment, on 29 September, 2003 the largest pharmaceutical retailer, Medicine Shoppe International Inc., entered the Chinese market (ibid.). China also approved the first foreign multinational, Roche Pharmaceuticals, to enter Chinese retail market, on 16 May 2003, which demonstrated China's fulfilment of its WTO commitments. Prior to this deal, Roche had already set up a subsidiary in Shanghai (in the early 1990s), which covered more than 100 cities and 400 hospitals. The framework of Roche's entry was through a joint venture with the Chinese pharmaceutical company Shing Hsing, in which Roche provided 49 per cent of the investment. The possible targets of this joint venture included hospitals, retail pharmacies, and pharmaceutical imports and wholesaling. It was also noted that foreign investment accounted for a higher growth rate in China's exports (*China Pharmaceuticals*, 2003).

As mentioned earlier, the Chinese government also provides support for research institutes and universities. The major agency in charge of science and technology policy and resource allocation is the State Science and Technology Commission. With an overall R&D budget of US$18.7 billion in 2003 (1.31 per cent of GDP), China has increased its annual investment in science and technology. This rapid progress in science and education since 1978 arose from the policy directive issued by the Chinese Communist Party Central Committee and the State Council, on 6 May, 1995 entitled the 'Decision of the Central Committee of the Chinese Communist Party and the State Council on the Acceleration of Progress in Science and Technology'. The 'Decision' aimed at both public and private sectors reaching Chinese R&D spending equivalent to 1.5 per cent of GDP by the year 2000. This was a breakthrough decision that urged scientific academies and institutes of higher education to establish their own high-tech companies. The 'Decision' paid attention to special development issues, such as population control, food security, environmental protection (including pollution abatement technologies), and public health (such as pharmaceuticals development). The State Council also suggested that science should move out of the institutes and into private enterprise. Government research institutes should join Chinese and foreign companies in co-operative ventures, decide their own research focus and be responsible for profit management. The flow of personnel, information and capital are expected to improve to meet the market's need for research (Wikipedia, 2006; see also Louet, 2004; BGCG, 2002, p. 1). This policy was conducive to China's high-tech research.

The investment in biotechnology began in 1986 with the launch of the 863 Programme for high-tech investment, which has reached US$500 million per year and includes major infrastructure building in research institutes, laboratories, centres and universities. About fourteen of the eighteen genetically engineered drugs approved by the state were sponsored by the 863 Programme. Other programmes are the 'Torch Programme' and the 'Natural Science Foundation', which enabled China to strengthen its research capacity in genome sequencing, bio-agriculture, traditional Chinese medicine, tissue engineering and gene therapy, which have strong potential for future growth (BGCG, 2002, p. 12). In this environment, genetic engineering has made progress in China. China's Genome Project is headquartered in Shanghai. Since 1993, the Chinese Genome Project has carried out structural analyses of genomes, collected samples from Chinese minorities for a national depository, and developed techniques for human genome research informatics. The project started with the rice genome and expanded to human genome research, with a focus on disease-causing genes. A liver cancer gene project that began in 1993 is now focusing on chromosome 17. Other groups focus on genes associated with oesophageal cancer and psychological disorders. A research group at the Institute of Medical Biology at the West China University in Chengdu is looking for disease-causing genes in several cell lines. Twelve institutes and nineteen research groups are involved in the human genome project. Large cities with sufficient infrastructure have become major scientific hubs, thus, Shanghai has become a leading Chinese centre for biotechnology and human genome research (Wikipedia, 2006). The South Centre of Human Genome Research has participated in the international undertaking of the sequencing of the human genome, and the Beijing Global Biotechnology Centre has made a major investment in developing an international biotechnology research park in Hangzhou (ibid.).

China's participation in biopharmas is also worth noting. There are now 139 drugs in China's biopharma pipeline, 60 biologics, 43 generics, 19 antibodies and 11 vaccines (*China Pipeline*, 2004.). Of the 139 drugs, 96 (69 per cent) are at a preclinical stage, while only about 13 (9 per cent), are at Phase III, compared to 700 biologics in clinical development worldwide, 150 of which are in a late clinical stage (Anscomb, 2004). China's biopharmas are likely to expand in an environment of increased government-sponsored research, increasingly available private venture capital investment, and innovative R&D in the biopharma sector (BGCG, 2005, p. 1).

Transgenetic research

Innovative research thrives in a flexible policy environment. Chinese research institutes, such the Centre for Stem Cell Biology and Tissue Engineering in Guangzhou, are establishing a new primate research centre that aims to create transgenic primates for use as models of human disease and as a global source of primate stem cells. The USA used about 57,000 primates in 2000, and China is a major supplier, which is conducive to the clinical trials business that China is establishing. Conducting animal testing close to its source could save a large amount on the costs related to breeding and transportation. The use of non-human primates is a source of major political controversy and a target for attack by animal rights supporters in the West, which gives China the opportunity to become a major animal testing centre for clinical trials. However, it is also important that China develops mechanisms in transgenetic research that can answer the concerns of animal rights supporters.

Liberal attitudes and fewer ideological interventions in scientific research

The debate about stem cells and therapeutic cloning research in the USA is less contentious in China. When China approved Gendicine in December 2003, developed by Shenzhen's SiBiono GenTech, China was the first country in the world to officially approve a gene therapy for head and neck squamous cell carcinoma. In total, in 2004, there were about ten gene therapy products in development in China, compared to forty-three in the USA and ten in Europe (see *Nature News*, 2004; see also *Asia Pacific Biotech News*, 2004). Similarly, China's approval of genetic medicines for the treatment of cancer in 2006 also showed China's advantage in prioritizing scientific research without ideological baggage.

The changing demands of domestic markets

The demands for biomedicine have increased, especially for drugs that deal with ageing, chronic diseases and infectious diseases globally. To meet these demands, pharmaceutical research, especially biotech medicine, has also received increasing support for research and development. The case of Gendicine was instructive. It has become the first genetically modified medicine approved by China's regulatory authority. The growth in biomedicine in general has been steady over recent decades in China. The largest growth has been in biomedicine and the manufacture of equipment designed for pharmaceutical industry. The growth of traditional Chinese medicine was slower than the average rate because of difficulties in the modernization and industrialization process. Medical apparatus and equipment in manufacture decreased from a growth rate of 50 per cent in 2002 to 7.76 per cent in 2003. Sales revenue in 2002 was US$40.05 billion, a 16.4 per cent increase over 2001, with a profit margin of 22.02 per cent. Imports in these categories increased steadily from 2002 to 2005 (see *China Industry Development Report*, 2003).

Policy environment

As mentioned earlier, the Chinese government is supportive of multinationals conducting R&D in China. The most important policy was 'Item 863', which was approved by Chinese leader Deng Xiao-ping in March 1986 and encourages technology transfer from industrialized countries and scientific research in various sectors. Deng approved about US$1.2 billion of investment in scientific and technology research from China's public funds. This policy has important implications for China's pharmaceutical sector. For example, in 2000, China's SFDA allowed exemptions from import duties and other customs taxes, to encourage R&D by multinationals. China has also listed biotech as a priority sector to enlist foreign investment in its *Catalogue for the Guidance of Industries for Foreign Investment*. This will render foreign companies eligible for a lower rate of corporate income tax, about half of the 33 per cent paid by domestic companies. Foreign R&D can import equipment without tariffs, and the revenues reinvested in research are tax-free. It is believed that multinational investment in R&D can support the bottom line in their global budgets as well as strengthen the financial performance in their Chinese operation (BGCG, 2005, p. 12). The Chinese policy environment is believed to be one explanatory factor for the increase of R&D in drug development. About 96 per cent of the 8,000 new drug applications submitted to China's SFDA in 2003 were manufactured by local companies, and about 40 per cent of the new drugs are imitations (see Vasella, from BGCG, 2005). Since 2002, central government has mapped out a plan to encourage innovation in the pharmaceutical industry. The Chinese government set out to invest US$120 million between 2002 and 2005, ten times higher than the period 1996–2000, to strengthen research and development of new drugs, instead of duplicating current generics. Traditional Chinese medicine is treated equally in this investment. The pursuit of patent ownership should be a priority for the Chinese government because Chinese ownership of pharmaceutical patents is sparse. For example, in 2002, Chinese pharmaceutical developers owned only 2 per cent of the patents of the medicines sold on the domestic market (China Internet Information Centre, 2002).

Challenges

China's pharmaceutical sector is facing challenges in several areas, such as in the need for R&D, a lack of patented pharmaceuticals developed domestically, the enforcement of intellectual property rights, a scattered geographical layout, duplicated production processes, the need to modernize manufacturing technology and management structure, a lower market concentration in international trading competitiveness, and its position in the world's pharmaceutical industry and the regulation environment under WTO.

Policy and the legal environment

(i) Since early 2000, China has been moving steadily towards improving the legal and policy environment by encouraging innovation and increasing patent protection. By 2002, China was producing 1,350 types of crude pharmaceuticals, in 24 categories, among which 97 per cent do not have patent protection. To date, China has only two innovative drugs, arteannuin and sodium dimercapto-succinate, that had international patents (Hong Kong Development Council, 2002):

(ii) Manufacturers should decrease duplication of products and streamline the pharmaceutical business. By 2001, China had 5,164 or fewer companies producing crude drugs, medicine and chemical reagents, and preparations. It was believed that there was excessive duplication in the production of pharmaceuticals. At the time, questions were raised about the competitiveness of such a large number of indigenous pharmaceutical companies in the face of strong foreign competition. It was suggested that the government should raise the threshold for the entry of new pharmaceutical enterprises. The other solution – vertical and horizontal integration – is important to decrease the number of indigenous pharmaceutical companies. This strategy is working gradually. In the 1985–98 period, there was a sharp addition of 500 new companies to the list of pharmaceutical production. In 1999, there was an increase of only additional five companies; 17 in 2002, and 23 in 2001. It was also mandated by the new law that other institutions or companies would not be allowed to replicate similar production once a new application had passed the first step of the application process. Third, the new law also made it difficult for small pharmaceutical companies not meeting the GMP standard to continue by changing the drug production certification process or enforcing GMP authentification. In 2001, about 10 per cent of smaller businesses were eliminated in this way.

(iii) China should enforce GMP standards. Enforcing these standards has been crucial to upgrading the pharmaceutical industry in China. In 2002, China's State Drug Administration set a timetable for all Chinese pharmaceutical companies to qualify for GMP authentication by 30 June 2004. All medicines, preparations and crude drugs had to conform to GMP standards and gain GMP certificates. It was a crucial step for quality control in Chinese pharmaceutical companies. Although this has caused smaller, less competitive pharmaceutical companies into bankruptcy and forced mergers of others, it has been beneficial to the industry overall;

(iv) The government should facilitate the flow of distribution channels, implement a classified drug management system, and separate the medical treatment from drug management. Retail pharmaceuticals are mainly sold through two types of outlet: hospitals and pharmacies. It was estimated that about 85 per cent of drug sales were through hospitals. Since 2000, Chinese government has mandated the use of a classified drug management system, and the separation of prescription and OTC drug sales was tried out in a number of venues, to encourage the development of pharmacies/drug stores. There is also a policy that encourages retail drugstores to set up chains and large medical retail enterprises to expand trans-regional business. China has also gradually improved the OTC (over-the-counter) system. A system of 'medical insurance designated drugstores' with measures 'separating medical treatment from drugs' has also been introduced. Now, with doctors' prescriptions, patients can buy drugs outside hospitals. This encourages the expansion of retail pharmacies. These policy directions will also open up distribution channels for pharmaceutical companies;

(v) The government should improve centralized bidding and efforts to reduce drug prices. Centralized bidding through hospitals was designed to reduce doctors' backdoor dealings when purchasing drugs – so-called 'grey income' – and to decrease expenses for patients. But, this policy was found to have serious defects. As mentioned earlier, the Chinese government has made strong efforts to cut pharmaceutical prices. Since 1997, the State Development and Planning Commission has cut the prices many times of more than 200 varieties of centralized managerial drugs and reagents. The goal was to cut retail prices while wholesale prices remain the same. This policy was hard to implement because the reduction of retail prices hurt the profits of hospitals and drug wholesalers, shifting the loss of profits bade to pharmaceuticals producers.

Creating brand awareness

In this area, the major issues facing China are: the protection of intellectual property rights (IPR); a lack of finance; a lack of state-of-the-art drug development infrastructures; a lack of management talent; difficulty in exiting; poor corporate governance; currency exchange; reduction of tariffs; domestic harmonization and compliance with WTO regulations at the central and local levels; competitiveness of domestic pharmaceutical industries; product registration regulation; the regulation of the Chinese herbal industry; the competitive advantages of biochemical medicines; and the public–private sector partnership (BGCG, 2005, p. 1).

IPR protection

According to the Pharmaceutical Research and Manufacturers Association, the IPR situation in China remains a concern. Major challenges include 'a lack of date exclusivity protection, counterfeiting, and inconsistent administrative protection'. In 2004, Pfizer's patent on Viagra (Sildenafil/citrate) was overturned in July 2004; and GlaxoSmithKline abandoned an attempt to defend its patent on Avandia (Rosiglitazone maleate) in August 2004 (BGCG, 2005, p. 1). The case of Pfizer aroused some concerns. In 2001, Pfizer's patent of Viagra was invalidated by China's State Intellectual Property Office after it was challenged by Chinese drug makers on the basis that Pfizer had not supplied enough laboratory data in its original application (*Business India*, 2005, pp. 92–3). The resolution by the Chinese Court that Pfizer should be awarded its Viagra patent in 2006 was a good sign for the Chinese government's credibility in IPR enforcement.

Under the WTO, the Chinese government has worked hard to improve IPR-related issues. It has had the positive effect of encouraging major global companies to build upon their initial involvement in China. In a survey (BGCG, 2005), more than two-thirds of the thirty-five senior executives of multinational pharmaceutical companies questioned said that they expect the WTO agreement to strengthen IPR protection in China. The fact that multinationals are expanding the R&D capabilities – multinationals such as Novartis, Roche and Eli Lilly, who have operated in China for a significant amount of time – suggests that China's IPR issues are not serious enough to diminish China's strengths (BGCG, 2005, p. 1). Chinese government officials believe that intellectual property rights issues are improving in China and that they have been overly politicized (*Sina News*, 2006).

The issue of R&D merits an in-depth discussion

The major challenge facing all pharmas operating in China is R&D: (i) domestic producers need to harmonize their R&D practices. It has been noted by some analysts that Chinese researchers engaged in different R&D processes from the multinationals in drug development, such as developing detailed research plans, establishing well-defined targets and timetables, and discussing progress with colleagues (BGCG, 2005, p. 11); and (ii) China needs to strengthen its drug development capabilities. It was noted that most of its drug development facilities do not reach global standards. GLP was recently introduced in China, but the end of May 2005, the total number of GLP-compliant facilities in the country was still fewer than twenty. It was pointed out that China lacks innovative drugs, and most domestic producers in China still rely on copying existing drugs rather than developing new ones. Between 1985 and 1996, most patented drugs were raw materials or herbal medicine products. As mentioned earlier, China has had only two drugs, arteannin and sodium dimercapto-succinate, approved internationally (Wang, 2002).

The issue of R&D is particularly important in biopharmaceuticals. China's biopharma industry is highly fragmented, with 4,000 producers. The fact that few domestic manufacturers are large enough to run effective R&D programmes shows that integration is necessary. The domestic bio-pharmas need to spend a higher percentage on R&D, given the fact that leading multinational companies spend around 15 per cent of their revenues on R&D. On average, Chinese companies spend less than 5 per cent (ibid.).

The niche of traditional Chinese medicine

Traditional Chinese medicine has been found to be effective in treating some long-term, chronic diseases, but it needs major research investment as well as improvements in marketing and manufacturing, which will be further discussed later. For example, in 2002, active ingredients of only 2,000 (out of 10,000 or more popular medicines) were known to the researchers. In the Chinese herbal industry, local researchers own more than 80 per cent of the patents, but most of them are about a combination of herbs (China Internet Information Centre, 2002).

Enforcement of pharmaceutical laws and regulations

The issue of counterfeited drugs merits discussion in China. Worldwide, counterfeiting is a major issue facing global health. It affects the legitimate pharmaceutical industries; wastes health care resources; causes increased health care expenses; decreases medical effectiveness; it can cause fatal results. In the environment of globalization and internet trade, conventional regulations on pharmaceutical trade are no longer powerful enough. The internet makes it much easier for consumers to compare prices and obtain prescriptions. The global pharmaceutical counterfeiting business, without effective control, will be a serious threat to global health. It has been estimated that 10 per cent of drugs in the global market and 50 per cent of the drugs sold in developing countries are counterfeit. Most counterfeit drugs are advertised as cures for obesity, impotency, baldness, or malaria. The production chain for counterfeit drugs is complex: the ingredients might be found in country A, while the final product is manufactured in country B. Counterfeiting requires global collaboration. The World Health Organization (WHO) has established an emergency communication system providing a platform to update information on counterfeit drugs, and this can provide a model for monitoring Chinese counterfeit drugs (Lee, 2005).

Counterfeit drugs are a major public health issue in China. For example, in Suanzhou City, the local FDA confiscated twenty-seven illegal drugs that claimed to have therapeutic effects in cardiovascular diseases, prostate problems or impotency. The labels were misleading, and frequently the companies listed on the labels do not exist (*World Journal*, 2005).

In a major city in China's North-west region, Viagra was sold for the equivalent of US60¢ per tablet. With similar packaging as that produced by Pfizer, Chinese counterfeit Viagra cost thirty times less than the American version. In another pharmacy in Henan, Viagra was sold for US$20 per pack and no prescription was required. The Chinese medical authorities have increased their surveillance over counterfeit drugs yet challenges remain formidable. For example, collaborating with the police, the provincial Food and Pharmaceutical Supervision and Management Office reported 17,664 violations, and confiscated illegal medical equipment and pharmaceuticals worth a total of US$900,000. Yet counterfeit drugs are now sold in health food stores. Locally-made Viagra is a major source of profit for sellers of counterfeit drugs. It was reported that, by August 2000, about 500,000 counterfeit Viagra pills had been produced in Zhejiang Province, and by the time the manufacturer was arrested, 80 per cent of the pills had already been sold in the market. Counterfeiters usually buy real Viagra from licensed sellers, analyse the active ingredients and counterfeit the drug in their own factories. In many cases, the counterfeit Viagra is just coloured sugar pills.

In particular, Henan Province has become a major centre for counterfeiting, with counterfeiting manufacturers even gaining name recognition among Chinese consumers. Some consumers have mistaken the 'Henan made' mark for quality assurance. The counterfeit drugs have also gained some share of the overseas market via mail order to about ten countries including the USA, Britain, and as far as Israel. The king of counterfeit Viagra, Mr Mo Huei Biao, sold most of it via the internet. He was able to produce 10,000 pills a day, at a production cost of US$0.28 per tablet. Local post office clerks, who were part of the operation, received a commission from the counterfeiters. Some local government clerks even became accomplices in this business. Now, local food and drug supervision and management authorities work with a wide range of government offices to stem the flow of counterfeit drugs. These include the police department, the post office, telecommunications, banking and mobile communications. In the face of the government's high-pressure tactics, the counterfeiting operations have also diversified their operations. The manufacturing, packaging, transportation and payment are now dispersed to different locations (*Sina News Beijing*, 27 September 2005).

Related to counterfeiting is the issue of the recall and disposal of expired drugs. This problem is widespread in Chinese villages despite the efforts by the Chinese government to issue a national mandate to recall and dispose of all expired drugs. Some recalled drugs have been repackaged and sold in remote villages (*Sina News Beijing*, 24 May 2005). The price attracts poorer consumers because it is usually some 50 per cent less than the drugs' original price (*Sina News Beijing*, 16 May 2005).

Control of classified drugs

On 6 November 2005, 1,360,000 pills of triazolam were sold to the black market by the 'Jinling Pharmaceutical Company' in Jilin Province. Triazolam, a Class I classified drug, is one of the most strictly regulated pharmaceuticals in China because of its anesthetic effects. It is used clinically to treat insomnia but it is often used as a rape or robbery drug by criminals. Jingling Pharmaceutical Company was one of only two companies permitted by the Chinese government to produce triazolam. In a routine inspection in May, 2005, local authorities found that only 18 per cent had been sold to licensed pharmaceutical wholesalers; the rest went to illegal sellers. The problem stemmed from the lack of vigilance on the part of the sales agents at the pharmaceutical company. The sales agents did not inspect the licences of the buyers, and most were counterfeits sold on the street for US$1.7 (*World Journal,* 6 November 2005).

Evidence-based pharmaceutical tracking and consumer protection

China needs a system to supervise retailers in the tracking and monitoring of drug use. In the past, consumers could not sue pharmacists for malpractice when suffering severe side effects caused by pharmacist error in dispensing drugs. The experimental application in a Guanzhou drug store of tracking patients' drug reactions history can improve this problem. Monitoring and tracing side effects is especially important when assessing the effectiveness of pharmaceutical products.

Misuse and abuse of prescriptions

Abuse of prescription drugs is on the rise in China. For example, it was reported that prescriptions used for human problems were sold at veterinary clinics at ten times the original prices. The overpricing and misuse of veterinary medicine is prevalent, especially in large cities such as Beijing. Beijing city mandates that all pet dogs should be vaccinated in public clinics, as private clinics often use illegal vaccines. The danger of using human prescriptions for veterinary problems is that, once the disease crosses the species barriers, it poses a grave risk to humans. The epidemics of SARS and avian flu, where viruses have crossed the species barrier, should be instructive to Chinese pharmaceutical control officials.

Regulating clinical trials

China has become a major clinical trials centre for multinational pharmaceutical companies. Yet this trend might have an adverse effect on China's participation in this business if it is not closely monitored. As mentioned earlier, it was estimated that more than 800 drugs in Phase IV of clinical trials are tested annually in China, directly or indirectly involving more than 500,000 Chinese in the process. There has been a lack of coherent policy and regulatory framework to monitor the clinical trials business in China. It is reported that many multinationals engaged in Phase III and IV trials labelled 'free physical examinations' or 'free cures', with the collaboration of local state health agencies. The victims were often poor farmers. The most appalling incident involved a Korean drug manufacturer. The Korean cancer drug manufacturer reportedly engaged in clinical trials on a group of 593 farmers between 1997 and 2001. All of them became seriously ill or died during the process (*World Journal,* 22 May 2005).

Pharmaceutical pricing control

Pricing is a challenging issue facing Chinese pharmaceutical regulators and other stakeholders. It has serious implications for all parties involved. In May 2005, the Pharmaceutical Association in twenty-one provinces in

China appealed to the Chinese government for pharmaceutical discount (*Sina News Beijing*, 19 May 2005). An issue related to pricing is access. There need to be more pharmacies in rural and remote areas offering affordable medicines. Large cities and towns benefit compared to small towns and rural villages in the quality and quantity of services they receive, while rural health care is falling apart. Access to quality medicine is a serious issue in the villages. There needs to be major infrastructure building and public–private partnerships to improve the distribution channels of pharmaceuticals in remote areas (*Business India*, 2005, p. 92).

The Chinese authorities are in a difficult position *vis-à-vis* pharmaceutical price controls. On the one hand, they have to meet public health objectives and social solidarity goals; but on the other, they are concerned about the impact of such measures on local pharmaceutical producers. For example, in June 2005, the Chinese government took measures to lower the prices of six antibiotics and six other drugs on the state health insurance list. The rate of reduction reached more than 60 per cent for domestic drug manufacturers, but less for joint ventures or foreign ventures. On, average, the reduction rate on brand names was 20 per cent. The main purpose of this was to lower drugs costs in hospitals, but it was said to have had a major impact on local drug manufacturers rather than on the foreigner pharmas, because antibiotics sales accounted for about 30 per cent of pharmaceutical sales. It was estimated that most large Chinese pharmaceutical companies saw their profits from antibiotic sales reduced by around 50 per cent (*World Journal*, 23 May 2005). More often than not, the well-intended price control measures did not achieve the intended effect of reducing the burden on the patients, as hospitals might in fact recommend more profitable drugs to patients.

China's public health objectives cannot be ignored in this discussion. On the whole, the Chinese Medical Reform Commission has made a deliberate plan to improve pharmaceutical access, and the lowering of prices for antibiotics was just the first step. The Medical Reform Commission aims to solve the issues of pharmaceutical overpricing, providing more pricing flexibility, and stopping the abuse of antibiotics. The role of doctors and hospitals in the use of pharmaceuticals is a major issue in overpricing. Generally, doctors and hospitals tend to charge a commission for pharmaceutical products. Unlike the situation in the USA or the EU, medical practice is not separate from pharmaceutical sales in China. Since China's economic reforms, hospitals receive fewer subsidies from the government and have to rely on the profits made on pharmaceuticals to pay for hospital operations. The lower discount rate for joint ventures and foreign drug makers is to take into account the high R&D cost for those producers. Yet these public health measures have not achieved their intended effects.

This plan resulted from consultations with experts and local pharmaceutical vendors, the Ministry of Health and China's State Department. The publicly-owned Chinese pharmaceutical industries are apprehensive that this measure would allow their competitors to erode their discount drug market and shrink the share of the domestic pharmaceuticals market held by publicly-owned pharmas in China. The domestic pharmas believed that shrinking profits would force them out of the market while joint ventures or foreign pharmas would maintain their profit margins. According to the China Pharmaceutical Sales Association, in 2004, the average sale prices for pharmaceuticals decreased overall; for example, in three major pharmaceutical categories prices were lowered by 4.98 per cent. Pharmaceuticals produced by Chinese domestic manufacturers showed the greatest rate of decrease, which seriously affected their profit margins. This trend was felt painfully by such major domestic pharmaceutical industries as Ha Pharmaceuticals, Northern China Pharmaceuticals and New China Pharmaceuticals. In the first quarter of 2005, profits of twenty-three state-owned pharmaceuticals decreased by 12.1 per cent compared to the first quarter of 2004. These industries face the combined challenges of rising prices of raw materials and policy pressure. Some were forced to decrease antibiotics production, streamline or change that product structure, reduce production costs by moving facilities to the villages, increase exports, or move into health foods businesses. In fact, the health foods industry can be a potential growth area for domestic state-owned pharmas if they cannot cope with the competition in the conventional pharmaceuticals sector. One major potential market is villages, which house for some 80 per cent of the Chinese population. New policies by the Chinese government to support a reformed health care system in the villages provides room for discounted drugs. According to one study, the market at the country and village level reached about US$630 million by 2005. The other possibility is to enlarge the export market (Jing, 2005).

In consequence, pharmaceutical pricing reforms are likely to:

(i) filter out domestic pharmas that are not competitive;
(ii) lead to a concentration of ownership of antibiotic makers, allowing for horizontal integration;
(iii) allow pharmaceutical producers that are strong in R&D to gain larger market share;
(iv) increase partnerships between multinationals and domestic pharmaceutical companies;
(v) change the marketing strategy among competitors; and
(vi) this will also be likely to increase generics and decrease the effort made to produce branded drugs.

Yet, it is important to note that the pricing issue is just the tip of the iceberg. The main problem is the financing of China's health system, especially the use of pharmaceutical profits to support the cost of hospital operations.

In conclusion, this chapter has offered an in-depth analysis of China's pharmaceutical industry, its potential in the global market, and the major advantages of and challenges facing the Chinese pharmaceutical sector. Overall, global pharmaceutical development is supportive of China's position in the global market place. China's domestic market also offers tremendous opportunities for global stakeholders. It is widely anticipated that within fifteen (around 2020) years, China's will be the largest pharmaceuticals market in the world. China's advantages lie in the size of its market; lower costs for labour, production clinical trials and quicker drug approvals; a talent pool; policy environment and commitment to health care improvement; and emerging health issues. Yet the challenges are also enormous, such as a need for R&D, a lack of patented pharmaceuticals developed domestically, the enforcement of intellectual property rights, a scattered population geographically duplicated production processes, the need to modernize manufacturing technology and management structures, a lower market concentration in international trading competitiveness, and a weak position in the global pharmaceutical industry, and the regulatory environment under the WTO. The next chapter will offer an analysis of the ways in which the WTO would have an impact on the major stakeholders in China's pharmaceutical sector.

4
The World Trade Organization, and the Present and Future of China's Pharmaceutical Industry

Mei-ling Wang

China's pharmaceutical industry is experiencing a period of high growth, in which global stakeholders have played an important role. The WTO framework has opened up new opportunities and challenges for the stakeholders in this sector. The purpose of this chapter is to examine the WTO and Trade Related Aspects of Intellectual Property Rights Agreement (TRIPS) rules related to the pharmaceutical industry as a whole; the WTO's challenges to the regulatory and legal system in China, especially surrounding the patents issue, pharmaceutical quality control, price control, and the potential of Chinese herbal medicines; and the WTO's overall impact on the development of indigenous pharmaceutical and biotech industries.

The WTO, TRIPS and pharmaceuticals

In the WTO framework, the TRIPS Agreement has had the most impact on the pharmaceuticals industry, mainly through the regulations on pharmaceutical patents (WTO, 2005). WTO definitions on patents and related issues affect the way the pharmaceutical industry operates across the globe.

The foundations of the TRIPS agreement are: Uruguay Round negotiating objectives for TRIPS, 1986 Punta del Este Declaration, and the 1988/89 Mid-Term Review.

A patent is defined as 'an exclusive right granted for an invention, which is a product or a process that provides, in general, a new way of doing something, or offers a new technical solution to a problem'. The patent protects the inventor so that the new invention cannot be commercially made, used, distributed or sold without the patent owner's consent. The enforcement of the patent rights resides in the authority of the court. A third party can challenge the original patent owner, and if the challenge succeeds, the patent to the original owner will be declared invalid.

The right of patent ownership: a patent owner has the right to decide which party may – or may not – use the patented invention for a specific period of time in which the invention is protected; twenty years in TRIPS.

Licensing allows the patent owner to grant permission to other parties to use the invention on mutually agreed terms. The owner may also sell the right to the other party, who will then become the new owner of the patent. The protection of the patent rights ends once it expires. Once the invention enters the public domain, others can use the invention commercially.

The overarching principles for the WTO are national treatment (treating one's own nationals and foreigners equally) and most-favoured-nation treatment (equal treatment for nationals of all trading partners in the WTO). It is important to note that national treatment is honoured in other international intellectual property rights agreements.

TRIPS is also underlined by the principle that it encourages innovation, technology transfer and social development. Article 7, entitled 'Objectives', according to which the protection and enforcement of intellectual property rights should contribute to the promotion of technological innovation and to the transfer and dissemination of technology, to the mutual advantage of producers and users of technological knowledge and in a manner conducive to social and economic welfare, and to a balance of rights and obligations. Article 8, entitled 'Principles', recognizes the rights of Members to adopt measures for public health and other public interest reasons, and to prevent the abuse of intellectual property rights, provided that such measures are consistent with the provisions of the TRIPS Agreement.

Related to the previous point is that there are exceptions to the patent protection. One is for inventions contrary to public order or morality (Article 27.2). Patent protection is exempted if the protection is dangerous to human, animal or plant life or health, or seriously prejudicial to the environment. Accessing HIV medicine is a most significant case in point. The use of this exception is to protect public order and morality. The second exception is on diagnostic, therapeutic and surgical methods for the treatment of humans or animals (Article 27.3(a)). The third is that Members may exclude plants and animals other than micro-organisms and essential biological processes for the production of plants or animals other than non-biological and microbiological processes. However, any country, in exercising exceptions in plant varieties from patent protection, must provide a *sui generis* system of protection, which is also subject to review four years after the coming into force of the Agreement in a WTO Member Country (Article 27.3(b)). Members may provide limited exceptions to the exclusive patent rights if the exceptions do not conflict unreasonably with a normal exploitation of the patent and do not prejudice unreasonably the patent owner's and the third parties' legitimate interests (Article 30).

The exclusive rights that must be conferred by a product patent are the ones of making, using, offering for sale, selling, and importing for these purposes. Process patent protection must give rights not only over the use of the process but also over products obtained directly by the process.

Patent owners shall also have the right to assign, or transfer by succession, the patent, and to conclude licensing contracts (Article 28).

Other treaties governing pharmaceutical production that are equally important are: the convention of the World Intellectual Property Organization, the Paris Convention for the Protection of Industrial Property, the Berne Convention for the Protection of Literary and Artistic Works, the International Convention for the Protection of Performers, Producers of Phonograms and Broadcasting Organizations (Rome Convention), and the Treaty on Intellectual Property in Respect of Integrated Circuits (IPIC Treaty).

The persons or parties protected by the agreement: Article 1.3 defines who these persons are. These persons are referred to as 'nationals' but include persons, natural or legal, who have a close attachment to other Members without necessarily being nationals.

On the technical terms of intellectual property rights, Articles 3, 4 and 5 include the fundamental rules on national and most-favoured-nation treatment of foreign nationals, which are common to all categories of intellectual property covered by the Agreement. These obligations cover not only the substantive standards of protection but also matters affecting the availability, acquisition, scope, maintenance and enforcement of intellectual property rights, as well as those matters affecting the use of intellectual property rights specifically addressed in the Agreement.

It is also required that patents be available and patent rights enjoyable without discrimination as to the place of invention, and whether products are imported or locally produced (Article 27.1).

Patent applicants must disclose the invention in a sufficiently clear and complete manner for the professionals to carry out the application (Article 29.1).

Compulsory licensing and government use without the authorization of the patent right holder are permitted if they meet the conditions of protecting the legitimate interests of the rights holder, such as an attempt to obtain voluntary licensing not being successful and adequate compensation.

The protection of undisclosed information is particularly relevant to the pharmaceutical industry. The TRIPS Agreement requires the protection of undisclosed information, such as through trade secrets. It also stipulates conditions on undisclosed test data and other data whose submission is required by governments as a condition of approving the marketing of pharmaceutical or agricultural chemical products using new chemical entities. The government concerned is legally obligated to protect the data against unfair commercial use. In addition, WTO members must protect such data against disclosure, except under such conditions as the protection of the public.

Doha Declaration, 2001*

Several stipulations are important to the pharmaceutical industry in this declaration:

1. WTO rules should not pose a barrier to the protection of human, animal or plant life or health, or of the environment. The WTO will continue to co-operate with the United Nations Environment Programme (UNEP) and other international agencies regarding sustainable development issues.
2. The WTO continues to work toward the liberation of services. The General Agreement on Trade in Services (GATS) are to regulate, and to introduce new regulations on, the supply of services with the goal of promoting the economic growth of all trading partners and the expansion of developing and least-developed countries by continuing the work started in January 2000 under Article XIX of the General Agreement on Trade in Services.
17. The TRIPS will be interpreted in such a way as to support public health by promoting both access to existing medicines, and research and development into new medicines.
19. In accordance with Article 27.3(b), Article 71.1 and paragraph 12 of the Doha declaration, the WTO will examine the protection of traditional knowledge and folklore, and other relevant new developments. The WTO will take into account Articles 7 and 8 of the TRIPS Agreement in examining the development dimension. (This is pertinent to the producers of traditional medicines, such as Chinese medicines.)

Specifically, on health-related issues:

1. The WTO recognizes the gravity of the public health problems afflicting many developing and least-developed countries, especially those resulting from HIV/AIDS, tuberculosis, malaria and other epidemics.
2. The WTO Agreement on Trade-Related Aspects of Intellectual Property Rights (TRIPS Agreement) should be part of wider national and international action to address these problems.
3. The WTO recognizes the effects of intellectual property rights on the prices of medicines.
4. The TRIPS Agreement should not prevent members from taking measures to protect public health. Accordingly, the TRIPS Agree-

*Doha WTO Ministerial 2001: Ministerial Declaration. WT/MIN(01)/DEC/1, 20 November 2001; Ministerial declaration, adopted on 14 November 2001.

ment should be interpreted and implemented in a manner supportive of the WTO members' right to protect public health and, in particular, to promote access to medicines for all.

Most importantly, the WTO patent rights provisions should be interpreted flexibly in accessing important medicines for developing countries. That is, WTO members have the right to grant compulsory licences and the freedom to determine the grounds for such licences. The members have the right to determine what constitutes a national emergency or other circumstances of extreme urgency, such as public health crises, including those relating to HIV/AIDS, tuberculosis, malaria and other epidemics that can represent a national emergency or other circumstances of extreme urgency. WTO members are free to establish their own regimes for the exhaustion of patent rights without challenge, subject to the MFN and national treatment provisions of Articles 3 and 4. For countries with insufficient or no manufacturing capacities in the pharmaceutical sector in making effective use of compulsory licensing under the TRIPS Agreement, WTO were to find a solution by end of 2002. The solution was generated in 'the 30 August decision'.

The WTO also encourages developed-country members to provide incentives to their enterprises and institutions to promote and encourage technology transfer to least-developed country members pursuant to Article 66.2, and that least-developed country members will not be obliged, with respect to pharmaceutical products, to implement or apply Sections 5 and 7 of Part II of the TRIPS Agreement, or to enforce patent rights, until 1 January 2016.

Taken as a whole, the Doha declaration provides flexibility for developing countries to access medicines in a more liberal framework. Developing countries can collaborate to improve pharmaceutical access to life-saving medicines if they can further improve this framework. This portends opportunities for developing countries, such as China, India and Brazil, which have pharmaceutical production capacities, as well as multinationals.

China's commitment in WTO and pharmaceutical regulation

China's accession to the WTO was a major concern for the global community. To prepare for entry to the WTO, China reached an understanding with the USA on critical issues, especially on intellectual property rights, in a memorandum (see BBC News, 15 November 1999). In 1993, China implemented a new patent law to protect medicines and reagents and promised administrative protection to foreign patented drugs not sold on the Chinese market between 1986 and 1992. Therefore, since 1993 it has been illegal for Chinese pharmaceutical companies to copy foreign patented drugs registered in China. As a rule, a party applies for a patent after it discovers a molecule with a pharmacological function and, within a year, the party also needs to apply to other countries for patent protection. It usually takes 10–12 years to undergo the clinical trial process before a product reaches the marketing stage. The 1993 intellectual property rights agreement between China and the USA offers a 10-year protection for China's pharmaceutical companies.

The five major commitments by China related to pharmaceuticals are: the IPR of pharmaceutical inventions; removal of import tariffs; the discontinuation of administrative control of imported medical equipment; the opening of pharmaceutical sector from 1 January 2003; and the opening up of the health care services (*China Pharmaceuticals*, 13 August 2001).

Specifically:

(i) China had allowed more imports of pharmaceuticals. China's SFDA had allowed multinationals to invest, up to 70 per cent of the market share.
(ii) China allowed multinationals to enter domestic distribution and retail by 2003, but entry was limited to 11 November 2004 (*Chinapharm*, March 2002).
(iii) China allowed more intervention of the market in determining drug prices.
(iv) China promised to enforce pharmaceutical IPRs and allowed compensation of US$400 million – US$1 billion if pharmaceutical IPR was breached.
(v) A reduction of tariffs. After China's entry to the WTO, the average rate of tariffs for medicine and reagents was reduced from 9.6 per cent to 4.2 per cent. The price of medicines and preparations decreased to 4 per cent (Hong Kong Development Council, 15 July 2002). China also reduced its import tariffs from 8–15 per cent to 3–6 per cent by 2004 for pharmaceutical raw materials. A similar reduction was offered to imported Chinese herbs, such as ginseng (see also *China Pharma*, 21 June 2002).

For imported pharmaceuticals, the multinationals still have to comply with China's Pharmaceutical Regulation Law, effective since 28 February 2001, and its Imported Pharmaceutical Regulation Law and Pharmaceutical Pricing Law, also since 2001. According to Imported Pharmaceutical Regulations, an imported medicine has to obtain an imported medicine registration certificate before it gains market entry. The conditions for registration are:

(i) the imported medicine has to be approved by China's pharmaceutical manufacturing authority;
(ii) it has to meet the requirement of GMP regulation, which regulates the quality of pharmaceuticals;

(iii) it has to undergo clinical trial test procedures outlined by GCP regulations, which mandate that clinical trials have to be conducted within Chinese territories; and
(iv) pharmaceutical products from Taiwan, Hong Kong and Macao are required to follow the same rules as other imported medicines.

Imported medicines should be sold through business agents who have a Pharmaceutical *Sales Agent Permit*. These agents should also be legally registered with the Chinese pharmaceutical regulation authorities (Hong Kong Development Council, 15 July 2002).

The full impact of the WTO on China's pharmaceutical sector remains to be seen. Yet a positive outlook was postulated before and during the initial phase of China's accession. Many believed that the WTO would open up more markets for Chinese pharmaceutical producers. Chinese producers would be forced to update their innovations, technology and management resulting from competitive pressures. WTO membership would open the markets in prescriptions and OTC drugs for foreign producers.

These predictions have been largely true. Sales in all categories of the pharmaceutical sector have increased since China's entry to the WTO. It is estimated that prescription drugs will rise to US$6.5 billion by 2010 (*Chinapharm,* 2001). WTO membership has opened up government-approved pharmaceutical retailers. By 2001, China had 16,000 retailers, only 1,000 of which were large sellers. They accounted for 70 per cent of the market share, with an average profit rate of 12 per cent. After entry to the WTO, their market share has reduced, replaced by foreigner sellers or joint ventures (ibid.).

It is also important to note that China's WTO membership has inevitably posed a challenge to all stakeholders in the pharmaceutical sector. For example, it was noted that, prior to WTO entry, some widely used medicines produced by domestic manufacturers, mainly OTCs, was already experiencing excessive supply. This has intensified the price wars between domestic and foreign medicine. The foreign pharmaceutical companies were advised to avoid competition in this area and pursue their respective market niche (Hong Kong Development Council, 15 July 2002). These kinds of challenges will inevitably continue to intensify as China further opens up its pharmaceutical sector. This will be discussed later in this book.

China's developments in pharmaceutical regulation under the WTO framework

The major impact brought about by WTO entry is in the changes that the Chinese legal and regulatory system has had to make to comply with WTO requirements of non-discrimination and transparency. It is worth noting that China has made rapid improvements in legal and regulatory frameworks in pharmaceutical-related issues, such as clinical trials, quality control and intellectual property rights, to accommodate WTO rules.

Historically, drug-related regulations were administered by the former Bureau of Drug Policy Administration (BDPA) within the Ministry of Public Health; drug production and distribution were regulated by the former State Pharmaceutical Administration (SPAC); and traditional Chinese medicine was supervised by the State Administration of Traditional Chinese Medicine (SATCM). The function of the BDPA was similar to that of the US FDA, in charge of enforcing Chinese pharmaceutical law in general. Specifically, it implemented China's Drug Administration Act in 1995, and regulated pharmaceutical manufacturing, distribution, sales and advertising. In addition, it approved domestic and imported drugs and biologics, and formulated and issued national drug standards. A major function of BDPA was pharmaceutical quality control through the National Institute for the Control of Pharmaceutical and Biological Products (NICPBP), the most important gate-keeper of pharmaceutical quality control. The other agency closely related to the function of the BDPA was the Centre for Drug Evaluation, whose main charge was pharmaceutical regulation, such as the technical review of applications, and technical and scientific guidelines for drug development. The SPAC, created in 1978 under the direct supervision of the Ministry of Public Health, supervised pharmaceutical R&D, manufacture, sales and distribution. As the state allowed more autonomy by private companies, SPAC's duties have been reduced to reviewing and approving the administrative protection of pharmaceutical products (Gross, 1998). This old structure was believed to have major problems: contradictory administrative behaviours and standards among different agencies, neglected areas that are not regulated by any agencies, and conflicts of interest (see Zhen, 2003).

The reforms starting from 1998 paved the way for today's pharmaceutical regulation system. In 1998, China founded the State Drug Administration (SDA), similar to the US FDA. In 1999, China reformed its health insurance system. In 2000, China established the system categorizing prescription from non-prescription drugs. This reform sharply increased the sale of non-prescription drugs. In 1999, the sale of non-prescription drugs was US$600 million and in 2000 US$1.5 billion, six times more than the volume in 1990. It was estimated that sales of non-prescription drugs in 2005 was worth more than US$7.3 billion (see also *China Pharma*, 21 June 2002).

The 1998 reform focused on the centralization of responsibilities and power. As a result, the State Drug Administration agency was created to combine the responsibilities of drug administration, production, distribution and traditional Chinese medicine by the SPAC and BDPA, and some responsibilities by the State Administration of Traditional Chinese Medicine (SATCM). The creation of the SDA has helped to streamline and centralize regulatory authority by replacing the SPAC and BDPA, and facilitating collaboration with SATCM for pharmaceutical regulation. As an entity, the SDA engaged in pharmaceutical regulation, the supervision of research, registration, production, market circulation/advertising, the use of chemical drugs and antibiotics, traditional Chinese medicine and preparations, biological products, radiopharmaceuticals, biochemical drugs, diagnostic products, medical devices and material, and medical packaging material. Under the SDA, the Department of Drug Registration closely supervised the technical operations of the registration of new drugs, biologics, generics and imported drugs (for example, narcotics and radiopharmaceuticals), conducted drug evaluation, and guided China's other drug control institutes through the Division of Chemical Drugs, Division of Traditional Chinese Medicine, Division of Biologics, and Division of Special Drugs. In this structure, pharmaceutical regulation was also controlled by the Department of Safety and Surveillance, Department of Market Supervision, Department of International Collaboration, and Department of Personnel and Education (Gross, 1998).

In March 2003, another administrative reform paved the way for the system currently used in China. In that reform, the SDA was reorganized into the State Food and Drug Administration (SFDA). Previously, the SFDA had only been in charge of food safety (Zhen, 2003). The major challenge since then has been to separate administration and execution. The 1998 Food and Health Law stipulates that the SFDA should be in charge of food control, but because of its limited staff members and equipment, its implementation ability is limited. As a result, food control is carried out by Epidemic Prevention Stations (ibid.).

Initially, the new system created confusion because of the uncertainty as to the responsibilities of each of the new departments. Reduction in the numbers of support staff has also caused some delays in reviewing some drug applications and clinical data. At the time, the restructuring of the local provincial and local pharmaceutical regulatory system was uncertain. Vertical integration was a challenge to the reform.

Now, the major Chinese agencies that regulate the pharmaceutical industries are the SFDA, the State Development and Reform Commission (SDRC), and the Provincial Administration for Industry and Commerce, which cooperates with the Provincial Food and Drug Administration to regulate drug advertisements. The SFDA takes charge of drug administration, while the SDRC oversees drug price administration (ibid.).

Specifically, the reformed SFDA has expanded its responsibilities beyond the 1998 regulations to include: pharmaceutical regulation; supervision of research; registration; production; market circulation/advertising; use of chemical drugs and antibiotics; traditional Chinese medicine and preparations; biological products; radiopharmaceuticals; biochemical drugs; diagnostic products; medical devices and materials, and medical packaging material; drug standards; the national essential drugs list; the control of non-prescription drugs and traditional Chinese medicines; quality control of manufacturers and distributors; supervision of controlled drugs; bulk chemicals; standards for registration of pharmacy practitioners; and international collaboration and liaisons (Rui, 2001). The SFDA oversees eleven functional departments, includes seven departments covering drugs administration: General Office, Department of Drug Registration, Department of Medical Devices, Department of Drug Safety and Inspection, Department of Market Compliance, Department of Personnel and Training, and Department of International Co-operation. Since its reorganization, it has made progress in two major areas: (i) improving drug regulation. Since 1998 the SFDA has been given major responsibilities in the design and implementation of drug administration rules and regulations that address legislative gaps in harmonizing with international practices in medical devices regulation, pharmacist law, prescription and non-prescription drug administration systems, and a drug adverse reaction reporting system; and (ii) The SFDA has also abolished new drug administrative protection in the current Drug Registration Regulations and strengthened the punishment for the manufacture and distribution of adulterated or misbranded drugs under the current Drug Administration Law. These rules and regulations have effectively 'confronted, restrained, and decreased unhealthy or unlawful practices in the pharmaceutical industry'. The SFDA also reinforces the legal management of administrative staff (Zheng, 2003, p. 10).

The SFDA is also instrumental in fostering the growth of the pharmaceutical economy. For example, the SFDA has expedited environmental policy by harmonizing its laws and regulations to make them consistent with the WTO regulatory framework, and standardizing the rules and regulations governing the pharmaceutical industry. This was designed to encourage the sustainable growth of the pharmaceutical industry in China (Chinese Medicine and Commerce Association, 2003; see also Cheng, 2003).

Reimbursements

Pharmaceutical reimbursements are payments from the Chinese Government to public hospitals for prescriptions to patients. The pharmaceutical reimbursement system in China, based on the 1998 reform, shows the involvement of the public sector in pharmaceutical access in hospitals. The principles underlying pharmaceutical reimbursements were: clinical need, safety, efficacy, price comparisons, convenience, and a balance between Chinese herbs and biomedicine (see also *China Pharma*, 21 June 2002). Under this structure, pharmaceutical reimbursement schedules were maintained at both national and provincial levels. Around 1,400 pharmaceuticals received reimbursements from state-controlled insurance organizations. About 90 per cent of the drugs on this list were identical to those on local government reimbursement lists. Because of price controls, most of the reimbursed drugs were made by local manufacturers (ibid.).

Provincial and municipal governments were allowed a 10 per cent local readjustment to alter the national reimbursement list, but this system was criticized by foreign pharmaceuticals as inconsistent. The demand for low-priced drugs makes it hard for foreign companies to qualify. It was pointed out that the drugs on the list were not consistent with the regulations. The local adjustment was often found to be on a different system from that of the central government which encourages multinational participation. One solution that foreign pharmaceutical companies found to address this dilemma was to enter into joint ventures with local partners to facilitate their involvement in the regulatory process and to gain a greater market share. It was also pointed out that this reimbursement might have little effect on the competition for market share, since most of the population did not have health insurance. By 1998, national health insurance only covered some 10–15 per cent of the population, government insurance covered 7–8 per cent, and local labour insurance covered 13–20 per cent of the local population (Gross, 1998).

Classification of domestic drugs

The classification system derived from the 1998 system, which had the following framework:

Class I: new pharmaceuticals that have not been approved in any country (such as those reported in a foreign pharmacopoeia);

Class II: products currently in process of being approved by a major regulatory agency (FDA, EU, Japanese government) but not specified in a foreign pharmacopoeia;

Class III: preparations made of two or more compounds;

Class IV: synthetic products of natural compounds, approved drugs, and modified formulas that have long been approved and in use in international markets; and

Class V: adopted drugs with a new indication.

Foreign drugs belong to a separate class.

In the old system, the SDA regulated Class I, II, III and imported drugs, and provincial governments dealt with Class IV, and V. Now, the SFDA makes a distinction between OTC and prescription drugs.

Registration

The current system derives from the 1998 reform. In the 1998 reform, two separate processes existed for locally manufactured drugs and imported drugs. Both required the submission of a registration data package. This package required the following information: application form, technical data, chemistry, manufacturing, standard and analytic methods, stability, quality control, non-clinical pharmacology and toxicology, local clinical data, labelling, and three samples testing.

In this system, Class I manufacturers may apply directly to the Centre for Drug Evaluation (CDE). Other manufacturers needed to submit an application to the provincial Department of Health, which then forwards it to the Centre for Drug Evaluation. A CDE advisory committee performs a full review of the drug, identifies possible deficiencies in the application, and sends queries to to the manufacturer for a response. After the CDE's review, the results are communicated to the BDPA. BDPA reviews an new drug under investigation, while MOPH (Ministry of Public Health) decides whether to approve of a new drug application (Gross, 1998).

On 28 February 2005, new Administrative Measures for Drug Registration were issued and implemented on 1 May 2005. These measures aim to further streamline the pharmaceutical regulatory processes. However, pharmaceutical registration and obtaining production and sales permits still involves the co-ordination and co-operation of numerous different central, provincial and local authorities, and this process can be cumbersome.

Approval of imported drugs

The current system retains the major elements of the 1998 framework. In the original regulations, the manufacturer first sent an application to the MOPH's International Co-operation Centre's pharmaceutical division, where the Imported Drug Evaluation department reviewed the application. The committee could request the manufacturer to conduct a local registration/clinical verification study. After reviewing the report submitted by the manufacturer, the BDPA would give its decision. Imported drugs were required to provide the following information:

1. Name of the drug, purpose, and proof.
2. Chemical composition.
3. Technological and manufacturing conditions.
4. Quality assessment.
4. Pharmacodynamic data and literature.
5. General pharmacological investigations.
6. Acute toxicity, long-term toxicity, and toxicity of a topical new drug.
7. Impact of each ingredient on the efficacy or toxicity of a compound preparation.
8. Mutagenicity tests.
9. Reproductive toxicity.
10. Carcinogenicity tests.
11. Drug dependency data.
12. Pharmacokinetic investigations on animals.

13. Preliminary stability tests on drug substances and their singular or compound preparations.
14. Quality standard of drug used for clinical investigation.
15. Drug sample, clinical investigation plan and preclinical review.
16. Clinical pharamcokinetic investigation.
17. Bioavailability or dissolution tests.
18. Stability test results and dates of expiration.
19. Protocol and remarks of production quality standards.
20. 3–5 sample batches produced in succession, with analytic reports.
21. Clinical reports and summary.
22. Samples of packaging material, labelling material and package inserts.

China has made attempts to harmonize its drug approval system with international standards. A new drug requires about five to eight years to be approved, shorter than the eight to ten years' average length in the USA. New drug approval requires:

(i) Investigational new drug application: besides the application materials, a sample of the drug is required to be submitted to the drug administration at the provincial level. Foreign biopharmaceutical manufacturers may apply direct to the SFDA.
(ii) Preclinical and clinical trials: China introduced its first GCP guidelines in 1998, as mentioned earlier; multiple designs, including single or double-blinded randomized controls are allowed.
(iii) Trials in China are generally not placebo-based. Instead, they compare the drug's performance with existing methods of treatment. In 2000, the SFDA issued new rules stipulating that at least 50 per cent of the work for Phase I–III clinical trials must be conducted by accredited National Clinical Trial Centres.
(iv) Quality testing: once clinical trials have been completed, the manufacturer should provide enough product samples, which have to be manufactured in three consecutive batches, for random tests.
(v) Certification: a registration certificate is issued once the quality test process has been completed successfully. Chinese provincial governments may require additional procedures to be carried out, which may not be transparent or consistent.
(vi) Post-market surveillance: the level and quality of post-market surveillance activity is increasing. All of the phase IV trials must be carried out at the same site as earlier trials (BGCG, 2005, p. 1).

Clinical trials

Drug approval is closely related to clinical trials. In the 1998 reform, clinical trials for domestic manufacturers were a separate process from that for foreign producers. The procedures for foreign producers were:

1. All foreign drugs need clinical trial data in China. China has gradually harmonized with the international clinical trial system since 1998 by the adoption of good clinical practice (GCP), which was compatible with international standards. These GCP standards were intended for drug-registration-related issues in clinical trials in China. After the clinical trials, all foreign drugs must undergo an initial two-year trial/review involving periodic comparative studies with locally manufactured products.
2. The study must be comparative, with randomized, double-blind parallel groups.
3. The minimum sample size is usually sixty samples per group.
4. Open-label studies must be evaluated on a case-by-case basis.
5. For ethical reasons, active controls over placebos are preferred for the control group.
6. Clinical and/or surrogate endpoints should be used for efficacy endpoints, depending on the drug (for example, blood pressure reduction, intraocular pressure reduction and so on)
7. Data concerning both clinical and laboratory adverse events should be collected at the safety endpoints (Gross, 1998).

This system was criticized because: (i) the uniform testing system did not take into account specific conditions of different diseases or specific population characteristics; (ii) it lacked statistical standards and specification of sample size; (iii) the hypothesis testing was not sufficient to detect population-level effects; and (iv) the standard was somewhat different for domestic producers. Domestic manufacturers have to submit one drug sample that is the exact product the company intends to manufacture; and drug stability data and the specification of OTC or prescription categories. (Gross, 1998).

Some modifications have been made and the clinical trials system in China is now more in line with international standards.

Now, under China's GCP, health authorities are responsible for approving new drugs by assigning clinical trials to investigational centres. It has been estimated that the Chinese government has given permission to 50–60 hospitals and medical centres for clinical trials. In addition, each study must be carried out at a minimum of three different sites, and of these, one must be in North China and one in South China. Furthermore, a foreign company may not conduct clinical trials itself; it must go through its Chinese counterpart. In addition, the determination of sample sizes varies on a case-by-case basis. In this system, the principal investigators of clinical trials play a significant part in determining the process of the clinical trials and the final reports for the review committee (*see* Pacific Bridge newsletter, 2005, and interview with Dr Wei Zhang, Assistant Professor, Bejing University, 20 January 2006).

Approval of non-prescription (OTC) products

The information (from the SFDA) relevant to manufacturers includes:

1. OTC drugs must be clearly identified on the labels and data insert sheets and must be conform to the National Catalogue of OTC Products list.
2. The SFDA is the authority to approve and regulate the use of OTCs.
3. Manufacturers can use a special OTC mark once it has received the Certificate of Examination and Registration for Non-prescription Drug Products.
4. Manufacturers should print this special mark on the product's label, data insert sheet, and interior and exterior packaging within 12 months of it obtaining the Certificate of Examination and Registration for Non-prescription Drug Products.
5. The red label is used for Class-A OTCs and green lake used for Class-B OTCs.
6. When using monochrome printing, the Chinese characters meaning Class A or Class B should be printed on the base of the products.
7. Penalties for violations have been regulated since 2001 by the Pharmaceutical Administration Law of the People's Republic of China.

Price controls

The Chinese government plays an active role in pharmaceutical price control. The basis of current price control is the 1999 reform, which had several stipulations: (i) the distinction was made between brands and generics, (ii) the criteria of price comparisons derived from developing countries are comparable to levels in China; (iii) a distinction was made between GMP-compatible and non-GMP compatible drugs; and (iv) a distinction was made between copies and innovative drugs. In this framework, the government did not allow any arbitrary reduction or increase in drug prices. It also mandated a special discount prices for autonomous regions. It granted high profit margins to more innovative drugs – 25–30 per cent for Class I drugs and decreasing profit levels for Class II, III and IV. It was criticized because this system excludes marketing expenses from profit calculations (Gross, 1998; see also *China Pharma*, 21 June 2002).

The regulatory mechanism for price controls was the State Development and Reform Commission (SDRC). In its scheme, only a small number of prices are regulated by the market (Guo *et al.*, 2003). This system is based on the following principles:

(i) prices are established by the SDRC. The SDRC plays a major role in regulating the drugs on the National Medical Insurance Drug List, and those manufactured or distributed by monopolies or restrictively (for example, patented drugs, Class I and II new drugs, narcotics, and category A psychotropics. Price factors include average cost, supply and demand, and affordability for the general public;

(ii) prices are guided by the SDRC: the SDRC controls drug prices indirectly by implementing a policy of purchasing/selling price differences and profit margins. Price formulations are based on: setting an intermediate price that allows the drug price to increase; setting an intermediate price that allows the drug price to increase and decrease within a fixed range; setting a ceiling price below which the drug price can only decrease; and setting a threshold price above which a drug price can only increase. The drugs in the last category listed have more price elasticity than those established by the SDRC;

(iii) prices adjusted by the market: these include drugs that are of low value and small-yield products, such as tinctures, vulcanized fatty oils and syrups. For these drugs, the manufacturers, distributors and medical institutions must report to the SDRC the actual purchase and selling prices, as well as quantity, and establish prices according to the principles of impartiality, reasonableness, honesty, and the match between price and quality. This policy allows the supply of drugs at reasonable prices to consumers (*China Pharmaceuticals*, 2002).

The central government constantly monitors pharmaceutical prices and adjust these in response to public concerns. For example, in June 2004, the state lowered the prices of twenty-four antibiotics by 30–50 per cent. On average, pharmaceutical prices in hospital pharmacies were much higher than those of retail pharmacies, on average by 39.5 per cent. In an estimate of the most-used 100 pharmaceuticals, hospital pharmacies priced them at 1.85 per cent higher than the national average, while in contrast, retailers priced them at 16.15 per cent lower than the national average. (*Chinapharm*, 2004).

Advertising control authorities

The main agency regulating food and drug advertising is the Provincial Food and Drug Administration (PFDA), while the Provincial Administration for Industry and Commerce (PAIC) supervises all advertisements, including those for drugs. All drug advertisements must be regulated by the local Food and Drugs Administration to verify their authenticity and legitimacy consistent with the package labels approved by the SFDA (Shang, 2001). In this practice, review and supervision responsibilities are separate. To co-ordinate the possible loopholes caused by this gap, a law introduced in November 2000 stipulates that the local Food and Drug Administration has the authority to supervise and urge the PAIC to sanction unlawful drug advertisements. The revised law says that the Provincial Food and Drug Administration should monitor drug advertisements, report breaches to the PAIC and suggest penalties for those who disobey the law; or, and prosecute offenders after investigation (Cai, 2001).

Intellectual property rights

The prospects for China's pharmaceutical business are closely linked with the enforcement of intellectual property rights (IPR). IPR-related issues are critical to China's scientific and technology development as a whole. By 2004, it was estimated that China owned the IPR of only 0.3 per cent of the core technology; 99 per cent of enterprises have not applied for IPR protection; and 66 per cent do not have their own trade marks. But, since then, Chinese IPR capacity has improved and in most of the recent IPR law suits, the plaintiffs have won their cases (China State Intellectual Property Rights Office, 2005). The history of IPR regulation in China demonstrates the country's attempt to integrate with the international system since occassion to the WTO. In April 1985, China implemented the People's Republic of China Intellectual Property Rights Law; on 1 January 1993, this IPR regulation was extended to cover pharmaceuticals; the People's Republic of China Trademark Law was passed by the People's Congress and implemented on 1 January 1983. It was further amended in 1993 and 2001. The People's Republic of China Pharmaceutical Management Law was passed on 20 September 1984 and implemented on 1 December 2001. The Approving a New Drug Law and Regulations on the Protection of New Drug and Pharmaceutical Technology Transfer were implemented on 1 May 1999. On 12 December 1992 and 14 October 1992, the State Council passed the Regulations on Administrative Protection of Pharmaceuticals and Protection of Chinese Herbal Medicines Laws, which were implemented on 1 January 1993. On 2 September 1993, the People's Congress passed the People's Republic of China Anti-Illegal-Competition Law to further strengthen intellectual property rights protection. In this new climate, pharmaceutical patent applications have increased since 2000. On 2001, pharmaceutical-related and raw chemicals patents numbered 2,487, about a 14.4 per cent increase; in 2002, the total number was 3,050, about a 22.6 per cent increase; and in 2003, the number was 3,423, about a 12.2 per cent increase over the previous year. Across those three years, the average rate of increase was 16.4 per cent. Biomedicine-related patents during those three years were 1,806 applications (a 13.3 per cent increase) in 2001; 2,342 applications (a 29.7 per cent increase) in 2002; and 3,263 (a 39.3% increase over the previous year) in 2003. Biomedicine-related patents increased by an average rate of 27.4 per cent over 2001–3. Patent applications for Chinese herbal formulas were 3,247 in 2001 (a 63.9 per cent increase over the year 2000); 2,865 applications in 2002 (a 11.5 per cent increase over 2001); and 4,030 applications in 2003 (a 40.7 per cent increase over 2002). Chinese herbal patent applications have increased 31 per cent on average. Biotechnology patent applications were 884 in 2001, a 37.7 per cent increase over 2000; 1,075 in 2002, a 23.8 per cent increase over 2001; 1,476 in 2003, a 41.3 per cent increase over 2002. The average increase rate for biotechnology patents between 2001 and 2003 was

34.3 per cent. Patents for genetic engineering numbered 2,331 in 2001, a 47.1 per cent increase over the year 2000; 2,077 in 2002, an 11.9 per cent increase; and 2,144 in 2003, a 3.2 per cent increase over 2002. The average increase rate for patents for genetic engineering was 18.6 per cent between 2001 and 2003 (*Chinapharm*, 2004).

In terms of administrative structure, China's State Intellectual Property Rights Office (SIPO) was established in 2005 to strengthen the enforcement of intellectual property rights issues in China. This move derived mainly from the policy changes in 1980, when the State Council required the Patent Office of the People's Republic of China (CPO, the predecessor of SIPO) to 'protect intellectual property, encourage invention and creation, help popularize inventions and their exploitation, promote the progress and innovation in science and technology, and meet the needs of socialist modernization' (see China's SIPO website). A series of changes including those in 1985, 1992 and 2000 led to a more complete structure. In 1985, the Patent Law of the People's Republic of China was proposed and came into force during the same year. The patent law was further amended twice by the Standing Committee of the National People's Congress, on 12 March 1992 and 25 August 2000. In 1998, a reform in government agencies changed the CPO (China Patent Office) into the SIPO (State Intellectual Property Rights Office). Now the SIPO is under the direct control of the State Council and is the main government authority dealing with patent-related enforcement and foreign intellectual property rights issues with China.

The major responsibilities of SIPO are:

(i) to receive and examine patent applications of inventions, utility models and designs, granting patent rights to inventions and creations according to the patent law; and the examination and determination of requests for re-examination and invalidation;
(ii) to participate in the revision of the patent law and its implementation regulations;
(iii) to formulate an examination guide, working procedures and regulations;
(iv) to participate in the study of patent rights discretion and infringement determination; accept the entrustment of the people's court and patent administrative authorities to provide advice on the settlement of rights discretion and infringement;
(v) to join the organization of patent education and training and;
(vi) to manage patent documentation, provide a patent information service to the public, assist with patent documentation and patent information work in departments and local areas, and promote the dissemination of patent information at all levels of society (ibid.).

Administration offices that concern the pharmaceutical industry are the following:

(i) The Patent Affairs Administration Department deals mainly with the examination of patents, the formulation and implementation of patent procedures, laws and regulations, and the publication of patent applications.
(ii) The Preliminary Examination and Flow Management Department deals with initial procedural and examination matters related to patent applications, such as receiving patent applications and fees, patent-related inquiries and requests, the management of patent-related archives, issuing of patent certificates, etc.
(iii) Chemical Examination Department 1 processes the classification of patent applications in the fields of food engineering, medicine, biological engineering, chemical engineering, petroleum chemical engineering and metallurgy, and the substantive examination of patent applications.
(iv) Chemical Examination Department 2 processes the classification of patent applications in the fields of non-organic chemistry, organic chemistry, polymer chemistry, biochemistry, agricultural chemistry and electronic chemistry, and the substantive examination of patent applications.
(v) The Patent Re-examination Board of the SIPO deals with re-examining applicants who were not satisfied with decisions made by the patent office; examining invalidation requests; defending cases in court relating to patent litigation; participating in research into patent rights discretion and infringement determination; and accepting the decisions of the people's court and patent administrative authorities to provide advice on the settlement of patent infringement.
(vi) The Patent Documentation Department processes the collection and international exchange of patent documentation; establishes, prepares and manages search files for examination (including patent and non-patent documentation); manages the patent library, which provides a patent information service to the public; offers professional guidance to the national patent documentation network and information service; and is responsible for patent documentation research (ibid.).

It is important to note that China has made attempts to harmonize with the intellectual property rights requirements of the WTO and other major international conventions. A historical review of major events shows that China has made significant changes in intellectual-property-rights-related issues. For example, in the patent law implemented on 1 April 1985, pharmaceuticals or chemical derivatives were not allowed to be granted patents. In July 1987, the Regulations on Pharmaceutical Protection and Technology Transfer changed this regulation by mandating that new pharmaceutical inventions would be protected by patents for ten years. On 2 January 1993, amendments to the patent law extended the protection of pharmaceutical inventions from ten to twenty years. In another regulation, Article 10 of the Anti-llegal-Competition Law stipulated the criminality of the violation of trade secrets, such as in counterfeiting Chinese herbal medicine formulae (*Chinapharm*, 2001)

China has also gradually harmonized its IPR practices with international norms (China SIPO 2005). For example, on 3 June 1980, China acceded to the Convention supported by the World Intellectual Property Organization. China is also a practising member of the Paris Convention for the Protection of Industrial Property, the Patent Co-operation Treaty (PCT), the Budapest Treaty on the International Recognition of the Deposit of Microorganisms for the Purposes of Patent Procedure, the Locarno Agreement Establishing an International Classification of Industrial Designs, and the Strasbourg Agreement Concerning International Patent Classification. On 1 January 1994, after becoming a member state of the PCT, the SIPO began to serve as a Receiving Office, International Searching Authority and International Preliminary Examining Authority. Chinese became one of the PCT working languages (ibid.).

In 2004, the National Copyright Administration (NCAC) participated in a WTO transition review of intellectual property protection in China, the APEC (Asia-Pacific Economic Cooperation) Experts' Conference, and the intellectual property negotiations between China and the EU. In March, the NCAC attended the bilateral consultations and negotiations between China and the USA at the working party level. NCAC provided opinions on copyright legislation, enforcement and policy for the Leading Workgroup on Commerce and Trade with the USA, and promoted the successful solution to the IPR problems between China and the USA.

The government's action to enforce intellectual property rights

Despite international criticism, the Chinese government has taken measures to comply fully with IPR protection in spite of the difficulty of implementing laws at the local level. In 2004, under the leadership of Vice-Premier Wu Yi, a Lead Group of IPR Protection of the State Council was set up. The Lead Group of IPR Protection comprised twelve related central authorities including the Supreme People's Court, the Supreme People's Procuratorate (SPP), the Ministry of Commerce (MOFCOM), the Ministry of Public Security (MPS), the State Administration for Industry and Commerce (SAIC), the National Copyright Administration (NCAC), the SIPO, and the General Administration for the Customs of China (GACC). The Lead Group aimed to direct and co-ordinate IPR protection issues at the national level, and to resolve IPR cases. Under the aegis of this Lead Group, enforcement by multiple departments was established. This determination to enforce IPR issues at the national level has also trickled down to local levels. Similar IPR protection working groups to those at the national levels were set up in every provincial local government. This decision to enforce IPR protection was supported by Vice-Premier Wu, who said in a speech on 13 January at the National Patent Conference that IPR enforcement is crucial to the nation's economy (China SIPO, 2005).

On 26 August 2004, the General Office of the State Council issued an Action Plan for Special Operations of Intellectual Property Protection, which aimed to conduct a special IPR protection platform across the country to combat IPR (patent, trade mark, copyright) infringement, raise IPR protection awareness, promote innovation in science and technology, and educate the public about WTO-related issues. This message was re-inforced in a National IPR Protection Special Operation Teleconference on 27 August, presided over by the Lead Group of IPR Protection, the State Council. This was endorsed by the Committee for Education, Science, Culture and Health (CESCH) of the National People's Congress.

Legal enforcement

The legal framework of enforcement was emphasized by China's Supreme Court on 22 December 2004. The Supreme People's Court and SPP jointly issued the Interpretations on Several Issues on Application of the Law for the Trial of IPR Criminal Cases by the Supreme People's Court and the Supreme People's Procuratorate (or Judicial Interpretation), for the purpose of prosecuting criminal actions of IPR infringement, and maintaining the order of the socialist market economy. The penalty for IPR infringement was clearly defined by the Judicial Interpretation, with standards being stricter than before. For example, the penalty for counterfeiting a registered trademark, counterfeiting a registered trademark design and infringing copyright was 50,000 yuan (US$6,000). This development was an important step for the Chinese judicial system in reinforcing the legal framework to protect intellectual property rights 2005.

In 2004, the public security authorities across the country continued to take action against infringement and piracy. A total of 30,000 infringement and piracy cases were resolved; 21 assembly lines for illegal disc production; and 130 million infringement and piracy publications were seized (ibid.).

IPR judicial protection in China is enforced by civil, administrative and criminal judicial protection, where the civil system serves as the foundation of the entire system. The trials are usually conducted by People's Courts at each level of China to deal with IPR disputes and infringement. The mechanism of juridical organs handling IPR related cases is relatively complete in China. By the end of 2004, various divisions specializing in the trial of

IPR cases had been established. At higher levels, IPR cases are also tried by Higher People's Courts at the provincial level, Intermediate People's Courts in all provincial capital cities and some other large cities, and even in certain Primary People's Courts in small towns and cities. The IPR Trial Division in the Supreme People's Court was set up in October 1996, and later (in 2000) renamed the Third Civil Division (ibid.).

The jurisdiction over IPR cases in China is relatively centralized. In respect of cases involving patents, new plant varieties and layout designs of integrated circuits, a designated jurisdiction has been adopted. The Supreme People's Courts have appointed 49, 34 and 43 Intermediate People's Courts to try patents, varieties of new plant, and layout designs and integrated circuits, respectively. In general, civil cases involving other kinds of IPR are handled by Intermediate Courts, or courts above the level of People's Courts. In 2004, about 90.76 per cent of IPR cases were tried by Intermediate Courts or courts above the level of People's Courts.

Statistics on IPR prosecution reported by the Chinese government showed that, despite the challenging nature of the issue and the difficulties in implementation, it was determined to tackle the issue head-on. From 1985 to 2004, local People's Courts have accepted a total of 69,636 IPR civil cases in the first instance, and concluded 66,385 of these. Of all the accepted cases, 18,654 involved patents, 14,708 were copyright disputes, 6,629 were trademark cases, and 8,368 were other kinds of IPR cases (ibid.). The Chinese authorities reported that IP civil cases accepted by People's Courts have increased at a high rate. In 2004, People's Courts across the country accepted 12,205 IPR civil cases covering first instance, second instance and retrial proceedings, an increase of 31.65 per cent over the previous year. Most of these cases (about 11,113) were concluded with a total settlement of 2,980 million yuan (US$3,70 million). Most cases involved ownership and infringement of IPR: about 86.86 per cent. The foreign/unique territories involved were Hong Kong, Macau and Taiwan (ibid.).

For IPR criminal judicial protection, it was reported that a total of 387 IPR criminal cases were accepted by the People's Courts across the country in 2004, of which 385 were concluded, and 528 of the accused were found guilty. Most of the cases were trademark violations – about 82.94 of all cases in 2004. The IPR criminal cases shared the following characteristics: (i) there was a major involvement of private companies; (ii) most crimes were complex and clever; (iii) the crimes were repeated in several regions; and (iv) penalties involved prison terms (usually for less than five years), and fines. In addition to the IPR crimes, the Chinese authorities reported that 932 and 1,434 cases were related to counterfeiting of commodity or illegal business operations (ibid.). About 1,961 individuals were convicted for commodity IPR infringement; 2,526 were charged for illegal IPR businesses (ibid.).

IPR protection and increased innovation

The statistics on patent applications in general showed that China's improved patent system has resulted in increased numbers of applications for patents. For example, by 31 December 2004, a total of 2,284,925 patent applications had been accepted by the China Patent Office (CPO). Of these, 1,874,358 were from domestic applicants and 410,567 from overseas applicants, accounting respectively for 82 per cent and 18 per cent of the total (ibid.). By 31 December 2004, the total number of patents granted by the CPO were 1,255,499. Of those granted patents, 1,093,268 were from domestic applicants and 162,231 from overseas applicants, accounting respectively for 87.1 per cent and 12.9 per cent of the total number of patents granted (ibid.). The CPO received 518 requests for an international preliminary examination, and completed 534 international preliminary examination reports. By 17 March 2004, the CPO had already accepted 2 million patent applications. On 12 March 2004 the CPO formally inaugurated its Patent Application Electronic Filing System, and by 31 December 2004 a total of 4,239 electronic patent applications had been accepted by the CPO (ibid.).

The reports from China's CPO were important indicators of the inventors' participation in Chinese intellectual property rights' framework. It reported that: (i) the process for patent applications and approval had become less complex; and (ii) there had been an increase in invention patents, accounting for more than 20 per cent of the applications. The rate of increase was significant from domestic applicants and averaged more than 20 per cent over five years. The overall numbers and percentages of invention patents have increased, achieving a 32.9 per cent increase over the previous year. The review process has also been speeded up. The increase in numbers of invention patents, especially from the domestic sector, was a particularly positive sign, a possible indication that the Chinese IPR system has spurred innovation, and there was growing confidence among the public in the system to protect their inventions (ibid.).

In addition, (i) overall, applications in all categories of IPR have increased. In the first half of 2005, the CPO witnessed an 18 per cent increase in patent applications – 81.6 per cent (2,028,053) from domestic applicants and 18.4 per cent (456,764) from foreigners. Invention patents accounted for 31.5 per cent. Among the applications, 86.5 per cent and 13.5 per cent were awarded to domestic and foreign applicants, respectively (*Chinaip*, 2006; *Economy Daily News*, 2005); (ii) the number of foreign applications were greater than domestic applications; (iii) most of the invention patents (about 85.7 per cent) came from foreigners; and (iv) patents granted increased by 35 per cent in the first half of 2005, compared to the same period in 2004 (ibid.).

Overall, foreigners have played a major role as participants in the patent system. From 1 April 1985 to 28 February 2005, China awarded 193,843 invention patents, of which 123,948 (64 per cent) came from foreign applicants, excluding those from multinationals, joint ventures or Chinese research institutes (*Chinaip*, 2006).

Requests for re-examination have also increased. For example, in 2004, a total of 2,768 requests for patent re-examination were accepted by the CO, 955 more than in 2003 (52.7 per cent increase), among which more than half (1,447) were settled. Most cases questioned rejection in the essential examination process and the decision in the invention patent revocation process. Most of the cases involved in patent dispute at the provincial level, and 1,215 out of 1,455 were settled.

The IPR protection for pharmaceutical business in China has important implications for all stakeholders. The IPR framework for pharmaceutical businesses evolved gradually. As mentioned earlier, in 1993, China's patent law extended its protection to pharmaceuticals. Prior to the 1993 patent law, chemicals and pharmaceuticals were only covered by 'process protection'. Now, China's patent law has been harmonized with the WTO's and patents are protected for twenty years. Patent protection is different from the administrative protection that was used sometimes in the old system, which grants exclusive marketing rights to pharmaceuticals.

The major specifications in the patent process are:

(i) Disclosure of drug information is necessary when applying for patents.
(ii) Local governments have the authority to issue manufacturing permits to medical factories and distributors. Gradually, this authority is being transferred to central government agencies, in order to offer stronger patent protection for high-tech pharmaceuticals.
(iii) The central government has mandated local governments' intellectual property law enforcement to crack down on illegal licensing practices or counterfeiting.
(iv) Registered product protection is another item on China's legal reform agenda. The 1993 Product Quality Law, for example, prohibits producers and sellers from counterfeiting products or falsely using others' trademarks, such as certification marks and famous brand marks or marks of excellence. It also prohibits producers and retailers from falsifying a product's origin, or using another factory's name and address. Violators face severe punishments and are liable for damages.
(v) China's State Intellectual Property Office (SIPO) is strengthening international property rights for new fields, such as microelectronic technology and biological engineering. The estimate from one Western investment analyst showed that SIPO expects to receive 100,000 applications each year and 150,000 patent applications every year until 2010 (Pacific Bridge Medical).

Despite all the improvements, intellectual property-rights-related issues will continue to challenge the Chinese government and society because of conflicting cultural assumptions and a lack of enforcement power. These issues were at the centre of trade disputes between the USA and China in early 2006.

Positions of the stakeholders in the WTO framework

Multinationals

To multinationals or joint ventures, China remains a challenge with a major market potential. The following factors are likely to affect their position:

- The timing of investments. Early investors have fared much better than latecomers because: (a) early investors have developed brand loyalty among consumers and therefore have much lower costs for marketing and advertising; (b) they already know how to manage labour costs; and (c) the early arrivals are in a strong position to enlarge their market share.
- Scale of investment in the early stages. Early investment in capital equipment, facilities, technology and management tends to have a larger return later. It has been estimated that it takes 5–10 years to reap the returns of a given investment. Most of the successful arrivals have been in China for more than two decades (see also *China Pharma*, 21 June 2002).
- Models of local partnerships. After China's entry to the WTO, multinationals are entering the Chinese market through either joint ventures or by creating subsidiaries in China. The former model is believed to be a safe approach, because of the knowledge the multinationals need in terms of local consumer culture, needs, market and distribution channels, which is linked directly to a reduction in production costs. Before China's entry to the WTO, most multinationals chose to develop low-cost medicines – for example, by making copies or low-cost generics. GlaxoSmithKline and Pfizer used a combination of two approaches: making copies for general markets and producing high-priced brands for selective markets (see ibid.).
- Understanding of the local culture, and business and management environment. It is crucial that multinationals understand the cultural norms in health maintenance practices, the health needs of changing demographics, government policies, business practices in pharmaceutical sales, and the organizational structure in production, marketing and distribution. These factors have a direct or indirect impact on pharmaceutical consumption. Most pharmaceutical sales representatives deal directly with hospitals and retailers in China, and therefore pharmaceutical promotion has been focusing on these venues. It is also important for foreign distributors to balance a global, universal management style

with local unique needs; centralization versus decentralization; and developing formal distribution and informal channels. It was noted that adjustment to local factors is a more important consideration than lowering cost by centralized marketing and distribution. A centralized management and decentralized distribution network seems to be a better model for pharmaceutical management in China. A well-known case in point was the multi-domestic geographical structure used by Johnson & Johnson, where finances and accounting were controlled from the head office, and local branches (possibly with local partners) were in charge of retail and distribution (see ibid.).

The other culture-unique management model was the use of polycentric staffing policies: that is, using local personnel for field operations while retaining decision-making power in the hands of executive managers. It was noted that some management models in the globalization framework by multinationals have been quite successful. For example, the partner of Johnson & Johnson, Xian-Janssen, was lauded as the 'Janssen University' for pharmaceutical and related management training for Chinese personnel. The maturing of China's WTO membership has also provided multinationals with more opportunities in China. In 2005 there was a deepening of the global structure by the multinationals into Chinese society in terms of (i) establishing their subsidiaries in China; (ii) taking full advantage of the global localization management model; and (iii) using China as a global strategic base and for the global standardization of practices.

- Understanding the legal environment and procedures. China's laws and policies are changing rapidly. It is important that stakeholders are familiar with this environment as well as playing a constructive and active part in the legal, regulatory and policy processes by consulting and having a direct dialogue with the public authorities.
- Capitalizing on labour costs. China's labour costs are already among the lowest in the world. In addition, the tax incentives provided by the Chinese government make it more attractive for foreign companies to set up their facilities in remote provinces to further lower their production costs. Special tax breaks apply to investment in inland provinces. Smaller pharmas, especially some Western start-up biopharmaceutical businesses, also see opportunities in the Chinese markets because of the lower costs, which allow them to buy time to prove the viability of their drug prospects before seeking more stable funding commitments from Western venture capitalists. Venture capital is now considered to be an important investment instrument in Western support of portfolio companies, to take advantage of the pool of research talent in China as well as looking for investment opportunities in Chinese markets.
- Vertical and horizontal integration. A business strategy considered by some multinationals is to increase their partnerships with local com-

panies through mergers and joint ventures, as discussed earlier. A typical operation model is: The companies first establish their base, including their sales force and market share; next they they set up manufacturing facilities, and then increase their local partnerships. In 2004, mergers in pharmaceutical sectors reached a peak, and most of the mergers totalled more than US$6 million (*Chinapharm*, 2005). Novartis, which developed an innovative approach using mergers and collaborations, is a case in point (ibid.). It established its manufacturing base in Beijing in 1987 and has invested another US$15 million in expansion. Its sales increased by 49 per cent in 2004, the highest rate of increase among all its global subsidiaries. The brands that will expire in 2008 and that will become generics account for 18 per cent of Novartis's total sales (*Chinapharm*, 2005).

Novartis's strategy to deepen its involvement when Chinese manufacturers play a larger role in the generics market is a well-timed move. The major issues with such horizontal integration, such as mergers, are the hidden costs associated with changing and integrating the management system and the culture, as well as the costs associated with improving efficiency.

The multinationals are also increasing the R&D capabilities of their Chinese partners as their involvement in China deepens. Increasing local R&D can have potential benefits that go beyond cost savings; for example, GlaxoSmithKline was the first multinational pharma to establish an R&D centre in China, in 2002, after it observed that the Chinese market accounted for 7 per cent of its total global business (*China Health Sciences Newsletter*, 12 June 2002).

Roche invested US$11 million in their facilities, with the aim of building strong ties with the Chinese regulatory authorities. Roche's R&D centre is the fifth-largest in its global operation and supports the Chinese National Human Genome Centre in its work on diabetes and schizophrenia. This move is likely, in the long term, to strengthen Roche's operations as well as to explore new market opportunities in China (see Agres, 2006; see also *Chinapharm*, 2005).

Novartise is also partnering the Shanghai Institute for Materia Medica to identify compounds derived from traditional Chinese medicine. This partnership allows Novartis to develop new products. Other major pharmaceutical companies also have similar plans. For example, Pfizer, which has manufacturing facilities and a marketing operation in China, plans to establish a R&D clinical trials centre in Shanghai. GlaxoSmithKline, which has manufacturing facilities and joint ventures in China, has already established an OTC medicine R&D centre; developed a recombinatorial chemistry lab with the Shanghai Institute of Materia Medica; and has invested over US$100,000 per year to support long-term antibiotic sensitivity studies since 1990. Eli Lilly, which has a manufacturing facility, has established a research lab in co-operation with its Chinese partner, Shanghai ChemExplorer. Merck and Company, which has manufacturing and joint development projects in China, has some joint research initiatives with leading domestic Chinese stakeholders, such as the Yangzi River Pharmacy Group. AstraZeneca has signed agreements with the School of Management at Beijing University, to invest US$37,500 to establish a research centre on pharmaceutical management and economics, focusing on pharmaceutical policies, hospital and pharmacy management, counselling and training that will provide feedback on the government's health care reforms, pharmaceutical pricing, health insurance and hospital management. A Chinese pharmaceutical manufacturer will also provide a further US$2.5 million research fund for similar projects (*Chinapharm*, 2003).

- Using China as a major centre for clinical trials. China has been approved by the US FDA to conduct clinical trials for US pharmaceutical companies. This is a business opportunity for both multinationals and their Chinese partners. AstraZeneca, for example, sees China as a critical component of its future global clinical trials because it allows possible access to data that include different ethnic populations and genetic variations. AstraZeneca has established a clinical trial operation and participated in a joint study with Shanghai Jiaotong University to identify the genes linked to schizophrenia. It has also agreed to fund a new centre for pharmaceoeconomics and outcomes research at Beijing University. The US pharmas are shifting their strategies from making traditional blockbusters to developing individually targeted drugs. The Chinese population offers access to a wide gene pool. The individually targeted drugs aimed at patients with specific genetic polymorphisms require a large pool of genetic data from diverse populations, which the Chinese population can offer. AstraZeneca claims to be the first international pharmaceutical company to locate its R&D centre in China with the hope of developing closer relations with Chinese health institutions and organizations (Santini, 2004).
- Finding unique niches for smaller pharmas. Smaller foreign drug manufacturers cannot compete with the big pharmas. They have to consider finding their niche and specialized markets, generating a diverse product portfolio, creating brand name awareness, partnering with local companies that have sales expertise, and exploring the vast untapped markets in rural areas or neglected satellite towns near big cities. The most important consideration for the smaller pharmas is to focus on a few innovative products. The greatest challenge for them is that they have to concentrate on the marketing and promotion of their products. For example, a joint venture between Dr Reddy's Laboratories, a company originating in India, and China's Kunshan Double-Crane Pharmaceutical Company was established at with total investment of nearly US$43 million to produce large volume of bulk formulations, tablets, capsules,

ointments, gels and other products across a limited range of 6–7 products, while in comparison, Dr Reddy's Laboratories in India produce 200 products. Companies have to choose between producing a wide range of products or focusing on fewer products in limited geographical regions. For this joint venture, 150 employees, out of a work force of 270, work in sales and marketing. The strategies that joint ventures usually employ are: building strong connections with health care professionals and providing professional seminars, medical education programmes and symposia for doctors. As mentioned earlier, hospital doctors are the major decision-makers about pharmaceutical recommendations, and in China some 85 per cent of pharmaceuticals are sold through hospitals, after going through a prolonged registration process that can take as long as 2–3 years. The registration process starts with the medical authorities in each province and, after their approval sales representatives apply for approval at the hospital level. In the case of KRRP (Kunshan Rotam Reddy Pharmaceuticals Ltd – a health care product company), its products are sold in eighteen provinces, through more than 100 distributors, which are accepted by 500 pharmacies, 800 hospitals and 5,500 doctors. The company's investment broke even and registered a turnover of US$9 million in 2004–5, the fifth year of its investment in China. A turnover of US$12 million is required before any profits are generated (*Business India*, 2005, p. 98).

Innovation remains the key to the competitiveness of the smaller pharmaceutical companies, and relying on only one or two products can be a risky undertaking. The story of Aurobindo Pharma, a major Indian pharmaceutical manufacturer and one of the largest of the small pharmaceutical ventures in China, is instructive. A major reason for its inability to make a profit is a fall in the price of Penicillin G, the mainstay of its production. The lesson learned in this case is that it is important not to rely on traditionally profitable pharmaceutical products but to diversify (ibid.).

- Using China as a re-export centre. The strategy of gaining a market share in China and using China as a manufacturing base to export to other countries is being used by some manufacturers. Indian companies have already learnt that they can use China as a manufacturing base and re-export to other middle-income or low-income developing countries (China Internet Information Centre, 2002). Other multinationals also find that China is a major hub for exporting to other BRIC countries: Brazil, Russia and India.

  Orchid Chemicals and Pharmceuticals, a joint venture between Indian and Chinese companies, uses China as a base for exports. It takes advantage of the low labour costs in China and targets the more regulated markets such as the USA and Europe with high-value generics that are out of patent. Orchid predicted that China would be a most competitive exporter in the near future. The diversifying strategy that Orchid uses is informative: a wide spectrum of pharmaceutical products, including semi-synthetic antibiotics, vitamins, fermentation-based products, recombinant DNA products and formulations as well as traditional Chinese medicine, veterinary medicine and pesticides, and market sterile cephalosporin bulk actives and formulations. It also partners with locals who fit with its strategy of diversity. The strategy of integration from upstream to intermediary products also helps. The business is profit- and efficiency-driven and has become a globally positioned company that is also competitive in local markets (*Business India*, 10–23 October 2005, p. 99).

- Understanding the pharmaceutical consumption culture. According to a study conducted by the Chinese Medicine Regulation Bureau on the need and utilization rate for Chinese medicine, a third of respondents surveyed said they would prefer to go to a practitioner of Chinese medicine when health problems arose (Central Daily News Agency, 2003). Among the chronically ill, the rate was as high as 48 per cent. There was a higher utilization rate than the national average among those who suffer from high blood pressure, heart diseases and diabetes. The level of confidence in Chinese medicine practitioners among Beijing residents was also higher than in other regions. This survey also pointed out that residents who wished to receive Chinese medical treatment or a combination of Chinese and Western treatment was about 30 per cent, especially among those who sought treatment by internal medicine. It was estimated that Chinese medical practitioners supported a third of the volume of clinical care in Beijing City. According to this survey, as of 2003, 664 clinics in Beijing practised Chinese medicine, or a combination of Chinese and biomedicine or other forms of herbal medicine (ibid.). A creative partnership between biopharmas and herbal product makers might be the next step in sustaining a win–win situation.
- Imports of quality herbal medicines. Imports of foreign-manufactured Chinese medicines, especially those made in Japan and Southeast Asia, accounted for more than 20 per cent of the herbal medicine market in China by November 2004. More than 10,000 patents for Chinese herbal medicines were filed by foreign companies, while, in comparison, the patients filed by Chinese manufactures in foreign markets were about only 3,000 by 2004. A Japanese manufacturer who imported raw herbal materials from China and exported the final products back to China achieved a sales record of US$100 million in 2003, when total Chinese exports in herbal medicines were only US$700 million. The major exporters of finished Chinese herbal products to China were Japan, Korea, the Southeast Asian region and Western European countries. Chinese consumers' confidence in foreign-made Chinese medicines lies in the stability of quality and more advanced technology. These trends

apparently point to the need for Chinese manufactures to use scientific processes in the production of Chinese medicines, to regain domestic consumers' confidence (*World Journal*, 21 November 2004).

Overall, the major challenge facing the multinationals is sustainable competitiveness. It was estimated that the attrition rate for foreign pharmas was about 30 per cent. Other challenges include: finding a more cost-effective way of developing new drugs; adapting to global as well as local markets; containing hidden costs, such as the costs and efficient returns from the promotion and marketing of products. In addition, understanding the local business environment and consumption culture remains a major barrier for newcomers to local pharmaceutical industries.

Research and development

As mentioned earlier, R&D is a challenge to all pharmaceutical manufacturers, and this is particularly true for local stakeholders: on average, multinationals invest a minimum of 10–15 per cent on R&D, while in comparison, Chinese manufacturers invest less than 2–5 per cent (*Chinapharm,* 2001). The existence of a large number of small-sized pharmas competing in a small generics market in China in the past was a major barrier for local pharmas to make larger profits. For example, it was noted that more than 100 pharmas were competing for the production of one antibiotic. The competition for a narrow list of generics leads to the fact that generics are often priced at a-tenth or a-twentieth of their brand's counterparts. In contrast, generics are priced at 7 per cent to 80 per cent of the prices of brands in Western markets, with fewer competitors for one drug (*Chinapharm,* 2005).

The key challenges to the local pharmaceutical industry as a whole are: innovations, IPR protection of their innovations, and how to market their innovations to the global community. On innovations, China needs to: (i) continue producing innovative products; (ii) strengthen training, recruiting, retaining and upgrading R&D talents; (iii) increase investment through various domestic and global financial mechanisms, such as through venture capital; (iv) commercialize innovative products; (v) upgrade R&D equipment and facilities; (vi) integrate R&D upstream and downstream development; and (vii) employ modern managerial skills in R&D. It was noted that before China's accession to the WTO, between 1991 and 1996, China approved 1,546 new drugs, most of which were Class II (copied drugs) and Class IV (changes of forms). Class I drugs (that is, new inventions) accounted for only 2.6 per cent of the total approved (*China Pharmaceuticals*, 13 August 2001). It was obvious that there was a general lack of invention or lack of registration for new pharmaceutical developments prior to China's entry into the WTO. Under the WTO, China's pharmaceutical companies can no longer copy foreign patented drugs. If this practice does not change, it will mean a tremendous loss of profit for the majority of local pharmas. It was pointed out that the gross sale volume of all Chinese local pharmaceutical companies totalled US$40 billion, which was less than the US$45 billion sale volume of the US-based Pfizer Pharmaceutical Company (*World Journal*, 28 April 2006). R&D investment will be a major factor determining competitiveness for Chinese pharmas. It is crucial that the Chinese pharmaceutical industry increases major R&D spending on finding new products or partners among other global players for R&D collaboration. In the past, most new investment went to the purchase of equipment, the building of facilities or assembly lines, with companies vying for the production of the same drug. This trend became a vicious cycle for the local pharmas: increased competition among them led to decreased profit margins, which affected innovation. These together become restricting factors to their competitiveness in global markets (*see* some of the discussions in *China Pharmaceuticals*, 13 August 2001).

It will take some time for China's R&D to be at the same competitive level as the multinationals. Nevertheless, local pharmaceutical manufacturers should not be underestimated. Their competitive potential has gradually been realized. As mentioned earlier, the cost advantage can be an important determinant of Chinese competitiveness. A new drug typically costs more than US$800 million before it is allowed to be marketed in the West; in comparison, its cost is a-tenth of this or less in China. In addition, China's R&D capacity has already shown some potential. China's biotechnology expertise was recognized when an advanced cancer drug was approved in China. A cancer therapy that uses a virus to attack tumour cells but not healthy cells is the first to be approved in the world. This therapy, H101, a modified version of Onyx-015, which was tested in the USA in 2003, attacks only cells with the particular genetic defect that characterizies the cancer cells (Pollack, 17 November 2005).

Chinese investment in these kinds of US-abandoned drugs has proved to be rewarding. The anti-cancer drug H101 was originally developed by an American biotechnology company but was discontinued for a number of reasons. The Chinese company Shanghai Sunway Biotech continued the research, and developed the therapy after going through China's clinical trial process. China is also the only country that has approved gene therapy. The other example is the approval of Endostar in China. Endostar (based on the endostatin invented in the 1990s), similar to the FDA-approved Avastin, which was based on the theory of 'starving' the blood supply to malignant tumours, was first developed in the USA by Boston-based scientist Judah Folkman. Before Avastin was allowed to be commercialized by Genentech in February 2005, EntreMed already owned the patent rights of endostatin but abandoned the drug because of high production costs, and because it did not pass clinical trials in the USA. Dr Folkman then allowed a Chinese scientist, Professor Luo Yongzhang, to have endostatin undergo clinical trials in China and it was approved by China's SFDA. The initial results from clinical trials were said to be encouraging in China but the drug's efficacy needs to be further proved by a larger scale of clinical trials and more rigorous studies published in internationally credible journals. Despite the fact that it might take Chinese manufacturers a long time to gain approval from the US FDA or from other countries, the drug itself already has a large market. In China, it has been estimated that more than 1.5 million individuals die of cancer every year, and the need for ground-breaking cancer treatment has never been greater (*World Journal*, 9 January 2006; see also *World Journal*, 23 December 2005). In addition, the recent discovery by Hong Kong scientists of a channel regulating the electric activities of stem cells, as in cell regeneration and multiplication, was considered a breakthrough in understanding the growth of tumours and possibly offering an effective cure. These developments in biotechnology among Chinese affiliates are conducive to the expansion of China's pharmaceutical sector if the public and private sectors continue their investment in these little-researched areas (*World Journal*, 4 December 2005).

Overall, these cases demonstrate that: (i) China's domestic pharmas should focus on niche areas in pharmaceutical innovation; (ii) they can increase their R&D capacity by acquiring smaller pharmas or drug research centres in other countries who are developing promising new drugs; (iii) they should build partnerships with already highly developed R&D sectors in Taiwan and Hong Kong, both of which have very close cultural, social and economic ties with China. Chinese pharmas should take advantage of the scientific expertise and infrastructure in both regions to grow China's domestic R&D; and (iv) domestic manufacturers should work jointly with multinationals to develop new drugs. Related to this approach is that a large number of Chinese scientists are already working in the pharmaceutical sector in the West. China should develop a framework to collaborate with these scientists in a mutually beneficial manner, and with the Western companies for, whom these scientists are working. (For example, collaboration with smaller, promising pharmaceuticals overseas, such as Tanox, could be a possible approach. Presided over by a Chinese scientist, Tanox is in the process of rolling out a new HIV drug, TNX-355, using amAb antibody that can be attached to CD4 cells and acts to prevent HIV from entering the lymph system. It has passed Clinical Trials stages I and II and is moving on to Clinical Trial stage III in 2006. This approach is a departure from the conceptual basis underlying all the existing anti-retrovirals.)

Retail pharmacy

The challenge to local pharmaceutical manufactures and distributors from 2006 onwards will be the volume of sales to retail pharmacies. The multinationals' entry into the retail market has already put immense pressure on local retailers. It was noted that, by 2003, there were only eleven local retail businesses, accounting for only 15 per cent of total sales volume. In comparison, in the USA, the top ten retail pharmacy businesses owned more than 15,000 retail pharmacies and grossed more than 60 per cent (interviews with Dr Phil Gerbino, President of the University of the Sciences in Philadelphia, 17 March 2006; see also *China Pharmaceuticals*, 6 June 2003). The competition between hospital pharmacies and retailers can further complicate this picture: most profits derive from branded pharmaceuticals that only hospitals are allowed to sell, which makes it more difficult for local retailers to compete. It was noted that a hospital pharmacy could easily gross more than US$100,000 a day while, in contrast, a retailer's total sale volume is less than US$1,000 a day. The profit margins for brands in some cases are three times higher than for non-prescription drugs. Competitive strategies for local pharmacies would be: maintain a cost advantage and customer loyalty; upgrade their scale; improve their management style and collaboration framework; capitalize on their competitive advantages, such as familiarity with local health needs; and deepen their presence in remote areas (*Chinapharm*, 2006).

Generics

For now, the most promising area for local biomedical pharmaceutical manufacturers is the production of generics. The generics market bodes well for local pharmas because first, they account for 40–50 per cent of local sales. Second, a range of the most popular brands on the global market will expire between 2001 and 2005, and more between 2005 and 2009. It has been estimated that about fifty brands with leading sales records expired between 2000 and 2005, and each of these drugs grossed more than US$500 million in the past. This list includes Prilosec (Omeprazole) by AstraZeneca, which grossed more than US$6 billion in 1999 and 2000 (*Chinapharm*, 2 December 2001). In another estimate, a large number of brands expiry between 2004 and 2008 will be worth about US$6–10 billion to the market globally (*Chinapharm*, 12 February 2005). Third, half of the drugs sold by foreign pharmas on the Chinese market since the beginning of 2001 were generics. It was also noted that half of the US pharmas relied on the production of generics as their major source of profit (*Chinapharm*, 2001) Local pharmaceutical companies can expand their generics production by conducting an exhaustive survey of those brands that will be off patent in the near future; and acquiring the rights to produce the generic form of these drugs (*China Pharmaceuticals*, 13 August 2001).

OTC

China set up its regulatory framework for OTC drugs through the Regulations on Prescriptions and OTC Drugs, and published *A National*

Catalogue of OTC Drugs in January 2005. It was estimated that the OTC market had grown by more than 30 per cent and had reached some US$2 billion (*Chinapharm*, 2005). The OTC market is likely to be contested by all the stakeholders in China. This market can be a niche for local manufacturers if they can develop a more sophisticated mode of production and marketing for selling OTCs. It was noted that, in China, the most critical issues facing the consolidation of the OTC market are brand name recognition, credibility and customer loyalty (*China Pharmaceuticals*, 13 August 2001).

It was noted that OTC customers usually follow a process of decision-making that includes needs, previous information, price comparisons, proven efficacy of OTC products, and after-sales services. The efficacy of the core products and derivatives of core products are the two major factors in sustained customer loyalty. The major OTC drugs sold in China since early 2000 are antibiotics; medicines to relieve symptoms of influenza or colds, calcium deficiency, cardiovascular problems, respiratory infections, bronchitis, skin irritations, digestive problems and eye problems; and analgesics. The increase in demand for calcium supplements is worth noting, because it is closely related to demographic trends in China. According to China's fifth census (1 November 2000), the population aged over 60 years will number around 410 million by 2050, accounting for 27.4 per cent of China's total population. Calcium deficiency and osteoporosis-related issues are already a major health problem among this age group. As indicated in a survey in 2005, 16.1 per cent of men and 19.9 per cent of women aged over 40, and 15 per cent of men and 28.6 per cent of women aged over 60 are suffering from osteoporosis. Calcium supplements account for 16–18 per cent of the food supplement market in China (*Chinapharm*, 2001). Most OTCs are not likely to be distinguished by the efficacy of the core products, and competitive strategies will need to capitalize on their derivative services.

The derivatives of OTCs are likely to make a major difference in terms of brand loyalty. Derivatives of OTCs are a new concept in the marketing of OTCs, but are believed to be correlated with sustained brand loyalty. Derivatives include information on the OTC labels and after-sales services. After-sales service is rare but can be a competitive strategy, since most of the public in China lack health and pharmaceutical literacy. These derivatives can include: free or discounted physical examinations, free prevention services, information and referral services, home deliveries, or post-sales monitoring. Health literacy and education can include: personal hygiene and health maintenance, family health, nutrition, disease prevention, drug interactions, and reactions and side-effects. Monitoring and tracking side effects for customers, which is already being implemented in some Chinese pharmacies, can also offer a competitive advantage. Yet the ethical issues involved in offering derivative services must be monitored closely to avoid fraudulent practices, such as the recommendation of unnecessary medicines to vulnerable patients. At the macro level, local pharmaceutical manufacturers need to expand their scale of operations by: (i) merging with multinationals; (ii) breaking geographical barriers by merging with other local retail chains; and (iii) expanding the internet retail market (*Sina Net*, 13 May 2001; see also *Sina Net*, 10 April 2001).

Pharmaceutical raw materials

China has been one of the largest producers of pharmaceuticals-related raw materials since 1997. By 2000, China was already exporting about US$2.25 billion in raw materials, more than sixty categories of which are globally competitive. China's potential has increased greatly since its entry to the WTO. China's major strengths in this area in the past have been: low production costs, including low labour costs; competitive labour skills; volume and scale of production; and global market share. The major weakness is quality control and competitiveness. As a whole, China's potential in this area is increasing, for a number of reasons. Because of its implications for pollution, most of the pharmaceutical producers in North America have relied more on imported raw materials than locally derived ones. In the early 2000s, this demand for raw materials was worth more than US$1.5 billion. Japanese producers were largely self-sufficient, but because of rising labour costs and the need for environmental protection, Japan has increasingly looked to foreign producers, especially China, for supplies. The EU countries are major producers and exporters of raw materials. In the early 2000s, the EU was exporting more than 80 per cent of its production of pharmaceuticals-related raw materials, with a value of more than US$3.6–4 billion, making it the top producer of pharmaceutical raw materials in the world. Indian pharmaceutical strengths are in formulations and generics, but India has always relied on foreign producers for raw materials. For example, India's antibiotics are a major export item but it has relied on China for most of the raw materials to produce these. Other potential competitors of China are the former USSR, Eastern European countries, Israel, South Africa and some Latin-American countries (*Chinapharm*, 2001).

Several global trends are conducive to China's competitiveness in this area:

(i) the low-cost raw materials suppliers account for a small proportion in the US/Western market. This is advantageous to Third-World producers;
(ii) because of environmental concerns and increasing quality control, the EU is planning to terminate the production of certain raw materials and move its production bases to developing countries;
(iii) the need for the raw materials for OTCs is increasing globally;

(iv) competition to obtain raw materials to produced generics from expired brands is growing and will improve the position of the suppliers in countries such as China and Brazil;
(v) profit margins are higher in pharmaceuticals-related raw materials than those in other chemical industries, such as petrochemicals and synthetic fibres. This trend will be a positive incentive for investors and producers in China (*Chinapharm,* 2001);
(vi) China's labour in this sector costs much less but is better-trained than in other countries;
(vii) at the time of writing China is only realizing about a third of its production potential;
(viii) production costs in this sector are much lower than in pharmaceutical production and as a result, profit margins are higher for Chinese producers; and
(ix) WTO membership has eliminate the tariff barrier and enlarges global market opportunities for Chinese producers.

Overall, the most promising markets for Chinese producers are in artemisinin and Vitamin C. In the early 2000s, China's artemisinin accounted for 30 per cent of the global market and production was increasing by 10 per cent annually. Vitamin C accounted for 30 per cent of the global market, and 90 per cent of Chinese production was for export. Production was concentrated in the hands of some five Chinese producers, and the average production cost was US$5 per 1,000 grams. Despite the fact that the international market for Vitamin C is saturated, the domestic market for this vitamin remains very large. On average, in the industrialized countries, the consumption of Vitamin C is 60–90 grams per capita, of which 55 per cent is in pharmaceuticals, 35 per cent in food and drinks, and 10 per cent in other areas. In contrast, in China, the per capita consumption is less than 4 grams, in which 90 per cent is used in pharmaceuticals and 10 per cent in food and drinks. There remains plenty of room for growth in China's domestic market (*Chinapharm,* 2001).

The major challenges for China's competitiveness in crude materials are:

(i) developing high-end, patent-protected products;
(ii) the need to diversify its global markets – at present, China is overly reliant on North American and EU markets;
(iii) the need to improve its distribution and marketing strategies in a global context;
(iv) the need to upgrade production technology in niche areas of raw materials, such as vitamins and proteins, and develop their derivatives; and
(v) the need to focus on low-pollution products.

Innovative products

Despite their lack of competitiveness in the conventional pharmaceutical market, Chinese producers have shown major potential with other innovative products, especially those in the biotech sector. As mentioned earlier, China has selected biotech as its key area of development in pharmaceutical sector since 1980, and is expected to own the patents of 10–15 biotech products in the coming years. The key areas of development are: upgrading technology in translation and molecular modification to improve the efficacy of antibiotics, vitamins and protein products to treat cancer, cardiovascular diseases, neurological problems, digestive problems and AIDS; diversifying the forms of vaccines, testing and screening devices, and therapeutics; using genetic and molecular engineering to increase the production of rare or nearly extinct herbal medicines; and developing new formulations through the use of biotechnology (*Chinapharm*, 2004).

The growth and profit-return rates in the biotech sector in China are worth noting, as discussed earlier. China has experienced rapid growth since the mid-1990s in infrastructure building in the biotech sector. For example, it has developed twenty-one genetically-engineered products and vaccines (*Chinapharm*, 2004). Among the top-ten best-selling genetically engineered products and vaccines, China is able to produce eight of them. China owns the patent of the recombinant p53 injection as a cancer cure and became the first in the world to approve it, as discussed earlier. China had more than seven genetically engineered products, to treat various intractable diseases, at the clinical trials stage in 2004. Vaccine development is also encouraging. New regulations by the SFDA in China mandates that vaccines and blood products cannot be re-processed overseas and be re-imported for domestic use. This ruling would increase the market share of domestic pharmas or foreign joint ventures of locally-needed vaccines (*Beijing Sina*, 29 November 2005).

The major challenges in China's biotech sector are: reorganizing its fragmented structure and integrating resources, recruiting top talents and searching for cutting-edge technology, capacity building, narrowing the gap between upstream and downstream production, building sustainable policy support, and capital investment from public and private sectors, and from domestic and international sources.

Capacity building

China has the potential to become a manufacturing centre for global pharmaceutical supplies and clinical trials, and Chinese domestic pharmaceuticals can be a direct beneficiary of this process. Certain steps taken by the government were important to moving in this direction, the most important being quality control. As discussed earlier, GMP, GLP and GCP were important steps for standard-setting. Since 1 July 2005, China has required all manufacturers to be GMP certified. By February 2005, about 60 per cent were GMP certified, and they controlled 90 per cent of China's pharmaceutical production (*Chinapharm*, 2005). Enforcing rigorous standards is important for China's pharmaceutical development because the regulations filter out inefficient and uncompetitive manufacturers; they increase horizontal integration (such as mergers); they improve safety and efficacy; and are important in the battle against counterfeit or expired drugs. The other important improvement is that China has gained approval from the US FDA to conduct clinical trials for multinationals. Chinese pharmaceutical companies thus have the opportunity to be a major competitor in this field because of low labour costs. As stated earlier, the prospect of being a major centre for clinical trials needs to be closely regulated because of its implications for public health. A lack of monitoring of clinical trials can seriously hamper the prospects for Chinese operators in global markets. The standards set by the US FDA should be upheld and harmonized in China. Quality control should also be applied in the monitoring of traditional Chinese medicines.

Chinese herbal medicines

Chinese herbal medicines and their derivatives are the major strength of domestic pharmaceuticals producers, yet most of their potential is not realized in the global market. It has been estimated that the total sales volume is US$13 billion across the world, in which Japanese pharmaceuticals manufacturers account for 80 per cent; Korean pharmas account for 10 per cent and Chinese local pharmas accounted for only 2–3 per cent by 2005 (*World Journal*, 28 April 2006). The search of a cure for malaria shows that, if the Chinese local pharmas improve their competitive position, they can take a major lead in this area.

The case of malaria medicine is instructive for Chinese herbal medicine producers. The urgent need for the Chinese herb artemisinin to cure malaria shows the promise of the Chinese pharmaceutical industry. The increasing need for malaria medicine by forty developing countries has led to a threefold price rise. Malaria is the major cause of mortality for 1 million children globally. Since some populations in malaria-prevalent countries have developed resistance to existing therapeutics, major donors such as charities, non-governmental agencies and inter-governmental agencies in the West are convinced that artemisinin is the most effective and cost-effective drug against malaria.

The shortage of artemisinin has caused a major problem for the WHO and the Global Fund against HIV/AIDS, TB and malaria. This shortage has led to a major crisis among those infected in poor countries, for several reasons: other new drugs need to undergo a lengthy process of registration;

and medical professionals need to be informed about the pharmacotoxicity and side-effects of these new drugs. This trickle-down process in information transmission can be time-consuming and might well delay the efforts to save the lives of those infected. Artemisinin has been used as an effective therapy in Asia since ancient times. Chinese medical professionals who assisted the North Vietnamese during the Vietnam War proved that artemisinin could treat malaria. The natural plant containing artemisinin grows only in the hills of China and Vietnam. It is usually planted in January and is harvested in the autumn. A group of donors, including the Global Fund, the WHO, the World Bank, UNICEF and USAID recommended in April 2004 that those developing countries most affected by malaria should gradually replace chloroquine and sulfadoxine-pyrimethamine with antemether and artesunate.

Immediately after this announcement, a shortage of artemisinin was discovered. Before this announcement about the efficacy of artemisinin, about 30 tons of artemisinin, costing US$115 per pound, was consumed globally. Since April 2004, the price has risen rapidly, to US$180 per pound. When it was estimated that global demand for artemisinin was to rise to 220 tons, the unit price increased from US$365 to US$455. Now, it is not even a matter of price. The severe shortage of artemisinin is affecting all countries and has caused some tension between nations: for example, Ipca, an Indian pharmaceutical maker, has accused the Chinese producers of hoarding artemisinin.

According to *Chinapharm*, globally, by 2004, the market for Chinese herbal medicines grossed more than US$16 billion, in which Japanese products accounted for 80 per cent; Korea produced 10 per cent; and other countries, especially India and Singapore, accounted for 7 per cent (*Chinapharm*, 2004). In this slightly different picture, Chinese herbal manufacturers accounted for only 5 per cent of global production. The finished products were mainly in the form of food supplements. Interestingly, though, In 2004 China also imported more than US$100 million worth of herbal products from Japan, Korea, Southeast Asia and Western Europe (ibid.).

Most of the high-value-added herbal products were manufactured by foreign producers. For example, China produced an average of only 4,000 formulations annually, compared to 150,000 in the USA and 40,000 in Japan. The gap is even bigger for compounds (ibid.).

It was estimated by the Chinese Customs Bureau that, in 2005, exports of Chinese herbal medicines reached US$734 million, a 15.06 per cent increase over 2004, and it was estimated that the actual volume was worth more than US$1 billion. Raw herbal materials, totaling US$338 million, accounted for 46.05 per cent of total herbal exports, but was 3 per cent less than in 2004, while in contrast refined products and extracts continued to expand. Extracts totaling US$226 million accounted for 35.69 per cent of all herbal exports, 4 per cent higher than in 2004. The average unit price per kilogram decreased from US$2,802 to US$2,726. Exports have increased to all regions, and the major market for Chinese medicines for 2005 was Asia, which imported 67.03 per cent of China's total herbal products, a 14.97 per cent increase over 2004. For other markets, exports have increased by 23.76 per cent in Europe, 5.06 per cent in North America, 33.85 per cent in Latin America, and 25.52 per cent in Africa (Liu, 2006).

Chinese herbal medicine derives from a comprehensive ethnomedical framework. Among the four major traditional systems, the Chinese ethnomedical system is the most widely used and practised. The clinical effects of Chinese herbal medicines have been well documented for more than 3,000 years in the medical literature. For example, currently, 12,870 types of herbal medicines are being used. By the end of the Ch'ing Dynasty early in the twentieth century, more than 100,000 prescriptions were issued. Since the mid-1990s, among the Chinese medicine formulae approved by the Chinese SFDA, more than 90 per cent have been derived from those ancient formulae (*China News Net*, 4 March 2005). The use of Chinese herbal medicine to control the symptoms of SARS in China demonstrated the need to find more innovative and scientific ways to realize the full potential of traditional Chinese medicine (*World Journal*, 13 November 2005). And, as mentioned earlier, the Chinese herbal derivative artemisinin has been found to be a most effective treatment for malaria.

Because of its potential for chronic diseases and possibly emerging infectious diseases, Chinese herbal medicine is arousing major interest in the West. For example, Novartis initiated a joint research programme with SIMM to develop natural herbal compounds in 2006. Bill and Melinda Gates Foundation granted US$42.6 million to three institutions to develop the malaria drug artemisinin. Artemisinin, despite being most effective as a treatment for malaria, is still unaffordable for most developing countries when produced in its natural form. The search for a synthetic counterpart for artemisinin is now under way. A recent project unites three partners in this undertaking: Amyris Biotechnologies Inc., a company focused on synthetic biology to make chemicals for drugs and other uses; One World Health, the first non-profit pharmaceutical firm in the USA; and UC-Berkeley. UC-Berkeley will conduct the research necessary to create a microbial factory for artemisinin. Amyris will develop the process for the industrial fermentation of the drug, and One World Health will provide drug development and regulatory support, hoping to prove bioequivalence of the synthetic drug with its existing natural counterpart.

The prospects of Chinese medicine are positive if their potential can be fully realized, with the following improvements:

(i) the trend of using high technology to purify and extract Chinese herbal medicine is conducive to the establishment of a standardized system and to enlarging the global market share;

(ii) new inventions specifically target difficult-to-treat chronic diseases, such as cancer, AIDS, malaria and hepatitis. These can offer competitive advantages for the Chinese herbal industry because these diseases prove hard to tackle in the existing Western biomedical framework;
(iii) new sources of medical treatments are being sought from plants, minerals and animal parts by researching the therapeutic effects of their active ingredients, such as ginseng. The Chinese herbal industry is also searching for substitutes for body parts of protected species, such as the polar bear, rhinoceros and hippopotamus;
(iv) preventive therapeutics is a promising area, which could be built on the abundant resources in the existing Chinese ethnomedical repertoire. The emphasis on prevention in Chinese ethnomedical knowledge can help to promote such products in food supplements and related health foods. The fact that the Shaolin Temple, an ancient centre of Chinese martial arts, is applying for a range of patents and trade marks for its martial arts and fitness knowledge is setting an encouraging precedent for local health product manufacturers.

The Chinese herbal industry is well positioned to enlarge its global market share given global regulatory trends and needs, both of which are favourable to this industry. For example, both the EU and the USA have relaxed their laws on the regulation of herbal medicines (*Chinapharm*, 2001). The global need for herbal medicine is also encouraging for Chinese manufacturers. Worldwide, the total volume of sales of herbal medicines has averaged more than US$60 billion since 2002, but Chinese herbal medicines only accounted for some 5 per cent of the market share. However, as mentioned earlier, it was noted that the profit margins for Chinese herbal producers were higher than for biomedical pharmaceutical makers in China (see *China Pharmaceuticals*, 6 March 2002).

The interest in herbal medicines has been growing rapidly in both the USA and the EU. In October 1994, the US Congress passed a law that allowed herbals to be included as 'food supplements'. This stipulation opened the door for Chinese herbal medicine on the US market, the US FDA has been studying the possibility of also registering herbal pharmaceuticals. The US market remains very attractive, for several reasons. There has been an increasing interest in natural herbals in the USA since the early 1990s, evidenced by the fact that sales of natural herbal products increased from US$6.5 billion in 1996 to US$12 billion in 2000, with an average yearly increase of 15–20 per cent, much higher than the 8 per cent increase in sales for biomedicine. In 2003, the herbal supplements market totalled more than US$400 billion in the USA (see *China Pharmaceuticals*, (6 March 2002).

In addition, the USA has also paid attention to the possibility of using the active ingredients of Chinese herbal medicines to cure chronic diseases.

By 2004, it was reported that more than 200 Chinese herbals had been permitted by the FDA to enter the clinical trials stage. More than half of the applications came from US domestic research institutions, and only ten came from Chinese research centres (*Chinapharm*, 2004).

The law relating to traditional medicine legislated by the European Union formally took effect on 30 April 2004. Before that, both Germany and Australia have approved the entry of some fifty Chinese herbals to their respective markets. The natural herbal market has been growing by 15 per cent a year in the EU.

This legislation significantly lowered the threshold for herbal medicine to enter the European Union. It recognizes the legitimacy of Chinese medicine and allows it to gain entry to the European market. Before this legislation, Chinese medicine could only be imported into the EU as food supplements or raw medical materials. The legislation allows for the broadening of pharmaceutical registration to include traditional herbal medicine, from active ingredients in a single herb, to vitamins and minerals and non-biomedical ingredients. It also allows for a change of wording in efficacy explanations: from 'its effectiveness has not been clinically proven' to 'its safety and effectiveness derive from information from long-term use and experience'. This will possibly lead to an increase of Chinese medicine on the EU market. This legislation mandates a transition period between May 2004 and April 2011, with strict conditions:

(i) exporters of Chinese herbals have to apply for a pharmaceutical sales permit;
(ii) their quality should meet EU standards;
(iii) individual EU members can mandate their pharmaceutical regulation authorities to conduct separate pharmaceutical quality testing;
(iv) exporters also need to generate a framework and mechanisms to trace the origin of poor products and record side-effects; and
(v) the exporters also need to provide facilities for recalling or recycling herbal medicines.

Serious challenges to Chinese herbals in global markets remain, however. For example, it was noted that the raw herbals and OTC herbals that were allowed into foreign markets were less than 10 per cent of the complete list (*Chinapharm*, 2001). The other issue is market share, as mentioned earlier. Chinese herbal products totalled more than 2,000 on the Chinese market, twice the number of biomedicine brands, but their share of the domestic market is only 20 per cent. Most producers are small-scale; products are repetitive; quality monitoring and control are lacking; and there is no organized management system (ibid.).

The EU framework poses major challenges and opportunities in quality testing for Chinese exporters. Because of the diverse kinds and production processes of Chinese medicine, it is almost impossible to specify the active ingredients so the new EU requirement is likely to force the smaller, less well-equipped and less provisioned exporters out of the EU market. However, the advantage of the new legislation is: it provides a greater profit margin for Chinese herbal medicine producers because they can raise their prices. If Chinese herbal medicine passes the quality test and is allowed to be included in the EU's universal health care system, it will give the Chinese pharmaceutical industry a major boost (Zhih and Shao, 2004).

Overall, the major issues facing the Chinese herbal medicine industry are: the need to preserve effective formulations and to create new ones deriving from existing formulations; to modernize, standardize and modulize the production process; to enhance the quality and quantity of production; to preserve the environmental resources for Chinese herbal medicines standardize cultivation; and to upgrade processing and extraction methods and the commercialization process. Specifically, these concerns make it imperative for local producers to pay attention to the following issues.

Quality control

Quality control is a major challenge for Chinese herbal medicine. The major problems are lacking consistent quality, the difficulty in monitoring heavy metal and toxic residuals, and the need to upgrade extraction technology. The Chinese herbal medicine industry needs to demonstrate its quality by meeting rigorous standards: according to a sample quality testing of seventeen Chinese herbal medicines from specialized retailers in July 2003, more than 70 per cent did not pass the test.

Many factors affect the quality of traditional Chinese herbal medicines. According to the Chinese National Food and Pharmaceuticals Supervision and Management Bureau, the major issues with the Chinese herbal market are: disorganization, high turnover rate for specialists, uneven quality, counterfeits, and the lack of a clear boundary between Chinese herbal medicines and food supplements. Biomedical medicine, in contrast, had a pass mark of 97.9 per cent, when subjected to quality testing (*Sina News*, 31 July 2003).

Patent Application and Protection for Chinese Herbal Medicines

It was noted that Chinese government has made serious attempts to modernize IPR protection for Chinese herbal medicines. For example, in 1993, the State Council announced Chinese Herbal Medicine Protection Regulations to reinforce IPR protection of Chinese herbal medicines. The length of protection varies from 10, 20 and 30 years for Class I herbal medicines; and 7 years for Class II. Article 13 mandated that the ingredients and manufacturing methods are protected as trade secrets during the legal period of protection. By 1996, the Chinese patent authorities had accepted

981 applications, and authorized protection for 523 Chinese herbal formulations, 54.5 per cent of which were made by local producers (*China News Net*, 4 March 2005).

In general, Chinese domestic pharmas need to catch up in patent applications, and this is especially urgent for Chinese herbal producers. Among pharmaceutical patent applications, it was noted that foreign applicants tended to outnumber domestic ones, and there were very few applications from Chinese herbal medicine producers (*Chinapharm*, 2001).

The prevailing IPR problems facing the Chinese herbal industry are: ignoring patent protection for new drugs, a tendency to copy drugs, and little innovation and little motivation to innovate (ibid.). These IPR related issues expose other long-existing problems and affect the prospects of the herbal industry (ibid.). Most producers lack the knowledge of how to use IPR mechanisms to protect their formulations effectively. Some of the research published in international journals or conferences which could result in the development of effective therapeutics were attended by researchers in other countries and IPR-protected products were developed.

The need to improve the current situation has never been greater. Chinese producers need to:

(i) Establish a patent protection system for all related knowledge, procedures, equipment and devices, and derivatives in the modernized Chinese medicine framework. Lack of patent protection tends to lead to the duplication of formulae, which means that the original developer is often not the beneficiary of the market. In the past, once a formula, had been developed, it was easily copied by other manufacturers.

(ii) Increase IPR education for Chinese herbal manufacturers. Ignorance of patent mechanisms leads to the loss of valuable herbal knowledge to other competitors. Multinational competitors have often obtained valuable formulae from their joint-venture partners and then used IPR mechanisms to protect their acquisitions against local Chinese producers. The development of artemisinin was the most prominent example of this. Artemisinin was developed by the Chinese Herbal Medicine Institute after more than ten years of research. It was the first patent for a new Chinese herbal medicine granted by the Chinese patent authorities since the new patent law came into force in 1985. A more potent derivative of artemisinin was approved by the Ministry of Public Health and was ranked as one of the top ten new drugs in China. Yet, in neither case was global patent protection applied for, and this resulted in tremendous financial loss for its developers. Similar experiences were reported by producers of a certain Vitamin C derivatives technology. A foreign enterprise was interested in buying the technology for US$5 million, but, because the Chinese originator had never applied for patent protection the deal fell through. The foreign business eventually obtained the technology from a published article for US$80. The story of Viagra was even more intriguing. Various perspectives were presented by different parties. Yet, in China, it was reported that more than ten Chinese enterprises had been studying the therapeutic effects of the active ingredients long before Pfizer applied for the Viagra patent in 1994 in China as well as in 111 other countries. The patent protection in 1994 for Pfizer prohibited Chinese domestic producers from benefiting from their research results. These instances show that Chinese manufacturers really need to catch up with the application of the new IPR mechanisms in the TRIPS framework, but the fact that applications by foreign producers for Chinese herbal formulae have been increasing was a positive sign for local producers (*Chinapharm*, 2001).

(iii) Form a collective force. From the perspective of fair competition, it is critical that Chinese herbal manufacturers form a collective force to use the IPR mechanisms to operate in the WTO environment to market their herbal products. It is equally important that their competitive position is not reduced by bilateral and trilateral agreements, which sometimes contradict TRIPS (ibid.).

(iv) Have a unified strategy towards the global market. The industry as a whole needs to decide its strategic position in global markets and generate effective solutions to meet challenges from global competitors. For example, to improve their weak infrastructure, a possible solution is horizontal or vertical integration via mergers among local small and medium-sized producers. Other strategies are: increasing collaboration between research institutes and industry; initiating international collaboration and patent applications in global communities; and creating their own named brands. They also need to participate actively in bargaining for IPR protection for their industry at international meetings.

(v) Increase technical capacity. There is an unwillingness or lack of the knowledge needed to apply for patents, or for re-application. It was estimated that 70 per cent of state-owned manufacturers and 95 per cent of small enterprises have never applied for a patent. Again, this is mainly because of the lack of IPR knowledge; lack of IPR expertise; or fear about the expense related to patent applications (ibid.). It has been noted that patents granted to Chinese herbal formulae are comparatively fewer than biomedical patents. One major explanation is that applicants were sometimes not familiar with IPR application procedures; some did not re-apply; others did not pay the renewal fees and then lost their patents; and others did not know how to write the application to prove novelty and utility (*Sina Net*, 27 May 2005).

(vi) Create brand name awareness. The public and private sectors need to make a major commitment to invest in innovations in Chinese herbal products, and create global brand names for them. There needs to be a major change of traditional practices among Chinese herbal producers. For example, many effective formulae handed down for thousands of years were kept as family secrets by some experienced herbal practitioners and these would be lost if they did not apply for patent protection (*Chinapharm*, 2001).

(vii) China still needs to harmonize its IPR protection system with international standards in the existing legal and regulatory framework. Herbal formulas were kept secret in patent applications for fear of counterfeiting, and Chinese herbal producers were usually not required to list the full ingredients of the formulation on the labels. This practice is inconsistent with the labelling requirement of patent application regulations in an international framework, and herbal producers are usually penalized if this practice is discovered by the importing countries. And harmonizing Chinese herbal IPR is important for another reason: so that it can extend the protection not only to its domestic herbal industries but also to outside producers of Chinese herbal medicines, especially in Taiwan, Hong Kong and Southeast Asia.

(viii) China needs to speed capacity-building in supporting a comprehensive IPR framework for Chinese medicines. There needs to be IPR education and knowledge-sharing at all levels of the government, between state agencies, industries, communities and non-governmental organizations (NGOs), establishing free IPR services for herbal producers, and increasing the education and training of IPR experts for the industry. (*Chinapharm*, 2001)

A coherent management system

The modernization of Chinese herbal production requires a coherent and systematic framework. There is an urgent need to establish a coherent upstream and downstream Chinese herbal production and management system, including the cultivation of herbal plants; storage; identification of the therapeutic effects of active ingredients and compounds; and a standardized production system (and related issues in preservation, facilities management, efficient equipment, automation, disposal of residues, and the handling of pharmaceutical pollution); quality control (standard setting, monitoring and surveillance systems and equipment); establishing theoretical pharmacology models; clinical trials; establishing Chinese herbal informatics; and integrating Chinese herbal medicines with biomedicine (ibid.).

Standardization

Establishing a GMP process for Chinese herbal medicines is critical to the competitiveness of Chinese medicines in the global market. China, Korea and Japan are all major markets and producers of integrated Chinese medicines. The competition to set quality and production standards among these three entities will affect the leadership positions of these countries in global markets. Korea, which imported more than 80 per cent of Chinese raw herbal materials in 2005, has proposed a new law to regulate the standards of heavy metal content and pesticide residues in all Chinese herbal medicines. Similarly, Japan has proposed to extend such monitoring from an original list of three products to cover fourteen products, the major ingredients of more than 300 herbal formulae. The Chinese domestic herbal industry needs to take the initiative in regulating such issues to enable the industry to grow (Liu, 2006).

In conclusion, this chapter has offered a review of the way in which the WTO has had an impact on major stakeholders in China's pharmaceutical market. In this fiercely competitive environment, the multinationals can capitalize on their R&D position, quality standards, leadership in branded biomedical products and niche markets, their capital advantage, and management efficiency. Yet strategies might vary between multinationals and small pharmas in different areas. Chinese manufacturers are facing very severe challenges, but their potential cannot be underestimated. For example, they can capitalize on their familiarity with generics and OTCs, local marketing and distribution channels, the consumer culture, raw materials and Chinese herbal medicines. Their competitive position in biotechnology can also not be ignored. The WTO's regulatory framework can be a positive force for both domestic and multinational producers if they take full advantage of the market entry mechanisms and IPR framework. It can be a win–win situation if vertical and horizontal integration is facilitated among different stakeholders. In this regard, the potential of the Chinese pharmaceutical sector is unlimited in the WTO framework, and it also increases the dynamic momentum of global pharmaceutical interaction.

5

The World Trade Organization, Hospital Reform and Health Service Provision in China

Mei-ling Wang and Xiao-wan Wang

At the time of writing, health provision is the central social concern in China, and the complexity of the issue presents a direct threat to the cohesion of the Chinese social fabric and political discourse. This chapter discusses the ways in which the WTO affects health service provision in China. Specifically, we shall provide a historical review of health provision; details of the current health needs of the Chinese population; trends in health care financing, investment and spending; the distribution of public and private health services across urban and rural populations; monitoring mechanisms in health provision; and major changes in health provision brought about by WTO membership.

To begin, China's WTO commitments in health-provision-related issues are in the process of largely being fulfilled. Regarding distribution services, since 2002, China has allowed foreign service suppliers to establish joint ventures to engage in selected and wholesale business of imported and domestically produced product categories (with some exceptions). Regarding architectural services, such as hospital design and construction, the Chinese government has mandated that multinationals may co-operate with Chinese organizations for cross-border supply of materials; yet, for commercial purposes, China only permitted the formation of joint ventures with foreign majority ownership in 2001. After 2006, the wholly foreign-owned enterprises are now permitted to enter this market. Regarding medical and dental services, the Chinese government allows multinational providers to form joint-venture hospitals or clinics with Chinese partners, with quantitative limitations, in areas that fulfil Chinese needs. In this area, the Chinese government also allows foreign ownership. In accordance with the Interim Regulations on Administration of Sino-Foreign Joint Venture and Cooperative Medical Institutions, issued jointly by the Ministry of Health and the Ministry of Foreign Trade and Economic Co-operation (or, now, the Ministry of Commerce – MOFCOM) in 2000, the Chinese party in joint ventures and co-operative medical institutions shall hold no less than 30 per cent and foreign investors shall hold no more than 70 per cent of the investment (Murphy and Li, 2005).

Historical overview of Chinese health provision

Health provision in China went through rapid changes between 1949 to 2005. It is generally agreed that China made impressive progress in its public health work prior to the reforms (World Bank, 1984). The health care system is controlled and regulated mainly by the Ministry of Health, which provides technical supervision through an interconnecting chain of agencies reaching down to the village level. The decisions made centrally are usually implemented without modification (Chen, 1989).

Prior to the 1980s, the major characteristics of the Chinese system were the emphasis on prevention, easy access to basic curative care, health services tailored to local needs and conditions, affordable services, and the integration of Chinese and Western medicine. In 1984, there were 2,458 people per doctor in China, as compared with 9,900 in other low-income countries, and about 4,310 in middle-income countries (World Bank, 1984). By 1984 China had made major gains in life expectancy, infant mortality, nutrition and calories intake, distribution of food, and population control; although the gap in the health services between urban and rural areas is widening. Health-related indicators in China show that its efforts in health care since 1949 have resulted in a healthier population.

As discussed earlier, the major policy directive for establishing public health for all in China was issued by Mao Zedong on 26 June 1965, in which he mandated the importance of building a rural public health infrastructure by transferring public health professionals to villages. He also mandated the increase of hospital beds in rural areas. It was estimated that, between 1965 and 1980, about 40–60 per cent of hospital beds were in rural areas.

During this period, China's health care system was characterized by four major principles: (i) medicine was at the service of the people; (ii) prevention played a key role in public health; (iii) health education was carried out through mass campaigns; and (iv) there was a close integration of biomedicine and Chinese medicine (Rosenthal, 1987). There was also special attention paid to women's health. It was noticed that there was a female health worker in every work unit. There were special health policies that protected women's health; for example, pregnant women were prohibited from engaging in hazardous work. A five-tier system was developed from these principles. The government was the source of financing for China's health care system.

The rural health system

One of the major dimensions that determine access to and quality of care in China is geographical location. Most progress in health care in China between 1950 and 1979 was made in rural areas. During this period, the rural health system operated on a five-tier system. On the first tier, the major innovation by Mao was the creation of the 'barefoot doctor' system in 1965. Paramedics, the so-called 'barefoot doctors', assisted by midwives and community health workers, were affiliated with the production brigade health stations and posted in every village (Dong, 2001).

In this system, some 1.3 million peasants were trained as health care providers as a basic prevention and intervention effort in the countryside. They had to pass a national examination before they were allowed to practice (ibid.; see also Leslie, 1976). These barefoot doctors, paramedics in traditional health care as well as basic modern health care and sanitation practices, were instrumental in reconstructing the health care system and improving the health of the population between 1949 and 1978.

At the next level, the commune hospitals were staffed with Western-style and traditional doctors, nurses and health workers, with a limited number of in-patient beds. On the third tier, district commune hospitals offered specialized services to its own commune and four to six others. The fourth tier, the county hospitals, had the best rural facilities. On the fifth tier, the County Bureau of Public Health were the centre of health care management for the entire county (Rosenthal, 1987; Chen, 1989).

The urban system

In the urban areas of China, the health care system was structured hierarchically into three tiers: street health clinics and workplace clinics providing preventive and primary care; district and enterprise hospitals and specialist clinics providing secondary care; and provincial and municipal general hospitals and teaching hospitals providing tertiary in-patient care. Prior to the reforms, these health care institutions were managed and financed by the institutions in the public sector. The three-tier system serves a different clientele in different settings. For example, in large cities, the municipal hospitals addressed the needs of the employees of state-owned enterprises, institutions, municipal government agencies, retirees, disabled veterans, and university faculty, staff and students. District hospitals took care of the employees of large and medium-sized state-owned companies, district and street-level government organizations, district government affiliates, retirees, and middle and primary school teachers and staff. The street hospitals undertook the health care of small state-owned companies, and health centres. Beyond these three tiers, most large work units owned hospitals, while smaller work units or institutions owned clinics or health-care stations. All neighbourhoods had health centres, supervised by neighbourhood committees, providing basic health promotion and education and home care (Dong, 2001).

This universal health care system established by Mao proved to be effective in addressing major health issues, making it possible for the government to provide free basic health services for all in the republic. It was widely agreed that, between 1965 to 1980, the Chinese made impressive gains in many areas of public health (World Bank, 1984).

Overall, the health status of the Chinese population, as evidenced by major health indicators, showed substantial improvement during this time. When the communist government was first established, there was half a billion people in China. The population then showed a sharp increase after 1949 because of the dramatic decline in population mortality. This was considered to be a major success among Mao Zedong's policies. The official death rate in 1953 was 14 deaths per 1,000 people (Coale, 1984; Riley, 2004). The government's efforts in improving the socioeconomic conditions of the population, such as improving the food supply, famine relief, reducing income disparity, bridging the urban – rural gap in accessing social resources, and the intensive upgrading of the public health infrastructure to improve access, generated positive results. Inexpensive but intensive grass-roots prevention campaigns waged by local health workers and political operatives proved to be effective in eradicating major public health problems and increasing life expectancy. This public health effort was interrupted several times by political events, the most notable of which were the Great Leap Forward and the Great Proletarian Cultural Revolution. The Great Leap Forward, designed to increase agricultural and industrial production, and the Great Cultural Revolution, aiming at eliminating the political rivals of Mao, caused major population dislocation and famine, and the consequent deaths of 30 million people between 1958 and 1961. In the years not interrupted by political upheavals, life expectancy at birth increased from 35 years in 1949 to 72 years in 2001 (*People's Daily*, 28 March 2002).

As mentioned earlier, China made impressive public health gains between 1950 and 1984. Infant mortality has declined dramatically, although the precise magnitude of the decline is uncertain because data on infant deaths are incomplete. The most reliable estimates suggest that the infant mortality rate fell from 139 infant deaths per 1,000 live births in 1954 to about 41 infant deaths per 1,000 in the late 1990s (China Population and Information Research Centre, 2001). China has combated successfully infectious diseases of children, and wide-reaching immunization programmes have reduced the prevalence of encephalitis, meningitis and hepatitis. In addition, improvements in water quality, especially in rural areas, have helped to prevent intestinal diseases such as diarrhoea, typhoid and cholera, which affect children in particular (Banister, 1992).

Expanding health care

Preventive care was a major achievement during Mao's rule. Immunization programmes were widespread: by 1990, 98 per cent of infants had been immunized against polio and measles. The Chinese government also financed all health services and made health care affordable for all citizens. Since the economic reforms of the 1980s, however, fewer citizens have had access to public health care, contributing to a rise in illness and mortality among some groups.

Health care after the market reforms between 1978 and 1990s

The change in China's health care system occurred as a result of the larger social and economic reform ushered by the Chinese leader Deng Xiao-ping. The introduction of a market-driven economy had a major effect on the structure of health care financing. The economic reforms of the 1980s that pushed China toward a market economy altered the country's health care system in ways that may have affected population health. In the early years of communist rule, universal access to health care was a top priority, but the shift towards a market-orientated system since the early 1980s has meant the demise of guaranteed access to health care. Poor people cannot afford health care, and rural residents might not have access to health services, making those groups particularly vulnerable. Regional, gender, and other differences in mortality are increasingly visible.

The principles underlying health policy during this time are to: (i) build and improve both urban and rural primary health care services; (ii) effectuate the prevention principle of disease control; (iii) integrate traditional Chinese medicine with Western medicine; (iv) establish maternal and child health institutions and enhance technical guidance in family planning; (v) upgrade medical education and training of health professionals; (vi) strengthen biomedical research; and (vii) improve health management by upgrading the managerial skills of health managers.

In addition, China's Ministry of Health developed national health reform measures for, which were approved by the Chinese State Council in 1985. The major objectives of these reforms were to: (i) decentralize responsibilities in health management and regional development; (ii) expand existing facilities and improve productivity through financial incentives to medical staff; (iii) encourage the privatization of health care provision in the form of private practice or family patient beds; (iv) increase staff support from city hospitals to rural and smaller hospitals; (v) create a health legislation system; and (vi) reform the health insurance system.

The 1985 measures initiated some changes in health care provision. The government limited the public sector's support for health care to basic personnel wages and restricted new capital investment to about 25–30 per cent of hospital expenditure. It allowed more financial independence for hospitals and health centres, and facilitated the privatization of health facilities and the establishment of private clinical practices (Hsiao, 1995).

Urban and rural health care provision

Prior to the reform, the urban health care institutions fell mainly into two major employer-based systems: the Labour Insurance Programme (LIP) and the Government Insurance Programme (GIP). Employees and retirees in state-owned enterprises are covered by LIP, with medical expenses being reimbursed from the employees' pre-tax income. To address the issues of inefficiency in health resource allocation and health care provision, and the lack of risk pooling across enterprises, the Chinese government instituted a major reform, executed in two stages – from the 1980s to 1991, and from 1991 onwards. The objective of the first stage reform was to contain cost from both supply and demand sides. On the supply side, cost-sharing mechanisms were established, such as pre-payment to hospitals according to the number of beneficiaries in their areas, and setting a fixed fee for services. Hospitals were allowed to retain earnings when hospital revenues were greater than payments (Dong, 2001). The hospitals in this scheme have to assume financial responsibility by improving efficiency. A second reform was to define a list of pharmaceuticals eligible for reimbursement. Improvements to GIP and LIP were also made, to increase risk pooling at district or corporate level – for example, by establishing medical expenditures for catastrophes.

In the second stage of reform, the primary goal was to expand the risk-pooling capacity, in conjunction with cost-containing considerations. For example, the city of Shanghai initiated a pilot programme requiring participating partners to allocate 3 per cent of total wages to health benefits for catastrophic and emergency care. The other example is that several cities experimented with city-wide universal health care by combining individual savings accounts and social risk-pooling funds to pay for health care costs. Individuals were required to pay expresses from their savings and a fixed amount of payment before being allowed to access social risk-pooling funds. This experiment was expanded to fifty other cities in twenty-seven provinces under a 1991 policy directive entitled 'Opinions on Expanding the Number of Pilot Cities for Reform of the Employee Health Protection System', drafted jointly by the State Commission for Economic Restructuring, the Ministry of Finance, the Ministry of Labour, and the Ministry of Health (ibid.).

Health issues and the needs of the Chinese population

The major health issues of Chinese society have changed rapidly since the founding of the People's Republic of China. Between 1949 and 1978, the overall health issues were mainly malnutrition, infectious diseases (TB and other respiratory diseases), hepatitis, parasitic diseases, and maternal and child health. Between the 1980s and the early 2000s, the economic boom in the cities and the rapid development of a market economy led to the emergence of a totally new set of issues. In 2005, according to the Ministry of Health, the most frequent causes of death among residents of Chinese cities are cancer; heart disease; stroke; respiratory diseases; injury and intoxication; digestive problems; endocrinal, urinary and reproductive problems; mental illness; and neurological disorders, which together account for 92 per cent of all mortality in 2005. In contrast, the ten major causes of death in villages were respiratory diseases; stroke; cancer; heart disease; injury and intoxication; digestive problems; endocrinal, urinary and reproductive problems; nutritional and metabolism issues; TB; and mental illness, which together accounted for 91.9 per cent of all mortality statistics (*Sina News*, April 2006, 'Cancer tops the major causes of death among Chinese residents'). This list reflects the results of the fast pace of economic growth and inequity in social determinants of health; yet it is also important that in the years ahead there will be increased mortality caused by emergent infectious diseases such as HIV/AIDS.

Changing population issues

The changing patterns of morbidity and mortality are also related to changing population issues since the 1950s:

Fertility trends and population health:

China's demographic changes and efforts to control its population size have exerted a direct influence on the population's health. Contrary to some criticism against China's population policy, the country has engaged in serious efforts to improve maternal and child health through various family planning campaigns. In the 1950s, starting from the first birth planning campaign espousing fertility control to improve maternal and infant well-being, China's family planning efforts have been conducive to the health of its population. The second family planning educational campaign, which ran from 1962 to 1966 was also designed to lower fertility, particularly in rural areas. This campaign propagated the ideas of later marriage, longer birth intervals and smaller families by providing easier access to contraceptives and abortion. However, this campaign did not result in much reduction in fertility in rural areas because of poor capacity and infrastructure. During this period, China began to manufacture its own contraceptive devices.

Population control continued after the Cultural Revolution. The third campaign, from 1971 to the end of the 1970s, spread a similar message of later marriages, smaller families and longer birth intervals. It was more successful than the previous one in that it provided easier access for rural women to the family planning services and established birth targets throughout the nation. This paved the way for the later single-child policy. A more rigid population policy was implemented in 1979, in the belief that rampant population growth would cancel out all the positive gains of economic growth. Controlling population growth in rural areas was a particular challenge because rural areas had the highest rate of population growth among all regions (about 75 per cent), and more difficult access to health services (White, 1994, pp. 137–58; Greenhalgh, 1990). This policy closely monitored population growth: every couple had to apply for approval before having a child, and individuals who abided by this policy would be rewarded by preferencial treatment in educational opportunities, health care, housing and job assignments; but children who were born out of quota would have reduced access to education and other social privileges. The implementation of this policy has been criticized heavily in the international community; yet it is important to note that the Chinese government relaxed the way that the population control policy was implemented since the 1980s. In the first phase, the government used more forceful measures to reach its targeted goal, such as by requiring women to use contraceptives and sterilization, especially after two births. However, a policy change announced in 1984 in 'Document 7' allowed more flexibility in implementing this policy, such as asking officials to adapt it to local circumstances (Greenhalgh and Winckler, 2001).

Past family planning efforts were successful in reaching the population goal of keeping the size of the population to 1.2 billion by 2000 (Greenhalgh, 1990, pp. 191–229), and at the time of writing, China has one of the lowest fertility rates among developing countries. Yet the fertility rate varies across different regions of China. Fertility rate in urban areas had started to decline in the 1960s, while the rural rate did not reduce until the 1970s. By the mid-1980s, rural rates were still 30–50 per cent higher than urban rates (because of government policy of allowing families with two children in rural areas (Peng, 1991, p. 228; see also Lavely, 1986). In 2001, the urban fertility rate was 1.22 children per woman, contrasting with 1.98 in rural areas.

As noted earlier, gender and socioeconomic status-related factors have a particular influence on fertility and population health. These include: education, income, social and professional status, and geographical location. It was noted that regions differ in fertility. The decrease in fertility was first noted in the more affluent Eastern provinces, but not in the rural and Western provinces (Birdsall and Jamison, 1983, pp. 651–75). In 2000, provincial fertility rates ranged from 0.9 and 1.0 children per woman in Guangdong Province in the south, and Liaoning Province in the north, respectively, to 1.7 in Ningxia Province in the west and 2.2 in Guizhou Province in the south west. The variation is even greater within provinces than among them (Poston and Jia, 1990). In addition, education as a whole and women's education, in particular, as well as income, marriage and childbearing patterns, and women's roles in family, society and the labour force were all contributors to social and population health in China (Wang M.L., 2006; Peng, 1989, pp. 1–38).

Improvements in life expectancy and infant mortality

China has made major improvements in most health indicators, such as life expectancy and infant mortality, since the 1960s. According to the latest estimates by WHO (2003), China's annual population growth rate was 0.9 per cent; the percentage of the population aged 60+ years, was 10.5 per cent; total fertility rate was 1.8 and; life expectancy was 70 years for males and 73 for females – this was 35 years in 1950. Child mortality was 32 per 1,000 for males and 43 per 1,000 for females under five years old (WHO, 2003). China has one of the lowest infant mortality rates among the developing countries (WHO, 2000). The improvements in the economy and overall living standards are believed to have been a major contributor to the improvement of major health indicators.

Imbalance in sex-ratio

An important side effect of restricting births was the unexpected imbalance of sex ratio because of the preference for boys in rural areas – the so-called 'missing girls' phenomenon (Johansson and Nygren, 1991; Coale and Banister, 1994, pp. 459–86; Zeng *et al.*, 1993, pp. 283–302; and Gu and Roy, 1995, pp. 17–42). It was noted that the increasing imbalance in the sex ratio would be 'missing' girls from the population registry. The close-to-normal ratio – 105 boys to 100 girls in 1989, was tilting increasingly towards the number of boys by 2000, which reached 120 to 100 girls, the highest in the world. There were regional differences: most provinces were abnormal, with Hainan and Guangdong provinces of reaching ratios of 135 and 138, respectively, while only Tibet and Xinjiang were close to normal. It was estimated that the sex ratio for first births in 2000 was closer to normal, at 107: 100, but rose much higher with second births, to 152: 100, and to 160:100 for third births. In the villages, gender discrimination was prevalent. In China's fifth census, in 2000, the sex ratio was 119.2: 100 and boys were still preferred in the villages (*World Journal*, 2005), ('The next fifteen years saw major changes in population structure') The explanations for the preference for boys in most villages were that the villagers wanted boys to carry the family name (36.2 per cent), followed by livelihood security (28 per cent), and emotional security (16.7 per cent) (*World Journal*, 2005, 'Boys are preferred in reduced births among villagers'). In general, the missing-girl phenomenon was evidenced by excess deaths of female babies through infanticide, neglect or abandonment; the under-reporting of female births; the putting up for adoption of female children; and sex-selective abortions. There is little knowledge about the exact statistics on these different options, since infanticide and sex selection is forbidden by Chinese law (Zeng *et al.*, 1993, pp. 283–302). Yet services for sex selection were believed to be widely available in private clinics, and have often escaped government surveillance (Gu and Xu, 1994, pp. 417–31; and Zeng *et al.*, 1993).

Neglect of the needs of the increasingly ageing population

The other phenomenon is the increase in the ageing population and lack of resources to take care of the aged. Several related phenomena are occurring in China. The rate of China's population increase is one of the lowest in the developing countries. In the 1980s, the number of newborns averaged 16 million per year but decreased to 7 million per year by 2004 (*Sina News*, 2005, 'Three major crises in China'; see also *The Blue Paper on Social and Economic Conditions of China*, China Social Sciences Sinica). The rate of decrease in newborns has been much faster than expected, which has a direct effect on the operation of schools. It has been estimated that in the year 2004 alone, more than 30,000 primary schools were eliminated in China, and a large number of them were being considered for conversion to nursing homes for the elderly (ibid.). Liuyang City in Hunan Province is a pertinent case in point. In 1995, there were 1,099 elementary schools but by 2005 there were only 326 remaining as the total of the student population had decreased by 61 per cent. Similar trends are occurring everywhere in China (*World Journal*, 2006, p. 50, 'China is on the threshold of an ageing society'.

In contrast to the reducing birth rate is the increase in the elderly population (see the analyses in ibid.). According to China's 2000 census, about 10 per cent of China's population was aged over 60 years, with 7 per cent being over 65 years of age. The rate of ageing is increasing by 3 per cent per year. By 2015, the demographers estimate that China will enter a 'population deficit' stage, caused by the immense pressure brought about by pensions for the rising elderly population. It was estimated that, by 2035, about 20 per cent of China's population will be over 65 years of age, and by 2040, China's ageing population will reach 25–28 per cent – greater than that of the USA (*World Journal*, 2005, 'The next fifteen years will see major changes in population structure'). By 2040, China's elderly population will reach 397 million, more than the total elderly population of France, Germany, Italy, Japan and Britain combined. China's working population will reach its highest point in 2015, but will gradually decrease to 18–35 per cent mid-century. In the 1970s, the ratio of children to elderly was 6:1, but in the next thirty-five years this ratio will be reversed. In addition, three-quarters of the Chinese working population have no pension plans. With no reform, the Chinese population will face a large elderly group with no family support, pensions or medical care, which will pose a serious threat to China's social and economic system.

The need for an effective pension system is urgent. Most state-run companies provide good pension and health care plans, but private companies do not provide any retirement and health plans. China is not oblivious to this issue, however. Since the late 1990s, China's State Council, equivalent to the State Department of the USA, has required private enterprise to provide pension plans. The new system has two components: taxes from the current working population are used to pay for those who are retired; and the government had established private retirement accounts for those retiring in the future. But a problem remains in that private enterprises are refusing to participate in the private accounts project because most of their funding has already gone on paying for the deficit in state-run pension plans, leaving no funding for private accounts, and the funds already collected in private accounts were often appropriated to pay for current retirees. Reforming this system is critical to China's economic success. If the reform is successful, the ageing population will not be a social barrier. The pension fund can be reinvested in the economy through various financial instruments (stocks, bonds and so on) and will thus become a powerful engine for economic development. It can thus improve China's investors' position in the global capital markets. But most important, it increases social solidarity, reduces the government's financial burden and decreases social cost. Ultimately, the reform is likely to increase the political capital of the government (see related discussions in Zhang, 2004).

If the current pension system is not reformed, the elderly will receive less support from the working populations in 2040 than it they do now. That is, only 2 per cent of the working population instead of the 6.4 per cent as in 2000, will be included in the safety net (WHO 2004).

Increasing presence of the 'floating population' in the cities

It was estimated that China now has a floating population of 150 million, accounting for one-eighth of the total population (communication with Xu Hua, Secretary General, China AIDS Foundation, 20 December 2005). Floating populations have made major contributions to China's economic development. It has been estimated that migrant labour has contributed 21 per cent of China's GDP since 1978, and about 100 million migrant labourers have accounted for 57.6 per cent of the work force of the labour-intensive sector, including 52.6 per cent in food and commerce, 68.2 per cent in manufacturing and processing, and 79.8 per cent in the construction sector (*Sina News*, 2006, 'Beijing will invest more than $RMB100 billion in the new "Eleventh Five-Year Plan"'). It was believed that, by the mid-1990s, there were already over 100 million floating populations living in cities, but the numbers are increasing. What began as a small urban population (about 20 per cent) at the end of the 1970s grew to be a much higher percentage in the early 1980s, after Deng Xiao-ping's economic reforms. Causes of this have been the government's relaxation of migration policy, the fast pace of urbanization, and increasing economic and employment opportunities in the cities. Between 1978 and 2005, population in Chinese townships and cities increased from 170 million to 540 million; cities having more than a million population increase from 13 to 49; and urbanization increased from 17.9 per cent to 41.8 per cent. It was estimated that, in 1978, there were fewer than 200 cities in China and in 2005 there were 661

(*Sina News*, 2005,) 'Fast urbanization in China leads to 49 million-people cities').

Between 1990 and 2000, urbanization was increased by 1 per cent, and between 2001 and 2005, by 1.4 per cent. Concommitantly, Neighbourhood Mutual Support Committees, which used to strengthen social solidarity have reduced, from about 100,000 to 77,000. This has had a serious effect on public health because in the past these committees shouldered major responsibilities in maternal and child health, public health alerts, and disease monitoring and surveillance (*Sina News*, 2005, 'Three major crises in China'; see also *The Blue Paper on Social and Economic Conditions of China*, China Social Sciences Sinica). Another cause of urban growth has been access to more and better social resources in urban settings. Urban–rural development in China is uneven and urban centres can often offer much better opportunities for villagers. For example, the City of Shanghai had over 17 million residents by 2005 in an area of 664 square kilometres, with a population density of about 15,000 persons per square kilometre. The suburban area around Shanghai is nine times larger than the City itself, but has a much weaker infrastructure, therefore most migrants choose to remain near the city centre, rather than in the suburban areas (*World Journal*, 2005, 'Shanghai plans to control the population at under 9 million').

Since the migrants are not in mainstream public or private employment sectors, they generally take up temporary jobs as construction workers, nannies, factory workers, or other posts in menial, labourers markets, which are often low-paid and risky, with no health insurance. Some have been forced to move between cities and villages – the so-called 'circular migration' or 'return migration', tending to move back to villages after a few years in the city. It was estimated that more than 40 per cent of the construction workers in Beijing in the mid-1990s were migrants, and the rate has been much higher in the 2000s (Lei, 2001, pp. 471–93). The state regulations on housing, hiring, health care, urban employment, public safety, schools and taxation, which did not take into account the situations of the floating regulations in the past, are now gradually catching up with necessary policies or programmes (Solinger, 1999).

A complicated employment structure and market

The unemployment picture is complicated by the increase in the ageing and floating populations. The year 2005 saw an increase of 9.6 million new jobs, and the recorded unemployment rate was less than 4.2 per cent in small towns and cities. Yet, according to a World Bank expert who formerly directed the Beijing office, the real unemployment rate was greater than 10 per cent in these settings (*Sina News*, 2006, 'Fluid labour market challenged the rights protection of labourers'). The labourers face major issues of social security, health care, unpaid wages, and children's education because of the lack of unions and rights' protection. The employment structure is also uneven: there is an oversupply of the unskilled but a shortage of skilled workers. A general college education is no longer a guarantee of employment (*Sina News*, 2005, 'Three major crises in China'). In a report by the National Development and Reform Committee on 14 February 2006, the Chinese authorities pointed out that the employment picture was complicated in 2006, and more than 14 million people, mainly in cities and towns, will face major employment issues. Unskilled college graduates will have to settle for jobs that are below their educational credentials, are low-paid and with decreased benefits. In 2006, the labour force over the age of 16 is estimated to be more than 17 million, and the job seekers will number more than 25 million, with the employment market offering work for only 11 million (*Sina News*, 2006, 'More than 14 million will face employment difficulties: new graduates will face decreased salaries and benefits'). The employment market is also unstable, sometimes varying with the seasons or trends. For example, for 2005, the need for a stable supply of menial labourers was heightened as China's labour-intensive industries increased. The Chinese New Year holidays in 2006 witnessed high-level anxiety among labour-intensive producers, when the rural migration workers resigned or left their jobs in the cities temporarily to return to their village homes for the Chinese New Year. The recess affected China's overall productivity for three weeks. Many employers had to provide the incentive of free round-trip transportation for these migrant workers so that they could return to their employment, and many employers set up recruiting centres near train stations after the New Year holidays to recruit a new batch of migrant workers.

Changing the social, economic and cultural environment

The economic reforms have also led to unprecedented social changes that have affected China's population, social and environment health. The opening of the economy in China has led to an increasing emphasis on economic growth without always foreseeing negative consequences. The exhaustive use/abuse of human resources, land and natural resources has led to serious environmental degradation, such as air and water pollution, violations of occupational safety, and rural discontent. The liberalization of the economic system and related changes in social values has produced some negative health consequences, such as an increase in commercial sex and arising incidence of STDs and HIV/AIDS. The capitalist mode of production, which requires efficiency, maximization of profit-making and expediency has also caused a decrease in social capital and an increase in social exclusion. This has resulted in some unexpected social health issues, such as the exclusion of the elderly, and an increase in the incidence of mental illness and psychological problems. The economic changes have also produced profound cultural changes that can have an affect on population health. In urban areas of China, globalization has led to increasing exposure to an unhealthy diet, especially to fast food. Compounded by an affluent economy, this exposure has increased the intake of high-fat, high protein and high-sugar foods at the expense of the much healthier traditional Chinese diet. This effect, which is particularly pronounced in urban populations, is a contributory factor to the increasing prevalence of obesity, hypertension, cardiovascular disease and strokes. The concentration of urbanization in major economic centres has increased population density and is also the conduit for the spread of infectious diseases and epidemics, such as avian influenza, SARS, HIV/AIDS, and an increase in violence.

Examples of major life-style issues include the changes in marriage and family stability. The floating populations in particular face major challenges in marriage, which has a direct effect on the family stability that Chinese society has valued for thousands of years. The floating workers often have to rely on matchmakers to arrange their marriages, and the arranged marriages often do not last. The men who provide a 'marriage guarantee fund' for their marriage often cannot claim it back after a divorce. In larger cities, 'eight-minute' matchmaking has become popular among singles (*World Journal*, 2005, 'Arranged marriage is the new way to find a spouse for village youths'). The divorce rate is also rising rapidly, in some cases, much faster than in industrialized countries. There are positive and negative consequences of this trend. It is conducive to gender rights, as most women believe that the right to divorce is a civil right. For example, about 70 per cent of the divorces in Canton are initiated by women. From October 2003, the Chinese government has simplified divorce procedures and made it easy to divorce in ten minutes. In 2003, China's divorce rate was 19 per cent, five times higher than in 1979. In 2004, the divorce rate was 21 per cent, 60 per cent of which were fast-track divorces in a Civil Affairs Bureau, which requires only the marriage certificate, personal identification, a photograph of both parties and a divorce application. Among younger generations, there is heightened interest in fast-track marriage and divorce: there have been cases of couples getting married in the morning and divorced in the afternoon. For example, a 24-year-old woman got married in September 2003, left for work a thousand miles away, and was shocked after coming back for a conjugal visit to discover her husband wanted a divorce. The couple only spent a few days together during the entire period of their marriage. This kind of fast-track marriage is especially prevalent in larger cities and has both direct and indirect consequences for social and individual health. A survey found that the divorce rate in Beijing was 50 per cent (*World Travel Journal*, 2005). Extramarital affairs have been cited as a major reason for divorce. In Canton, extramarital affairs accounted for 30 per cent of divorces, especially among well-to-do men, who followed the fashion for taking a mistress. On the negative side of sexual liberation, both men and women are paying the price for the liberalization of marriage and sexual attitudes. These cultural phenomena are tied directly to the spread of hepatitis, TB, HIV/AIDS and STDs (*World Journal*, 2005, 'Divorce rate rises fast in China. Chinese women choose foreigners for their second husbands!').

Major health issues in China

In general, the major health issues in China are different from those in the 1950s and 1960s, as mentioned in Chapters 1 and 4, and also differ between rural and urban areas. For urban residents, the major diseases are ranked in the following order: cancer and malignant tumours; stroke; cardiovascular disease; respiratory diseases; and injury and intoxication, while for rural residents, the major diseases are respiratory diseases; stroke; malignant tumours and cancers; cardiovascular disease; injury and intoxication; and digestive disorders. For the government, the immediate challenge is infectious diseases. The beginning of the twenty-first century saw an increase of infectious diseases in all regions of China. In a report released by China's Ministry of Public Health on the causes of mortality for October 2005, the most prevalent infectious diseases are were TB, hepatitis B, amoebic dysentery, syphilis and gonorrhea, which together accounted for 87.71 per cent of morbidity. The top five causes of mortality were TB, rabies, AIDS, hepatitis B and meningitis, which together accounted for 89.94 per cent of all reported cases (*World Journal*, 2005, 'Pneumonia is number 1 cause of mortality'). In 2004, according to David Ho, a leading global AIDS expert, the three major infectious epidemics in China are: SARS, AIDS and avian influenza. After SARS was controlled effectively in 2004, AIDS and avian influenza remain major challenges (*Sina News* 2004, 'Warnings from David Ho: China is facing three major infectious epidemics').

Respiratory diseases. In a report released in October 2005 by China's Ministry of Public Health on the causes of mortality, respiratory diseases were the major causes of mortality, with about 1.6 million people dying of them by October 2005 (*World Journa*l, 2005, 'Pneumonia is number one cause of mortality'). It was estimated that more than 100 million Chinese are infected with various kinds of influenza each year. And respiratory diseases, including an extremely prevalent degenerative type of pneumonia, were the fourth largest cause of mortality among the whole Chinese population, between January and October 2005, and a major cause of mortality among villagers, because of smoking, air pollution and hereditary factors, despite the fact that this degenerative disease is curable. Overall, the rate of prevalence was 12.4 per cent among males and 5.1 per cent among females. About 8.8 per cent of urban residents and 7.8 per cent of rural villagers have suffered from this disease (*China News*, 2005, 'Respiratory disease ranked number one as major cause of mortality for rural villagers').

Among the emergent respiratory diseases, SARS was the most serious public health threat since the year 2000, and China was the worst victim in this crisis. During November 2002–July 2003, a total of 8,098 probable cases of SARS were reported to the World Health Organization from twenty-nine countries, including thirty-eight cases from Canada; 812 SARS-related deaths (case-fatality rate: 9.6 per cent) were reported 38 cases of which were in Canada (Centre for Disease Control, 2003). In China, SARS claimed 348 lives, with 5,327 probable cases reported during this period (Cui *et al.*, 2003). It was estimated that China's tourist industry lost more than US$2 billion during the SARS crisis (*Xinhua News*, 2003) 'SARS inflicted nearly 2 billion dollars loss on Beijing tourism industry'.

SARS was a shocking wake-up call to the Chinese government as well as the world at large about the vulnerability of the Chinese population to the new wave of intractable infectious agents whose transmission was spearheaded by the free flow of migration and globalization. When SARS first appeared in South China, it was mis-identified as a typical influenza. Even when the symptoms and toll of casualties in China began to cause alarm among global health agencies, the seriousness of the disease was played down, and related information suppressed. This initial lack of action proved to be costly for the Chinese government.

The other example is avian influenza. Since the autumn of 2005, avian influenza has posed a serious threat not only to China but also to the rest of the world, and this threat is increasing every day. China was able to control the avian influenza outbreaks successfully in sixteen provinces between 27 January to 16 March 2004. But in 2005 there were newly reported cases of mortality caused by H5N1, the virus causing avian influenza in central, eastern, north-eastern, and western regions, such as Hubei, Shinjiang and Qinghai provinces. The World Health Organization warned China on 17, November 2005 that the country should be prepared for outbreaks of this influenza in all regions. China is vulnerable to this epidemic because: (i) China has the largest poultry industry in the world, with 14 billion chickens, ducks and geese; (ii) as in Vietnam and Thailand, which also experienced a high incidence of avian influenza, half of the poultry farmers in China, mainly in the villages, are free-range farmers. Poultry provides an important supplementary income as well as an importance source of nutrition for villagers. However, the intense contact between poultry and human beings in these settings provides the most direct channel of transmission for avian influenza (*World Journal*, 2005) 'WHO should be alarmed by the increasing incidence of bird flu, and Avian flu spread by birds and humans'.

Another example is porcine influenza. During the summer of 2005, porcine influenza was detected in the nine cities of the Western Provinces, such as Sichuan, causing 174 cases, with 34 deaths (*World Journal*, 2005,

'The quarantined areas in Sichuan saw an emergency delivery of vaccines' and 'Spread of porcine flu in Shih Shuan Province').

Tuberculosis. Tuberculosis remains the most serious respiratory health problem in China. The number of TB cases increased dramatically in the 1980s. A 1990 survey found that six in every 1,000 people in China had some form of the disease. Only half of those infected by TB who started treatment were cured, and the cost of long-term treatment hampered efforts to reduce the disease's prevalence and spread. TB prevention and control efforts, aided by WHO and the World Bank have helped to stem the resurgence of TB in some provinces, and have provided a successful model for combating other infectious diseases. Their programme involved diagnosing and treating cases at the village level with affordable drugs. The subsidized treatment and concerted effort has helped to bring TB under control in provinces served by the programme, but the disease is still widespread in many areas in China. The intractability of TB in underserved areas highlights deficits in China's public health capacity. The outbreaks of SARS, HIV/AIDS and various types of hepatitis have also further aggravated this picture.

Respiratory cancer caused by malignant tumours due to a variety of factors is also a serious issue. According to a survey of some 170 medical facilities in Beijing, malignant tumours are the major cause of mortality of the Chinese population in Beijing, with an incidence of 179 in 100,000 persons. Lung cancer took most lives, followed by cancers of the colon, liver, stomach and breast (*Sina News*, 2004, '20,000 have malignant tumours every year in Beijing').

Malignant tumours and cancer. As mentioned earlier, the prevalence of malignant tumours and cancer such as liver cancer is increasing both among urban and rural residents.

Sexually transmitted diseases (STDs). According to China's CDC (China Centre of Disease Control and Prevention), reported cases of STDs increased from 5,800 in 1985 to 750,000 in 2003, around 120 times higher, but it was believed that the total number of cases could be more than 7 million. Since 90 per cent of those infected went to private clinics for treatment, the actual statistics remain unknown, as these clinics do not normally report to China's CDC. People's ignorance of their disease status has also increased spousal or vertical transmission to foetuses (*World Journal*, 2005, 'STDs cases increase by 100 times in 18 years'). It was also noted that only a tenth of those encountering sexual problems sought clinical help. Most people first sought information from the internet, followed by books and only later from health professionals. The information obtained from their researches was often inaccurate and medicine ordered from the internet was often counterfeit. A source of concern is that the prevalence of STDs is directly related to the HIV infection. Controlling STDs should be at the top of China's public health agenda (*World Journal*, 2005, 'Only 10 per cent sought help from a doctor for sexual health').

Among all the STDs HIV/AIDS epidemic in China has caused the most concern because of the grave public health and social consequences it can inflict on Chinese society. Globally, HIV has infected a total of 40 million, with 5 million new cases in 2005 alone (UNAIDS report, 2005). In China, the total number of cases of HIV infection reported by September 2005 was 135,630, which included 31,143 AIDS cases and 7,773 deaths. However, it is believed that the actual numbers are much higher. In 2003, it was estimated that the number had reached 1 million cases, with only 5 per cent of cases detected (*Sina News*, 2003, 'HIV infected are 1 million and 95 per cent not detected'). It has been estimated that HIV transmission has increased by 30 per cent per year in China, and that by 2010 the number of people infected may reach 10 million (*Sina News*, 2003, 'Thirty per cent of HIV transmission in China').

The major causes of HIV transmission in China are drug use, blood transfusions and sexual contact, of which IV injections account for 40.8 per cent; blood transfusions accounted for 23 per cent; sexual contact 9 per cent; and other routes, most probably via sexual contact, were 27.2 per cent. The overall infection rate in China was low compared to other countries, but the prevalence and incidence rate was much higher among high-risk populations and in certain geographical regions. HIV transmission among commercial sex workers increased from 0.02 per cent in 1996 to 0.93 per cent in 2004. The rate for pregnant women in high-risk regions increased from 0 per cent in 1996 to 0.26 per cent in 2004. Vice-Minister Wang of the Ministry of Public Health admitted that under-reporting was a serious issue in some regions. It was estimated that the actual cases might have been more than 840,000 by 2004. Besides under-reporting, other problems are: (i) areas of HIV surveillance are limited, and usually excluded high-risk populations (homosexuals, drug users, and commercial sex workers); (ii) a fear of stigma and discrimination means that most high-risk populations do not want to be tested; and (iii) surveillance is difficult in floating populations, entertainment workers (including escorts in karaoke bars), students, military recruits and newlyweds. An estimate showed that there were 8,644 AIDS-affected orphans, including 4,730 school-age children, among whom 4,385 have received free education, close to the national enrolment rate of 98.93 per cent (*Sina News*, 2005, 'HIV/AIDS close to 135,000 cases, with 7773 mortality'). It is also worth noting that new cases of transmission among women have also increased.

Unlike in other countries, homosexual sex accounted for only 5–10 per cent of total HIV/AIDS cases in China (*Sina News*, 2005, 'Homosexual males rank the second high-risk populations in HIV transmission'). Sales of blood, a major source of income for villages in the early 1990s, became a major contributor to HIV transmission. Illegal blood stations made large profits as illegal agents brokered blood sales between the villagers and hospitals. Blood sellers were paid US$22.5 for 400 ml of blood. Most of the blood stations were not legal or sub-standard. For example, a speech by the Deputy Governor of Hebei Province on 8 April 1995, pointed out that out of twenty-two blood stations in Hebei Province, only one was legal, and out of 132 blood banks, only one was approved by provincial authorities (*Sina News*, 2005, 'The truth about HIV/AIDS in Shing Tai City of Hebei Province').

In the context of HIV increase in China and the taboo of sex related discussion, sex education is still very much needed. The contradictory results showed a gap between increasing prevalence of STDs and self-reported preventive efforts. In a survey of Chinese sexuality, sex education started at 15 years of age, compared to 13.2 years of age in the rest of the world; 34 per cent of Chinese do not use any protection, compared to 57 per cent in the rest of the world; 18 per cent of Chinese admitted to having had STD infections, compared to 13 per cent in the rest of the world; 17 per cent of Chinese have had one-night stands, compared to 44 per cent in the rest of the world; and 15 per cent of Chinese have had extramarital affairs, compared to 22 per cent of populations in other countries (*Sina News*, 2005, 'Global sex behaviour report').

What is disconcerting is that, among the Chinese surveyed, 34 per cent of males and 33.56 per cent of females did not use any protection with sex partners whose sexual history was unknown. Among individuals in the 16–55 age bracket, about 32–33 per cent of those surveyed do not use any protection. The Chinese survey respondents expressed a serious concern for HIV/AIDS, gonorrhea and herpes (ibid.). More educational effort is apparently needed in this area.

Overall, the challenges facing China in containing HIV are numerous, such as a weak and incomplete national HIV testing and surveillance system; a dysfunctional public health system, particularly in rural areas; a lack of qualified human and physical infrastructure; the need for more HIV education and prevention efforts; the need for a comprehensive post-testing follow-up programme; the lack of any co-ordinated effort on horizontal and vertical levels; and the need for government support for vulnerable groups in the population.

Life-style issues and chronic disease. Life-style-related issues are a major threat to Chinese health. It is believed that more than 40 million Chinese are overweight (*Sina News*, 2006, 'Forty million people are overweight, a large market for Hong Kong businesses'). In a study of the weight, blood pressure, cholesterol and fat composition of 190,000 people aged 35 to 74 in twenty cities and townships, about 10 per cent of Chinese residents were above the normal weight; 18 million were extreme cases of obesity; and 64 million suffered from cardiovascular disease caused by poor nutrition or a lack of exercise. Most of those who were overweight were women in urban areas in the Northern China. Based on this study, it was projected that more than 170 million Chinese are overweight (*World Journal*, 2005,

'Physical checkups show that 18 million are excessively overweight'). Chronic diseases caused by life-style-related issues are particularly serious among urban dwellers. Obesity is a serious health threat. Urban dwellers now exhibit the 'three highs' phenomenon: high blood pressure, high cholesterol and high glucose. This is particularly pronounced among the highly paid and those with high academic credentials. According to a report released by China's Ministry of Health, more than 160 million Chinese suffer hypertension; more than 20 million are inflicted with diabetes; and more than 160 million suffer from cholesterol issues. Cardiovascular disease is a health problem that kills 2.6 million people in China annually – a figure that is predicted to rise significantly by 2020 (see Chinese Ministry of Health, 2006).

Chronic diseases increase with increasing GDP per capita of more than US$800. According to a study undertaken in 2002, about 18.8 per cent of adults aged 18 or above were suffering from hypertension, a 31 per cent increase over a decade ago. An excessive intake of saturated acids is a major health threat for city dwellers. For example, the major sources of energy for Chinese urban residents are from dairy and meat products – some 35 per cent of their overall diet, and much higher than the WHO-recommended 25 per cent (*World Journal*, 2005, 'Gourmet diet makes Chinese city dwellers lose nutritional balance').

A report released by a physical examination centre in Beijing also showed the seriousness of the fitness problem in urban centres. About 70 per cent of 2,160 married males examined, 59.7 per cent of the examinees reported a lack of regular physical exercise and being overweight. This is the most important predictor of major illness, followed by hypertension, (suffered by about 34.4 per cent of those examined); cirrhosis of the liver serosis (32 per cent of those examined); and osteoporosis or bone loss. Among these examined, 67.5 per cent reported abnormal social relationships and 41 per cent suffered from chronic anxiety and depression, with major symptoms of headaches, back pain, fatigue and memory loss (*World Journal*, 2005, 'Sixty per cent of married males reported overweight').

Obesity is also problematic among children. According to a 2006 survey, about 17.6 per cent of teenagers aged under 18 were overweight and, among them, 5.6 per cent were obese. In large cities, about 16.7 per cent of boys and 9.6 per cent of girls were found to be overweight (see *Sina News*, 2006, 'Health survey shows poor nutritional status for Chinese children').

Nutrition is a complex health issue and imbalanced nutrition is a major factor in poor health at the time of writing. According to 'A 2006 survey on the Nutrition and Health Conditions of Chinese Residents', anaemia, malnutrition and obesity are three major nutritional issues facing Chinese children. For the better-off, the issue is excessive intake of proteins, fats and calories, while for the poor, it is a lack of an adequate and balanced diet. A study has shown that, for children aged 7–12, the incidence of malnutrition was 20.6 per cent in large cities and 26.4 per cent in medium-sized and small cities (*Sina News*, 2006, 'Health survey shows poor nutritional status for Chinese children'). A lack of basic micronutrients, especially iron and vitamin A, is a major issue in malnutrition, and Chinese children's calcium intake is estimated to be only a third of the internationally recognized standard. By March 2006, the calcium intake by Chinese girls aged 11–13 was 312 mg; and 338 mg by boys. Both are below the recommended amount of 1,000 mg. It was estimated that about 12.3 per cent of boys aged 7–17 in the cities and about 15.9 per cent of girls suffered from anaemia caused by iron deficiency. The rate of anaemia was estimated to be even higher in villages (ibid.). According to one estimate, anaemia affects 15–20 per cent of the whole population of China – about 200 million people, and mainly affects women and children (*Ohayo Network*, 2006, '200 million Chinese suffer from iron deficiency'). Diabetes, especially among children, has also seen an increase in China. It has been estimated that 5 per cent of Chinese diabetics are children (*Ohayo Network*, 2005, '5 per cent of Beijing's diabetics are children').

An increase in smoking also reflects changing lifestyles in China. It is a serious health problem China under the WTO framework has become the largest market for tobacco, with the Chinese tobacco market increasing to US$58 billion in 2004. According to a Chinese official estimate, about 180 billion cigarettes were sold to 320 million smokers in China. More than 50 per cent of smokers started smoking before they were 18 years old. Other smoking-related statistics were also alarming: 8 per cent of smokers started smoking by 10 years of age; 12 per cent start between 11 and 14; 34 per cent 15 and 18; 39 per cent between 19 and 25; 7 per cent after 26 (see *Sina News*, 2006, 'Most smokers start smoking by 18; monitoring mechanisms are not complete'; see also *World Journal*, 2005, 'Japanese tobacco maker is looking to the Chinese market'). The reduction of cigarette smoking in major industrialized countries, especially in Japan and the USA, has made tobacco producers look to the Chinese market as their major outlet. For example, the Japan Tobacco Company has been urging the Chinese government to open up the tobacco market more quickly. In general, tobacco smoking poses a serious threat to population health and in China at the current time, about 12 per cent of mortality is related to smoking. In a study of 500,000 residents in ten regions, it was estimated that about 50 per cent of smokers had died as a result of smoking-related disease. More than 80 per cent of Chinese males smoke, and it has been predicted that, by 2010, there will be a million Chinese dying from smoking-related problems; 2 million by 2025; 3 million by 2050; and 6 million or more after 2050, most of the victims being males (*Sina News*, 2005, '12 per cent of Chinese male mortality is related to smoking').

Rapid industrial development is contributing to environmental pollution in China, and this in turn affects population health. The most serious environmental issue facing China at the time of writing is water management. It was noted that the four major river systems in China are all highly polluted. The Long River, the largest river system in China, absorbed more than 16.4 billion cubic metres of polluted water each year; and the Yellow River, the second-largest river system, more than 4.4 billion cubic metres (*Sina News*, 2005, 'High cancer rate village'). The Minister of Water Resources, Wang Shu-tsen, has started that water shortages, floods, pollution and loss of water resources are major environmental threats to China. On average, the Chinese population has at its disposal 2,200 cubic metres per capita – about a quarter of the global standard, and each year there is a water shortage of 40 billion cubic metres. The management of its water resources is a major challenge to China during this social and economic transition (*Sina News*, 2006, 'Four major challenges in water resources and development').

A recent report has found that the drinking water for 700 million Chinese was polluted. Three-quarters of the lakes were polluted and it was estimated that about 80 per cent of the 60 billion tonnes of waste water poured into the major rivers had not been processed. In 2004, in the Long River alone, most of the waste water was dumped into the water system without filtering (*Epoch Times*, 2006, 'Environmental pollution is serious and 700 million Chinese are drinking dirty water').

Water shortage is often further aggravated by pollution. Among some 600 Chinese cities surveyed, more than 400 suffered a shortage of water supply, 110 of these suffering very high level of water shortage. These water shortages have been aggravated by pollution, making this a major life-threatening issue for China. Among some 660 cities surveyed, around 400 cities suffered pollution to different degrees, with 136 suffering serious pollution. On the whole, about 50 per cent of the cities were polluted to different degrees. Water shortage aggravated by pollution is a real public safety issue in China (*Sina News*, 2005, 'Half of the Chinese cities suffer underground water pollution'). Of 118 cities investigated, about 75 per cent of 10,000 kilometres of underground water was polluted. In Beijing's underground water alone, about 300 of its 375 kilometres of underground water had various degrees of pollution, and 200 kilometres had serious pollution. The major factor of underground water pollution was unprocessed polluted water passing into river beds or underground water reservoirs. The Liao and Shonghua rivers in north-east China are among the most polluted in the country. In Harbin City, the pollution caused by seven toxins caused a public panic. A similar incident occurred on 14 February 2006 in the Yue River in Sichuan Province, where heavy contamination from three chemicals caused a temporary shutdown of the water supply system. The most toxic chemical in these cases was benzene. Most of the population uses below-standard volume of underground water. In villages alone, more than 300 million are forced to use unsafe drinking water every day.

These water shortages invoke a vicious cycle of environmental degradation. For example, in north-west China, water shortage has contributed to the rapid disappearance of some oases. The Mingching Oasis has lost 94 per cent of its original size, which has seriously implications for the climate of the Northern Hemisphere. This trend has already affected other oases in China, such as Lobu Lake in Xinjiang Province (*World Journal*, 2005, '94 per cent of oasis has gone').

The soil and the ocean also face major threats from pollution. Regarding soil pollution, more than a third of China's soil has been polluted by acid rain. The case of black soil is also a concern. China's area of black soil accounts for a fifth of the total area of black soil in the world. With a depth of 60–100 cm, China's black soil is disappearing by some 0.7 to 1 cm annually. The black soil area is a major agricultural resource in northern and north-east China. As far as the ocean is concerned, there are reduced fishing activities over more than 90 per cent of the ocean floor close to China, caused by pollution. A large number of fish have been contaminated with pollutants such as mercury or PCP (Pentachlorophenol) (*Epoch Times*, 2006, 'Environmental pollution is serious and is threatening the ecosystem in China').

Most often, both air and water are polluted by chemicals issuing from industrial areas (Tremblay, 2005). These include PCP, pesticides, herbicides, food additives, detergents and mercury, and chemicals in vegetables, seafood, air, water, grains and textiles. A recent case was that of a chemical plant explosion which severely polluted one of China's biggest rivers and caused a cut in water supplies to millions of people. It also caused panic among the public in neighbouring Russia. The explosion, at a PetroChina factory in the north-west province of Jilin, deposited a large amount of the carcinogen benzene into the 1,897-km-long Songhua River, according to China's Environmental Protection Administration. Benzene levels in this incident were 108 times above national safety levels. An emergency summons was issued to fourteen hospitals to treat possible cases of poisoning. The city of Harbin needed 80,000 tons of clean water on the first day of the disaster. The pollution also affected the Far Eastern region of Russia, with its several million population (*World Journal*, 2005, 'Shonghua residents were evacuated for fears of pollution').

Incidents of environmental pollution on a smaller scale take place every day. A car transporting sulphur dioxide, which exploded in Shanghai led to the leaking of 10 tonnes of sulphur dioxide and water pollution over an area of 1,000 square metres (*Sina News*, 2006, 'Nearly ten tons of sulfite caused serious pollution near Shanghai'). Another incident of an explosion involving propane, caused a major alarm in the city (*Sina News*, 2006, 'Very toxic chemicals exploded in Jiangxi Province'). Another environmental and occupational disasters are related to mining. Mine disasters have been occurring more frequently than in the 1990s (*Sina News*, 2005, 'Mine disasters exposed problems in state-owned mines'). It has been estimated that there were thirty-three mining accidents in China between 1 January and 21 August 2005 alone, an increase of 43.5 per cent over the same period in 2004, with mortalities totalling 951, an increase of 134.2 per cent (*Sina News*, 2005, 'Three major crises in China'; see also *China Social Sciences Sinica*, 2005).

Waste disposal is also a major source of environmental pollution. The accumulation of rubbish in major urban centres has reached 600 million tonnes and is increasing by 4.8 per cent per year. It was estimated that two-thirds of Chinese cities are facing major problems with waste disposal. The capacity for disposing of waste and rubbish reached 149,000,000 tonnes in 66 cities, 4.96 times greater than 1980, but is still insufficient. A study has shown that the capacity for disposing of non-toxic waste was less than 15 per cent of what was needed in 2002 (*World Journal*, 2005, 'Two-thirds of cities engulfed by garbage').

Another environmental concern, resulting from globalization, is the increase in harmful micro-organisms, plant varieties or insects that has incurred a loss of more than US$125 million in the agro economy. There are more than 380 harmful plant varieties, 32 insects and 23 micro-organisms. Among the hundred internationally defined most harmful living organisms, more than fifty have been found in or transported into China and have caused major damage not only to agricultural products but also to environmental integrity and safety (*Sina News*, 2006, 'Foreign organisms damage China's ecosystem').

A major consequence of environmental problems is reflected in the threats to the health of the population, especially in the rise of the prevalence of cancer, which has been rising rapidly. By March 2005, China had 20 per cent of the world's total of new cancer cases – some 2.2 million (Parkin *et al.*, 2005). The emergence of 'high cancer prevalence villages' is plaguing every province of China. In one village, the cancer rate was 1.3 per cent in 2004. In one case, more than 30 out of 100 family members died from various kinds of cancer caused by pollution. The victims were all in their forties (*Sina News*, 2005, 'High cancer rate village'). Lead poisoning is another controversial issue. An estimated one third of Chinese children suffer from lead poisoning (*Sina News*, 2006, 'One-third of children suffer lead poisoning').

Other emerging health issues also pose a challenge to China's health systems: (i) *Mental health*. At the beginning of the 2000s, China was already seeing a rising prevalence of mental health problems, especially depression, neurosis, alcoholism, drug dependence and senile dementia. This can be attributed to physiological, genetic, social and occupational factors, such as rapid social and economic development and related population *dislocation*, increasing urbanization and ageing of the population, intensified competition, and a rising unemployment rate. The prevalence has increased from

0.54 per cent in the 1970s to 1.347 per cent in 2001 (*People's Daily*, 2001, '16 million Chinese suffer from mental illness'). In 2001 it was estimated that, compared with the 400 million cases across the world in 2001, more than 16 million Chinese suffered mental illness. Mental illness has been increasing by more than 100,000 cases per year in China. Some 16–20 per cent of college students had suffered various psychological problems, and it was predicted that mental illness would be a major health problem over the next two decades in China, higher than the prevalence of heart disease, respiratory diseases and cancer. The capacity for treating mental illness was inadequate by international standard, but is improving. In 2001, there were 575 hospitals, 110,000 beds, 77,000 doctors and 13,000 specialists. This was 43 times below the level and capacity in the USA. China, at the beginning of 2000s, had 2.4 psychologists per million population, while in the USA, there were 550 per million population. However, the Chinese government's efforts at improving capacity has gradually paid off and clinical visits for treating psychological problems have increased. With more attention being paid to this aspect of health care, and investment from both private and public sectors, the capacity is likely to increase to meet the demand for treatment (*China Daily*, 2001, 'Psychological health stressed'; see also *People's Daily*, 2000, 'Mental health problems on rise'). (ii) *Occupational health issues*. Although the 2001 law on occupational health clearly stipulated the protection of workers' health, its implementation is still inadequate. It was noted that this regulation has been ignored by managers in small factories or private companies (*Xinhua News*, 2001, 'New law to protect workers' health'). For example, all enterprises must participate in social insurance for pensions, unemployment, health care, work-related injuries and maternal leave, according to state regulations. They are mandated to pay the full amount of social insurance premiums to social insurance agencies and are also required to participate in making payments for pension premiums. The trade union may participate in establishing a collective contract with the enterprise for such matters as work remuneration, work hours, holidays, workplace safety and hygiene, and insurance and welfare. Yet in actuality, a large number of enterprises have never complied with the law. (iii) *Violence*. Violence in different forms has been on the rise in China, such as villagers confronting local officials, crime, violence against women, and violence against children. It was estimated that two-thirds of Chinese children were victims of domestic violence in 2004. About 71.38 per cent of children reported corporal punishment by their parents before reaching the age of 12 (*Central Daily News*, 2004, 'An internet survey shows that two-thirds of Chinese children have suffered domestic violence'). (iv) *Treatable but neglected diseases*. There are a large number of treatable diseases that receive inadequate support from the public health sector, for example, eye diseases such as blindness and glaucoma. Glaucoma is a most relevant case in point. It was estimated that about

30–40 million individuals need glaucoma surgery but only an eighth – 400,000–500,000 can afford it. Of 2,700 townships, 40 per cent do not have eye specialists, (*World Journal*, 2004, 'Five specialties in one doctor in China').

Health provision and trends in health care costs

Health provision in China is undergoing many changes and facing many challenges. According to one estimate, there are about 65,000 health providers in China, but distribution of public and private health services in the urban and rural populations is uneven.

Before the reforms, the division of labour in health provision was clear between small health clinics and hospitals, with health clinics shouldering the bulk of responsibility for health promotion and disease prevention. Since the 1980s reforms, most health care provision has been concentrated in the hospitals, and the management and operation of these has also undergone rapid changes. There are two kinds of hospital in China: non-profit/public and private/for-profit. Public hospitals are usually government-owned. It has been estimated that, by 2005, China had more than 16,000 hospitals, 90 per cent of which are categorized as being public. It was also estimated that more than 80 per cent of Chinese medical resources were concentrated in urban areas, with less than 20 per cent in rural areas (Wikipedia, 2005).

Government-controlled/public hospitals received their guidance from the healthcare department of a province, city or county. In comparison, private hospitals and publicly trading hospitals are operated as private enterprises. Similar to the situation in the USA, profit-orientated hospitals are allowed to retain their profits, but non-profit hospitals are required to reinvest their earnings into the infrastructure or to pass them to affiliated government agencies. As a rule, non-profit hospitals are given special tax incentives and government subsidies, plus low-cost financing from public authorities for their capital investment. After WTO membership, the entry of large investors has led to an increase in large hospitals, but a decrease in small-scale hospitals. The entry of JV (joint-venture) hospitals has also imposed tremendous pressure on the non-profit hospitals (Wikipedia, 2005; see also Wang and Chen, 2005).

Health professionals

Nurses must be qualified, but support staff are low-skilled workers with very low pay. Nursing education offers a range of programmes. It usually takes about four years to complete after a middle school education and three years for senior high school graduates. Starting from the 1980s, some universities also offer a bachelor's degree in nursing. Some medical schools, such as that at Beijing University, offer five-year programmes. Most hospitals are staffed with full-time licensed nurses and staff, but more hospitals, especially private ones, are hiring part-time support staff to reduce costs. The Chinese government has intensified the quality control of health care professionals, primarily in large cities. For example, the City of Beijing has recently established a regulatory framework on training and hiring of qualified hospital support workers (Zhang, 2006).

In the training and education of doctors, the Chinese medical education system follows the British model. In total, there are more than 130 medical schools, about 120 of which are recognized by the USA. Most of these are located in large cities, such as Beijing, Shanghai, Tianjin and Chongqing, and in other large cities in the provinces or in secondary cities. The most highly rated are: Peking (Beijing) Union Medical College; Beijing University Medical School; the Fudan University Medical School in Shanghai; Zhongshan University Medical School, Guangzhou; and Sichuan University Medical School, Chengdu (Wikipedia, 2005).

Medical education takes about five years after passing a competitive examination after high school. Some medical education programmes take fewer than three years to complete but these are not regarded as highly as those from schools with five-year programmes. Most hospitals hire graduates from five-year programmes. A medical school graduate begins as an assistant doctor; after three years' practice, the graduate will have to pass a certification test, equivalent to the US board exam, to become a fully licensed doctor. Exceptions are made for physicians with a master's degree in medicine. Having had seven years of training in total, the candidate with a master's degree can shorten the cycle by taking the certification test after one year practising medicine. Residency is not practised uniformly. In fact, it did not start until 2003, when the Huaxi Hospital of Sichuan University established a residency requirement for new medical school graduates. Similar to the US model, on this programme students have to complete their medical education first, which is followed by the residency, during which students must pass the certification test (Zhang, 2006; see also Wikipedia, 2005; Wang and Chen, 2005).

Most of the medical students were trained as generalists, despite the fact there are specialist hospitals and clinics, such as those for treating hepatitis, cancers, infertility, dental diseases, dermatitis, nephritis and diabetes. Students focus on a speciality after their training has been rotated through several different departments. Yet it is worth noting that there is no system for developing speciality physicians in China. In addition, all Chinese medical students have to study traditional Chinese medicine. This provides market niches for joint-venture hospitals when they enter China's health provision market. The classification of specialities at a Chinese hospital is similar to that at a US hospital (Wikipedia, 2005).

After graduation, most candidates work for public hospitals, but they are encouraged to have their own private practices or also to work in private practice. Practitioners of traditional Chinese medicine usually graduate from specialized programmes in colleges or universities, but many of them also follow an apprenticeship system, where they learn their trade from their parents based on skills and ancient formulas handed down from their ancestors (ibid.).

There are wide variations in salary levels among doctors. Salaries for doctors at public hospitals can be as low as US$120 per month but for those at the better-known hospitals, they are several times higher. Hospitals are ranked 1–3, (3 being the highest rank) with a sub-classification system A–C, (A indicating the highest rank). As such, the elite hospitals are ranked as 3A+, and those who work at the highest-ranked hospitals are paid the most. Generally, though, their incomes derive from multiple sources and the base salary is not a clear indicator of their total income. Most doctors have a 'grey income', and can increase their salaries by working at other hospitals or owning private clinics. However, 'grey income' is controversial because it also contributes to rising health costs. In the face of increasing health needs in China, the need for medical professionals is also rising (Zhang, 2006).

Health care financing

China's overall health expenditure, including both public and private sources, increased from 3.86 per cent in 1995 to 5.33 per cent of China's GDP in 2001. Facing rising population pressure, this figure is likely to increase at a higher rate in the years to come. In addition, at the time of writing, Chinese health care consumption totals more than US$500 billion every year, about 4 per cent of the country's GDP. This figure is likely to to grow to US$2,000 billion by 2010. Health expenditure per capita in China is US$36 (Wang and Chen, 2005; *Sina News*, 2004, 'The government should improve the public health system. Delegates made three suggestions').

Among the population as a whole, overall out-of-pocket health spending increased from 23 per cent to 60.6 per cent between 1980 and 2001 (ibid.). In another estimate, according to the Third National Health Survey in 2005, in the context of a lack of health insurance for the majority of Chinese people, they spent an average of US$13.5 on every visit they made to a doctor, a 57.5 per cent increase since 1998; in-patient one-off treatment has reached US$500, an increase of 76.1 per cent since 1998 (*Sina News*, 2005, Vice-chair of People's Congress reveals that the Ministry of Health will not allow an increase in pharmaceutical prices').

The conceptual, legal and regulatory framework of financing and investing in health provision has undergone many changes since the 1950s. The government financed the total operation of all hospitals before the 1980s. After the economic reforms, reduced public sponsorship in the 1980s and 1990s has now been replaced by more forceful intervention from the government to improve public health, with increasing partnerships with the private sector and intergovernmental agencies and foreign governments.

The regulatory framework for health provision is based on: (i) the directive from Chairman Mao in the 1950s to improve China's public health infrastructure; (ii) the policy on health reform in 1985 that allowed the entry of private providers to health care. The health reform in 1985 was designed to resolve the so-called 'three difficulties': difficulty in seeing a doctor; difficulty in getting access to surgery; and difficulty in obtaining in-patient care. The 1985 reform opened up the participation of the private sector in financing health care after forty-five years of being financed by the public sector. The private sector was encouraged to invest in the building of new hospitals, improving existing hospitals by adding beds, purchasing equipment and providing surgical facilities. In 1998, another reform targeted health insurance, access to pharmaceuticals, and health care provision; (iii) WTO regulations allowed foreign ownership of hospitals and the entry of foreign investment in health-care-related services and products after 2003.

In the 1980s and 1990s, the public hospitals operated in both non-profit and for-profit modes. In general, they relied on government funding to finance such expenditure as staff salaries and capital costs – for example, buildings and capital equipment. The government determined the charges for health services without taking into account the cost of financing. In general, health services, such as diagnostic and other non-pharmaceutical categories, were below cost while the pharmaceutical charges were much higher than the cost. As mentioned in Chapter 3, the Chinese government has established a complete essential medicine list and reimbursement system. Hospitals are reimbursed by the government on a fee-for-service basis and therefore cannot make a profit from the reimbursement system. As discussed earlier, most hospitals now rely on pharmaceutical sales to provide additional profits to cover the inadequate government finance (Wikipedia, 2005; see also Wang and Chen, 2005).

The year 2000 hospital reform

In the year 2000, the Chinese government announced a major reform of the hospital system. The Ministries of Health and Foreign Trade and Economic Co-operation participated jointly in the regulatory framework. The two ministries will examine the qualifications of all JV hospitals established without the permission of these two ministries, and multinationals have to obtain approval from these two ministries before they build JV hospitals. Those hospitals that are 100 per cent foreign-owned would not be allowed to operate. Prior to China's opening up to to WTO, the JV hospitals should follow internationally established standards regarding equipment, technology and management, and would only be allowed to provide services that local hospitals could not provide. The initial investment of all JVs should be at least US$2.4 million, with a no more than 70 per cent foreign share, over a term of twenty years, but there were special incentives and exceptions for hospitals in inland China (central and western regions), and remote and poor areas. Investors from Chinese regions, including Hong Kong, Macao and Taiwan, had to follow the same rules.

Health costs

As mentioned earlier, the Chinese insurance system has undergone rapid changes. Most Chinese, about 45 per cent of the urban population and 80–90 per cent of the rural population do not have any form of insurance (in another estimate, the overall uninsured rate was 70–90 per cent). The health insurance scheme developed under Chairman Mao for the whole population in the 1950s has been completely dismantled. In different regions, new modes of health insurance are being experimented with constantly. Between 1980 and 1994, the state-owned enterprise (SOE) and collective insurance covered about 140 million workers, plus 60 million family members were also covered. In 1994, a major health insurance reform was initiated by the State Council. In December 1998, a National Medical Insurance Scheme was launched by the State Council and managed by the Social Insurance Fund Administration Centre, a department of the Ministry of Labour and Social Security. By the end of 2002, this had covered about 100 million of the population in most of the country's enterprises as well as government employees in both cities and counties. This plan covers up to 70 per cent of medical expenses and replaces other forms of government-sponsored insurance scheme, such as GIP and LIP. In addition, multinational enterprises are obliged to provide health insurance but do not have to participate via this programme, or they can choose to participate through a broker or third party. WTO membership also allows the entry of multinationals to commercial health insurance. The entry of high-end commercial medical insurance offered by Chinese and Western companies, such as China Life Insurance, Ping An Insurance, AIG and other big insurance companies is of benefit mainly to high-income individuals (Wang and Chen, 2005).

In general, the basic medical insurance programme covers only basic medical treatment and is limited in relation to chronic illnesses or very expensive health care items, and does not cover most of the rural and/or excluded populations. The premium is shared by employers and employees for both individual and aggregate accounts. The individual accounts pay for out-patient services and a limited amount of in-patient services. Certain approved medications are eligible for reimbursement, and patients are free to choose which institutions they use. The existing framework of health insurance is not perfect but has improved rapidly since the 1980s; however, it is still not a flexible system that adjust to the needs of different segments of the population. At the time of writing, health care costs are paid from several sources: government-sponsored insurance, employer-sponsored insurance, and most commonly, individual out-of-pocket payments.

Regulatory mechanisms of health provision and quality control

China has a framework for addressing malpractice through its 1987 'Regulations on Medical Incidents' and the 'Amendments to the Regulations of Medical Incidents', published on 4 April 2002 and implemented on 1 September 2002. With the rapidly changing medical environment at present, the latter needs further amendment to meet the rising needs of both health care practitioners and patients. At the time of writing, patients can choose private arbitration procedures or engage in civil procedures to seek compensation.

Despite these provisions, the need for an improved legal and regulatory framework for health provision in China has never been more urgent, to improve not only the quality of care but also efficiency, health outcomes, and most important, global competitiveness.

On patients' rights, the major issues are: (i) a lack of guidelines on grievance and legal procedures for victims complaining about malpractice; (ii) a lack of a dispute-settlement mechanism between hospitals, patients and health care providers before a case reaches the courts; (iii) a lack of an effective public arbitration regulatory framework; and (iv) a lack of free legal assistance for victims of malpractice. Most important, there is a lack of education regarding patients' rights as a whole. In China, medical liability suits incur major costs on the part of patients and it often takes a long time for arbitration to generate results (*Sina News*, 2004, 'There should be a buffer between the patients and health care providers'). Also, there is no effective legal and regulatory system to protect patients' rights.

Regarding protection for health care providers, there is a lack of ethical education in doctor–patient relations and interaction. In addition, there is no medical liability or malpractice insurance to protect the provider and support compensation for victims. This issue is closely related to the discussions of other issues, such as the establishment of a monitoring system by the public sector and non-governmental agencies, ethical capacity building and health insurance provision, which will be analysed in Chapter 6.

The status of health provision under the WTO: major changes and trends

WTO membership has brought with it a high level of energetic, dynamic and creative partnership as well as complications to China's health provision market. The momentum for these charges have mainly been brought about by global interest in the size, needs and long-term potential of the Chinese market. After China's fulfilment of its commitment to open up the health care provision sector in 2003 to WTO members, the government has eliminated almost all barriers for private and multinational capital to enter the health care provision market. Most of the stakeholders in this sector are multinationals and domestic IPO (Initial Public Offering) companies.

As with pharmaceutical supplies, the health care construction market has shown a large market potential for all stakeholders. It was noted in 2005 that China's investment in health care construction has been growing by about 20 per cent annually. In 2003, China invested US$4.5 to US$7.5 billion in building health care facilities, and this investment has been increasing every year (Murphy and Li, 2005). Even so, China's health care facilities still cannot accommodate all its needs. It was estimated that, in 2005, China's capacity was far below the world standard, with an average of 2.4 beds per thousand population. Given the fact that China accounts for 22 per cent of the world's population, it has only 2 per cent of the world's medical resources (ibid.). Other factors also support the expansion of the health care construction market: (i) about 80 per cent of existing Chinese hospitals need reconstruction work; (ii) all Chinese Centres of Disease Control (of which there are more than 300) need to be rebuilt; (iii) the need for health care facilities is acute across all populations and all regions, including remote inland and poor rural areas, and for excluded populations and the elderly. It was noted that China had built an average of 270 hospitals annually during the period 1950 and 2000, and 519 hospitals between 2000 and 2004 (ibid.). This has given the medical equipment industry a major boost. It was noted that, by 2005, 25–35 per cent of expenditure on health care facilities was devoted to the purchase of medical equipment. Most new hospitals need high-tech equipment to operate, including but not limited to: diagnostic imaging equipment; surgical and therapeutical equipment or systems; biosafety laboratory equipment or instruments; anti-cross-contamination equipment for critical care units (CCUs); intensive care centralized safety air conditioning and filtration systems; negative air flow systems; hospital information systems and Post Acute Systems (PACS); hospital materials flow and handling systems; testing instruments for food and environmental safety and occupational health; and rapid test instruments for communicable diseases (ibid.). This explains the multinationals' intense interest in this area. For example, Sanhsing (Tri-Star), a domestic investor, has invested US$35 million in establishing a 500-bed hospital in the south-eastern province of Jze-jian on 236 acres of land. The interest of the Taiwanese capital in the health provision market has been significantly higher than that of other stakeholders because of the saturation of health providers in Taiwan, which makes realization of profits within the country inefficient. Since 2001, the Wang Group, the country's largest conglomerate, has generated a plan for investing US$3.7 billion in a chain of three hospitals with a total of 11,000 beds in China. Other Taiwanese investors, such as Sichuan Health System and Mingshen Health System, have similar plans to establish leading positions in the provision of regional health care. The legal and regulatory trends under the WTO are most favourable to mega investment in hospitals. Yet, for smaller domestic investors, there are major challenges facing stakeholders (Wang, 2002). The fact that, by 2005, among more than 290,000 medical institutions of all kinds, only forty-five belonged to Sino-foreign JVs shows that the overall health care construction market was still relatively untapped by multinationals (Murphy and Li, 2005).

The WTO has encouraged all kinds of partnerships in China. In 2004, Beijing Aikang Medical Investment Company acquired a state-run enterprise, a 50-bed, AAA hospital (the highest rated), the first of its kind in China. The dominant position in Aikang Medical Investment Company is SK Conglomerate from South Korea, one of the top 500 businesses in the world, although its core business had previously always been in telecommunications. The SK is the largest telecommunications company in South Korea, and it operates one of the most advanced mobile technologies in telecommunications. The SK group is also the largest energy provider, controlling 50 per cent of Korea's gasoline provision market. SK's involvement in health care dates back to 1975, when it established a pharmaceutical R&D centre in the USA. It also controls a pharmaceuticals manufacturer in Korea. As early as 2000, SK established a life sciences enterprise in China, and in 2002, it invested another US$1 billion to expand this. The Aikang Chinese hospital was the first overseas hospital among SK's health care investments, and it took the Chinese government two years to approve this acquisition. The Chinese partner was an affiliate of the Ministry of Health – the International Exchange Centre – with a 20 per cent shareholding. Another 10 per cent of the ownership is a private enterprise from Fuzhou. The company plans to acquire twenty hospitals between 2004 and 2009, and fifty by 2014. Compared to the Wang Group from Taiwan, whose hospital investment has been delayed, the success of SK's acquisitions lies in it filling the void in the Chinese health provision market, such as in plastic surgery and other health services such as fitness services, housekeeping and membership service. The other reason for its successful entry into China is that, like other JV hospitals, Aikang does not compete with local markets. Most JV hospitals target very affluent sections of the Chinese population – whose percentage is small, but volume is large by international standards. Aikang's strategy is to target a small, focused market with 50-bed units (compared to the unrealistic ambitious of the Wang Group's plans to build 6,400-bed hospitals with, 20,000 visits per year), The Wang Group's plan has posed a serious threat to local stakeholders because it aims to penetrate the local markets on which local stakeholders have had a strong hold for many years. Similar trends of privatization have also occurred in regional hospitals. In Fuzhou, the capital city of Fujian Province, private investors have also acquired four government-owned hospitals (see Lee, 2004, p. 48; Wikipedia, 2005; see also Wang and Chen, 2005).

Several trends have increased the momentum of investing in China's health provision market:

The government has renewed its commitment to reinforcing health provision through the Hospital Classification System, which mandates that the government provides basic health care services, and that top-ranked regional and national hospitals are designated as not-for-profit hospitals. The government has also made major efforts to increase health insurance coverage, as mentioned earlier. Despite the small volume of health insurance as a percentage of the total population (about 70–90 per cent of the population has no health insurance and two-thirds of health payments are out-of-pocket expenses), it increased by six times between 1999 and 2004. During the same period, total combined health insurance premium grew at the 4 per cent rate of reaching US$312 billion (Burrill & Co., 2005).

Increasing need for health provision. Starting from the year 2000, the Chinese population is expected to increase by 10 million every year. Population density, economic growth and liberalized lifestyle will increase major health threats. In addition, the ageing members of the population will account for at least 10 per cent of the total by 2015. This will be further discussed in Chapter 6. Compared to the year 2000, these demographic trends are predicted to increase the need for treatment of chronic disease by 55 per cent by 2015, especially the treatment of such chronic diseases as cardiovascular conditions, cancer, diabetes and mental illnesses.

The potential for growth. China has 20 per cent of the global population, but accounts for only 3 per cent of total global health expenditure (ibid.). As mentioned earlier, China's overall health expenditure, including public and private sources, has increased from 3.86 per cent in 1995 to 5.33 per cent in 2001. Chinese health care consumption now totals more than US$500 billion every year being about 4 per cent of its GDP, compared to more than 14 per cent in the USA, 9 per cent in Sweden, 5 per cent in the UK and 6–8 per cent for Korea, Japan and Hong Kong. The potential for growth is enormous and this figure is estimated to grow to US$2,000 billion by 2010 in China, which suggests the arrival of an even larger health provision market. For now, health expenditure per capita in China is US$36, compared to US$4,090 in the USA, US$2,339 in Germany, US$1,741 in Japan and US$587 in Korea. It is estimated that, with the rising income from a booming economy, China will easily reach the level of Hong Kong or Korea, but there are major issues to be addressed in this growth scenario. (Wang and Chen, 2005). These will be discussed later in this chapter. It is believed that the Chinese health provision market has become a coveted target for global investors. The elevation of health care on the Chinese government's policy agenda and its determination to increase its public commitments has also increased the investment momentum in health provision in China (see Wang and Chen, 2005).

The introduction of new financing mechanisms and creative partnerships. It was noted that the government, as the only source of financing between the 1950s and 1980, has serious limitations in improving the quality, efficiency and coverage of health care provision. The centralized mode of planning, financing and operating health care provision had led to some problems, including an inflexible management style, overlaps of functions and responsibilities, lack of competition, and a related lack of quality assurance. The financing generally went into payments for personnel and staff. The reforms of the 1980s generated diverse forms of partnerships, such as private hospitals, JV hospitals and specialty hospitals. WTO membership has further introduced foreign capital that is conducive to the presentation of a wide range of products and services in health care provision. Under the WTO, health care is categorized in the 'services' sector. China is committed to opening up health care provision and dental services. Multinationals are allowed to enter the Chinese market in the form of joint ventures, collaborative health services, and clinics. Ownership by multinationals is not allowed to exceed 70 per cent; but multinationals are allowed to be majority owners in a given health care enterprise. This stipulation has given rise to an increase of in private and joint-venture hospitals, which has forced the government to develop a more sophisticated regulatory framework for these new enterprises – that is, drawing a clearer distinction between not-for-profit and for-profit businesses, although major efforts are still necessary to clarify this distinction. For example, the Chinese government has completed a classification system for clinics and hospitals in villages and townships; according to preliminary results, in 2005, the for-profit hospitals accounted for 44.2 per cent and not-for-profit hospitals 55.8 per cent. The investment flowing into the hospital market has helped to diversify the services and scale of health provision. For example, Chungmeihua Hospital was allowed to take over more than ten other hospitals and form a hospital chain. In this picture, the public/non-profit hospitals still offer most of the health provision, while the private or collaborative hospitals offer services that compete or complement those of the public/non-profit hospitals, based on market competition principles.

It is obvious that the WTO has been the major impetus behind the enlargement of health provision market in China, through the unprecedented infusion of investment capital and the opening up of the Chinese financial market. The government has also developed creative ways of financing in this environment. The entry of the stocks and bonds market has provided the flexible financing mechanisms for health care provision. In addition, the Chinese savings rate is unprecedented in the world. From early 2002, Chinese savings have totalled more than a third of its GDP. These funds also provide an abundant source of health care financing (Wang and Chen, 2005). As with pharmaceuticals, health care provision is also considered to be a promising target for investment. Its potential is believed to be unlimited and has not yet been realized. For example in the USA, health care services and products account for more than 30 per cent and health care expenditure per capita was more than 14 per cent because of rising population health needs. In comparison, Chinese health expenditure is less than US$36 per person per year. With rising government investment, an increase in population income and health needs, the infusion of private investment, and the involvement of charities, health provision has much room to develop.

This trend was evidenced by the close interaction among investors and health care providers over several events. For example, in June 2000, there was the first alliance between three top-ranked hospitals – Tung-ren, An-tsen and Dze-suei-tan. By 2005, there were four major alliance hospitals. The largest merger was between the top-ranked Hsieh-heh Union Hospital and Telecom hospitals the total value of which was more than US$800 million. The enthusiasm for integration was further evidenced by the 2002 China Hospitals Investment Exposition, and various forms of vertical and horizontal integration. The participation of Taiwan's Wang Group, Harvard University and Hong Kong's top businessman Jia Tsen Lee in the market of health care provision has further sustained the momentum of takeovers, mergers, restructuring and partnership formation. It is believed that the concentration of investment capital is also likely to promote efficiency/cost-effectiveness, quality of care, and the diversification of services in health care provision. Many hope that this trend will lead to a more efficient allocation of health care resources and an improvement in health provision that satisfies populations of different demographic strata.

In this competitive environment, the opportunities for multinationals and domestic health care providers are unlimited, but the stakes are also very high. For multinationals, including those from Hong Kong, Taiwan and other Asian regions, the opportunities lie in: health care construction markets (including hospitals, CDCs and clinics); speciality/high technology hospitals; chain hospitals or clinics; integrated hospitals for biomedicine and traditional chinese medicine; hospital management; hospital data and informatics management; health professionals training and brokering; infrastructure building, such as of hospital equipment and facilities; and hospital waste disposal).

For domestic stakeholders, the government will continue to play a strong role in regulating the health care provision among not-for-profit hospitals, which are in fact operated in a for-profit mode. They can still gain if they can improve their management and financing issues through creative and effective partnership in several areas: discount hospitals and clinics; medical record management; medical supplies; outsourcing of Chinese health care professionals; the Chinese medical and health care education market; health prevention and promotion services, and health literacy; health provision services for rural populations; low-tech hospital equipment; low-tech hospital cleaning services; derivative patient services, such as care of the elderly, postnatal care, and nursing homes; health test services; and discounted drugs through collaboration with pharmaceutical partners.

The use of creative partnerships and diversifying health care products will be crucial for both domestic and multinational stakeholders. The example of Tuonen Enterprise is instructive. Tuonen specializes in an expensive cancer treatment device valued at more than US$10 million. Hospitals often cannot afford this device. The creative strategy Tuonen suggested is that, rather than selling the device, it will be rented out and the company will sell the services needed to operate the equipment. In addition, the company provides certified physical therapists and its own health care teams to the hospitals. It also has plans to establish a global health care network that allows patients to receive health care services anywhere in the world. In a creative way, Tuonen has become a highly flexible and diversified health care provider (Wang, 2002).

Major issues facing stakeholders in the WTO framework

Some challenges remain for health care provision stakeholders:

Issues of classification, ownership and management between not-for-profit and for-profit hospitals. Lack of regulatory control over classification and related responsibilities inhibits the normal operation of market mechanisms. Overall investment is still not sufficient. The public sector subsidy mechanism is not efficient, and misallocated; for example, not-for-profit hospitals are given enormous tax incentives while for-profit hospitals have to deal with operational risks, management, revenues and changing health care and insurance policies. Not-for-profit hospitals are operating like for-profit hospitals in terms of charges for their services, yet they follow the bureaucratic mode in service provision, capital management, and monitoring and quality control, because they lack profit incentives. They now need a clear legal and regulatory framework of: (i) accountability and transparency; (ii) ownership reform and the introduction of private partnership; (iii) the separation of health care management and financial management between different state agencies; and (iv) the separation of ownership and hospital management. This can follow the example of US business. For example, in the USA, the board of trustees is often separate from the executive management team of the enterprise.

Uncertainties in profit incentives for-profit hospitals. It takes one to five years to obtain a return on a for-profit hospital, and most of the domestic for-profit hospitals are still on too small a scale to generate fast returns. Most important, many of the for-profit hospitals lack clear direction or identification of their niche markets. The utilization rate is low because most of the population cannot afford to use them: according to one estimate, on average, county-level hospitals have more than 16,000 beds in the whole country but the utilization rate is less than 60 per cent. They face competitive pressure from the public hospitals over fees and payments, therefore, their health care charges have to be lower or comparable with those of the public hospitals. They have limited funding and operating budgets, and the staff have to perform multiple tasks, which tends to reduce the quality of care. Without the support of tax incentives, they have had to rely on the sale of prescriptions, expensive tests, and recommending unnecessary health tests and services for revenues. Alternatively, they had to opt for 'rare diseases' niche markets. The services they offered were often exaggerated, which further discounted their credibility. If the government moves forward with its plan to separate medical consultation from drug dispensing services, the potential earnings for the for-profit hospitals will be even more seriously disrupted. It was estimated that the planned change will affect the turnover of a typical hospital by 45–58 per cent (Wikipedia, 2006; *see also* Wang and Chen, 2005). The implemention of medical insurance is not necessarily a positive incentive either for the for-profit private hospitals. The higher utilization rate of hospitals that medical insurance brings will put a greater burden on services, and hospital margins will be under pressure because insurance providers will demand more discounts from the hospitals to protect their own margins. As a result, the hospitals' bargaining power will be quite weak. In addition, to keep their clients, the hospitals will be pressured to upgrade their equipment and services. The capital investment cost will possibly be transferred to the medical insurance participants and most probably to uninsured patients (Wang, 2002, p. 54).

Hospital Management. Hospital management at all levels, and between not-for-profit and for-profit hospitals is a major issue and a source of waste, inefficiency, malpractice and poor quality of care. Corporate governance, financing, accounting and resource allocation, personnel management, medical record management, supplies, equipment and facilities management, waste disposal management, surveillance and monitoring, and quality control have posed major challenges to health care provision.

Issues of quality control. The intense competition brought about by WTO membership will help to improve the quality of care because of the need to attract and retain clients through high-quality services. The entry of large JV hospitals, especially chain hospitals, is posing a real challenge to less well-equipped and providers of lesser quality. The fact that patients are now free to choose providers via a basic medical insurance scheme, and increasing disposable income leading to a higher demand for quality in health care is intensifying this competition. At the time of writing, China has more than 65,000 health providers and most of the hospitals are already under-utilized. This demand for quality is a positive trend for patients, but the price tag for quality might further threaten access to quality care by poorer patients. Complaints of poor quality have been widespread. For example, carrying on physical check-ups is one of the largest businesses in health care provision, but the quality of the service is variable. In China, a physical check-up certificate is required for employment, migration and related housing, schooling and military service. Providing certificates is a major source of revenue for private hospitals. However, the poor quality of such services has led to many malpractice complaints. In one example, it was estimated that, in Guanzhou, some 3–4 million individuals use physical check-up services, worth of millions of US dollars: to make fast profits, about 160 tests were performed in 3–4 hours, which led to serious mistakes. The misdiagnosis rate is very high for such tests. However, with heightened competition from both multinationals and domestic players, this situation should improve (*World Journal*, 2004, 'Malpractice leads to serious mistakes. Wellness becomes illness').

China's health provision is facing many challenges, for which the stakeholders in health care sector are also part of the solution. The quality and quantity of health care provision has a direct impact on the population's health. This chapter has presented a historical analysis of China's health care provision, population health issues and needs, trends in health care financing, investment and spending, the distribution of public and private health services in both urban and rural populations, monitory mechanisms on health provision, and major changes in health provision brought about by WTO membership. The Chinese health provision system is undergoing such rapid changes that it is predicted that, in a matter of years, it will have an entirely new face. Under competition pressure brought about by the WTO framework, the Chinese health care system is in the process of engaging in a multi-sector-level reform of its current system. Yet other macrosocial issues should also be taken into account to examine the impact of the WTO on China's health system. These include macroeconomic growth and sustainable development, equity, access, infrastructure and capacity building, and public–private partnership, which will be further discussed in Chapter 6.

6

The World Trade Organization, Challenges and Opportunities for China's Heath Care System

Mei-ling Wang

The beginning of the twenty-first century has witnessed major events in China's health care system, such as the epidemics of HIV/AIDS, SARS, avian influenza, environmental disasters, and an increasing incidence of mental illness and chronic illness caused by socioeconomic changes. The country is facing public health challenges on all these fronts, which combine the problems of both developed and developing countries. This chapter aims to provide a long-term assessment of China's health care system and how these challenges can also be seen as opportunities for domestic and multinational stakeholders within the World Trade Organization (WTO) framework. And most important, how these challenges will help to improve the health of the Chinese people. This chapter will review: (i) China's position and commitments within the WTO framework; (ii) Chinese economic and development outlooks; (iii) major health-related issues facing the Chinese population; (iv) capacity building in meeting the changing health needs of Chinese society, and required investment and infrastructure building in health and related areas; (v) assessing the initial impact of China's WTO membership on China's health care sector; and (vi) China's potential to participate in the global health care market.

China's compliance with WTO commitments

The overall evaluation of China's initial fulfilment of its WTO commitments has been positive among international communities, despite some criticism raised by the USA and the EU. A 2006 WTO review gave high marks to China's efforts at economic liberalization and globalization under the WTO framework, and praised the country's efforts at poverty elimination, which has led to a ninefold increase in per capita GDP. According to the WTO, the major challenges faced by China are its currency policy, intellectual property rights protection, and the opening up of the services sector (WTO, 2006). In the WTO framework, the commitment to the opening up of the services sector are the most controversial among WTO members, but China is believed to have made significant progress in the services sector by the agreed deadline of 11 December 2005, meeting commitments in advertising, banking, foreign forwarding and insurance. Advertising and insurance are somewhat relevant to the health care sector. Regarding advertising, China allowed wholly foreign-owned enterprises (WFOEs) in advertising services when the Regulation on Management of Foreign-Invested Advertising Companies, issued by the State Administration of Industry and Commerce and the Ministry of Commerce (MOFCOM) in March 2004, took effect on 10 December 2005. Regarding insurance, starting from 11 December 2005, the China Insurance Regulatory Commission (CIRC) allowed foreign-invested insurers to operate directly in non-life, personal accident and health insurance without having to cede to the China Reinsurance Corporation a portion of the lines of the primary risk. The China Insurance Regulatory Commission has also lowered the asset threshold required for an insurance brokerage licence from US$300 million to US$200 million. These regulatory steps were indicative of China fulfilling its commitments in this area. Other commitments that remain unfulfilled are in courier services, hospitality, and technical testing and freight inspection. In other sectors, China is committed to allowing WFOEs and other foreign-invested wholesalers and commission agents to distribute chemical fertilizers, processed oil and crude oil. In compliance with this commitment, China will remove the last remaining prohibitions on all products apart from salt and tobacco (which currently remain under state control) for foreign-invested distributors (Overmyer, 2006). Overall, China has met most of its commitments to the WTO. However, the industrialized countries have not relaxed their scrutiny of China's compliance status. For example, following the US action of placing China on the Priority Watch List of countries that have a questionable enforcement record of intellectual property rights, Japan filed an Article 63 request to China for information on specific endorsement actions taken to protect intellectual property rights. The USA has asked China to provide evidence of judicial rulings and administrative decisions that have been published in public reports and WTO filings, which should demonstrate China's compliance with the WTO rules. If China fails to address the concerns behind this request, this might provide the USA with an opportunity to establish a case for dispute settlement (ibid.).

Macroeconomic and development outlooks in China

As mentioned earlier, China's economy has shown promising signs in recent years. Looking at productivity, it was estimated that China's GDP had averaged 9.6 per cent between 1979 and 2004. China's, GDP for 2004 was US$1.650 trillion. According to a report by the World Bank, China's GDP per capita reached US$1,100 in the first part of 2005, and according to

China's Statistical Bureau, it increased by 9.9 per cent over 2004, higher than its earlier estimate of 9.4 per cent. China's total GDP for 2005 ranked the fourth largest, followed by Italy, France and the UK. Total savings in 2005 grossed US$140 trillion (China National Statistical Bureau, 2005). The average inflation rate of commodities increased by 1.8 per cent, and energy prices have increased by 8.3 per cent. Energy consumption has increased by 9.5 per cent, the highest increase being for natural gas – about a 20.6 per cent increase over the previous year. Housing prices in seventy cities have increased by 7.6 per cent. China has become the fourth-largest economy in the world. Given the fact that China's currency has increased by 2.5 per cent against the US dollar and the economy in the informal sector was not included, the volume of GDP would be much larger (*World Journal*, 2005, 'China will become a major economic power'). Yet, there were also concerns that the ageing population would slow down China's economic growth from the current 9 per cent to less than 5 per cent by 2050. It was noted that the average age among the Chinese population was 24 years in 1950, compared to 22 years in Asia and 24 years in the rest of the world; in 1980, the Chinese average age was 22, compared to 21 in Asia and 23 in the rest of the world; but in 2005, the Chinese average age was 33, compared to 28 in Asia and 28 in the rest of the world. It has been estimated that, by 2015, the Chinese average age will be 37, the Asian average will be 31 and the global average 30. Obviously, the Chinese population is rapidly ageing. In 2050, Chinese average age is estimated to be 45, compared to 40 in Asia and 38 in the rest of the world (*World Journal*, 2006, 'China is ageing'). In 2006, it is noted that about eleven coastal provinces are already facing labour shortages, especially in Shanghai City. In addition to the holiday factor, the acute shortage of labourers during the Chinese New Year in February 2006 was also related to the phenomenon of an increasing ageing population and a reduced supply of labour in high-growth regions. This phenomenon is also likely to lead to the increase in wages, which in turn will put more pressure on production costs. In some regions, few professional wage labourers earn move than college graduates with skills.

China has become a major global trading partner, but this has also caused some international concern. As briefly mentioned earlier, China is the third-largest trading nation, and the fourth-largest trading partner of the USA. In contrast, the USA is the second-largest trading partner of China and its fourth-largest export market. In the first eleven months of 2005, US–China trade totalled US$191.55 billion, a 25.4 per cent increase over the same period in 2004. Exports from China to the USA totalled US$147.64 billion, a 31.7 per cent increase over the same period in 2004; and China's import from the USA totalled US$43.92 billion, an 8.1 per cent increase over the same period in 2004. China's trade surplus with the USA exceeded US$100 billion in 2005. This trend also caused some concern in the USA. Globally, China's import were 5.4 per cent and exports 5.9 per cent of the total volume of global trade: manufactured goods totalled 90 per cent and high-tech goods totalled 23 per cent both of which were higher than the global average of 78 per cent and 21 per cent, respectively. Between January and November 2005, the USA initiated four anti-dumping investigations against China, in total worth some US$572 million of China's exports. This explains why the USA has put tremendous pressure on China to loosen its control over Chinese currency policy. The USA believes that China's currency control has contributed to the rapid increase in the trade deficit between the USA and China (*World Journal*, 2006; see also *Sina News*, 2005 'Total China–US trade was close to 200 billion US dollars in the first eleven months of 2005'; 'China's seven major economic indicators ranked high among developing countries, according to the World Bank').

The market-orientated economy has taken root in China. A recent economic survey shows that around 60 per cent of enterprises are privately owned in China (*Sina News*, 2005, 'China's economic survey shows that 60 per cent are private enterprises'). The Chinese economy showed few signs of side-effects from the Asian economic crisis of 1997–8. According to a report released by Chinese Social Sciences Institute and State Information Centre, China's GDP has been increasing in a stable fashion at a rate of more than 9 per cent since early 2000s. In addition, most economic indicators have shown that China's economy seems to be developing at a steady pace. The rate of inflation was well controlled; production costs were stable; the flow of investment capital was growing at a steady speed; consumption had increased steadily; imports and exports had increased rapidly; employment was under control, with some 9 million new jobs; the unemployment rate was 4.2 per cent; food production had increased; there had been major improvements in transportation infrastructure; and stability in energy supply. It has been forecast that the economic picture will see an even greater improvement in 2006, with GDP continuing to grow at a rate of 5–9 per cent over the year. China's transition period with the WTO ends in 2006, which means that the country's market economy will be further stabilized, and its consumption structure will be upgraded. There will be increasing consumption in housing, motor vehicles and education; deflation is not forecast; the domestic market is seen as a major driver in the Chinese economy; there might be overproduction in certain sectors; there will be little increase in wages; the prices of industrial products are not likely to increase; the rate of increase for oil prices is likely to be below the level of 2005; but the prices for services might see a small percentage increase (*Sina News*, 2005, 'Three major crises in China').

As a whole, China has made rapid progress in socioeconomic development. Living standards in China have improved rapidly for urban residents. It was estimated that for these urban residents, in 2003, disposable income averaged US$500 per household, an increase of 9 per cent over

2002; and the average consumption per household was US$400, a 6.7 per cent increase over 2002. Major categories of consumption are: services, clothing, medical care, transportation, and culture and entertainment (*Sina News*, 2003, 'Income has increased for urban residents; consumption fluctuates; and disposable income has increased by 9 per cent'). Regarding poverty reduction, between 1979 and 2004, China successfully resolved food security issues for about 250 million people. By 2004, the country had invested more than US$38.5 billion in the poor among the population (*World Journal*, 2004, 'Poor population increases because of corruption'). As a result, the UNDP, in its 2005 Human Development Report, has raised the ranking of China from 94 to 85 among a total of 177 nations (UNDP (United Nations Development Programme, 2005).

Yet this overall economic progress needs to be put into perspective. China's GDP by 2005, (about US$1,500 per capita) ranked 107 in the world, and was only a fifth of the average global GDP. In addition, China has paid a colossal social and environmental price for its rapid economic development. Given the tensions brought about by a high-growth scenario, the Chinese government has intensified its efforts to address the social consequences of economic development. For example, at the annual meeting of People's Congress concluded on 14 March 2006, the government instituted a more sustainable model of the 11th 'Five-Year' (2006–2010) Plan for China (CNN News, 30 March 2006). For example, for 2006, the government has set a lower goal for GDP growth at a rate of 7.5 per cent per year; it will eliminate 10 per cent of polluting emissions; it will increase high-tech R&D capacity; and, most important, it will increase investment in the agricultural sector. In 2006, China will invest 1.7 per cent of its GDP on rural development, a 14 per cent increase over 2005. It will invest US$4.7 billion on rural health care, around seven times greater than 2005. Building an overall infrastructure for villages is the most important, including villagers' living standards, and agricultural production. In health care, the government is determined to improve villagers' access to pharmaceuticals and clinical care. By 2004, the Chinese government was already engaged in nationwide major infrastructure building. The length of China's highways was increased to more than 30,000 kilometres, and more than 532 million Chinese had a telephone line (Kynge, 2004; see also *Sina News*, 2004, 'China's GDP has increased by 9.1 per cent in 2003). Chinese cities have also intensified their participation in the information age. It has been estimated that Chinese internet users totalled more than 110 million, with more than 690,000 websites (*Sina News*, 2006, 'Internet users totalled more than 110 million, with more than 690,000 websites').

China has also absorbed a large amount of foreign investment. According to the *Far Eastern Economic Review*, a quarter of the world's foreign direct investment (FDI) of US$268 billion went to Asia in 2004. China alone received US$60.6 billion. In 2005, Beijing City alone absorbed

US$3.5 billion of FDI, mainly in the service sector, a 14.4 per cent increase over the previous year. By January 2006, China has absorbed a total of US$60 billion FDI, 35 per cent of China's total GDP, according to the country's Ministry of Commerce. There was also an increase in fund flows to research and investment businesses. The FDI resulted in total exports of more than US$125.57 billion from Beijing, ranked top among all Chinese cities. Overall, most of the FDI that went to Asia was invested in India and China, which together absorbed 45 per cent of global foreign total investment in Asia. FDI today differs from that of the past because of its involvement in local development. For example, it has created new jobs, export goods and new industries; and it has facilitated technology and knowledge transfer. Overall, it promotes growth. For example, China's high-tech export increased from 6 per cent in 1992 to a third of its total exports. In comparison, India's information technology products have increased from less than US$500 million in 1992 to US$17.2 billion in 2004–5. Foreign direct investment has had a direct impact on both India and China in major ways: for example, in poverty reduction and high-tech development. For three consecutive years up to 2005, global investors ranked China as the best target country for FDI. India's position is also improving rapidly and it was ranked from fifteenth in 2002 to sixth in 2003 and third in 2004 (*World Journal*, 2005, 'China and India have absorbed most FDI'). If the current growth picture continues, it has been estimated that the total volume of China's economy will be 2.5 times that of the US economy, and its GNP per capita will be 50 per cent of that of the USA by 2050 (*Sina News*, 2003, 'Economists predict that China will experience high growth in the next 30 years').

Yet China is also facing challenges in sustainable development: new trade opportunities have produced some negative consequences in social relations, and the increasing wealth gap is an alarming issue facing Chinese society. It has been noted that the income gap between rural and urban residents is US$1,000 on average, and in large cities the gap is even wider. For example, in Beijing, the population in the top 20 per cent income bracket – especially finance, information technology, science research and geology specialists – have an average salary of US$3750 per year, but those in the bottom 20 per cent, usually in the mining, construction and manufacturing sectors, earn about US$900 per year. This gap is particularly pronounced in rural areas. For example, the average gap is about US$100, while in the vicinities of large cities, it increases to about US$200. WTO membership has caused some negative impacts on the Chinese agricultural sector, and a lack of protective mechanisms in the public sector makes villagers particularly vulnerable (Jiang, 2006). For example, the opening up of trade in soya beans, corn, cotton and sugar cane is likely to benefit American farmers, but seriously hurt the economic position of Chinese farmers. In particular, the poor farmers in the inland provinces of China will suffer more negative consequences than those in the coastal provinces. China's economic surplus is still based on low-cost labour, with its workers earning about US$1 an hour in labour-intensive industries, compared to US$28 earned by German workers and US$0.5 by Sri Lankan workers in the global context, for example. Chinese workers work for long hours in hazardous environments, without social security or health care. This economic structure is thought to produce negative consequences for the wealth gap, social solidarity, the environment and health conditions. It has been estimated that, among the twenty most polluted countries in the world, China is ranked sixteenth. About 370 million Chinese have no access to potable water and the victims of environmental pollution have reached 180 million; China's desert area is increasing by more than 2,000 square kilometres every year. The country's economic structure remains in the midstream and downstream manufacturing sectors, and China still needs to catch up in up-scale, new technology development. Chinese manufacturers make slim profits of only around 1–2 per cent. China's economy is driven mainly by the US$1.1547 billion in exports. This shows that China's heavy reliance on exports can spell instability for its economy, by representing about 70 per cent of total GDP in 2004, around 60 per cent higher than 1978. This rate of reliance ranks as the highest among all nations. In comparison, the total percentage of exports among major industrialized countries, such as the USA, Japan, India and Germany, averaged between 14 per cent 20 per cent over the period 1980–2001 (*Sina News*, 2005, 'The two-edged sword of low-cost China-made products').

China's pro-trade policy since the 1980s has boosted the presence of global multinationals in China, and their investment is increasing. For example, General Electric (GE), which, in early 2006 faced financial strain in the USA, has made major financial gains in China and is increasing its investment in the country in health care, aviation, financial investment and energy, for an expected profit increase of 20 per cent every year. In 2001, the total sales of GE in China was US$1.5 billion, and in 2005 US$5 billion. By the end of 2005, there were 107 high-ranking managerial positions in China's GE office, about 46 per cent of whom were of native Chinese origin (*World Journal*, 2005, 'GE increases its investment in China').

The economic success spearheaded by the forces of globalization in the WTO framework generates a multitude of opportunities and issues for China, and health care takes a central position in this picture. According to a Blue Paper produced jointly by the Chinese Social Sciences Institute and the State Information Centre, the three major social crises in China are the wealth gap, financial crises, and the high unemployment rate. Related to these issues are three major public concerns. Health care, along with unaffordable housing and education, is a major political lightning rod. Overall, it has been estimated that the price of housing increased by 5.6 per cent in 2005, much higher than the rate of inflation. Education costs have increased by several times. Health care costs topped this list with their rate of increase. The public have commented critically that the business-mode operation of education and health care has cost the Chinese government major political capital. Payment for education and health care have become major contributary factors to poverty in rural villages. Other issues that are also public concerns over the negative consequences of the economic reforms are: environmental pollution, equitable economic development, an increase in crime, and threats to public safety (*Sina News*, 2005, 'Three major crises in China'; see also *China Social Sciences Sinica*, 2005.) These issues all have both a direct and an indirect impact on China's social and population health, the solutions to which will have a severe effect on China's chances for sustainable development.

Social health issues and challenges

The size of China's population already presents a challenge to its health care system. In February 2006, China had a population of some 1.3 billion. About 57.01 per cent of Chinese lived in villages and 42.99 per cent lived in rural towns and all sizes of cities. As mentioned earlier, the percentage of females in 2006, at 48.5 per cent of the population, was less than that of males – 51.5 per cent of the population. The average life span was 71.4 years, and the population aged over 60 years accounted for 11 per cent of China's total population. The largest city is Shanghai, with its population in 2006 being over 18 million. In February 2006, the birth rate was 12.40 per thousand, the mortality rate 6.51 per thousand; and the natural growth rate 5.89 per thousand. Infant mortality was 21.5 per thousand. The recorded unemployment rate in towns and cities was 4.2 per cent. By November 2005, national health insurance covered about 135.67 million people, including 98.62 million employed and 37.05 million retirees, with more than 50,000 participating providers and 30,000 pharmacies (China National Statistical Bureau, 2006).

Health care in China's current environment is facing unprecedented challenges and opportunities for Chinese society. The major health challenges are the social and environmental causes of health problems (for example, the wealth gap, gender inequality, social exclusion, and sustainable development); infrastructure readiness (for example, public health surveillance and response, the establishment of legal, regulatory and ethical frameworks, and public education); and equitable access to resources (in the social, economic and health sectors) to resolve health-related issues.

These challenges are the result of major social, political and economic policy changes since the 1970s, such as economic reform in 1978, family planning and fertility policy in 1979 (aimed at controlling population growth), and health care reform from the 1980s. These changes have all had an effect on the Chinese population's health, and it was believed by many that China's progress in public health in the 1960s was negated by the changes. In the 1960s, China's infant mortality was reduced by two-thirds, and the country had successfully eliminated polio, plague and cholera. Yet after the economic reforms, when the public health infrastructure was reduced, many feared that rural populations had become vulnerable targets for emergent infectious diseases (*Sina News*, 2003, 'Strengthening control over health care by the central government is needed').

As discussed earlier, major changes in population health since the 1950s in China were brought about by macroeconomic and social changes, such as an improvement in living standards and a change of economic system. These changes in the population's health are fertility trends, ageing, lifestyle changes, sex-ratio imbalance, and environmental and sustainable development issues. Despite the fact that rising income has improved the overall economy, the population's health is facing a different set of issues caused by socioeconomic changes.

Major issues in China's social health: equity and access for socially excluded groups

China's wealth gap and related issues have had a serious effect on the population's health, despite economic growth having contributed to an overall improvement in living standards. In 1978, at the start of the economic reform, China was one of the world's poorest countries. Between 1978 and 1996, per capita disposable income tripled in urban areas and quadrupled in rural areas (Bian, Y., 2002, pp. 91–117). The rate of increase has been even faster in urban areas since the late 1990s. Yet various social groups have become marginalized during this process.

Equity

Poverty and equity are major challenges to Chinese society, and will continue to have an impact on the population's health. The issue of poverty is complex. The wealth gap in China was reflected in the increase in the GINI coefficient, according to Dr Lee, Deputy Director of the China Social Science Institute. A GINI coefficient of 0 indicates absolute equity; 0.4 shows enlarging equity; 0.5 or move indicates unreasonable inequity. China's GINI is estimated to be 0.447, but in the cities it is approaching 0.5. It is believed that 5 per cent of the population have appropriated most of the economic resources, with some 84 per cent of the population remaining at the tail end of social resources distribution. The very rich owned 359 times more assets than the poorest families (*Sina News*, 2001, 'Commentary from Hong Kong: wealth gap is a dangerous social problem'). The major causes of poverty are expenditure on education and health care. The gap in access to educational opportunities is widening at an alarming rate. It was pointed out that tuition accounted for 32.6 per cent of income in villages, compared to 25.9 per cent in cities and 23.3 per cent in small towns (ibid.). This increase has occurred within the framework of major income disparity between rural and urban residents. As mentioned earlier, the urban–rural wealth gap has increased from 2.6 times in 1978 to 3.2 times in 2004 and the gap is increasing rapidly (*Sina News*, 2006, 'Wealth gap is a major social issue in China'). These figures suggest that the actual burden of educational expenses is much heavier for rural villagers than for urban residents.

The gap between large cities and small villages is beyond statistical calculation. For example, the largest city in China, Shanghai, will have a total GDP of more than 26,700 billion yuan (US$330+ billion) by 2010; in contrast, a large number of villages will continue to have a negative asset value (*Sina News*, 2006, 'Shanghai will be worth $US400 billion by 2010 in total worth of industries').

According to the government's own estimates, the number of the poor in the population decreased from 250 million in 1978 to 24 million in 2005. In the villages, the percentage of poor people was said to have decreased from 30 per cent to 2.5 per cent. Yet estimates from the World Bank in 2006 showed that there are still 200 million poor people in China (*Sina News*, 2006, 'Commentary from Hong Kong: wealth gap is a dangerous social problem'). China's own estimate in April 2006 was that there were fewer than 150 million of the population living under the poverty line. Despite Government investment in anti-poverty campaign – some US$162.5 million in 2005 – there remains major work to be done in this area. (Poverty in China is defined by an annual income of less than 668 yuan, about US$83.5 per year.) (*Sina News*, 2006, 'According to the State Council's Anti-Poverty Office, the basic needs of the poor will be resolved by 2010'). According to the Blue Papers on China's Social and Economic Conditions released by the China Social Sciences Institute, the wealth gap and related issues are considered to be political crises and of public concern. It is important to note, however, that China is not the only country that has wealth gap problem. It is also a major issue for all countries, including the USA. It was estimated that, regarding housing in China, there is a 60 times difference in the gap between the top 20 per cent and bottom 20 per cent and that 67.2 per cent of financial assets are in the hands of the top 20 per cent of wealth holders (*Sina News*, 2005, 'Three major crises in China'; see also Social Sciences Institute, 2005).

The rural–urban gap

The rural–urban gap in development is a major barrier to social progress in China. Most Chinese are still poor and the majority of them live in rural areas (Yao, 1999, pp. 104–30). Research carried out by the Social Sciences Institute showed: (i) the urban–rural income gap is 6 times. Between 1980 and 1984, the gap was minuscule; in 1985, the gap was 1.86 times; but in 2004, the gap went from 3.21 to 6 times, when all factors were considered (after taking into account social securities, benefits and subsidies, totalling 500–600 yuan difference per person per year). Social security payments for urban residents were US$220 per person, while they were less than US$2 per rural resident and there is a gap of 126 times; (ii) It was estimated that two-thirds of rural governments are in debt, which has forced them to seek revenues from rural villagers via all kinds of levies, taxes and forcible takeovers of villagers' land (*Sina News*, 2005, 'Three major crises in China'; *see also* China Social Sciences Institute, 2005). Another estimate showed that the actual gap in social benefits was in fact much larger after taking into account access to social resources in urban settings, such as health care, education, economic/employment opportunities and financial services (*World Journal*, 2004, 'There has been an income increase for high-wage earners; rural–urban gap has increased').

Government employees' salaries are a prominent example of the rural–urban gap. The rural–urban income gap for government employees is 13 times. The income of government employees has two components: basic salary and benefits. The basic salary is the same across the country, while benefits vary and are decided by local governments. The benefits in local provinces were much less and sometimes were even appropriated by corrupt officials. Some employees do not even receive regular pay cheques (*World Journal*, 2005, 'The rural–urban income gap is 13 times for government employees'; see also Brenner, 2001, pp. 245–75).

In urban settings, inequity is also severe. Class differences are developing and deepening. Managers and professionals have been able to strengthen their positions in the stratified economy. Some, especially business people involved in international trade, have benefited from China's new open-door policies and export-orientated development strategies, and many have attained enormous wealth. At the same time, however, many urban residents have difficulty in meeting basic needs. The social and economic positions of labourers, once honoured as the 'vanguard of the revolution', have been eroded, although it is believed that inequity among different groups of urban residents is less than that in other Asian cities. The people that faces the greatest risks to health are the migrants (Yao, 1999, p. 126). The major social concern is that this rising inequality might cancel the positive effects of rising income on poverty alleviation (ibid., pp. 104–30). Migrants and their children face the highest risks in HIV infection, STDs, other infectious diseases and drug addiction, but have the least access to health care.

The continuing, and even growing, inequality across China is evidenced in health and mortality data. As mentioned earlier, the effects of the disparity in health provision have been pronounced in several areas, especially in the increase of infant and maternal mortality. It was evidenced in the disease burden on the rural population, including increases in the prevalence of TB, hepatitis and other infectious diseases, and decreases in immunization rates. For example, with infant mortality, it was noted in 1999 that rural areas had a much higher infant mortality rate (37/1,000) than urban areas (11/1,000). In 2002, the mortality rate among rural children aged under five was also much higher at 39/1,000 than that in urban areas – 14/1,000. For maternal mortality rates, those in urban areas were much lower: 54/100,000 compared with 72/100,000 (Blumenthal and Hsiao, 2005). This is also true for the rates of infection from major diseases, such as respiratory problems, TB and cancer. It seems clear that social determinants of health, such as poverty, a lack of opportunities in employment and education, and gender and class discrimination, have also aggravated health inequity, and that rural poverty is a major reason why infant and maternal mortality has remained much higher in rural areas. Many infectious diseases that had disappeared before 1978 are now returning. Under the leadership of Hu Jintao, the government has announced plans to address poverty in China. These include economic development, infrastructure building and improved educational opportunites in the western parts of the country and rural settings, with the hope that this will encourage sustainable development. Government attention and intervention might help to alleviate poverty in some areas, but urgent action is needed to enhance sustainable development for all.

Socially excluded populations

The uneven pace of development across different geographical regions, genders, sectors, rural–urban areas and ethnic groups have increased the exclusionary status of traditionally vulnerable populations in access to social resources, which has had a serious effect on the health of the population. This trend also spells major problems for the country's leadership (see Bian, 2002, pp. 91–117). The effort to eliminate gender discrimination by Mao Zedong has gradually been eroded, albeit not intentionally, but simply because women have more difficulty in accessing social resources from rural areas, or accessing opportunities in the cities after economic reform. The equity achieved between 1949 and 1978 was commendable by international standards; however, the economic reform, which saw growth as a primary social goal, produced some unexpected burdens for already vulnerable populations.

Major excluded populations are: the poor in rural areas and the western and south-western pants of the country, the elderly poor, poor and uneducated women, floating populations, ethnic minorities, those affected by disasters, and those who are sick, especially those suffering from stigmatized diseases, such as HIV/AIDS. It was estimated that, in the spring of 2006 alone, more than 70 million Chinese need emergency aid because of various kinds of disaster (*Sina News*, 2006, 'More than 70 million need emergency aid this spring').

The poor in rural areas

This group has not benefited from economic liberalization. As mentioned earlier, their income has not increased in the face of rapid economic growth and inflation. It is not unusual that they sell their hard labour for US$0.50 a day that will buy just a simple meal (*World Journal*, 2004, 'Chinese villagers' survey exposes the truth about village life'). It is predicted that more than three-quarters of rural households, which still make up the majority of the Chinese population, will lose out from globalization because of decreased income and decreased access to economic opportunities (*World Journal*, 2005, 'China's economic miracle sacrifices the poor labourers'; see also International Confederation of Free Trade Unions (ICFTU), 2005).

The economic regression in rural areas has led to serious consequences: low income has led to low living standards; which in turn have led to reduced innovation in productive activities that affects agricultural supply; reduced investment in rural children's education and health; and unproductive, unhealthy and uneducated rural lives make the villagers the primary victims of major epidemics, such as HIV, SARS, avian influenza and so on. Ultimately their conditions become a major barrier to Chinese social progress. Unproductive and poor farmers also have a serious effect on China's economic progress because, instead of being productive members and active consumers in the Chinese economic programme, negligence of their issues has incurred major financial liabilities to Chinese society. It was believed that half of the economic growth in China was to pay the social costs of inequity facing those vulnerable populations (Friedman, 2005). They have often been asked to pay for the bloated bureaucracy in local administrative units, which imposes all kinds of taxes on the villagers.

Floating populations/urban labourers

As mentioned earlier, there is a more than 150 million floating population in Chinese cities. This floating population deserves attention from the public sector because, through all types of discrimination and the hazardous conditions in which they work, they are the most vulnerable to health risks (Solinger, 1999). It has been noted that unfair practices against the floating migrants are prevalent, and about a third of their contracts were discriminatory and unfair (ibid.). They have suffered an extreme form of discrimination. Even within state enterprises, the floating population does not receive equal treatment compared to those from the cities in the education of their children, in housing, household registration and health care. Although China's labour laws prohibit workers from work more than 44 hours per week, it is not usual that migrants work more than 96 to 112 hours. Second, their working conditions are often extremely toxic and hazardous, of which they know have little knowledge in order to protect themselves. According to a report released on

9 December 2005 by the International Confederation of Free Trade Unions, which has 145 branches and a membership of 25 million, China's economic achievements have been built on the sacrifices of the poor labourers, mainly from the vast rural areas, who have benefited only marginally from the economic boom. The suppression of the wages of the labourers and the elimination of related benefits, such as health care, has seriously affected their well-being. It has been estimated that the income of three-quarters of Chinese villagers has decreased, and poor villagers are often forced to go to the cities to find employment, where work conditions, as discussed earlier, often threaten their lives. More than 15,000 Chinese people are killed every year at work and they are paid much less than the country's minimum wage.

The employment market further complicates the picture. The unemployment rate in China has been estimated to be higher than in the rest of the world. Despite an official estimate of 4 per cent unemployed, the unemployment rate for migrant workers is believed to be more than 10 per cent. China will have to create up to 300 million new jobs by 2016 to prevent unemployment rising to unsustainable levels, especially for migrant workers.

The issues of unemployment are very complex. Although the seasonal shortage of labourers might increase wages temporarily, this has not contributed to the long-term improvement of the floating population's rights or well-being. The Chinese government must engage in more in-depth research of migrants' employment issues in terms of: (i) their unemployment rate; (ii) their employment needs; and (iii) how employment can address their health care needs and sustainable social goals. These issues will directly affect the population's access to social security, health care, and risks of major epidemics.

Poverty reduction for migrants is critical in this picture to maintain the population's health. China's successful eradication of poverty in the early 1980s has stagnated since the 1990s. It is believed that the health risks for migrants worsened further with the country's entry into the WTO, when China became part of the international stratification of production and division of labour. More than three-quarters of rural households, which still make up the majority of Chinese rural villagers and urban migrants, are predicted to lose out in economic growth scenarios (*World Journal*, 2005, 'China's economic miracle sacrifices the poor labourers'; see also ICFTU, 2005).

The issues regarding migrants are entangled with the dire conditions of the menial labourers' and the vast majority of such labourers are losing out in the face of globalization. Most private firms in China are not able to support the basic rights of employees, with more than 80 per cent of companies refusing to sign employment contracts with workers, according to a government survey published in the state-run *China Daily*. Even among the firms that do sign contracts with employees, many only protect the rights of the employers while imposing harsh obligations on workers (Media Corp Press, 2005).

The floating manual labourers are bearing the brunt of economic inequity. The wages of coal carriers is a case in point. For ten years, the wage for hauling a cart of about 500 kilos of coal remained at US$0.38 while coal price increased every year. In the year 2005 alone, coal prices increased by 40 per cent. On average, coal carriers are paid US$2 dollars a day for hauling six to ten carts of coal, payment that is barely enough to pay for three meals, let alone paying for health care (*World Journal*, 2005, 'For ten years, the payment for carrying 500 kilos of coal is US$0.38 in China').

The children of the floating populations/migrants are also direct victims of inequity and poor health. Their health, education and future are the most serious social concerns. It was estimated that 19.8 million children from the floating populations were living in urban centres in China, often living in the most squalid conditions. Often exploited by urban employees, they engage in hazardous work, such as house cleaning, cooking, and acting as carers while their parents were equally exploited in being required to do the most hazardous and menial jobs in the cities, such as collecting rubbish, disposing of toxic wastes, operating rickshaws, etc. The children often grow up in very unhealthy settings that affect both their physical and mental growth, and they often experienced discrimination, suppression and alienation in the urban environment. A survey showed that the floating children experienced severe discrimination and often exhibited passivity, introvertedness, a lack of self-esteem and social skills, fears of socialization and closed-mindedness. The schools for these floating children are often ill-accommodated and ill-equipped. These children are invisible social time bombs who carry the highest risks of infectious disease and mental illness because of abuse (*World Journal*, 2005, 'Children of the floating population').

The abuse of child labourers is a serious public health issue. Child labour is illegal in China, according to the Child Labour Law passed on 16 October 2002, but it has been estimated that about 246 million Chinese children are being used as illegal labourers, accounting for some 10 per cent of the total labourers in the world. About 179 million Chinese children engage in hazardous and physically demanding work that should be undertaken only by adults. As mentioned earlier, poverty is the major cause of child abuse, poor children being forced into wage labour by their parents. These children are often exposed to major occupational health risks, such as chemical poisoning, and suffer from eye irritations and headaches. Their typical diet is rice and, if they are fortunate enough, some vegetables. They are paid yearly, and if they leave their employment in the middle of a year, they will receive no compensation from their employers. These child labourers are often dropouts from high schools or have been forced to drop out of primary school (*World Journal*, 2004, 'Poor Chinese children engage in illegal, hard labour day and night').

Disparities in health and mortality

As mentioned in Chapter 5, mortality rates are noticeably higher in rural than in urban areas; among the poor; among ethnic minorities; and among women (see also Men, 1993, pp. 119–32). The most obvious disparity is the rural–urban infant and maternal mortality gap, which is persistent and growing. Rural health problems and higher mortality have long been recognized as being linked to lower living standards and inadequate health services. Malnutrition, preventable and treatable diseases of infancy, and serious gynaecological conditions are much more common in rural areas than in cities. In general, an area's mortality rate is closely related to its per capita net income and its per capita industrial and agricultural output. It is clear that many rural areas rank poorly on these indicators. In the 1990s, for example, respiratory diseases were the leading causes of death in rural areas; these often preventable deaths accounted for more than 25 per cent of all rural deaths, compared with 16 per cent of all urban deaths. In contrast, cerebrovascular diseases among older adults and lifestyle related issues were the leading causes of death in urban areas. They caused 22 per cent of all deaths in urban areas in the 1990s, but only 16 per cent in rural areas (ibid.).

Infant and child mortality

It is true that China has lowered its infant mortality rate since 1949, but there are no recent, complete data to document the way in which infant mortality has been affected by recent health threats or social issues. Yet, as mentioned earlier, documentary evidence has shown that infant mortality for girls and boys is different. Between 1973–5 and 1990, infant mortality rates among males fell more than those among females (43.1 a per cent decrease compared to a 24 per cent decrease), which has resulted in a decline in the sex ratio, which was 1.15 in 1973–5, 1.06 in 1981, and 0.86 in 1990). The cause was not made clear, but it might be health-related or socially or culturally related, however, sex selection has long been suspected of being a cause. Other causes of infant and child mortality are: infectious diseases, malnutrition, labour abuse, gender discrimination, and environmental hazards (Xu *et al.*, 1994; *see also* CPIRC, 2001). For example, in the wake of the HIV/AIDS epdiemic, the mortality and morbidity issues facing children and rural populations have worsened (information from Dr Xu Hua, China AIDS Foundation, 12 January 2006).

Access

Access to health care has been the most urgent issue in China since the 1990s. It has been estimated that, among urban populations, those who could not afford clinical care rose from 36.4 per cent in 1993 to 48.9 per cent in 2006. Among villagers, those who could not afford in-patient care rose from 63.7 per cent to 75.4 per cent. about 33.4 per cent of villagers have been bankrupted by health care costs (*Sina News*, 2006, 'Minister Kao points out six reasons for high health care costs'; see also *Sina News*, 2003, 'Health care access'). In 2006 it was estimated that the average annual income of Chinese villagers was US$320, similar to the cost of one off in-patient care. It has been reported that 60–80 per cent of rural mortality was a result of the unaffordability of in-patient care. There is rural saying 'One ambulance call costs a pig; one in-patient visit costs a year's livelihood' reflects the dire straits of poor villagers. Despite the new health insurance plan instituted by the government in 2004, 90 per cent of villages still do not have any form of health insurance (*World Journal*, 2004, 'Rural villagers wait for death at home because of inaffordability of health care').

The major issues in health inequity are: (i) the imbalance in health resources between cities and rural areas. It has been estimated that 80 per cent of health resources are in the cities, with only 20 per cent in rural areas; (ii) a lack of public financing. The government's financing for health care has decreased from 6 per cent in the 1980s and 1990s to less than 4 per cent at the time of writing. China's total expenditure on health care, including both private and public expenses in 2004 was 5.5 per cent of GDP, in which the government provided only 16 per cent and out-of-pocket expenditure provided 55 per cent of the total health expenditure; (iii) a lack of progress in health insurance. Among a 1.3 billion population, fewer than 200 million have some form of health insurance – less than 25 per cent of the total. There are more than 8,000 pharmaceutical wholesalers and 120,000 retailers, who rely solely on pharmaceutical profits to run their business, and transfer the cost burden to patients and consumers without any public or third-party intervention; (iv) a lack of organization and control in the sale and distribution of pharmaceuticals and medical equipment. Since the early 2000s, the government has lowered prices of pharmaceuticals seventeen times, but still does not seem able to resolve the issue of high-priced pharmaceuticals; (v) the profit-operation of non-profit public hospitals. Public hospitals were forced to compete for profits because the government pays only 7–8 per cent of the costs of running the hospitals; and (vi) a lack of monitoring of the health care market (ibid.).

One important indicator of access to health care is health insurance coverage at the general population level. In 1981, about 71 per cent of Chinese were protected by state-supported health insurance, but over the next twelve years, this coverage decreased to only 21 per cent. It was estimated that, while the actual data are unknown, most Chinese do not have any health care insurance, mainly because of their inability to afford the premiums. In another estimate, in 2004, the rate was thought to be as high as 90 per cent. It was also noted that market reform has caused a decrease in the quality and quantity of health care services in villages (*Sina News*, 2005, 'Three major crises in China'; see also China Social Sciences Institute, 2005).

A major reason for the public sector's retreat from health insurance is that government revenues in proportion to GDP have decreased. In 1995, these revenues accounted for only 10 per cent of total GDP, which means a decreasing ability on the part of the government to pay for social security and medical care for the Chinese population. Central government is now relying increasingly on local government for health financing and other related public projects. In addition, most of the government spending went into the hospital system, 60 per cent of which in turn went into the pockets of the pharmaceutical companies. In addition, the non-governmental organization (NGOs) and communities do not have a strong voice in protecting the marginalized populations (*Sina News*, 2003, 'Strengthening control over health care by the central government is needed').

This lack of health protection at the level of the populace leads to an increasing financial burden on individuals to pay for their health care. According to a report issued jointly by the Australian government and UNICEF in 1998, the gap between the haves and have-nots in accessing health resources was increasing in China. In the face of rocketing health care costs, out-of-pocket payments were increasing rapidly every year across all cities and regions. As mentioned earlier, according to the Third National Health Survey, in the context of a lack of health insurance for the majority of the Chinese people, the populace spent an average of US$13.5 on each visit to the doctor, a 57.5 per cent increase since 1998; one-off in-patient treatment has reached a cost of US$500, an increase of 76.1 per cent since 1998. The increasing cost of clinical care is related to several factors: the major reason is the updating of equipment and technology; a second is the tenfold difference in price between wholesale and retail pharmaceuticals (*Sina News*, 2005, 'Vice-Chair of People's Congress reveals that the Ministry of Health will not allow an increase in pharmaceutical prices'). In one example in 2004, in a small city, Nanchang in Jiangxi Province, out-of-pocket payments have increased by 37.6 per cent (*Sina News*, 2006, 'It is difficult to see a doctor and it is expensive too'.) The gap in the quality of care is also increasing. Health care provision in some regions, especially in large cities, can be as advanced as Singapore or Hong Kong, while poorer Chinese regions resemble the most underprivileged countries in the world, such as Bangladesh. What adds to the woes of health provision inequity is that corruption is rampant. After the market reforms, village doctors are now forcing unnecessary prescriptions and injections on to their patients, to generate income. The exception is in Tibet, which still receives free health care because of its special political status (Kennedy, 1999).

Vulnerable and excluded populations are affected the most by the lack of health protection and related issues. A World Health Organization (WHO) report in 2002 showed serious public health inequity facing vulnerable populations in China. More than 100 million Chinese did not have any access to any health services at that time, and more than 20 per cent of rural villages were not equipped with any infrastructure to provide basic health services. More than 100 million people had no access to potable water, and more than 400 million villagers did not have running water. Only 28.5 per cent of villages were equipped with waste disposal facilities. The number of women who died after giving birth or from related conditions was 177 per 100,000 in nine poor south-west and north-west provinces, 2.8 times higher than the national average of 56 per 100,000. More than 8 per cent of Chinese children did not receive any inoculations, among whom 13 per cent were from poor villages. This is against the national goal of reducing the unimmunizated rate to below 1 per 1,000 for the '3-in-1 vaccines'. Morbidity rate was much higher in poor central and western provinces, and life expectancy among those populations was much lower (*Sina News*, 2003, 'There remain more than 100 million Chinese who do not have access to any health care').

Professor Hu An Kang, Director of the China Science Institute, has noted that China's public health infrastructure still need major upgrades to enhance equity. The situations among the poor in the western regions need to be the focus of attention among policy-makers. Taking eye care as an example, more than 9 million Chinese have lost their sight because of poor health and poor living conditions. About 7 million of these are in rural areas, but 80 per cent of all the eye specialists are based in the cities. Thus, 80 per cent of the blind receive only 20 per cent of the eye care available. Government subsidies pay for only 20–30 per cent of hospital operations in the villages. The rest of the revenues must come from villagers' out of-pocket payments.

The government is trying to sponsor public health insurance programmes, but again only in larger cities in the western provinces. For example, the local government has sponsored a health insurance programme in Ta-li County, in which the local government pays more than half of the payments, but only two out of thirteen townships participated, the major reason being that even half of the cost was still considered as unaffordable by the locals. In a small city in the western province of Yuen Nan, Dr Shen of Hsian Yuen County Hospital noted that, out of all the glaucoma patients, only 1 per cent could afford to payment for treatment. In many rural areas, a doctor has to have 'five specialties', and can treat all ailments in 'the eyes, ears, nose and teeth' (*World Journal*, 2004, 'Chinese villagers in western provinces are losing their sight'). It was estimated that, of 2,700 counties in China, about 1,000 were not equipped with eye specialists. A medium-sized city such as Ta-li in Yuen Nan Province did not have a children's eye clinic until 2004, and within a year it was overburdened with the task of treating 6,000 patients. It has been estimated that, in China as a whole, there are 40 million patients who need eye surgery but only 500,000 who are able to afford it (*World Journal*, 2004, 'China is popular with 5-speciality doctors'). The rest are left to go blind. Overall, it was estimated that villagers on average spent an astronomical amount of US$279 for in-patient care, from their average annual income of US$350. As noted earlier, more than 79 per cent of villagers do not have any form of health insurance, and most of them do not visit a clinic unless in an extreme emergency. Again, the fact that about 65 per cent to 90 per cent of Chinese do not have any form of health insurance is the major cause of poor access to health care (*Sina News*, 2005, '2005 health care reform general analysis').

Health care cost

Access to health care and affordable pharmaceuticals is a central concern to the present-day Chinese government and society. Few societies have seen the friction this has caused between the health providers and patients in Chinese society. It is one of the most difficult and potentially explosive issues facing the Chinese government. According to a survey in 2005 on the status of Chinese health care, among all categories of public service, health care is ranked as the lowest in terms of public satisfaction. About 67 per cent of respondents believed that health care costs are unreasonable (*Sina News*, 2006, 'Public health services barely passes the mark, according to consultants').

Pharmaceutical costs

On average, in 2004, pharmaceuticals accounted for 15 per cent of total health care costs across the world, but in China the figure was more than 60 per cent (*Chinapharm*, 2005, 'Pharmaceutical sales in China in the framework of 2004 WHO report: Part II'). The seriousness of the issue is seen in several statistics. In an estimate, wages increased by twenty times between 1950 and 1982; in contrast, pharmaceuticals increased by 100–200 times in the same period. Nationwide, in 2003, 32.14 per cent of the sick could not afford to visit a doctor; and 63.13 per cent of sick people in need of in-patient treatment could not afford it. As mentioned earlier, relevant percentages are much higher for villagers and floating populations, the main reasons being the high costs of both medicines and clinical care (*Chinapharm*, 2004, 'A review of the planning of the pharmaceutical sector in the "Tenth Five-Year Plan" '). This rate has been increasing every year. In Beijing, in 2006 where the average annual income per capita was 17,653 yuan (about US$2,200), the residents paid an average of US$80 for medicines, a 14.5 per cent increase over 2004, and US$92 for clinical visits – a 9.2 per cent increase over 2004 (*Sina News*, 2006, 'Beijing residents made 17,653 yuan, a narrower wealth gap in the city').

Despite the fact that the central government has lowered pharmaceutical prices twelve times since 1997, totalling some US$2.5 billion in value, the profit margins for sellers were still high. Pharmaceutical sales were ranked in the 'top three fast profit' sectors. Several factors explain the high prices of pharmaceuticals in China. As mentioned earlier, 70–85 per cent of the revenues of public hospitals derive from pharmaceutical sales, which has made it difficult for hospitals to lower prices of pharmaceuticals. Pharmaceutical prices were determined mainly by the state, the market and other factors. These other factors include: the state determining that pricing must remain high; a lack of health insurance or third-party payments among most of the population, allied to a lack of collective bargaining power; insufficient public financing; and an excessive number of intermediaries in pharmaceutical marketing, distribution and sales. It was noted that there were several intermediaries involved before pharmaceuticals reach hospitals or retail pharmacies: the wholesalers, regional/provincial agents and city-level/local distributors. In addition, there is the cost of public relations. It was estimated that the number of intermediaries has increased from about 2,000 in the late 1990s to 17,000 in 2003, equivalent to the total number of county-level hospitals in China. In contrast, most industrialized countries have one to four major distributors. Even in the USA, there are only eight large-scale distributors, such as McKesson, Amerisource, Cardinal Health and Fisher Scientific, which together account for 95 per cent of the total market in North America. Most wholesalers across the world derive their profts from cost control in distribution, information management, production and patient services, and not from the gap between wholesalers and retailers. In China, most distributors derive their profit from the latter, which raises pharmaceutical prices. The cost for intermediaries' public relations with hospitals for every drug ranges from US$1,000 to US$6,000. Pharmaceutical agents have to get through four barriers before the final sale is completed: the pharmaceutical committee and its purchase plan; the director of pharmaceutical purchasing; the doctors themselves; and the pharmaceutical statistics bureaux. A recent scandal in Sichuan Province on illegal commissions paid to hospital staff by a pharmaceutical sales agent involved 128 individuals, who accepted about US$1 million in bribes. The staff involved included the CEO of the hospital, its directors, bureau chiefs, and section heads in the departments of financing, accounting and pharmaceutical purchasing. The staff who took the bribes had recommended expensive medications to their patients (*Sina News*, 2006, 'A scandal in Shih-tsua involves 128 individuals and more than US$1 million in bribes'). To please the buyers in the hospitals, the distributors have to maintain a certain price level to enable the hospitals to request budgetary assistance and compensation from the government. In addition, reimbursement to pharmaceutical sales agents takes at least three months to come into effect, so maintaining high prices supports the operations of the distributors. Pharmaceutical pricing is not an isolated problem but is related to the core issue of health system reform. It is widely recognized that there has to be a more comprehensive reform to resolve the dilemma, especially in the area of hospital financing, a clear distinction between for-profit and not-for profit hospitals, more effective price controls, reforming the distribution system, increasing market competition in pricing, third-party payments, and a separation between clinical care and pharmaceutical provision (*Chinapharm*, 2004, 'A review of the planning of the pharmaceutical sector in the "Tenth Five-Year Plan"').

Contradictions in pharmaceutical manufacturing are worth noting. First, the fact that the number of biomedicine manufacturers has increased from about 500 in the late 1990s to more than 6,000 at the time of writing should have the effect of lowering pharmaceutical prices; yet, smaller manufactures have to resort to high-price tactics to maintain their profit margins. Second, the fact that China ranks as the second most important producer of raw materials after the USA, and that it still has excessive production capacity, makes it abnormal for pharmaceutical prices to remain so high. Third, there are about 20–30 competitors for the production of a given medicine, much higher than the rate of competition in industrialized countries (*Chinapharm*, 2003, 'Diagnosis for the pharmaceutical sector: how to shake off the problem?').

It will be a daunting challenge for the Chinese government to balance public health needs and hospital financing to provide affordable pharmaceuticals. The Chinese government used to be the only party financing pharmaceuticals in the health care system. Reimbursements from the government were the major source of income for hospitals before the 1978 economic reform. After the reform, hospitals were asked to be responsible for their own financing, and their major source of income is from the sale of pharmaceuticals, as mentioned above. The Chinese government has taken this factor into account and allowed the hospitals to raise 15 per cent on all pharmaceuticals. Yet the government lacks an effective surveillance system to monitor the pricing practices of the hospitals. As noted earlier, at one time, pharmaceutical sales account for 60–85 per cent of the income of hospitals. Even after the government intervened, most of the hospitals still rely on 45–60 per cent of the income from pharmaceutical sales (*Sina News*, 2005, 'Vice-Chair of the People's Congress reveals that the Ministry of Health will not allow an increase in pharmaceutical prices').

Reducing the gap between wholesale and retail prices for drugs will be a major task for the government. It was estimated that in some cities the difference between wholesale and retail prices could be as high as 63 times. It is believed that the bidding system that began in 1999, was aimed at reducing pharmaceutical costs in hospitals, did not help the situation (Zhang, 2005). The problems are: (i) a lack of consistency in regulating the bidding system. The parties responsible for the bidding differed between different cities, provinces and regions. They ranged from local health departments, health providers, a bidding department within health providers to outside private companies affiliated with local health departments; and (ii) The bidding system has increased transaction costs. The range of brokering fees was enormously wide – such fees for as testing, sampling, labelling, documentation and brokerage. For example, documentation fees at the time of writing, according to standards set by the state, are US$20. It is not unusual for a large pharmaceuticals manufacturer to have more than 100 products up for bids, and the cost of bidding can be unreasonably high. There are also many hidden costs, such as internet bidding fees, which are at least US$600. All these costs are added to the cost of the pharmaceuticals sold to the hospitals, and the bidders often colluded with state agencies or health providers to raise these pharmaceutical costs. Sometimes, bidders could not deliver the pharmaceuticals promised and had either to withdraw their bids or to raise their prices later. Since 80 per cent of pharmaceuticals are sold through hospitals, it is hard to reform the system unless hospital financing is improved. Ending the bidding system will not solve the problem because there is no effective alternative at the present time. The system requires a complete overhaul. Making incremental changes might be the best way to reform the system (*Sina News*, 2002, 'Hospital pharmaceuticals are 63 times higher, severely hurting people's interests').

Price controls would be an important step in addressing this issue of affordable pharmaceuticals. As mentioned earlier, the Chinese authorities have already taken important steps in that area. The lowering of the prices of antibiotics in 2005 by the Medical Reform Commission reflect Chinese government's determination to tackle the issue, despite the difficult challenges.

The public also expressed its discontent with the costs of clinical care. As discussed in Chapter 3, according to a survey conducted by China's National Statistics Bureau, among 1,030 individuals surveyed, 81.6 per cent said they felt that medical costs were too high and the waiting time for treatment too long. Stress was a major reason for ill-health that needed clinical treatment. A third of those surveyed believed that stress was a major contributor to their health problems, especially among those working for multinational companies. About 70 per cent of those surveyed said that they did not usually go to see a doctor when illness occurred: 46.9 per cent surveyed chose to self-medicate and if that did not work, respondents would then see a doctor. Of those surveyed, 5.8 per cent never consulted a doctor. Only 32.5 per cent would go to a doctor as soon as they had a problem. Almost a third (31.1 per cent) believed that waiting time was too long and the appointment procedure too complicated. More than half of the respondents did not have a regular check-up, 47.6 per cent believing that the cost of a physical examination was too high (*Sina News*, 2005, 'More than 80 per cent of residents believe that medical and pharmaceutical costs are too high').

Health needs and capacity building in China's health care system

China's health system is in need of major, innovative and urgent reform. Given the fact that the government is already taking bold steps and making investments, the prospects in improving China's development and health issues are promising.

According to a recent report by the WHO, China is ranked 141 among 191 WHO member states regarding public health infrastructure (*Sina News*, 2003, 'More than 100 million Chinese do not have any access to health care'). In an estimate in 2006, equity in health care in China ranked 118th in the world, the fourth from the bottom among all countries surveyed, (*Sina News*, 2006, 'Hospital reimbursement and market system lead to costly health care after twenty years' reform'). These recent survey results were a contradiction of the grand achievements that the founders of People's Republic made in public health.

When agriculture was liberalized in the 1980s, communal welfare funds, which had up to that time provided the major source of health financing, were removed. The co-operative medical care offered to the villages dropped from 82 per cent in 1978 to 11 per cent in 1983 (Huang, 2005). Market reform in 1980s led to the decrease in public subsidies, and the health care public sector resorted to charging fees to users to meet its budgetary needs and public health institutions were transformed into revenue-producing machines. As mentioned earlier, public health providers rely on drug sales and extra service provisions to ensure revenue growth. China's health reforms in 1985 were blamed for the recent problems in access to health care. In fact, the health reforms of 1985 were well-intentioned and were designed to resolve the so-called 'three difficulties': difficulty in seeing a doctor;, difficulty in gaining access to a surgical procedures; and difficulty in obtaining in-patient care. As mentioned earlier, the 1985 reforms encouraged the participation of the private sector in financing health care after forty-five years of financing by the public sector; the private sector was encouraged to invest access the board, in infrastructure building, services and management. The reforms improved infrastructure but led to other problems, especially to the unaffordability of health care. As discussed earlier, in 1998, a further set of reforms targeted health insurance, access to pharmaceuticals, and health care provision. Yet these reforms did not address the fundamental issues of health care costs and access. The core issue is the financing of health care, especially for the public hospitals.

As mentioned earlier, China has more than 16,000 hospitals, 90 per cent of which are categorized as being public. The financing of public hospitals is derived mainly from pharmaceutical sales and health services (*Sina News*, 2006, 'Hospital reimbursement and market system leads to costly health care after twenty years' reform'). The percentage of pharmaceutical sales in hospital revenues has increased. Historically, between 1986 and the 1990s, more than half of the revenues of urban hospitals and more than 60 per cent of revenues from rural township health centres came from pharmaceutical sales, but the retreat of the public sector in providing affordable health care has led to drastic increases in individual health spending. In the years 1990–2000, out-patient fees per patient increased by and in-patient fees increased from US$57 to US$376, and health care costs continued to increase despite the 'significant' decrease in population-wide health insurance coverage. A survey in 1998 showed that 76 per cent of the total population, including 44.1 per cent of urban residents, had no access to health insurance. It has been estimated that, since 1995, more than half of all health spending has come from out-of-pocket payments. As mentioned earlier, this proportion is rapidly increasing. The lack of public sector involvement has contributed to an increase in the total burden of disease in rural areas. A 1998 study showed that half of villagers were living below the poverty line (if using the cut-off point of earning less than US$0.25 a day) consulted a doctor only in an emergency. This has seriously affected China's ability to respond to serious epidemics such as HIV/AIDS, SARS, porcine influenza, and avian influenza.

In the context of increasing individual out-of-pocket spending, the governments decreased role in health spending prior to 2003 was bad news, for the villages especially.

In terms of the government's health spending, there was a downward spiral in health spending in the 1990s, which reached its lowest point in 1995–6. The public sector's spending on health started to increase again only after the year 2000 (ibid.). Since 2001, health spending has accounted for 3–4 per cent of China's total GDP, much less than the 27 per cent among industrialized countries noted above, or 13–15 per cent in the USA (ibid.). When combining total government spending, health insurance protection and disposable income for personal health care spending, the villagers who make up two-thirds of China's population were allocated less than a quarter of the country's health resources. At the same time total health spending for villages from the public sector decreases every year. In 1993, rural health spending accounted for 34.9 per cent of GDP; in 1998, it accounted for 24.9 per cent; and in 2000, it accounted for 22.5 per cent (*Sina News*, 2004). Within seven years, rural health spending had decreased by more than 10 per cent (ibid.).

In another survey, it was reported that, in 1998, China spent US$47.2 billion on health care, but only 15.9 per cent of this was spent on the villages. The spending on urban residents per person was US$16.25 but only US$1.34 on rural residents (*Sina News*, 2004). The gap between urban and rural populations was 13 per cent. In 2000, the gap was 14.9 per cent. To put these statistics in perspective, in the year 2000, urban residents (who account for only 5.8 per cent of China's total population) were protected by health insurance while the majority of villagers did not have any form of insurance. In 2001, the income of urban residents was 2.9 times that of villagers. While being supported by health insurance, urban residents were also being allocated 3.5 times more resources for health care (*Sina News*, 2004).

There is a double barrier facing villagers in poor provinces. In one estimate, a large gap was found between rural and urban areas, and between rich and poor provinces (the coastal and inland provinces). There was a ten times greater gap between the highest amount of per-person health spending from the public sector in 1998: for example, US$11 in Shanghai but only US$1 in Henan Province (ibid.). Regarding hospital beds, the gap between rural and urban areas was 4.2 times in 1998; the highest number being 6.28 beds per thousand people in Beijing and the lowest at 1.51 beds per thousand in Guezhou (ibid.). Hospital beds for villages decreased from 60 per cent in 1982 to 3.42 per cent in 2001 (ibid.). These gaps have increased further since 1998.

This emphasis on profit and a neglect of the importance of prevention by public health workers has contributed to the deterioration of village health, and the lack of co-ordinated efforts to improve health is also a major deficiency. For example, in many villages, the free vaccines provided by the government were useless because villagers were asked to pay user fees for taking the free vaccines, and most villagers could not afford the user fees despite their low cost.

This deficiency in the public sector's involvement in health care is likely to produce negative effects on major health indicators. An increase in mortality and morbidity will be inevitable in the long term. In the 1990s, it was estimated that about 10 per cent of Chinese were infected with hepatitis B (compared to 1 per cent in the USA and Japan); 30 million Chinese suffered the chronic effects of hepatitis B; and 31 per cent were infected with tuberculosis, resulting in annual deaths of some 150,000. Most of those infected lived in rural areas. As discussed earlier, more than 10 million people in China might be infected by HIV by 2010. China's lack of public health resources to respond to HIV/AIDS before 1998 – thirteen years after the disease was identified – has contributed to the rapid transmission of HIV in the population. The public health issue is also a political catalyst for social unrest. The rise of Falun Gong has been claimed to be related to unfulfilled needs for health care. The leaders of Falun Gong protested against the unaffordability of health care. In April 1999, some 10,000 protesters gathered around the central government compound to protest about related issues (Huang, 2005).

A report by the Centre for Development and Research of China's State Council concluded that China needed major health reform work. In 2005, the United Nations Human Development Report also pointed out that the Chinese health care system was not addressing the problems of the needy. The interrelated issues facing Chinese villagers are that they cannot afford either education or health care (*Sina News*, 2005 'The hope for China's rural health: the Kanong Project').

It is clear that China needs to engage in major capacity building in the health and development-related sectors to improve overall social well-being. As mentioned earlier, in a WHO survey of 191 member states, China ranked 144th in terms of health improvement, government responsiveness, and fairness of health financing, behind India, Indonesia and Bangladesh. Our analysis shows that major issues are: capacity in policy design, implementation and evaluation; financing; infrastructure building (facilities, equipment, laboratories, personnel, and so on); technology upgrades; pharmaceutical and vaccine delivery and management; vertical integration in health expertise between central and local governments; technical capacity in disease surveillance and monitoring; quality of care; ethical and regulatory framework; human capacity building (training of public health practitioners and managers); development; and the balance between public health intervention and profit seeking.

Urban capacity building

Urban capacity building includes discussions about establishing disease surveillance and monitoring, emergency response, building of facilities, efficient use of human resources, evidence-based research, community health work (such as prevention, public health, basic care and referral to upper-level hospitals), vertical integration from clinics and general hospitals to upper-level, high-tech health care. Most important, there need to be special programmes to address the needs of vulnerable, excluded members of the population, especially migrants. The focus on the floating population cannot be over-emphasized, because most of the recent epidemics started in the cities, with the migrants being the most affected.

Rural capacity building

Capacity building is an urgent concern in rural areas. The most urgent needs are: upgrading the village-level health system; establishing village-level disease monitoring and surveillance; a sustained commitment and financing from the public sector; direct intervention by the government to support the needy and excluded; improving inefficiency; evaluation of the efficiency of resource allocation; quality of care; transparency; and accountability. The abuse of financing deserves attention. As discussed earlier, most of the health financing from the government has been used to pay for staff, and not for health care provision. The socioeconomic gap is especially serious in the villages. In March 2006, the average annual net income for villagers was less than US$400, compared with more than US$1,400 in the cities and US$30,000 in developed countries. The rural population living in absolute poverty (with an annual income below the range US$83.5 to US$115) numbered over 26 million equal to the total population of

Canada, (*World Journal*, 2004, 'Poor farmers cannot even afford a pack of cigarettes'). To put this statistic in perspective, a college education costs US$1,000 a year. Four years' college education is equal to a villager's income for thirty-five years. Most villagers have to borrow to pay for health care and education. In a survey of 20 provinces, the major source of loans for villagers was loan sharks, accounting for 55 per cent of villagers' loans. From loan sharks, the villagers in the west of the country borrowed 62.43 per cent; those in the eastern provinces borrowed 56.45 per cent; and those in central regions borrowed 55.47 per cent of their total loans. Loan sharking is not uncommon, and villagers have to pay much higher interest rates for these loans (*Sina News*, 2005, 'Agricultural tax is eliminated'). The villagers are lagging behind those who are living in the larger cities, preventing their participation in the economic boom.

Human capacity building

China needs to increase the training of public health professionals in both the government and the community, especially those involved in public health policy-making, as well as in disease control, surveillance, and monitoring, information systems, community health, and health provision. As mentioned earlier, it was estimated that in China, among the public health personnel in the government, less than 1 per cent have the MPH qualification that is considered necessary to provide leadership and technical support within China's health system, compared to 10–20 per cent in the USA (Lee, 2003). There also needs to be a major increase in the numbers of health professionals serving the vast rural areas. The 'barefoot' doctors that engaged in major preventative efforts in China's rural areas in the 1960s and 1970s, and who were instrumental in improving the health status of villagers, are a useful model, based on which China can improve its human capacity for health care in rural areas. In addition, there needs to be a major increase in a wide range of health care professionals serving the rural areas. The need for specialists is felt most acutely in the poorer provinces.

Food safety

Food safety is one of the most challenging and complex issues for China's public health system, and urgent action is in order. The food industry is considered as a pillar industry, with a total worth of US$2,500 billion and a high profit margin of US$137.5 billion (*World Journal*, 2006, 'Food security: a commentary'). Yet, this industry is plagued with life-and-death issues. The amount of contaminated meat, milk, cooking oil, vegetables and snacks in 2005 has led to public outrage. Contamination has derived from: (i) contamination at within the production process, such as in the water, soil and air, which causes contamination of agricultural products; (ii) contamination during the processing of food because of insanitary procedures and the excessive use of harmful additives and preservatives; the overflow of fake or counterfeit products on the market. Given the public health implications of food safety, the Chinese government is in the process of strengthening public surveillance over food production. The most important first step is to increase the regulatory capacity in food safety, especially through the implementation of an effective surveillance system. This is not a new issue for the government; as early as 2002, China's State Council published a notice on the importance of the issue. The notice called for co-ordination among related government departments to establish safety standards for food production, transportation, storage and circulation. The notice paid particular attention to infrastructure construction and the management of the markets for grain, meat, vegetables and other agricultural products. The notice required government departments at all levels to provide policy and directives on food issues, and reinforce examination procedures on food quality. Furthermore, the public were to be informed about food safety issues. The notice also ordered the government at all levels to establish information services, for farmers regarding food supply and demand, for food-producing enterprises, and for the public at large (*Sina News*, 2006, 'China intensifies regulations on food safety'). In addition, China plans during 2006 to set up quality standards and certification processes for all categories of food, which will be an important step towards an improved system of food regulation. The Chinese government's reorganization of some twenty agencies into six to oversee food safety was an important step, involving agencies responsible for imports and exports, agricultural production, monitoring, commercialization, and public health. However, it is important that these agencies should have clearly distinct responsibilities and tasks that are co-ordinated in a collaborative framework (*World Journal*, 2006, 'Many problems with China's food safety'). In addition, the food surveillance agency needs to work closely with the environmental monitoring agency to remove contamination at its source. These policy measures are critical to safeguard the health of the public and to save the economic costs incurred through the consumption of unsafe foods. Yet the problem remains whether the government has the power to implement these well-intentioned policies at provincial and local levels. The local capacity is still lacking to enforce policies from central government. A good number of incidents of food poisoning or unsafe foods have been reported, such as the fake milk incident in Henan, or the poisoned fish from coastal cities (*Sina News*, 2005, 'Fake milk in Henan'). There are serious issues with the food safety regulations. For example, some manufacturers have used pig feed to make soybean products for human consumption, or applied insanitary procedures in the production of soybean cakes. Certain food manufacturing facilities have been set up next to waste disposal sites, and the products often contain carcinogenic ingredients (*World Journal*, 2005, 'Pig feed used for human tofu').

Related to food regulation is health food safety. The volume of health foods/supplements is increasing in the Chinese market, as in the rest of the world. Illegal advertisements exaggerating the therapeutic effects of health foods have become a serious public health issue in recent years (*Xinhua News*, 2005, 'China to ban uncensored health food ads'). The Chinese government has increased its controls over health food advertisements. China's State Food and Drugs Administration (SFDA) announced on 12 June 2005 that the 'Interim Rules for Health Food Advertisement Reviewing' that came into effect on 1 July 2005 state that health food advertisements must be approved by provincial food and drug administrations before being published. In addition, these advertisements would not be allowed to be disguised as news reports. In addition, the SFDA requires that the statement 'this product cannot be a substitute for any medicine' must be marked clearly on printed advertisements and made clear in television commercials. The SFDA would closely scrutinize and ban any food supplements advertisements that are expressed in such a way that they can be confused with medicines; that their therapeutic effects are exaggerated; that false testimonies have been created as though from medical institutions, well-known doctors, experts or actors posing as consumers claiming specific efficacy. The SFDA will also regularly publish a list of health food advertisements on its official website that meet the requirements. Similarly, the SFDA at the provincial level will publish monthly notifications of illegal health food commercials and advertisements.

Financing: public and private sources

Financing and efficiency are major problems in China's health care system. The key issue is that China should allocate resources where they are needed most, not just to the health providers, through major public intervention. There are several related issues: (i) priority setting requires a major assessment of the population's health needs across all sectors. It was noted that, in China, a fifth of hospital care was intervention while the remainder was prevention. There also needs to be a demographic and geographical assessment in this process to identify the most urgent health issues facing the most vulnerable populations in rural and urban areas, as well as the subpopulations within these areas; (ii) it is necessary to identify sources of financing and how funds should be allocated. In this endeavour, the involvement of multiple stakeholders is also critical; (iii) there is a need to recognize the importance of prevention, which is the key to dealing with many infections or chronic diseases. China has ample experience in these areas and has achieved major milestones in the past. Prevention is also more cost-effective in the long term (*Sina News*, 2004, 'The government should improve the public health system. Delegates made 3 suggestions'; see also *Sina News*, 2005, '2005 health care reform general analysis').

Major investment in public health care financing will be a crucial step. China's public health infrastructure at all levels is much lower than that recommended by the WHO (*Sina News*, 2003, 'There remain more than 100 million Chinese without access to any health care'). As mentioned earlier, the total expenditure on health as a percentage of GDP since 2002 is less than 3 per cent (WHO, 2003). For example, in 2005, the rate was about 2 per cent of GDP, less than the global average of 2.5 per cent, and the general government expenditure on health as a percentage of total general government expenditure in 2002 was 10 per cent. Social security expenditure on health as a percentage of general government expenditure on health in 2002 was 50.8 per cent, while private expenditure on health as a percentage of total expenditure on health in 2002 was 66.3 per cent. In terms of sources of private health expenditure, out-of-pocket expenditure on health as a percentage of private expenditure on health in 2002 was 96.3 per cent (ibid.). For public health expenditure, its percentage in the total government budget decreased from 6 per cent to 4 per cent between 1980 and 2005 (ibid.).

Priority setting in financing will have a crucial impact on the health of China's population. Major areas of population health that need immediate attention were summarized by Professor Hu An Kang, Director of the China Science Institute in 2003. He pointed out that China's public health infrastructure needs serious work in all major areas, such as access to sanitary water and waste disposal, health services, and morbidity and mortality control, as mentioned earlier, and he made several recommendations on building public health infrastructure, including: China needs to improve basic care and increase efficiency in its health system; Public health funding should derive from multiple channels, especially increasing the funding from charities and social organizations. China needs to upgrade its public health services and infrastructure in all regions, and improve facilities and equipment. Universal services should be made available to the whole population. There is a serious gap in public health resource allocation and quality of services between rural and urban areas. The main focus should be on the villages. Major attention needs to be paid to the poorest people in the poorest regions and in the cities (*Sina News*, 2003, 'There remain more than 100 million Chinese without access to any health care').

The financing of health care poses a formidable challenge and requires innovative solutions. There needs to be a framework of public – private partnership; in fact, China's public health funding potential from private sources is unlimited. According to a survey on global philanthropy, the gap in charity donations from individuals is 7,300 times greater in the United States than in China; and less than 1 per cent of Chinese enterprises have made donations to charitable causes. According to the same survey the Chinese nation donated about US$0.11 per person to charities, a total of around 0.00001 per cent of its GDP. Scandals associated with the misuse of donations were major factors in the lack of willingness of private donors to give to charity. Possible solutions include: levies of the 'sin tax' on alcohol or tobacco to pay for health care, providing tax incentives, establishing oversight over private donations, and the establishment of private foundations (*Sina News*, 2005, 'Chinese lack willingness to donate to charities. Compared with Americans, the gap is 7,300 times less').

Disease surveillance, monitoring, evaluation and health information collection systems.

The SARS epidemic in 2003 initiated major concerns about China's capacity for disease surveillance, monitoring, evaluation and speedy response. It was clear that China needed a monitoring and surveillance system at every level: in villages, townships, counties, regions, provinces and in central government. It is worth noting that, since SARS, China has shown a rapid improvement in capacity building in this area. A new system called the 'National Infectious Diseases and Sudden Public Health Emergencies Direct Reporting Network' began its operations in January 2004. Public health departments now produce daily reports on morbidity and mortality data on emergent infectious diseases, and regularly update the public with data about infectious diseases. By the end of 2004, 93.21 per cent of county or upper-level hospitals and 42.7 per cent village clinics had been included in this system. In 2004, China invested US$ 1.4 billion in a disease surveillance, monitoring and reporting system that included more than 30,000 local CDCs at provincial, regional and county levels, and in 2005, a further US$500 million was invested in this system. Special emphasis was put on the prevention of and intervention in cases of HIV/AIDS, TB and hookworm.

The disease surveillance and monitoring system in China offers major potential for public and private sectors – of more than US$1.2 billion of business for the private sector. The major issues in response to emergencies in China's information system are: epidemiological reports, efficiency in data transmission, information system coverage, the establishment of oversight, and effectiveness in the system of emergency care, monitoring and evaluation, and a unified platform for the public health information system. The improvement in the surveillance system after the SARS epidemic is impressive; it used to take twenty-nine days for local epidemiological reports to reach to the China CDC headquarters; at the time of writing, it takes less than a day. On 2 June 2006, China's Ministry of Health announced that health professionals must report Class I and II diseases (such as anthrax, SARS, poliomyelitis and avian influenza) to local CDCs within two hours. China has also invested US$700 million in building an information system for sudden health emergencies: 95 per cent in the western provinces and the remaining 5 per cent in the poor coastal provinces. Major projects for the future involve: horizontal and vertical integration across all departments in the central government, local government and villages; upgrades in China's CDC; improving efficiency and speed, and reducing barriers to communication; and building a three-level (central, provincial and city) emergency response and stewardship platform. What is also needed is to build a computerized database in hospitals. According to one estimate, investment in hospital information systems and technology in China increased in 2002, and a faster pace of increase was noted in 2003, by up to 32 per cent. This also provides many of opportunities for the information technologies businesses of the multinationals (*Sina News*, 2003, 'CIO health information system conference in China in 2003').

Population informatics

The improvement in health information system to gather data on population informatics is crucial for China's disease surveillance, monitoring and emergency response. China began its investment in a health information system in 1995. According to a 2002 survey on 6,921 hospitals, about 2,179 had already established a health information system (HIS) (some 31 per cent of those surveyed (ibid.). The highest percentage was in the coastal provinces (about 80 per cent) but only 20 per cent in the western inland provinces were provided with such a system. About 10 per cent of China's hospitals have built clinic-based information system (CIS), and it was noted that the system in the large hospitals has reached the standard of developed countries. It was estimated that the Chinese have spent more than US$80 billion on health services and the rate is increasing by 13 per cent a year. If the hospitals spent 1 per cent of their budgets on health information system upgrades, the business potential cannot be ignored. Barriers are: a lack of sufficient investment and funding commitments by the state because of delayed returns, an over-emphasis on hardware over software, and a lack of standardization in the information platforms, which has posed a barrier to maintenance (*Sina News*, 2003, 'CIO health information system in China in 2003').

Facilities and equipment

In terms of health care facilities, the construction of modern hospitals is an important first step in improving health care infrastructure. Stories of overcrowded hospitals are reported daily in major cities, and the capacity of the hospitals remains limited. For example, patients had to camp outside the Beijing Children's Hospital overnight in ten camps provided by the hospital so that their children could be treated. This hospital treated 1.11 million to 1.2 million children in 2004; and more than 1.5 million between January and October 2005 (most recent available data). Another maternity and children's hospital in Beijing regularly sees more than 500 patients daily, much higher than the 50–100 ceiling in middle-income developing countries (*World Journal*, 2005, 'Beijing Children's Hospital is overstretched').

The construction of new hospitals is helping to relieve this shortage of beds. Under the WTO framework, this will provide the multinationals with many opportunities. For example, Peking University is investing US$360 million to build a not-for-profit, 2,400-bed hospital in Beijing. This hospital will use modern approaches to ownership, management, operational and patient services. It is a shareholding entity jointly owned by Peking University and affiliated companies. Parts of the hospital, such as the luxury medical services sector, will be open to investors. The doctors and nurses will work on a contract system, and will receive payment for quality service. Employees will be protected from malpractice. Patients who cannot afford treatment will benefit from the setting up of a special fund to cover their medical costs (*People's Daily*, 2003, 'New hospital concept introduced in China's capital'). The Wang Group from Taiwan, which has published ambitious plans to build modern mega-hospitals in China, has also obtained approval from the Chinese authorities to build a 3,000-bed hospital 1.2 squ. km. of land in Hsiamen, southern China, which will also be covered by Taiwan's universal insurance. This is just one of three mega-hospitals that the Wang Group is building (*Sina News*, 2005, 'China approves Wang's hospital in Hsiamen'). Multinationals have much to contribute to Chinese health care provision. Collaboration with local experts can also facilitate their entry into the local market.

In terms of equipment, it was obvious from the early 1990s that medical equipment is one of the fastest-growing imports to China. China's products remain low-tech, but it is not unusual for modern hospitals in major Chinese cities to use the same kinds of high-tech equipment as are used in the USA and other industrialized countries. Yet the major issue is inequity – that is, modern technology has not trickled down to the smaller hospitals in the cities or to rural clinics because of the lack of public financing and budgetary commitment. This gap has had a particular pronounced effect on the poorer sections of the population in urban and rural areas. Again, some form of public–private partnership here will generate a large number of opportunities for the multinationals.

Rural investment

China needs to invest major resources to address the social determinants of health in rural areas: decreasing poverty, improving universal education, and building a rural infrastructure. Other specific areas of work needed are: access to educational opportunities; vocational skills training opportunities; the protection and improvement of working conditions; a sustainable financial commitment from the government; a guaranteed minimum wage; access to health care and health insurance; and the integration of the floating population into the safety net of an urban social security system (*World Journal*, 2004, 'Survey of Chinese villagers exposes the truth about village life').

A new development plan from the central government appears to be designed to address just these issues. In China's 'Eleventh Five-Year Plan', starting from 2005, one of the major goals for the country's social development is to improve rural health provision. China plans to invest at least US$7.5–12 billion in rural development, which is termed the 'New Village Movement'. In 2006 alone, the Chinese government has invested more than US$420 billion to improve agricultural output, rural infrastructure, and villagers' living standards, which accounted for 21.4 per cent of the expenditure in the central government's total budget. Specific goals included: improving seed protection; establishing large-scale commercial agricultural centres; supporting high-end/niche agriculture; and upgrading large-scale irrigation systems. In improving the villagers' lives, the government will focus on the improvement of 'water, gas, roads and electricity'. With regard to infrastructure, more than US$21 billion will be invested in road building. In addition, measures will be taken to protect farm land. The government will also invest more than US$272 billion in free universal education. Given the enormous scale of this plan, these measures are expected to address social determinants of health, and are likely to improve population health if they are executed with transparency and accountability. Most important, by the end of 2006; China plans to cover 40 per cent of rural health care through a collaborative health insurance scheme; 60 per cent by 2007; and 100 per cent by 2008. In 2006, financing from the public sector has already reached US$509 million, a sixfold increase over 2005 (*Sina News*, 2006, 'In 2008, rural health care will be completely covered'). However, this is still a drop in the ocean and, again, the participation of private partners will be more sustainable in the future.

Capacity building in the ethical, policy, regulatory, and legal environment

Capacity building in ethical, policy and regulatory frameworks is central to improving China's health system with the aim of improving access to and equity of health care in China. Major technical areas in the existing bureaucracy in need of regulating are: establishment of an administrative structure with a clear central chain of command and division of labour and responsibilities; improving price controls and cost containment in health care provision; regulating health care providers' practices and ethical conduct, improving the position of consumers in negotiating prices and quality for health care provision; establishing a coherent fee payments scheme and cost structure; increasing transparency in the process of payment and provision; protecting patients' rights to be informed; establishing a system of checks and balances; monitoring quality of care; and improving management and accounting system (*Sina News*, 2005, 'Shocking loopholes in Harbin Hospital scandal'). The overarching goal of the improvement is to address equitable access to health care in the short-term and social determinants of health, such as exclusion, in the long term.

Political will. The major issue in China's capacity building in health care is political will and commitment from the leadership. In this regard,

China's recent response to the HIV epidemic has served as a positive example for other health issues. Despite the criticism from the global community that the Chinese government's actions were far from being satisfactory, the government has committed itself to addressing the needs of the HIV infected and affected. These measures reflect the progress that the political leadership has made in cognizing the HIV issue. These include: increasing collaboration with global partners, such as the Global Fund, to establish the China Comprehensive AIDS Response (*see* the 2004 CSIS report); and taking proactive measures by instituting the State Council Working Committee on HIV/AIDS in February, 2004, which generated 'Five-Commitment Policy', the 'Four-Frees' action plan, improved relevant laws and regulations, and protected the legitimate rights and confidentiality of HIV/AIDS patients. These policy measures gave birth to some successful models of tackling the HIV/AIDS epidemic. For example, in March 2003, China established HIV Integrative Prevention and Intervention Demonstration Districts in eleven provinces and fifty county units. By the end 2003, the number of these districts will increase to 127. Additional increases are contingent upon funding availability (*People's Daily*, 2005, 'China's disease surveillance and monitoring system has made progress'). This programme provided a comprehensive framework in supporting the HIV infected and affected. For example, in these districts, HIV patients in financial difficulties will receive some financial support, such as in the form of 10 yuan coupons (*Central Daily News*, 2003). All patients who had been infected with HIV through blood transfusion would be treated free. Treatment is limited to four low-cost generic drugs that are off-patent, which China can produce itself. China's long-term plans are to offer free medicines to all infected by HIV. The major problem is that these free ARVs (antiretrovirals) tend to have strong side effects and most are not recommended any longer in the USA. Because of the side effects, the drop-out rate among HIV patient is more than 20 per cent. The positive result of these policies is that the mortality rate has improved since the use of ARVs.

The HIV epidemic clearly was an awakening call for the Chinese political leadership and it has prompted the government to strengthen its capacity to address the impact of infectious diseases in general. For example, in 2003 China instituted a Law on Prevention of Infectious Diseases. It has committed itself to investing in US$800 million in strengthening the provincial CDCs for disease surveillance; US$200 million in the prevention of and intervention in HIV transmission; and US$2.55 billion in strengthening the infrastructure of the blood stations in the North-western provinces. In the face of increasing occurrence of epidemics, the Chinese government was also forced to generate 'Policy Directives and suggestions from PRC State Department' in 2004 and 2005 to tackle avian flu. In this framework, the policy measures include: (i) increasing monitoring and surveillance in all regions. The Chinese government has forcefully implemented the policy that all chickens found within three kilometres of the infected location will have to be destroyed; (ii) generating a comprehensive compensation system for the poultry industry. For example, central government provides subsidies to the poultry farmers for all chickens slaughtered. It would provide a subsidy of 20 per cent in eastern provinces and 80 per cent in Western provinces to poultry farmers who had to destroy chickens; (iii) providing a tax relief. The state has waived income tax, value-added tax and part of local taxes for poultry farmers affected by the epidemic; (iv) reducing financial burden of the affected businesses. The government will reduce various fees, such as administrative fees and export fees, for large-scale or individual poultry farmers or poultry-processing industries between 1 November, 2005 to 30 June, 2006. In addition, the state will relax loan and subsidy policies to affected farmers or plants, and to vaccine producers; (v) adopting preventive measures and protecting the business viability of the poultry farmers. The state will secure, protect and increase the supply of vaccines to respond to any related emergencies. The state will also ensure their supply to the poultry industry to meet market needs as well as to enforce sanitary measures to prevent the epidemic from spreading. The state will protect the livelihood of poultry farmers and workers. The state will standardize monitoring and surveillance, management and sanitation systems of the poultry industry by standardizing and building the infrastructure in processing infected poultry and their remains and waste (China State Department, 2005). Nevertheless, despite the thoughfulness in this policy framework, the major barrier to the Chinese political leadership in addressing the prevailing health issues is how these policies can be harmonized and coherently implemented at all levels. There is often a disconnection in regulatory and legal enforcement between the central and local governments.

Despite these efforts targeting very specific challenges, there are many areas in health care that need improvement. The most urgent issue is to *improve access*, as our analyses in the earlier sections of this chapter have illustrated.

As noted earlier, unaffordability is a major issue in China's health care system and it occurs at all levels and to most of the Chinese population. The poor and underprivileged have suffered the most in this crisis. In general, in contrast to an increase in luxurious treatment for the better-off, there has been a lack of care for the poor. A most recent example occurred in Beijing. Beijing City government plans to build a super hospital for Olympic visitors, costing some US$40 million and occupying 1,000 hectares of land. The plan was heavily criticized because there has been a higher demand for resources for a basic public health infrastructure. This new hospital was seen as subsidizing the rich and misusing resources. The struggle between for-profit motivation and the achievement of public health goals is major issue facing China (*World Journal*, 2005, 'Luxurious hospitals ignore the poor', A-13). The phenomenon of rising fees for child-birth is experienced by all the Chinese families. It has been estimated that the fees associated with child-birth have increased more than 100 times since 1980s. In the 1970s, child-birth costs were less than US$1; by the 1980s, it cost US$200; it now costs some US$500–1,200 per birth. The fees can be as high as $15,000 in luxurious hospitals (*Sina News*, 2005, 'In Beijing, child-birth costs have increased more than a hundred times').

The tragic stories of the way in which the poor take health care into their own hands are most heart-wrenching because of their inability to pay for health care. They occur daily in Chinese society. For example, in the western city of Lanchou in Shaanxi Province, a 19 year-old youth, Ying, suffered frost bite in ten fingers while attending a female camel that had just given birth. The female camel had strayed from other camels Ying was minding. For fear of being reprimanded by his father, Ying traced the camel to the edge of the desert when the temperature was minus 45 degrees. Since the family could not afford the hospital visits, Ying's father used a saw to cut off all his son's fingers to relieve the pain. The villagers collected US$500 to pay for his hospital care, but this was far from the US$2,500 needed for the surgery (*World Journal*, 2005, 'Poor villagers used a saw to cut frost bitten fingers', A-13). Another 19-year old youth suffering from chronic heart disease was abandoned in the foyer of a hospital in Beijing. The father of the youth spent all of his savings on his child's health care. As a last resort, the father was forced to leave his son at the hospital door so that the boy's life might be saved (*World Journal*, 2005, 'A young man was abandoned by father due to inability to pay the hospital', A-13). Another story reported that a 47-year old man was sent to a mortuary awaiting cremation while he was still breathing. This man had suffered a stroke. Instead of sending him to hospital, the family made the decision to send him to the funeral home because they could not afford hospital treatment. The staff at the mortuary found that he was still alive and decided to send him to hospital. The hospital demanded payment of US$1,200, equal to the total of the income of all five members of the family (*World Journal*, 2005, 'Live man was sent to a funeral home to be cremated due to inability to pay the hospital', A-14). A similar incident has aroused outrage and sympathy. A security officer who had bravely chased and arrested a robber, commited suicide because he could not afford the cost of treating the wounds he suffered when apprehending the thief. He was afraid that the medical costs would be a burden on his family (*World Journal*, 2005, 'A security officer commits suicide because he could not afford hospital cost', A–13). It is also not uncommon that hospitals see desperate parents drop off very sick children at their doors. Tragically, hospitals usually have to terminate life support for abandoned newborns and watch them die because of a lack of funding.

Another incident that occurred in November 2005 sent shock waves across the the whole nation. A 74-year-old man, Mr Wung Wen Hwei, spent almost US$700,000 for 66 days in a Class I hospital before he died there. Mr. Wung had been diagnosed with lymphoma. Complications from chemotherapy treatment led to his being transferred to a teaching hospital. After receiving the enormous bill, Mr Wung's children filed a complaint to the government. During those sixty-six days in hospital, there had been 3,025 medical reports covering extremely unusual clinical activities: for example, on 25 July 25, Mr Wung was reportedly given a 78,604 ml blood transfusion and a further 69,307 ml on 1 August. During his stay in the hospital, there had been 588 analyses of Mr Wung's glucose level, 299 of his kidney functions, 968 blood transfusions, and 379 respiratory analyses. The hospital had charged him for eighty-eight days' in-patient treatment despite his stay of only sixty-six days. Among the 3,025 medical reports, only thirty-five were genuine (*Sina News*, 2005, 'Central Disciplinary Committee investigates the RMB5.5 million medical cost in Harbin').

These cases demonstrate the need for major reforms to improve access to the health system by the majority of the Chinese population. The key steps that need to be taken are: increase the involvement of the public sector in hospital financing; rebuild public health clinics; strengthen third-party payments. Intervention from the public sector is necessary; however, the issue remains the extent to which the public sector can and is willing to intervene. As mentioned earlier, the recent experiment of 'discount hospitals' can only address a small part of the problem (*Sina News*, 2006, 'Analysis of discount hospitals'). The idea of discount hospitals was encouraging but the extent to which it is able to solve China's health care problems remains to be seen. Yet this development is good news for the underprivileged. Discount hospitals serve excluded and marginalized populations, such as villagers, the unemployed, workers forced into early retirement, uninsured population, migrants, the elderly, and underprivileged children. In the case of Shang-Ti hospital, the first discount hospital in Beijing, the system seems to work well for the needy. In this case, there are separate tracks for revenues and financing. The major sources of financing are from the government and private charities. Pharmaceutical sales account for 30 per cent of the financing, much lower than in other Chinese hospitals, and the hospital is usually supplied with discounted drugs. The prices for all categories of health care are some 30–50 per cent lower than in regular private or public hospitals. For example, in terms of child-birth, it makes a charge of US$125, compared with US$300 or $ US1,000 in other hospitals. Doctors' salaries often derive from commissions from pharmaceutical sales or administering clinical tests.

The model of discount/welfare hospital operation offers a glimmer of hope for Chinese society in addressing the questions of equity, access and cost; however, the sustainability issue requires special attention.

Government support is the key to sustainability. We are convinced that the Chinese government has to shoulder more than 5 per cent of its GDP for health care for its benefit to be shared by the whole population. For example, in the UK, the share of health care in the total GDP is 5 percent; it is 11 per cent in France, and more than 13 per cent in the USA. In fact, in countries that provide universal health care, the public sector manages more than 80 per cent of the resources for health care. The DSH (Disproportionate Share Hospital) payment in the USA, in which the financing of hospitals comes from the government, in the form of Medicaid and other government programmes, can also provide a useful lesson for China. In this case, the Chinese government can finance the health care to the poor and underprivileged through public programmes or grants. In addition, the participation of the philanthropy sector will be critical in the future to ensure sustainability.

In the case of Mr Wung discussed above, a lack of an objective monitoring system for health care provision and the absence of effective financing mechanisms, such as third-party contributions, were major factors in the tragedy. It was noted that, for the accused hospital in Mr Wung's case, the main increase in revenues since 2002 had been from the increase in the number of patients and out-of-pocket payments. Compared to 2001, the number of patients in this hospital had increased by 69.73 per cent and fees had increased by 30.27 per cent. It was also noted that a clinical visit by a specialist cost US$4,000 in this setting, much higher than the fee charged in any industrialized country. In this hospital, inpatient treatment was also a major source of revenue in 2002, increasing by 61.46 per cent in 2001. Two factors contributed to the high hospital care costs in the case of Mr Wung and across the board: (i) profit motivation and (ii) fear of malpractice charges. In many cases, recommending unnecessary medical tests was used as a protective mechanism for doctors against future liability suits. It was obvious that third-party contributions to this picture are urgently needed (*Sina News*, 2005, 'Investigation into the financial situation in the Harbin hospital scandal: unchecked power got bloated').

The need for health insurance is urgent in China to resolve situations like Mr Wung's. As mentioned earlier, at the time of writing, most Chinese people do not have any form of health insurance. Even for those who have insurance, the coverage is often meagre and only pays for a small part of the medical costs. In most cases, the yearly allowance is usually spent on one consultation (*Sina News*, 2005, 'Retired physician also suffered the slaughter of overpricing by hospitals'). Striking a balance between affordable insurance, population inclusiveness, sufficient coverage and the avoidance of abuse is a formidable task for the government.

The issue of how to implement health insurance is widely discussed. Minister of Health Kao Chian has pointed out the need to reform the current hospital system by: (i) privatizing some hospitals. The contradiction of a profit motive and public health responsibilities in public hospitals is a major cause of poor quality and high health care costs. As mentioned earlier, more than 90 per cent of Chinese hospitals are owned by the government but these are most aggressive in pursuing profits, despite being given a wide range of subsidies and tax incentives. In contrast, privately owned hospitals have to pay all taxes and do not receive any subsidies; (ii) separating the sales of prescription drugs and hospital care. As mentioned earlier, an important problem leading to high health care costs is that hospitals rely on pharmaceutical sales as their major source of revenues; and (iii) separating health care provision from the collection of payments. The insertion of a third-party payments system into health care is necessary; that is, the hospitals provide care while insurance companies meet the costs of the service. This system will improve health-care financing; control pricing of health care provision; and provide a monitoring framework for health care consumption behaviour. At present, health care consumers have no bargaining power in price negotiations because of the weak third-party payment system. The insurance company can be a better negotiator for affordable care because of the volume of the services purchased from health care providers (*Sina News*, 2005, 'Urgent reform is needed behind the hospital cost scandal in Harbin').

A number of experiments on third-party payments are being conducted to improve the existing system. For example, an experimental system of monitoring medical insurance costs was conducted in about fifty cities. Department of Labour Insurance has further expanded this programme. It is the goal of the Chinese government that the rate of participation in health insurance should be greater than an average of 60 per cent, including 70 per cent in cities under the direct control of the central government, and at least 50 per cent for mid-sized cities. By June, 2003, there were already 100.94 million participants with national health insurance. The Labour Department would be responsible for monitoring: types of payments by participants, payments for essential medicines, the use of the health care insurance fund, and the balance of payments in the fund. It has also focused on the monitoring of the hospitals contracted by National Health Insurance governing pharmaceutical costs, management, and the reimbursement system. The hospitals that do not meet the stated standards will be required to relinquish their contracts with the Department of Labour (*Sina News*, 2003, 'Health cost monitoring will expand to 30–50 cities in China'). The challenge, however, is to extend the coverage of this kind of programme to the remote villages, in which the majority of the poor Chinese population reside and where the need is greatest.

The regulation of pharmaceutical quality control, sale, and management should also be a priority for Chinese society because problems in these areas directly impact on the health of the population.

On *pharmaceutical quality control*, Chapter 4 has provided a detailed discussion of the challenges facing China's pharmaceutical quality control. Infrastructure and capacity building in this area are the most critical tasks facing both private and public sectors in health care in China because: (1) they affect patient safety; (ii) they have major implications for the efficacy of public health policies; and (iii) they affect China's global competitiveness. Recent steps taken by the Chinese government towards improving pharmaceutical quality are encouraging, but the possibility of thorough implementation at all levels is challenging. For example, by the end of 2004, China's SFDA decreed that all provinces must establish surveillance, monitoring and regulatory systems for pharmaceutical control, distribution and retails (*Chinapharm*, 2005, 'An analysis of IPR (Intellectual Property Rights')). By Feburary 2005, the central government had also established thirty-two province-level ADR (Adverse Drug Reaction) monitoring centres, which together have collected more than 70,000 reports on population informatics of pharmaceutical side effects. From 1 July 2005, the Chinese government requires that all pharmaceutical manufacturers must be GMP (Good Manufacturing Practice) certified. Without this certification all manufacturing activities would be terminated (ibid.). Other issues in quality control are: control of the abuse of antibiotics and control of illegal pharmaceutical sales, such as counterfeits. In China, each year, more than 80,000 individuals died from misuse of antibiotics. It has been estimated that some 35 per cent of the hospital revenues come from antibiotics and this rate is increasing. Abuse of antibiotics was a major factor in this increase (*Chinapharm*, 2005, 'An analysis of IPR (Intellectual Property Rights')).

In addition to regulating legal drugs, the Chinese government is also in the process of reinforcing the control of illegal sales of drugs. For example, a new law controlling illegal pharmaceutical sales, such as counterfeit and time-expired drugs, came into effect on 1 July, 2006. In particular, drug counterfeitng will continue to be a major problem for China's pharmaceutical sector. The counterfeits not only generate negative health effects but also affect the global position of the Chinese pharmaceutical industry in the WTO framework.

On *pharmaceutical management systems*, given the fact that large pharmacy chains are being established in every province in China, there is an urgent need for computerized systems in the drug stores. An innovative system established at a discount drug chain for patients in Guanzhou could be an exemplary model. At those stores, a patient's pharmaceutical history is reviewed when new drugs are ordered. The pharmaceutical review includes medication use and dosage, any history of allergies or adverse reactions and side effects. Monitoring side effects is the focal point. The drug store is able to track the side effects of certain high-risk drugs, such as those for heart disease, diabetes and weight loss via regular telephone interviews with the patients (*Sina News*, 2005, 'A Guanzhou discount drug chain traces pharmaceutical history of consumers'). This system, if implemented more widely, could prevent many unnecessary incidents related to inappropriate pharmaceutical use.

On *pharmaceutical sales regulation*, China has made some progress in its regulatory framework for pharmaceutical sales. The decision by the State Food and Drug Administration to implement 'pharmaceutical permit regulations' from 1 April, 2004 was an important first step. The food and pharmaceutical supervision and management authorities at provincial, district and city levels will be responsible for the issuing, renewal, and amendment of permits, and the monitoring of the daily operations of pharmaceutical retailers. This measure aims to improve the quality, management and operation of local retailers, and to ensure the standardization of retail practices. The regulations also clearly stipulate: application for the wholesale licence, qualifications for obtaining a sales permit, performance assessment and procedures, quality assessment and control, and the application process for retailers. It states that pharmaceutical retailers have to be in operation 24 hours a day. In addition, only licensed pharmacists are permitted to dispense prescriptions and some OTC medicines. Quality control personnel have to have at least one year's experience. Pharmacies are also allowed to operate in supermarkets. From 1 July, 2005, all retail pharmacies can only sell prescription drugs with the permission of a licensed physician (*Chinapharm*, 2005, 'An analysis of IPR'). These steps are important changes for China's pharmaceutical operation because they are being brought into line with the systems used in most developed countries.

For pharmaceutical wholesaling, the law requires that businesses are to be equipped with an information management system that can process information on purchasing, storage, sales, inventory monitoring and quality control. The system should be able to manage the information required by the new regulations. Wholesale agents are also required to employ a certain number of licensed pharmacists, and are required to have facilities to refrigerate, store, classify, deliver and transport pharmaceuticals. Despite the fact that this system was well-designed, the challenge is to reinforce its implementation and ensure that this system also covers the technologically backward areas in villages.

Besides pharmacy and pharmaceutical regulation, clinical care has also caused a great deal of controversy since the economic reform in the 1980s and needs a major reform,

On *clinical care management*, technical, systematic and scientific management skills are urgently needed at all levels in China's clinical care. These include appointments for clinical visits, accounting, maintenance, personnel, record keeping and health information systems. For example, the appointments system for clinical visits is seriously flawed. It was reported that even for those who can afford clinical care, it is hard to obtain an appointment because of the monopoly by hospital scavengers. The scavengers take up all the quotas for appointments and resell them for high prices. Patients have to pay a fee of US$29 to obtain an appointment from the scavengers. The scavengers also forge specialist physicians' signatures to bypass the appointments system. The illegal trade is hard to eradicate because the penalties are small, usually limited to 10 days' imprisonment or a small fine (*World Journal*, 2005, 'Appointment scavengers sneak through the loopholes and cannot be stopped', A-13).

On *regulating malpractice* in clinical settings, a more comprehensive legal and ethical framework is needed. Malpractice by unlicensed doctors was frequent in 2005. For example, in Shenzhen City of the Guanzhou Province, more than twenty people died as a result of malpractice, and there were more than 2,600 illegal clinics in that year alone. These clinics, most of which treated venereal diseases, hired unlicensed doctors, and illegally performed sex selection of the foetus for pregnant women, or carried out abortions (*World Journal*, 2005, 'Canton engaged in serious attacks against illegal clinics and unlicensed physicians', A-13). Malpractice occurs in every category of health care in China but one area that has witnessed a large volume of malpractice claims is plastic surgery because of its large profit margins and lack of regulation. Although only a certain number of hospitals in the Class III A category are allowed to perform breast enlargement, a large number of women have used unlicensed doctors and have suffered serious side effects without compensation (*World Journal*, 2005, 'Quality of care is uneven for breast enlargement', A-13).

There are a number of explanations for the rise of malpractice incidence. The blurred line between for-profit and not-for-profit health care is the main reason for the increase of malpractice and has led to major conflicts between health care providers and patients. For health care providers in public hospitals, pursuing a profit has become a dominant concern for them. They often engage in unethical conduct in health care settings, such as raising the prices of medicine, receiving illegal commissions from pharmaceutical companies, receiving illegal 'rewards' or 'grey money' from patients, recommending unnecessary tests, procedures, and services, using excessive amounts of medicines, and engaging in illegal surgery.

The patients often lose when they choose to sue the provider. A law suit for malpractice brought by a 9-year-old leukaemia sufferer who became infected by HIV while a patient a Beijing University Hospital showed that patient protection, especially of the very vulnerable, needs to be strengthened. This patient lost the case but the parents suspected that their child had been infected with HIV through contaminated blood. The case was closed without resolving the patient's questions (*Sina News*, 2005, 'The first case of a law suit by an HIV infected was closed. The plaintiff lost').

Owing to the lack of protection of their rights, patients often resort to extreme measures. A doctor was stabbed to death by a patient in Fuzhou,

Fujian Province. The patient was angry because over a period of ten years, the doctor had not been able to cure the patient's prostate problem (*World Journal*, 2005, 'A physician was stabbed to death by his patient in Fujou', A-13). Another similar incident occurred in Sichuan, where a doctor was seriously injured by being stabbed by a patient. It is not unusual for doctors to have to hire bodyguards to protect them at work (Zhang, 2006).

The many health care scandals that have occurred recently demonstrate the need to establish an ethical and regulatory framework in health care practices to protect both public health and patients' rights. As noted earlier, China already had a rudimentary framework for addressing malpractice through its 1987 'Regulations on Medical Incidents' and 'Amendments to the Regulations on Medical Incidents' published on 4 April, 2002 and implemented on 1 September, 2002. Facing a rapidly changing medical environment, the latter regulation needs further amendments to meet the increasing needs of both health care practitioners and patients. At the time of writing, patients can choose private arbitration or engage in civil action for compensation, and the Chinese government has made some attempts at addressing malpractice in this area. For example, as early as 2001, there was a national inspection campaign by the Ministry of Health, the State Administration of Traditional Chinese Medicine, the State Drug Administration, and the State Administration of Industry and Commerce, to investigate false diagnoses and illegal treatment. This campaign also attempted to address coercive sale efforts by drug producers and pharmaceutical wholesale companies. These coercive efforts were often carried out during 'health consultations' and 'free treatment' sessions, to persuade patients to buy unnecessary and expensive medicines (*China Daily*, 2001, 'Medical services receive check-up'). The government's action was commendable; nevertheless, it is essential that: a rigorous monitoring system is instituted permanently to regularly evaluate the performance of health providers in all different categories; and a comprehensive legal framework of arbitration, penalties and compensations needs to be in place to protect the patients' rights. The protection of the rights of the vulnerable populations, such as the disabled and mentally ill, also needs urgent action because they are often abandoned by their families and community. An attempt at legislation in 2001 was a good start in addressing the rights of mental patients to receive services and the protection of their privacy and confidentiality.

On the other hand, for law-abiding providers and patients, there is no framework to protect their legitimate interests, either. The major issues in this area are: (i) no dispute settlement mechanism between hospitals, patients, and health care providers before a case is heard by a court; (ii) no effective public arbitration regulatory framework; (iii) no medical liability and malpractice insurance to protect providers and support compensation for victims; and (iv) no free legal assistance for victims. In general, medical liability suits incur major costs for patients and providers, and it can often take a long time before arbitration generates any results (*Sina News*, 2004, 'There should be a buffer between the patients and health care providers'). Without a clear legal framework, it is now a lose–lose situation for both the patients and health providers.

Another area of medical practice that has aroused serious ethical concerns in the global community is the trade in body organs and tissues in China, mostly the sale of hearts and kidneys. It is widely known that China is one of the largest organ markets in the world. It has been estimated that, in China, more than 2 million of the population need organ transplants each year but because of a shortage of donor organs, only 20,000 transplants can be carried out (*Xinhua News*, 2006, 'China issues human organ transplant regulation'). Despite the organ shortage, body parts, legally or illegally obtained, are being regularly sold to foreigners from Chinese nationals and this trade is increasing. In addition, the number of foreigners who receive organ transplants is also increasing because of the low cost. For example, by March 2006, about 100 foreign patients had received organ transplants in Chinese hospitals. In comparison to the US$1 million required to perform this kind of surgery in hospitals in the industrialized countries, it costs only US$110,000 in China (*World Journal*, 2005, 'Taiwanese were the brokers in China's organ trade', A–11). As a result of the high demand for organs from developed countries, an illegal trade has also been burgeoning. In some cases, hospital staff or military personnel have been implicated. China needs to take major steps to improve current laws and regulations to prevent this illegal trade and protect the rights of the legitimate interests as well as the safety for sellers and buyers. The Laws passed in March 2006, ban the sale of organs and introduce a set of standards for organ transplants to protect public safety. The provisional regulations require the medical institutions to obtain the written agreement of donors before a transplant takes place. Donors are entitled to refuse the donation at the last minute, a regulation that became effective on 1 July, 2006. All hospitals staffed by doctors with clinical transplant qualifications have to register with the provincial government. Unregistered hospitals are prohibited from performing organ transplants. The regulations also require organ transplant cases to be reported to and discussed by the ethics committee. The operations cannot take place without the committee's approval. This framework was a good start in addressing the organ transplant issue; yet additional steps need to be considered to address the commercial market of the organs' sale, such as: (i) establishing a legal commercial framework to stop the illegal organ trade; (ii) providing medical and legal guidelines to administer the processes; (iii) strengthening the surveillance and monitoring of the health of the parties involved, as a way of monitoring the spread of infectious diseases that can be transmitted in this process, such as BSE (or the commonly known 'mad cow disease'), HIV, hepatitis, and so on.

Lack of ethical guidance has a direct impact on the quality of care, a concept that has been widely discussed in the USA. New measures are being introduced to improve quality of care, to enhance health care outcomes and to improve efficiency. In the USA, it has been found that improved quality of care is often conducive to efficiency, cost-effectiveness, and improved health among patients. It is a win–win situation for all parties. China can avoid the mistakes that have occurred in developed countries by addressing ethical issues in health care as a first step towards improving quality of care. In China, there is a need to integrate ethical principles into the regulatory framework of clinical care. The fact that China does honour internationally sanctioned principles of health care, such as dignified, controlled, careful, just, fair, affordable, and economically sustainable treatment, is a good starting point from which to design and implement policies and laws to regulate ethical conduct among the clinicians (*Sina News*, 2005, 'A live lesson in the Harbin Hospital scandal for medical ethics').

Addressing social determinants of health. Ultimately, to address equitable access to health care requires long-term, multi-lateral collaboration to address social determinants of health. To be specific, all sectors in the Chinese society need to take immediate action to build a solidarity framework for the vulnerable populations to address social determinants of health.

This solidarity framework should strive to eliminate social exclusion of the vulnerable populations and its success will be judged on the basis of the health of those populations. There are several critical elements in this framework. First, China needs to build a protective framework, including, most importantly of all, a pension system, to accommodate the needs of a rapidly increasing ageing population. There has been a lack of effective social policies to address the needs of the vulnerable elderly. For a long time, pensions were only offered to urban workers in the state-owned sector of the economy. In 2002, the 'basic pension system' included only 45 per cent of the urban workforce, mainly employees of state and collectively owned enterprises. Participation in the pension systems of the private sector remains minimal. The civil servants, some 10 per cent of the urban workforce, are covered by a more generous pension system. Only 11 per cent of villagers are covered by a small, voluntary rural pension system. Overall, it has been estimated that only 25 per cent of China's total workforce, both urban and rural, receives some form of pension that includes some health care coverage (Jackson and Howe, 2004).

Despite the Chinese government's commitment to improvement in the pensions system, the participation of the private sector remains a challenge. Since the late 1990s, the Chinese State Department has asked private enterprises to include pension plans. This new system has two components: the taxes from current working populations are used to pay for those who are retired; and the government has established private retirement accounts to pay for those retiring in the future. However, there is a problem in that some private enterprises are now refusing to participate in the private accounts project because most of their funding has already gone to pay for the deficit in state-run pension plans, leaving no funds to provide for the private accounts. The money collected in private accounts has often been appropriated to pay for those who are currently retired. This reform is critical to China's economic success, however. If the pension reform is successful, China's ageing population will not be a barrier to China's sustainable growth; the pension fund can be the engine for economic development and investment momentum; it can increase the political capital for development; and it can increase China's global economic position by effectively leveraging and investing the pension fund in global projects (Zhang, 2004).

Second, there needs to be a protective framework for the floating population. The issues facing the floating population are complex but are also urgent. For this population, there needs to be an overhaul of every aspect of the Chinese social sysem to address their health needs. This includes major changes in: the household registration system, social security, education, employment, work conditions, social integration, civil rights, social organization, the migration system, financial help, housing, and political participation. A starting point would be to integrate the floating population into the urban household registration system or to combine rural and urban registration. It is also important to monitor the health of the migrants and to provide regular health services for their children. The education and health care of 'floating' children, which should be integrated, cannot be ignored because of the large size of this population. The urban education system needs to accommodate their nutritional, immunization and hygiene needs (*World Journal*, 2005, 'Children of the floating population').

Third, there needs to be a more sustainable policy commitment to poverty reduction for the rural populations. China has engaged in serious poverty elimination measures since the start of the 2000s. For example, by 2004, China had invested a discretionary fund of more than US$38.5 billion in the poor population. Yet, because of corruption, a tenth of the fund was misused (*World Journal*, 2004, 'Poor populations increase because of corruption', A-13). The announcement by the Chinese prime minister, Wen Jia Bao, on 18 November, 2005 that China will eliminate all fees and payments associated with 9-year free mandatory education in rural areas is a critical step towards improving the social health of rural areas. In 2003, China had already spent 3.61 per cent of its GDP on education and with increasing revenue. Rural education reform is workable within the existing budget (*Sina News*, 2005, 'A commentary on the implementation of free mandatory education in rural villages'). Addressing the issue of affordable education helps to improve the social determinants of health facing the vast poor rural populations in China. Other ongoing projects would also help the health of this group.

There are some positive policy commitments and models for poverty reduction in rural areas and these models have long-term implications for the social health of the underprivileged, poor villagers. The main model was the 'Nine Action Plans' for the rural economy, announced by the Chinese government on 29 December, 2005. This plan aims to improve the livelihood of the populations in rural and far-flung provinces. The key measures in this plan include: increasing overall agricultural productivity and quality of major staples; strengthening infrastructure to promote quality products; upgrading technological and technical capacity; increasing productivity for the dairy and fishing industries; promoting agricultural commercialization and increasing added-value products; establishing national certification and standard building for organic products and increasing organic production; increasing the use of clean and alternative energy; increasing the surveillance and monitoring of poultry diseases (*Sina News*, 2005, 'China implements Nine Action Plans for villagers').

The other policy in poverty reduction was the elimination of agricultural tax, as announced on 29 December, 2005, by the Chinese government. This policy had been established 2,600 years ago. Before this announcement, the three major taxes in rural areas were: the agricultural tax, a special agricultural tax, and a dairy tax, with the agricultural tax being a major source of revenue for the local government. Elimination of this tax was more symbolic than substantive in addressing the root causes of poverty for Chinese villagers. Other related taxes are a heavier burden than this one, and so should also be reduced.

In addition, the Kanong Project in Luchen Township, Shaanxi Province, aimed at improving access to health care, is a successful model of public-private partnership in addressing social determinants of health and should be scaled up. In this model, the Chinese government implements the policies; while private enterprises provide the management; the communities provide network support; and health care providers offer health services. This project was financed by the An-shen Medical Group, which invested US$150,000 in eighty-eight village health clinics and implemented the reform in two months. Now, all the clinics in Luchen have 'four assets': computers, air-conditioning, refrigerators and telephones; four 'unifications': unified designations, facilities, titles, and filing systems. To ensure its sustainability, the private enterprise company has also built on village land a herbal industry that provides jobs for local villagers. This programme is in the process of being scaled up in another city Jiangxi. It is expected that over four years, the project will cover 60 per cent of health services in Jiangxi, including more than 3,000 health clinics, but the clinics will not be under any obligation to purchase products from the sponsoring company, the An-shen Medical. All the health clinics in the programme will be responsible for the primary care of villagers and collaborate with major hospitals to treat chronic and emergent diseases. The information system established as part of this effort will be crucial to bridge the health data gap between villages and cities (*Sina News*, 2005, 'The hope for China's rural health: the Kanong Project').

Despite these arduous efforts in poverty reduction from all the stakeholders, the challenge for the Chinese society is formidable. The government needs to generate a governance and accountability framework so that the resources are not wasted in the inefficient or corrupted bureaucratic process. It should also ensure these projects are sustainable in the long run by engaging in multi-lateral and multi-sector partnership.

The WTO and China's health care system: opportunities for all stakeholders

As a whole, China's WTO membership has brought new challenges, competition and risks as well as innovative ideas, products and solutions for the stakeholders in China's health care system. In one study by a consumer group on the profit margins of all businesses in China it was estimated that, among all industries surveyed, the health care industry in China today was ranked at the top of the most profitable sector. In some cases, the rate of return for initial investment is 13 times. For example, antibiotics are regarded as the most profit-making item in pharmaceutical industry, with a return rate of 20 times the initial investment. Health care professionals, especially the doctors, charge commission as high as 30 per cent for recommending pharmaceuticals to patients. Another example is medical equipment: a cardiac bridge that sells for US$300 in Hong Kong sells for US$3,000 in China. Food supplements, such as vitamins, also see a profit return as high as 100–200 per cent, usually a result of heavy investment by the advertisers (*World Journal*, 2006, 'Top ten profit-making industries include health care and funerals'). These are both positive and negative signs for China's health care system. On the one hand, they show the high-growth momentum of the Chinese health care industry; but on the other hand, they also illustrate the abnormal profit margins that have contributed to the increasing disparity in access and health outcomes. These issues will continue to be a major challenge to Chinese society. The role of market mechanisms in the WTO framework and the public sector's supervision will play an important part in reducing the negatives and promoting the positives.

Major areas of growth under the WTO framework are:

(i) Pharmaceutical R&D and exports of Chinese traditional medicines. As stated earlier, the size of the Chinese market, the low labour costs, the research talents, and the dynamic resulting from local and multinational collaboration will combine to provide the pharmaceutical producers with enormous competitive advantages in the global context. The internet pharmaceutical trade is also a potentially booming business since China's Food and Drugs Authority (SFDA) has approved a sales permit for the first internet pharmacy, Weita Pharmacy of Beijing, which sells mainly non-prescription drugs. The prices from this internet pharmacy are lower than those of non-internet pharmacies. Beijing's FDA will be involved in monthly surveillance of all drugs sold by the internet pharmacy (*World Journal*, 2006, p. 54. 'The first internet pharmacy opens in China').

(ii) Health care provision, especially hospital care. The fact that the Chinese government has placed improving access and equity of health care at the top of its policy agenda, and its commitment to increase public investment in this area, will offer a wide range of opportunities for health care providers. For multinationals, the primary advantage will be in the entry of high-tech clinical care, such as that used in treating cardiovascular problems and cancer. For local providers, their best positions are in providing affordable care to the vast rural population or other socially excluded populations through a public–private partnership. Partnership with charities and the government to invest in this area is likely provide them with a niche market.

(iii) Training and education of health professionals. The various public health crises, such as in HIV/AIDS, SARS, TB and avian influenza have exposed China's need for trained public health professionals at all levels, especially to serve socially excluded populations. Health care education can also be a niche market for both foreign and domestic stakeholders. For example, medical education in China costs much less than it does in Western countries, and even compared with India it is more affordable. This explains why the Chinese health care education market has attracted increasing attention from overseas students, especially from neighbouring countries, such as India. Similarly, the health care education expertise in industrialized countries, such as Master of Public Health (MPH) education in the USA, can also be transferred easily to Chinese settings. It is a mutually beneficial situation for both domestic and foreign health care institutions as it synergizes experience, skills and future research potential to solve Chinese health care problems. It is also instrumental in producing innovative (and possibly highly useful and profitable) products for both Chinese and global markets. The entry of Harvard University into the health care provision market in China through the building of a modern hospital in Beijing and the training of health care professionals is a good example.

(iv) Biomedical technology. As mentioned earlier, the policy and investment environment for biotechnology in China has given this sector a competitive edge in global markets. The trend of collaboration between domestic and multinational stakeholders augurs well for the future development of cutting-edge, ground-breaking treatments of cancer and other chronic or intractable diseases.

(v) Outsourcing of China's abundant labour for health care. China, like India and Brazil, has, through the prevalence of its mandatory education, trained a well-versed and hardworking workforce. Moreover, the increase in the ageing population, the very high cost of health care labour and a heightened need for caretakers for the elderly and chronically ill in developing countries present Chinese health care workers with a valuable opportunity to export this work force overseas if barriers in the 'health service provision' regulations in the WTO framework can be amended. The recent acute shortage of nurses in Western countries, especially in the USA, will eventually make it necessary to liberalize the health care services in the WTO framework. This will be a good opportunity for Chinese health care labour to expand its market. But China's own domestic needs have to be addressed before it can enter the global health provision market, to avoid a brain-drain problem.

(vi) Infrastructure building in software and hardware (in health care construction) for disease surveillance and monitoring. The size of China's population and the need to upgrade its informatics to monitor the health status and disease profiles of the populations will present tremendous opportunities for multinationals specializing in health-care-related information technology. China's determination to invest in public health surveillance and the monitoring of emergent health issues will give multinationals a major stake in this area, such as in the provision of software and hardware of population/medical informatics, medical facilities, equipment and testing devices, given the fact that, in those areas Chinese domestic health care providers still rely on imports to meet their needs.

(vii) Health insurance services. Health insurance services will present the biggest opportunity for both public and private, and domestic and multinational, stakeholders. The multinationals, mainly from the USA and the EU, or regional leaders, such as those from Hong Kong, Japan, Singapore and Taiwan, are well-positioned to gain major advantages if they present a diverse range of products targeting different segments of the Chinese population, such as rural versus urban residents, or white-collar versus blue-collar urban residents. Chinese domestic insurers can also benefit if they form partnerships with global stakeholders or the government that capitalizes on their familiarity with the local clientele.

China's role in global health care provision

China's role in global health care provision cannot be ignored. This points to China's potential to provide a wide range of health care products and services, including: the provision of low-price generics, low-end medical devices, raw materials, Chinese herbal medicines, holistic treatment (such as acupuncture and physical therapy), clinical trials, biotechnology, research and development expertise, affordable hospital care for foreigners, the export of inexpensive health care professionals for the overseas elderly care market, and affordable medical education for global students. China itself is becoming a manufacturing centre for global health care. Inexpensive labour, policy incentives, abundant R&D talent and the influx of direct investment from overseas investors have all enhanced China's competitive advantages in global markets and place it in a good position to provide creative solutions for the global community. It has been noted widely that Chinese health provision services cost only a fraction of the prices in developed countries. For example, as mentioned earlier, compared to developed countries, organ transplants in China cost only a tenth of the price. Other types of health provision services, including elderly care, cost even less. A large number of elderly people in other Asian countries, such as Japan, have already migrated to China's warmer provinces, such as Kunming City in Yunhan Province to retire.

Globally, health care needs in both developing and developed countries have never been greater. The West consumes most of the world's health care resources. With only 20 per cent of the population, Western countries consumed 50 per cent of all health care resources. This trend is increasing yearly and leads to the need to transport health care skills from developing countries. The brain-drain of health care professionals from developing to developed countries is a serious global problem and is getting worse. For example, in Malawi, there are only two paediatricians in the whole country, but it has been said that there are more Malawi paediatricians in Manchester than in Malawi (*United Daily News*, 2005, 'Twenty per cent of the population consumes half of the health care resources'). In this case, China's abundant labour force may be a possible solution to this problem after the country's domestic needs have been met. This is also true for other developing countries such as Brazil and India. The growth of China's health care capacity can help to relieve problems of inequity in global health care provision in both developing and developed countries. It is obvious that the risks and crises resulting from China's WTO membership have brought about the potential to synergize positive forces among foreign investors, NGOs and intergovernmental agencies. If China can capitalize on this positive momentum, it can play a constructive and active role in global health solutions.

In conclusion, WTO membership has generated a real challenge to China's health care system, but at the same time has produced a wide range of opportunites for all stakeholders and solutions to improve the health of the Chinese population. Within this framework, the disputes, agreements, competition and collaboration are likely to provide a win–win situation for all stakeholders if constructive dialogue and action is brought to fruition. For China, active participation and taking the lead in the WTO's legal, regulatory framework and negotiation processes will increase China's competitive advantages in the new global economic order. For multinationals, their presence has brought new energy, capital, innovative fameworks of operation and management, and alternative solutions for not only the health care system but also the Chinese development agenda. They will inevitably continue to be the driving force for improvement in China's health care system. They will also be instrumental in promoting China's deepening involvement in the global economy within the WTO framework. However, the downside of globalization and the WTO cannot be overlooked. This chapter has provided a detailed analysis of the status of China's compliance with the WTO commitments, sustainable development issues, social and population health issues and challenges, China's social determinants of health, especially those affecting socially excluded populations, infrastructural and capacity building needs, and China's participation in global health provision within the WTO framework.

Looking ahead, the health care of the most populous nation on earth is not a crisis but rather a bright prospect if all parties take advantage of the multiple channels of communication, interaction and action that the WTO framework affords, and tackle the possible negative side-effects, such as increasing inequity and the abuse of labour, head-on. China's WTO membership is the testing ground for all stakeholders in China's health care system in that globalization in health care either brings out the best products and solutions for the health of Chinese society or it generates the worst consequences of an enlarged health gap between the haves and have-nots resulting in vicious cycles for the poor and underprivileged. Failure to address the negatives might result in large-scale social discontent. China's WTO membership provides a litmus test to the current globalization ideology embraced by the major trading nations. The crux of the issue remains: whether the marriage between market mechanisms and public health principles is feasible. If the public sector strengthens its position in investing in the health of the needy and excluded, combined with the private sector's good use of market mechanisms to ensure product excellence and efficiency in health care provision and financing, the Chinese people will be the ultimate winners. They will be the direct beneficiaries of the most positive results of globalization. The challenges discussed in this book will, we hope, invite more reflection on the possibility of producing ingenuous solutions within the WTO framework that benefits all stakeholders in such a way that ultimately enhances the health not only of the Chinese population but also of the global community. That will be the true realization of globalization in the ancient Chinese 'universal' sense: 'The greatest means of solving social problems is to see that our resources are universal and our solutions are universal.'

Bibliography

1. China's Health Care System at a Crossroads in the World Trade Organization Framework

'A shortage of public health professionals in China after SARS' (Kong Kong wei shen Yen Tsai & dwanchiuch), *World Economics Report (Beijing), Sina Finance News* (10 May 2003) (http://finance.sina.com).

'Attention urged to people's health in Western areas', China Internet Information Centre (CIIC) (12 March 2001) (www.china.org.cn/english/2001/Mar/8899.htm).

Beach, M. (2001) 'China's Rural Health Care Gradually Worsens', *Lancet*, vol. 358, no. 9281, p. 567.

Birdsall, N. and Jamison, D. (1983) 'Income and Other Factors Influencing Fertility in China', *Population and Development Review*, vol. 9, no. 4, pp. 651–75.

Blackhurst, R. (1998) 'The Capacity of the WTO to Fulfil its Mandate', in A. O. Krueger (ed.), *The WTO as an International Organization* (Chicago, Ill.: University of Chicago Press), pp. 31–58.

Blumenthal, D. and Hsiao, W. (2005) 'Privatization and its Discontents – the Evolving Chinese Health Care System', *New England Journal of Medicine*, vol. 353, pp. 1165–70.

Chao, J. and Tyson, T. (1997) 'China's New Business Climate Warms Up', *Medical Device and Diagnostic Industry Magazine*, July.

Chen, C. C. (1989) *Medicine in Rural China: A Personal Account* (Berkeley, Calif.: University of California Press).

Cheng, L. K. (1999) 'China's Economic Benefits from WTO Membership', Unpublished manuscript, Department of Economics, Hong Kong University of Science and Technology.

China Population and Information Research Centre (CPIRC) (2001) 'Total Population, CBR, CDR, NIR and TFR of China (1949–2000)' (www.cpirc.org.cn).

'China's life expectancy averages, 71.8 years', *People's Daily* (28 March 2002) (Accessed online at http://english.peopledaily. com.cn/200203/28 /eng20020328_93017.shtml).

Coale, A. J. (1984) *Rapid Population Change in China, 1952–1982* (Washington, DC: National Academy Press).

Columbia Encyclopedia (2001–5) (6th edn).

'Does the Future Belong to China?', *Newsweek*, 9 May 2005, pp. 28–9.

Dong, W. (2001) 'Health Care Reform in Urban China', Working paper 2001/2, Munk Center for International Studies, University of Toronto.

Eaton, J. (2000) 'GATS and Public Health, Part I', *Lancet*, 9 December.

'Fragile public health care system in rural areas,' *Phoenix tv News* (7 November 2003) (www. phoenixtv.com/home/sms/renwu200311/07/143316.html).

'Great leaps of Chinese public health infrastructure in infectious disease reporting', *People's Daily* (15 May 2005), p. 1.

Groombridge, M. and Barfield, C. E. (1999) *Tiger by the tail: China and the world trade organization* (Washington, DC: AEI Press).

Henderson, G., Akin, J., Li, Z., Jin, J., Ma, H. and Ge, K. (1994) 'Equity and the utilization of health services: Report of an eight-province survey in China', *Social Science and Medicine*, 39, 5, September, pp. 687–99.

Hsiao, W. C. L. (1995). 'The Chinese health care system: Lessons for other nations', *Social Science and Medicine*, 41, 8, October, pp. 1047–55.

Huang, Y. (1994) *Health in China* (Zhongguo Weisheng Guoquing) (Shanghai: Shanghai Medical University Press).

IMS World Health Review (2000).

Jackson, J. H. (1998) 'Designing and implementing effective dispute settlement procedures: WTO dispute settlement, appraisal and prospects', in A. O. Krueger (ed.), *The WTO as an International Organization* (Chicago, Ill.: University of Chicago Press), pp. 161–80.

KPMG (19 January 2005) 'Medical device sector presents next big Chinese growth opportunity' (http://www.kpmg.com.cn/en/about/KPMG-News/05 0119_medical Device Sector. html/TopmenuOn=5&NoChinese=1).

Krueger, A. O. (1998) 'Introduction', in A. O. Krueger, *The WTO as an International Organization* (Chicago, Ill.: University of Chicago Press), pp. 1–30.

Leslie, C. (1976) *Asian Medical Systems: A Comparative Study* (Berkeley, Calif.: University of California Press).

Liu, X. Z. and W. C. Hsiao (1995) 'The Cost Escalation of Social Health Insurance Plans in China: Its Implications for Public Policy', *Social Science and Medicine*, 41(8), pp. 1095–101.

Lo, T.-P., Su, F. and Lo, H.-W. 'Public health system in Lai-yang village' (http://run-sniper.blogchina.com/398806.html) (Accessed 20 March 2004).

'Major Progress in Public Health Infrastructure Building and Prevention and Control of Major Diseases', *China Internet Information Centre* (May 11, 2005) (www.china-info.gov.cn/data/200501/1 20050110 101183.html).

'Mobilizing social resources to rebuild health infrastructure', *Sina News* (22 August 2004).

New China Economic Publishing House (1982) *New China's Population* (New York: Macmillan).

OECD (2005) *Economic Survey: China*, vol. 13 (Paris: OECD Publishing), September.

Porkert, M. (1983) *Chinese Medicine as a Scientific System* (New York: Henry Holt and Co.).

Porkert, M. (1983) *The Essentials of Chinese Diagnostics* (Zurich: Medicinae Sinensis).

Representative (2002) 'Report to congress on China's WTO compliance', United States Trade (www.usembassy.it/pdf/China WTO.pdf), p. 3.

Riley, N. E. (2004) 'China's Population: New Trends and Challenges', *Population Bulletin*, June (http://www.findarticles.com/particles/miqa3761/is200406/ai n9455376/pg 1).

Rosenthal, M. M. (1987) *Health Care in the People's Republic of China* (Boulder, Col.: Westview Press).

Siyuan, C. (2002) 'Will Globalization and the WTO Bring Rule of Law to China?', Center for International Private Enterprise, April 19 (www.cipe.org/whats new/events/webevents/cao.htm).

Snape, R. H. (1998) 'Reaching effective agreements covering services', *The WTO as an International Organization* (Chicago, Ill.: University of Chicago), pp. 279–96.

Song, L. (1991) 'Approach to the Reform of the Medical Care System in China', Paper presented at 'Issues and Options on Health Financing in China' Seminar, 27 May–1 June.

'Taiwanese were the brokers in China's organ trade' (Chung kuo chih kwan, tsuan you Taiwan dzong jieh), *World Journal* (2005) p. A-11.

'The first internet pharmacy opens in China' (Ta lu sho jiah wan shang yao tien kai dzan), *World Journal* (29 January 2006), p. 54.

'Three propositions to the government to improve public health infrastructure' *Southern City News* (10 February 2004) (http://www.sina.com./news).

Tu, T.-W. (1980) 'Health Care Services in China's Economic Development', in Robert F. Dernberger (ed.), *China's Development Experience in Comparative Perspective* (Cambridge, Mass.: Harvard University Press).

UNESCAP (2001) 'Infant mortality rates, 1985–1990, 1990–1995, and 1995–2000, and mortality under age 5 years, 1990–1995 and 1995–2000' (www.unescap.org/wid/).

US Department of State (2001) *Country Commercial Guide. Industry Overview: Ethical Drug Manufacturers* (Washington, DC: US State Department).

Vines, D. (1998) 'The WTO in relation to the fund and the Bank: Competencies, agendas, and linkages', *The WTO as an International Organization* (Chicago, Ill: University of Chicago Press), pp. 59–96.

Wachtel, H. (1998) 'Labor's stake in the WTO', *American Prospect*, vol. 37, March.

Wang, F., Ren, P., Shen, A. and Zhan, S. (2001) 'Staying Healthy in Shanghai: Study of Reproductive Health among Female Migrants in Shanghai, China', Paper presented at the Population Association of America's Annual Meeting, Washington, DC, 2001.

Wang, Y.-D. (2005) 'Special attention and reinforcement of China's Public Health Infrastructure', Chinese Social Science Academy, 11 May (http://www.cass.cn/webnew/file/2004072015501 html).

World Bank (1989) *China: Long Term Issues in Options for the Health Sector* (Washington, DC: World Bank).

World Bank (1997) *The World Bank Annual Report 1997* (Washington, DC: World Bank).

World Health Organization (2000) *2000 World Health Report* (Geneva: World Health Organization).

World Bank (2001) *China: Socialist Economic Development. Vol. III: The Social Sectors: Population, Health, Nutrition, and Education* (Washington, DC: World Bank).

World Trade Organization (1995) *International Trade: Trends and Statistics* (Geneva: WTO).

'WTO approved China's accession unanimously' (WTO wu yih yih tung kuo Beijing ru shih) (November 11, 2001), *World Journal*, p. A-1.

WTO (17 September 2001) 'WTO successfully concludes negotiations on China's entry', Press release (http://www.wto.org/english/news_e/pres01_e/pr243_e.htm).

WTO (World Trade Organization) (2006) *2005 World Trade Report* (April).

Yabuki, S. and Harner, S. M. (1999) *China's new political economy* (revd edn) (Boulder, Col.: Westview Press).

Yin, J. Z. (1999) 'The WTO: What next for China?', in A. J. Nathan, Z. Hong, S. R. Smith (eds), *Dilemmas of reform in Jiang Zemin's China* (Boulder, Col.: Lynne, Rienner), pp. 91–106.

Yuen, P. P. (1996) 'Reforming Health Care Financing in Urban China', *International Journal of Public Administration*, 19, pp. 211–32.

Zheng, Zeguang (2005) 'China's development and Sino–US relations', Presentation at Global Interdependence Center's 24th Annual Monetary and Trade Conference, 9 November.

2. The World Trade Organization and China's Health Insurance Sector

ABC News (29 May 2006) from Reuters Dispatch (http://abcnews.go.com/ Business/wireStory?id=2008239).

Ahmad, K. (2000) 'Patients Health Assembly debate effect of globalization on health care', *Lancet*, 356 (9247), p. 2077.

'Be well: 91 per cent of cities don't provide health insurance', *China Online* (26 June 2001).

Blumenthal, D. and Hsiao, W. (2005) 'Privatization and its discontents – the evolving Chinese health care system', *New England Journal of Medicine*, 353, pp. 1165–70.
Business Coalition for US–China Trade (27 June 2001) 'A terrific deal for American Coalition for US–China trade' (http://www.uschina.org/public/wto/part4.html).
China Insurance Almanac (1999) (www.circ.gov.cn).
'China unveils WTO details on opening insurance market', *People's Daily* (23 November 2001) (http://english.people.com.cn/200111/23/eng20011123 85130.shtml).
'China's risk revolution: Mass layoffs boost insurance industry', *Radio Free Asia* (29 May 2006) (http://www.rfa.org/english/news/business/2004/12/20/china insurance).
CIGMA 'Corp. helps set up health insurance test centre in China', *China Online* (26 June 2001) (http://www.chinaonline.com/industry/healthcare/NewsArchive/cs-protected/2000/september/C00090433.asp).
D'Arcy, S. P. and Xia, H. (2005) 'Insurance and China's entry into the WTO' (Urbana-Champaign: University of Illinois).
Economy Watch (2001) 'Economy in China' (http://www.economy watch.com/insurance/china.html).
'Impact on China Sectors after WTO Entry', Institute of Global Communications (19 September 2000) Reuters (www.igc.org/globalpolicy/socecon/bwi-wto/China/impact.htm).
'Industry overview: Pharmaceutical industry in China', US & Foreign Commercial Service and US Department of State, Country Commercial Guide, US Department of State (2006) FY1998–1999 (http://www.corporateinformation.com/cnsector/ Health.html).
'Insurance market to keep WTO promise', *China Daily* (24 May 2005) (http://www.china.org.cn/english/BAT/129805.htm).
Kuttner, R. (1996) 'Columbia/HCA and the resurgence of the for-profit hospital business', *New England Journal of Medicine*, 335 (5), May, pp. 362–67.
National Bureau of Statistics of China (2005) 'Statistical communique of the People's Republic of China on the 2004 National Economic and Social Development', February.
'Proceedings of high-level conference on China's health reform and development strategy', China Ministry of Health (2000), 22–24 July Beijing.
Stocker, K., Waitzkin, H. and Iriart, C. (1999) 'The exportation of managed care to Latin America', *New England Journal of Medicine*, 340 (14), pp. 1131–6.
Swiss Re/Sigma (2001) Cited by David Liu in his presentation to the Conference: 'China after WTO entry: Opportunities and Challenges', Harvard University, May 6.
'The beginning of legislative change', *China Online* (4 August 2001) (http://www.chinaonline.com/issues/wto/NewsArchive/secure/2001/August/C0108 0150.asp).
'US, China conclude WTO negotiations', *China Online* (26 June 2001) (http://www.chinaonline.com/issues/eco news/NewsArchive/secure/2001/June/C01061450.asp).
Wu, D. (2006). 'New market, new regulation and new prospect – The Chinese perspective', Geneva Paper on Risk and Insurance Issues and Practice, vol. 31, no. 1, January, pp. 17–24.
Wu, Y. (1997) 'China's health care sector in transition: resources, demand and reforms', *Health Policy*, 39(2) February, pp. 137–52.

3. The Global Pharmaceutical Industry and China's Position

'A breakthrough discovery to understand stem cells' (Li dze tung tao dzao tau, kang his bao yen diju tu puo), *World Journal* (4 December 2005), p. A-14.

'About 50 per cent of Pekingese prefer to see Chinese medicine practitioners' (Wu tsen Beijing ren ai kan chung yi), *Central Daily News* (28 October 2003) (http://news.sina.com.tw/articles/11/44/25/11442539.html?/china/20031028.htmal).

Agres, T. (2006). 'Foundations for Chinese pharma', *Drug discovery and development report* (Rockaway, NJ: Advantage Business Media).

'An analysis of the biomedicine market in China after WTO' (Ru shih hou hwa shiue dzih yao yeh chien jing fen shih: II), *Chinapharm* (3 December 2001) (http://www.chinapharm.com.cn/html/scfx/2002116113657.html).

'An analysis of chemical raw materials before WTO' (Ru shih hou hwa shiue dzih yao yeh chien jing fen shih: I), *Chinapharm* (2 December 2001) (http://www.chinapharm.com.cn/html/scfx/2002116113610.html).

'An analysis of China's generics market in 2005', (2005 nien wo kuo fan dzih yao yen jiou yu shih tsan fen shih), *Chinapharm* (26 December 2005) (http://www.chinapharm.com.cn/html/scfx/10222620051226.html) .

'Analysis of China's pharmaceutical IPR' (Wo kuo yih yao han yeh dzih shih tsan chuan bao hu hsien dzwan fen shih), *Chinapharm* (5 November 2004) (http://www.chinapharm.com.cn/html/scfx/09305420041105.html).

'An analysis of IPR' (Ban chiuen fen shih: Yih yao can yeh ban chiuen yung yuen deh tsao yan tsan yeh), *Chinapharm* (10 January 2005) (http://www.chinapharm.com.cn/html/scfx/16093420050110.html).

'An analysis of IPR in China' ('Jin nien shan ban nien wo kuo dwan li shen ching jih shou chuan dwan kwan jieh shih'), *Economy Daily News* (2005) (http://www.chinaip.net/news/1.jsp?id=113412441355).

'Analysis of OTC market and products' (2000 nien kuo nei OTC shih tsan leh Hsiao shou ping dzong fen shih), *Sina Net, Chinapharm* (3 May 2001) (http://www.chinapharm.com.cn/html/scfx/20010511180100.htm).

'An analysis of the status of China's domestic OTC market' (Kuo nei fu fen OTC yao ping yih yuen shi yung hsien dzwan tiao yen), *Chinapharm* (8 December 2005) (http://www.chinapharm.com.cn/html/scfx/20001204162706.htm).

'Analysis of strategies and markets for multinationals' (Wai shang jing ru chung kuo shih tsan deh tse lieu jih hwan jing fen shih), *Chinapharm* (21 June 2002) (http://www.chinapharm.com.cn/html/scfx/2002620155939.html).

Anscomb, A. (2004) 'Pharmaceutical outsourcing opportunities, post-contract manufacturing, and sales and marketing', in S. Heffner (ed.), *Kalorama Information Market Intelligence* (Kalorama Information) (Rockville, MD: Kalorama Information LLC).

'A review of the planning of the pharmaceutical sector in the Tenth Five-Year Plan,' (Hwei gu: yih yao han yeh shih wu kwei hwa, I), *Chinapharm* (2 July 2004) (http://www.chinapharm.com.cn/html/scfx/133370620040701).

Asia Pacific Biotech News (2004) vol. 8, no. 12.

Asia Pacific Biotech News (2005) vol. 9, nos 1 and 2.

'A slowdown of mergers in China' (Yih yao han yeh bing go fan hwan) *Chinapharm* (21 February 2005) (http://www.chinapharm.com.cn/html/scfx/09023520050221.html).

'Assessing China's pharmaceutical access in light of WHO reports' (Yih WHO pao kao kan chung kuo hsien dzwan), *Chinapharm* (26 December 2005) (http://www.chinapharm.com.cn/html/scfx/09393220051226.html).

'Because of inexpensive labour, China has become a global manufacturing centre of pharmaceuticals' (Ren kun di lien, ta lu chen chuan chiu tze yao yeh kung tsan), *World Journal* (6 August 2003), 'Local News Section, p. B-1.

Cai, W. S. (2001) 'Discussion of the Basic Principles of Drug Administration Law', *Chinese Pharmaceutical Affairs*, vol. 15, no. 1, p. 30.

Cheng, L. S. (2003) 'The Current Situation and Trend of Development in Chinese Pharmaceutical Trade', *China Pharmaceuticals*, 14(3), pp. 132–3.

'China accuses the US of exaggerating IPR issues' (Mei kuo kuo fen kwa tah chung kuo chih shih tsai tsan bao hu wen ti), *Sina News* (12 April 2006) (http://news.sina.com.tw/articles/13/75/92/13759278.html?/finance/20060412.html).

China Industry Development Report (2003) (http://ww1.cei.gov.cn/ce/e_report/hy/yy.htm).

'China pipeline', *General Biologic* (2004) (http://www.generalgiologic.com).

China State Intellectual Property Rights Office (2005) (http:/www.sipo.gov.cn/sipo_English/gysipo_e/lsyg/t20020305_33887.htm).

'China unveils WTO details on opening insurance market', *People's Daily* (23 November 2001), p. 4.

'China's increasing opportunities after WTO' (Chung kuo jiah ru WTO shih wai kuo chih yen ken dwo jih hwei), *Chinapharm* (25 October 2001) (http://www.chinapharm.com.cn/htmal/scfx/20011024135434.html).

'China's pharmaceutical industry gets major push', China Internet Information Centre (30 April 2002) (www.china.org.cn/english/2002/apr/31451.htm).

'China's pharmaceuticals industry in 2003', *China Industry Development Report* (2003) (www1.cei.gov.cn/ce/e_report/index.htm).

'Chinese herbal medicines for SARS can be used to cure bird flu' (Kan SARS chung yao, keh dzh chin liu kan) *World Journal* (13 November 2005), p. A-11.

'Chinese markets for cardiovascular drugs', AMID Co. (January 2003), p. 235 (http://www.researchandmarkets.com/reportinfo.asp?report_id=29861).

'Chinese pharmaceuticals industry', *Research and Markets* (February 2005) (Access China Management Consulting Ltd. p. 39) (http://www.researchandmarkets.com/reportinfo. asp?report_id=237931).

'Chinese pharmaceuticals industry: strategies, trends, and opportunities', *Research and Markets* (August 2005), Digital Vector, p. 360 (http://www.researchandmarkets.com/reportinfo.asp?report_id=305197).

'Competition for prescriptions in 2006 retail pharmaceuticals' (Er ling ling liu nien yao ping ling sho, tsen dwo tsu fan), *Chinapharm* (2006) (http://www.chinapharm.com.cn/html/scfx/11043520051226.html).

'Development of three ventures in a globalization framework' (Chiuen chiu hwa kwo tsen chung deh chung kuo yih yao shan tse chih yeh fah tsan shing shih fen shih), *Chinapharm* (2002) (http://www.chinapharm.com.cn/html/scfx/ 2002227144844.html).

'Digitalizing the pharmaceuticals sector in China' (Yih yao han yeh de shu dze hw ashen tsuen), *Chinapharm* (14 September 2004) (http://www.chinapharm.com.cn/html/ scfx/11032620040914.html).

'Experts point out that the Chinese pharmaceuticals sector is rapidly increasing its competitiveness' (Dzwan jiah dzih tsu: wu kuo yih yao han yeah jing tsen lin shiuen shu ti gou), *Chinapharm* (2 December 2003) (http://www.chinapharm.com.cn/ html/scfx/2003101953317.html).

'Features of China's current pharmaceuticals market', *China Pharmaceuticals* (2002), 11(10), p. 32.

'Foreign investment shows a hot fever in pharmaceuticals investment' (Kuo hwai dzih ben tsen hsien chih yao reh), *Chinapharm* (10 September 2003) (http://www.chinapharm.com.cn/html/scfx/200399234514.html).

'Foreign pharmaceutical enterprises expand investment', *China Health Sciences* (12 June 2002), Newsletter, vol. 3, no. 13 (http://beijing.lehmanlaw.com/newletter/pharma/20020612.htm).

'Foreign pharmaceuticals enter into retail business in China: much remains to be seen' (Wai tse sheh dzu yao pin fen hsiao, chung kuo yoa chih jin kwan chih bien), *Chinapharm* (6 June 2003) (http://;www.chinapharm.com.cn/htm/scfx/20036663918.html/).

General Biologic (2004) 'China Pipeline 2004' (http://www.generalbiologic.com).

'Generics are likely to account for 70 per cent of domestic market' (Fan dzih yao yu wan dzan jiu wei lai chih tsen shih tsan), *Chinapharm* (18 November 2005) (http://www.chinapharm.com.cn/html/scfx/1032372005 1118.html).

Gerbino, P. (2006) *Commentary on the Global Pharmaceuticals Industry* (Philadelphia; Pa.: University of the Sciences), 17 March.

Gross, A. (1998) 'Regulatory trends in China's pharmaceuticals market', *Pacific Bridge Reports*, December (www.pacificbridgemedical.com).

Guo, Y., Sun, L. H. and Li, C. H. (2003) 'Study of the current drug price management model in China', *China Pharmaceuticals*, 14(2), pp. 68–9.

'Illegal phase III and IV clinical trials have caused many deaths in Dzejian Province' (Fei fah ren ti shih yao, Dzejian dwo ren shih wan), *World Journal* (22 May 2005), p. A-13.

'Issues related to OTC and prescriptions' (Tsai OTC tsan ping heh fei ying lin yao wu shang dzwo wen dzan), *Chinapharm* (13 August 2001) (www.chinapharm.com.cn/html sefx/20010810165157.htm).

Jing, F. J. (21 May 2005) 'Medical Reform Commission initiate another price cut on pharmaceuticals' (Shing fang ang nei wei you bieh ying zhen yih), *Sina News* (http://finance.sina.com.cn).

Kemani, F. and Findlay, G. (2000) 'The Pharmaceutical R&D Compendium', *CMR International* (http://www.cmr.org).

KWA Pharmaceutical (2006) (http://www.healthcare-in-china.com/servicesimported-drugs.htm) (1 January).

'Kwanjou City went after 27 counterfeit drugs' (Kwanjou cha chi er-shi-chih dzong chia yiao, ta dwo biao bang dawn yan jien wei), *World Journal* (11 November 2005), p. A-13.

'Latin America's understanding of China is pragmatic. China is both a competitor and a partner' (La me dwei chung kuo ren shih wu shih, jih shih chu ko shih tsan you shing jing tsen dwei shou), *Sina News Net* (12 April 2006) (http://news.sina.com.tw/articles/13/75/92/13759282.html?/finance/20060412.html).

Lee, Shu-juan, 'Life-killing counterfeited drugs is a global challenge (Wei lieh yao sha ren, chuan chiu mien lien kao yen), *World Journal* (16 September 2005), p. E-8.

'Less than 70 per cent of Chinese herbals passed quality testing, showing disorganized management' (Chung yao zhaun yehn zhih tsan yao tsai heh geh liu bu dzu chih tsan, gwan li hwen ren), *Sina News* (31 July 2003) (http://chinanews.sina.com.tw/market/2003–07–31/291697/shtml).

Liu, Z. L. (2006) 'Two strengths and one worry for Chinese herbal medicine exports' (Chung yao chu ko de liang ta liang tien han yih ta ying hwan), Quoted from *Chinese Management Newspaper*, 18 February (http://news.sina.com.tw/articles/13/61/24/13612449.html?linkchina/).

'Living with counterfeit Viagra' (Yu jia wei geh kun shen), *Sina News* (27 September 2005 (http://news.sina.com.tw/articles/13/23/12/13231202.html?/linkchina/).

'Looking to China and cancer as cost containment slows growth', *IMS Health* (2006) (http://www.imshealth.com/web/content/0,3148,64576068 63872702 70260998 73052844,00.html) (accessed on 6 January 2006).

Louet, S. (2004) 'Can China Bring its Own Pipeline to the Market?', *Nature Biotechnology*, 6 December.

'Mergers combined with increasing capital investment strengthens Novartis's position' (Bing go yu tsen tse bing hsing, nuo hua chian shih jieh ru chung kuo shih tsan), *Chinapharm* (7 March 2005) (http://www.chinapharm.com.cn/html/scfx/10493920050307.html).

'Millions of class I classified drugs flow into the black market' (Jiling yao tsan, bai wan keh mi yao wai liu'), *World Journal* (6 November 2005), p. A-12.

'Miraculous possibilities', *Business India* (10–23 October 2005), p. 92.

Nature News (2004) (www.nature/com/news/2004/ 041206/full/nht1204–1497.html) Norwood, Mass, Biopharm Insight's Investigational Drug intelligence database.

'New cancer drug Endostar is revived in China' (Kan ai shing yao endo, ta lu dzai tsao shang shih), *World Journal* (23 December 2005), p. A-3.

'New cancer drug Endostar is revived in China' (Mei kan ai shing yao, dzai ta lu fu huo', *World Journal* (9 January 2006), p. C-4.

'New measures to reduce pharmaceutical costs starting in June 2005, affecting mainly antibiotics manufacturers' (Shih yi ren yao ping jian jian liu yue chih tung, kun shen shu chih yeh jian shout tson jih), *World Journal* (23 May 2005) (http:/finance.sina.com.cn).

Newsletter BGCG (Burrill Greater China Group) (2005) (second quarter, p. 17).

Newsletter Green Valley Financial Services (2005) (www.agedwards.com/arizona.green-valley.html).

Newsletter Pacific Bridge (2005) (www.pacificbridgemedical.com).

Newsletter Yangzijiang Network (2006) (www.bloon.com).

'Pharmaceutical companies strive for businesses related to health care reform' (Dzih yao jiu tou tsen chien chung kuo kai ge hsin jih), *Chinapharm* (9 December 2003) (http://www.chinapharm.com.cn/html/scfx/200312915322.html).

'Pharmaceutical industry in China, 2004–2005', Okokok Research Centre (2005) (www.okokok.com.cn/abroad/Abroad show.asp?ArticleID=110).

'Pharmaceuticals profits will concentrate in competitive manufacturers' (Yih yao han yeh shen tsan chih yeh li luen jian hsian you shih chih yeh jih chung), *Chinapharm* (12 February 2005) (http://www.chinapharm.com.cn/html/scfx/10291120050204.html).

'Pharmaceuticals regulations mandate that drug stores must remain open 24 hours a day' (Yao ping jing ying kwan lie fah gwei ting: ling shou yao tien shih er-shih-shih hsiau shih yinng yeh), *Sina News* (17 February 2004) (http://news.sina.com.tw/articles/11/72/71/11727188.html?/finance/20040217 2.html).

'Pharmaceuticals are a rising industry' (Ban chiuen fen shih: Yih yao han yeh ban chiuen yung yuen deh tsao yan tsan yeh), *Chinapharm* (10 January 2005) (http://www.chinapharm.com.cn/html/scfx/16093420050110.html).

'Pharmaceuticals sales in China in the framework of the 2004 WHO report: Part II' (Yih WHO pao kao kan chung kuo hsien dzwan II), *Chinapharm* (26 December 2005) (http://www.chinapharm.com.cn/html/scfx/09393220051226.html).

Pollack, A. (2005) 'China Approves a Selective Cancer Drug', *New York Times*, (17 November) (http://www.nytimes.com/2005/11/17/business/17sunway.html).

PriceWaterhouseCoopers (2004) *China: Prescription for Growth.*

'QFII pays attention to the pharmaceuticals sector' (QFII kwan jiu yih yao han yeh), *Chinapharm* (27 December 2002) (http://www.chinapharm.com.cn/ html.scfx/2002122685226.html).

Rui, M. (2001) 'Discussion on the structure and system for the administration of pharmaceutical affairs in China', *Chinese Pharmaceutical Affairs*, 15(1), pp. 28–9.

Santini, L. (2004) 'Companies Look to China for Cheap R&D', *Wall Street Journal*, Eastern edn, vol. 244, issue 101, 22 November.

'Science and Technology in China', Wikipedia (February 2006) (http://en.wikipedia.org/ wiki/Science and technology in China).
'SFDA prohibits the processing of vaccine and blood products' (Kuo jia yao jien chiu gwei ting yih miao bu de jie shou jing wai wei tuo jia kung), *Sina News* (29 November 2005) (http://news.sina.com.tw/articles/13/39/66/13396613.html?/linkchina/).
Shang, C. M. (2001) 'Strengthening the management and supervision of drug advertisements', *Chinese Pharmaceutical Affairs*, 15(5), pp. 294–5.
'60 per cent of China's invention patents awarded to foreigners', *Chinaip* (2006) (www.chinaip.net).
'Suggestions from local and foreign experts for Chinese herbal medicines IPR issues' (Chung wai dawn jian wei chung yi yao dzeh shih tsan chuan bao hu chu mao jih tseh), *Sina News* (27 May 2005) (www.sina.com).
'The derivatives of OTCs: a new competitive factor', *Chinapharm* (10 April 2001) (http://www.chinapharm.com.cn/html/scfx/20010410121959.htm).
'The development of three ventures in China in globalization framework: Series four' (Chieun chiu hwa kwo tsen chung deh chung kuo yih yao shan tse chih yeh fah dzan shing shih fen shih: 4), *Chinapharm* (6 March 2002) (http://www.chinapharm.com.cn/html/scfx/200235104438.html).
'The Importance of Innovative R&D', *Business India* (2005), 10–23 October, p. 98.
'The internal and external environments facing the domestic pharmaceutical industry', Hong Kong Development Council (15 July 2002) Industrial profile (http://www.tdctrade.com/report/indprof/indprof_20703.htm).
'The IPR for Chinese herbal medicine needs to be reinforced' (Chung yao dzih shih tsan chuan bao hu chih tai jiah chian), *China News Net* (4 March 2005) (http://www.pharmtec.org.cn/allpage/newsall/content1.asp?id=1701000064).
'The new trends for China's pharmaceutical economy', Chinese Medicine and Commerce Association (2003) *Pharmaceutical Economic Information*, 16(6), pp. 8–9.
'The Pharmaceutical Market Outlook to 2015: Implementing Innovative, Long-term Strategies for Sustainable Future Growth', *Business Insight* (May 2005), p. 131. (*See also* http://www.researchandmarkets.com/reportinfo.asp?report_id=302088).
'The sale volume of 5,000 local Chinese pharmas is less than that of Pfizer's' (Wu chien jiah yao tsan tsan dzih tih bu kuo yih keh ren hwei), *Central Daily News* (28 April 2006), Quoted from *World Journal*, p. C-4.
'The status, problems and solutions for Chinese herbal medicines IPR' (Chung yao dzih shih tsan chuan bao hu de hsien dwan, wen ti yu dwei tseh), *Chinapharm* (2001) (http://www.chinapharm.com.cn/html/scfx/200112139440.html).
Tufts Center for the Study of Drug Development (2002) 'Outlook 2002' (http://csdd.tufts.edu).
'Twenty-one pharmaceutical association in 21 provinces appealed to the state to lower pharmaceutical prices' (Er-shih-yih shen yih yao hsieh hwei lien ming shan shih, yao chiu jian ti yao ping jian jia fu tu), *Sina News* (2005) B (http:/finances.sina.com.cn/chanjing/b/20050519/01511600484.shtml).
Vasella, D. (2005) Chief Executive of Novartis AG, in 'China's Growing Drug Market: Will You Be a Contender?' (2002, cited from BGCG Newsletter, second quarter, 2005), Burrill Greater China Group, p. 12.
Verret, R. (March, 2006) *Commentary on the Global Pharmaceutical Industry* (Philadelphia Pa.: University of the Science).
Wang, J. (2005) 'The return of the "Sea Turtles": Reverse brain drain to China', *China Daily*, 27 September (http://www.chinadaily.com.cn/english/doc/2005–09/27/content_481163.htm).

Wang, J. (15 July 2002) 'The internal and external environment facing the domestic pharmaceutical industry' (http://www.tdctrade,com/report/indprof/indprof 20703. htm).

'Western Chinese medicine takes up 20 per cent of the Chinese market' (Yan zhou yiao, kung hsai ta lu liang zheh shih zhan', *World Journal* (21 November 2004), p. A-13.

'What Are Intellectual Property Rights?', World Trade Organization (1 May 2005) (http://www.wto.org/english/tratop_e/trips_e/intel1_e.htm).

'Who is in charge of regulating recalled drugs?' (Fei fa hwei shou yao ping, she lai gwan), *Sina News* (24 May 2005) (http:/www.sina.com.cn/o/2005-05-24/05005968631s.shtml).

'WTO hails China deal', BBC News (15 November 1999) (http://news.bbc.co.uk/1/hi/business/the_economy/521857.stm).

'WTO is no disaster for the Chinese pharmaceuticals industry' (WTO bu shih chung kuo dzih yao deh dzai nan), *Chinapharm* (7 November 2001) (http:/www.chinapharm.com.cn/html/scfx/20011107152954.htm).

Zhang W. (2006) Interview with Dr Wei Zhang, Assistant Professor, Beijing University, 20 January.

'Zhen Dzou City Discount Drugs paid $60,000 to recall expired drugs' (Zhen Dzou ping jiah yoa fan chu zhi wu shih wan hwei shou guo chi yao ping chih zhon hsiau hwei), *Sina News* (16 May 2005) (http:/finance.sina.com.cn/roll/20050516/08581589308.shtmal).

Zhen, L.-H. (2003) 'Drug control authorities in China), *The Annals of Pharmacotherapy*, vol. 38, no. 2, 19 December, pp. 346–50 (online publication). (www.theannals.com).

Zheng, X. Y. (2003) 'Facing with the challenge to improve the strategic transfer of China's drug administration model', *China Pharmaceuticals*, vol. 11, no. 3, p. 7.

Zhih, W. and Shao, L. (17 May 2004) 'EU recognizes the legitimacy of Chinese medicine, a positive example for other countries' (Oh men tsen ren chung yao heh fah ti wei, jian dwei chi ta kuo jia chi shih yin Hsiao yin), *Sina News* (http://news.sina.com.tw/articles/11/94/86/11958616.html?/linkchina/20040517.html).

4. The World Trade Organization, and the Present and Future of China's Pharmaceutical Industry

'An Internet survey shows that two-thirds of Chinese children have suffered domestic violence' (Chung kuo wan lu tiao tsa fa hsien yu shan fen dzih er er tung tsen tsao shuo jia bao), *Central Daily News* (6 December 2004).

'Arranged marriage is the new way of finding spouses for village youths' (Bao ban hwen yen, nong tsuen ching nien shing kwei shu), *World Journal* (11 December 2005), p. A-14.

Banister, J. (1992) 'China: Recent Mortality Levels and Trends', Paper prepared for the annual meeting of the Population Association of America, Denver, May.

'Beijing will invest more than 100 billion yuan in the new Eleventh Five-Year Plan' (Beijing shih yih wu chien yih yuen jien sheh shing nong tsun), *Sina News* (23 January 2006) (http://news.sina.com.tw/articles/13/54/62/13546275.html?/linkchina/20060123.html/).

'Boys are preferred in reduced births among villagers' (Nong min shen yu shao, nan hai ren shih bao), *World Journal* (4 May 2005), p. A-14.

Burrill & Co. (2005) Presentation at China Life Sciences Partnership Meeting, 18 June.

'Cancer tops the major causes of death among Chinese residents' (Er shing dzong liu chu chung kuo tsen shih jiu min dzih shih bin yin shou wei), *Sina News* (20 April 2006) (http://news.sina.com.tw/articles/13/78/14/13781488.html?/linkchina/).

CDC Mobility and Mortality report (2006), Chinese Ministry of Health.

Center of Strategic and International Studies (2004) 'Diffusing China's time bomb: sustaining the momentum of China's HIV/AIDS response', B. J. S. Morrisson and D. Thompson (eds) (http://www.csIs.org/media/CSIS/pubs/040 413-china_ aidz.pdf).

Chen, C. C. (1989) *Medicine in rural China: A personal account* (Berkeley, Calif.: University of California Press).

'China is determined to contain avian flu' (Wha shen twen yu bao: chung kuo tsen fu kan ching liu kan jiue shing jien ting), *Sina News* (23 November 2005) (http://news.sina.com.tw/articles/13/38/20/13382087.html?/linkchina/).

'China is on the threshold of an ageing society' (Chung kuo kwa jing lao ling hua sheh hwei), *World Journal* (5 March 2006), pp. 50–2.

China Social Science Institute (2005) Blue Paper on Social and Economic and Conditions of China.

Chinese Insurance Annual Statistics (1999).

'Chinese women choose foreigners as their second husbands'; 'Divorce rate rises fast in China' (Ta lu li hwen lu biao shen, dzai hwen bu tiao hang jiah lan), *World Journal* (5 October 2005), p. A-3.

Coale, A. J. (1984) *Rapid Population Change in China, 1952–1982* (Washington, DC: National Academy Press).

Coale, A. and Banister, J. (1994) 'Five Decades of Missing Females in China', Demography 31, no. 3, 459–86.

Communication with Xu Hua, Secretary General, China AIDS Foundation. 20 December 2005.

Cui, Y., Zhang, Z.-F., Froines, J., Zhao, J., Wang, H., Yu, S.-Z. and Detels, R. (2003) 'Air pollution and case fatality of SARS in the People's Republic of China: An Ecological Study', *Environmental Health*, November (http://www.ehjournal.net/content/ 2/1/15).

Dong, W. (2001) 'Health Care Reform in Urban China', Working paper 2001/2, Munk Center for International Studies, University of Toronto.

'Environmental pollution is serious and 700 million Chinese are drinking dirty water' (Shuei wu yen dzong, chih yih ren heh dzan shuei), *Epoch Times* (11 January 2006), p. A-3.

'Fast urbanization in China leads to cities of 49 million people' (Chung kuo kwai shu tsen tsen hwa, yuh bai wan tsen shih tah shih shi jiou keh), *Sina News* (10 November 2005) (http://news.sina.com.tw/articles/13/34/48/ 13344856.html?/ china/).

'5 per cent of Beijing's diabetics are children' (Beijing tan niao bing hwan dzeh, wu tsen shih er tung), *Ohayo Network* (2005) (http:/www.ohayo.com.tw/ohayo/medical/news_events/n_news_1_xv.asp?id=8873).

'Five specialities in one doctor in China' (Ta lu yih yuan shen shing wu kwan keh), *World Journal* (21 November 2004).

'Fluid labour market challenges the rights protection of labourers' (Lau kung shih tsan liu tung shih jia tah jian tsong jih chung kuo chiuen li jieh go), *Sina News* (17 February 2006) (http://news.sina.com.tw/articles/13/60/92/13609241.html?/linkchina/20060217.html).

'Foreign organisms damage China's ecosystem' (Wai lai shen wu wei shieh chung kuo shen tai an chiun), *Sina News* (21 February 2006) (http://news.sina.com.tw/articles/13/62/08/13620868.html?/china/20060221.html/).

'Forty million people are overweight, a large market for Hong Kong businesses' (Chung kuo shih chien wan ren tsau tsong kang shan fen fen chian tsan pan tah shih shan), *Sina News* (19 January 2006) (http://news.sina.com.tw/articles/13/53/75/13537509.html?/linkchina/).

'Four major challenges in water resources and development' (Chung kuo shue dzih yuen mien lin shih tah wen tih. Shuei li fah dzan ren wu jien jiu), *Sina News* (19 February 2006) (http://news.sina.com.tw/articles/13/61/42/13614290.html?/linkchina/20060219.html/).

'From birds and humans, avian flu spreads' (Tsong niao tao ren you bing), *Sina News* (23 November 2005) (http://news.sina.com.tw/articles/ 13/38/19/13381992.html?/linkchina/).

'Global sex behaviour report' (Chuien chiu shing tiao tsa bao kao), *Sina News* (7 November 2005) (http://eladies.sina.com.cn/z/2005sexreport/index.html).

'Gourmet diet makes Chinese city dwellers lose nutrition balance' (Tsih deh tai hao, tsen shih jiu min yin yian shih tiao), *World Journal* (10 July 2005), p. A-13.

Greenhalgh, S. (1990) 'The Evolution of the One-Child Policy in Shaanxi, 1979–88', *China Quarterly*, vol. 122, June, pp. 191–229.

Greenhalgh, S. and Winckler, E. (2001) *Chinese State Birth Planning in the 1990s and Beyond* (Washington, DC: INS Resource Information Center).

Gu, B. and Roy, K. (1995) 'Sex Ratios at Birth in China, with Reference to Other Areas in East Asia: What We Know', *Asia-Pacific Population Journal*, vol. 10, no. 3, pp. 17–42.

Gu, Baochang and Xu, Yi (1994) 'A Comprehensive Discussion of the Birth Gender Ratio in China', *Chinese Journal of Population Science*, vol. 6, no. 4, pp. 417–31.

'Half of Chinese cities suffer underground water pollution' (Chung kuo yih ban tsen shih ti hsia suei tsao wu ran), *Sina News* (1 December 2005) (http://news.sina.com.tw/articles/13/40/33/13403375.html?/linkchina/).

'Health survey shows bad nutritional status for Chinese children' (Jien kan tiao tsah hsien chung kuo ching shau nien ying yian tzwan kwan chien jieh), *Sina News* (14 April 2006) (http://news.sina.com.tw/articles/13/76/72/13767290.html?/linkchina/).

'High cancer rate village' (Ai dzen kao tsuen: bai shing bu nen tsen shou wu ran dzih tung), *Sina News* (29 April 2005) (http://www.sina.com.cn/).

'HIV/AIDS close to 135,000 cases, with 7,773 deaths' (Ai dzeh bing kan ran dzeh bao kao 13.5 wan ren, shih wan 7,773 li), *Sina News* (29 November 2005) (http://news.sina.com.tw/articles/13/39/70/13397056.html?/linkchina/).

'HIV infected number 1 million and 95 per cent not detected' (Wo kuo ai dseh bing kan ran ku jih you bai wan 95% tsuan ran yuen wei dzao tau), *Sina News* (1 December 2003) (http://news.sina.com.tw/articles/11/53/34/11533410.html?/linkchina/20031201_2.html).

'Homosexual males rank the second high-risk population in HIV transmission' (Nan tung shing lien dzai kan ran ai dzeh bing kao wei hisen ren chiun chung wei chu ti er), *Sina News* (2 December 2005) (http://news.sina.com.tw/articles/13/41/43/13414338.html?/linkchina/).

Hsiao, W. C. L. (1995) 'The Chinese Health Care System: Lessons for Other Nations', *Social Science and Medicine*, vol. 41, no. 8, October, pp. 1047–55.

'Japanese tobacco maker is looking to the Chinese market' (Reh ben jih yuh chung kuo yen tsao shih tsan), *World Journal* (14 August 2005), p. A-11.

Johansson, S. and Nygren, O. (1991) 'The Missing Girls of China: A New Demographic Account), *Population and Development Review*, vol. 17, no. 1, March, pp. 35–51.

Lavely, W. (1986) 'Age Patterns of Chinese Marital Fertility, 1950–1981', Demography, vol. 23, no. 3, pp. 419–34.

Lee, K. C. (2004) 'Aikang Hospital: Multinationals Compete for Health Care Market' (Aikang yih yuan wai dzih chian tan yih liao shih tsan), *World Journal*, 15 February, p. 48.

Lei, G. (2001) 'Reconstituting the Rural–Urban Divide: Peasant Migration and the Rise of Orderly Migration in Contemporary China,' *Journal of Contemporary China*, vol. 10, no. 28, pp. 471–93.

Leslie, C. (1976) *Asian Medical Systems: A Comparative Study* (Berkeley, Calif.: University of California Press).

'Malpractice leads to serious mistakes. Wellness becomes illness' (Kwandzou wu Iian yih yuan tih jien, mei bing bien dzong bing), *World Journal* (7 November 2004), p. A-10.

'Medicine China', Wikipedia (2005) (http://en.wikipedia org/wiki/medicine (China)).

'Medicine: China', Wikipedia (2006) (http://en.wikipedia.org/wiki/Medicine (China)# Number of Hospitals).

Mental health problems on rise', *People's Daily* (22 November 2000) (http://www.china.org.cn/ english/2000/Nov/4312.htm).

'Mine disasters expose problems in state-owned mines', *Sina News* (30 November 2005) (Kwan nan pu lu kuo you ta kwan lo tung).

'More than 14 million will face employment difficulties. Newly graduated will face decreased salaries and benefits' (Wo kuo jing nien yih chien shih bai wan ren jiou nan. Hsing tsen bi yeh shen shih tso hwei jien shau), *Sina News* (14 February 2006) (http://news.sina.com.tw/articles/13/59/82/13598276.html?/ linkchina/).

'Most smokers start smoking by 18; monitoring mechanisms are not complete' (Wu tsen yen min shih bah shuei chien kai shih jieh chu hsian yen, jien du jih dzih bu jien chuan), *Sina News* (2 June 2006) (http://news.sina.com.tw/articles/13/88/47/ 13884735/html?/linkchina/).

Murphy, R. and Li, S. (2005) 'China's health care construction market', Commercial Office, US Consulate General, Guangzhou (www.buyusainfo.Net/docs/x_8008917.pdf).

'Nearly ten tons of sulfite acid caused serious pollution near Shanghai' (Shanghai Putung shih twen liu shuen hsieh lou jing ping fun mi shuei ti wu ran), *Sina News* (6 December 2006) (http://news.sina.com.tw/articles/13/41/84/13418470.html?/ linkchina/20051206.html).

'New law to protect workers' health', *Xinhua News* (13 April 2001) (http://www.china.org.cn/english/2001/Apri/11101.htm).

'94 per cent of oasis has gone' (Shih bei tih chiu Mingching lu jou shao shih, 94% hwan mu hwa), *World Journal* (4 December 2005), p. A-11.

'One-third of children suffer lead poisoning' (Wo kuo shan fen dzih yih er tung hsie chien han liang tsao an chiuen dzih biao), *Sina News* (18 February 2006) (http://news.sina.com.tw/articles/13/61/28/13612883.html?/linkchina/).

'Only 10 per cent have sought help from a doctor for sexual health' (Yu tao shing wen ti kan yih shen dzh bu dzu yih tsen), *World Journal* (23 October 2005), p. A-14.

Parkin, D. M, Bray, F., Ferlay, J. and Pisani, P. (2005) 'Global Cancer Statistics, 2002', *CA: A Cancer Journal Clinicians*, vol. 55, pp. 74–108.

Peng, X. (1989) 'Major Determinants of China's Fertility Transition', *China Quarterly*, vol. 117, March, pp. 1–38.

Peng, X. (1991) *Demographic Transition in China: Fertility Trends since the 1950s* (Oxford: Clarendon Press).

'Physical checkups show that 18 million are excessively overweight' (Jieh kan shih tseh, yi chien ba bai wan tsen nine ren tseh fei), *World Journal* (17 April 2005), p. A-10.

'Pneumonia is number one cause of mortality' (Fei yen shih wan ren shu chiu ti yih), *World Journal* (11 November 2005), p. A-13.

'Presentation at China Life Sciences Partnership Meeting', Burrill & Co. (18 June 2005), Ritz-Carlton Hotel, Philadelphia, PA (www.burrillandco.com/docs/china_access_forums.ppt#85617,slide).

'Psychological health stressed', *China Daily* (26 March 2001) (http://www.china.org.cn/english/2001/Mar/9601/htm).

'Report on the Nutrition and Health Status of the Chinese population', US Center of Disease Control and Prevention (2003).

'Respiratory diseases ranked number one as major cause of mortality for rural villagers' (Hu shih jih bing dzih ming liu dze chung kuo non tsuen pai ming ti yih), *China News* (8 November 2005) quoted from Central Daily News Services (http://news.sina.com.tw/articles/13/33/92/1339228.html?linkchina/20051108.html).

Riley, N. E. (2004) 'China's Population: New Trends and Challenges', *Population Bulletin*, June (http://www.findarticles.com/p/articles/mi_qa3761/is_200406/ai_n9455376/pg_1).

Rosenthal, M. M. (1987) *Health Care in the People's Republic of China: Moving toward Modernization* (Boulder, Col.: Westview Press).

'SARS inflicted nearly 2 billion dollars loss on Beijing Tourism industry', *Xinhua News* (2003) (http://antisars.gianlong.com/8639/2003–6–17/208@902264htm).

'Severe Acute Respiratory Syndrome', *CDC Morbidity and Mortality Report*. Center for Disease Control (2003) (http://www.cdc.gov/mmwr/mguide_sars.html).

'Shanghai plans to control the population at under 9 million' (Hu chung shing tsen ren ko, kung zeh tsai jiu bai wan nei), *World Journal* (11 November 2005), p. C-4.

'Shonghua residents evacuated for fears of pollution' (Fan du hai, Song hua jian bien jiu ming tse li), *World Journal* (25 November 2005), p. A-11.

'Sixteen million Chinese suffer from mental illness', *People's Daily* (8 April 2001) (http://www.china.org.cn/english/2001/Apr/10586.htm).

'Sixty per cent of married males reported as overweight' (Beijing yih hwen nan shing liu tsen ti tsong tsau biao), *World Journal* (12 June 2005) (from Central Daily News Services), p. A-5.

'Spread of porcine flu in Shih Shuan Province' (Buo jih jiou tsen shih), *World Journal* (31 July 2005), p. A-1.

'STDs cases increase by 100 times in eighteen years' (Shing bing hwan shih bah nien tsen yu bai bei), *World Journal* (12 June, 2005), p. A-5.

'The government should improve the public health system. Delegates make three suggestions' (Cheng fu ying kai wan shan kung kung wei shen ti shih, tai biao ti chu shang ta jien yih), Quoted from *Southern City* newspaper, *Sina News* (10 February 2004) (http://www.sina.com.cn/c/2004–02–10/10162818227.shtml).

'The next fifteen years will see major changes in the population structure' (Wei lai shih wu nien, ren ko jieh koh kwan jien chih), *World Journal* (17 July, 2005), p. A-13.

'The quarantined areas in Shih Chuan saw an emergency delivery of vaccines' (Shih Chuan fen shuo yih chu, jing jih dze yue yuen yih miao), p. A-11; 'Spread of porcine flu in Shih Shuan Province' (Buo jih jiou tsen shih), *World Journal* (31 July 2005), p. A-1.

'There should be a buffer between patients and health care providers' (Shing lan shih pin: wei yih hwan kwan shih sheh dzeh yih tao hwan tsong tai), *Sina News* (2 February 2004) (http://news.sina.com.tw/articles/11/73/79/11737916.html?/linkchina/20040220.ht ml).

'Thirty per cent of HIV transmission in China' (Chung kuo ai dzeh bing yih mei nien bai fen shan shing shu du tsen dsan), *Sina News* (29 November 2003) (http://news.sina.com.tw/articles/11/53/16/11531609.html?/china/).

'Three major crises in China' (Wo kuo tan chien sheh whei mien ling shan ta fen hsien), *Sina News* (22 December 2005) (http;//news.sina.com.tw/articles/13/45/89/13458999.html?/linkchina/20051222.html).

'Truth about HIV/AIDS in Shing Tai City of Hebei Province' (Hebei shing tai shih ai tse bing tsen hsian tiao tsa), *Sina News* (30 November 2005) (http://news.sina.com.tw/articles/13/39/99/13399961.html?/linkchina/).

'12 per cent of Chinese male mortality is related to smoking' (Chung jui hsien yu nan shing shih wan dzeh chung bai fen dzeh shih er yu shih yen you kwan), *Sina News* (17 November 2005) (http://news.sina.com.tw/articles/13/36/42/ 13364272.html?/linkchina/20051117.ht ml).

'20 per cent of the population consumes half of the health care resources' (Oh mei ren ko chuan chiu lian tsen, youn tiu ban shu yi hu), *United Daily News*, Quoted from *Sina News* (24 May 2005) (http://news.sina.com.tw/articles/13/01/07/13010745.html?/living/20050524.html).

'20,000 have malignant tumours every year in Beijing', *Sina News* (19 August 2004).

'200 million Chinese suffer iron deficiency' (Lian yih chung kuo ren chiueh tie shing ping shieh), *Ohayo Network* (2006) (http:/www.ohayo.com. tw/ohayo/medical/news_events/n_news_1_xv.asp?id=8873).

'Two-thirds of cities engulfed by garbage' (Shan fen dzih er tsen shih shien ru tsong wei), *World Journal* (15 May 2005), p. A-12.

UNAIDS (2005) *UNAIDS Report, 2005.*

UNESCAP (2003) 'Infant mortality rates, 1985–1990, 1990–1995, and 1995–2000, and Mortality under age 5 years, 1990–1995 and 1995–2000' (Accessed online at www.unescap.org/wid/ 04widresources/01statistic/table2.4.pdf, on July 29, 2003).

'Very toxic chemicals exploded in Jiangshu Province' (Jiang shut u shih hwa kung tsan tswen fan jiu tu wu tsu kwan bao tsa), *Sina News* (2 December 2006) (http://news.sina.com.tw/articles/13/40/63/13406336.html?/linkchina/20051202.html).

'Vice-chair of People's Congress reveals that the Ministry of Health will not allow an increase in pharmaceutical prices' (Rent a fu wei yuan jian tou lou wei shen bu jian jih dze yih yuan yao ping jiah jia), *Sina News* (24 May 2005) (http://www.sina.com.cn).

Wang, M. L. (2006) 'WTO, trade, exclusion and global health inequity', Paper to be presented at the Global Health Society Conference, Rio de Janeiro, Brazil.

Wang, R. (2002) 'Top-ranked businesses target private hospitals' (Ta lu sho fu, liu yung shing miao tsuen ming ying yih yuan), *World Journal*, 24 February, p. 54.

Wang, X. W. and Chen, X. H. (2005) 'Theory and practice of capital operating in hospital financing', Research Publication 410078, Chung Nan University.

'Warnings from David Ho: China is facing three major infectious epidemics' (Ho ta yih jing kao: chung kuo dzan mien ning shan ta bing du wei hsieh), *Sina News* (24 November 2004) (http://news.sina.comtw/articles/12/49/85/12498534.html?/linkchina/20041124.html).

White, T. (1994) 'Two Kinds of Production: The Evolution of China's Family Planning Policy in the 1980s', Population and Development Review, vol. 20, suppl., pp. 137–58.

WHO (2000) *WHO Health Report* (World Health Organization).

World Health Organization (2003), *Country Health Indicator: China* 2003 (Geneva, Switzerland: WHO).

WHO (2004) *World Health Report* (World Health Organization).

WHO (2006) *2005 World Trade Report* (April) (World Trade Organization).

'WHO should be alarmed by the increasing incidence of bird flu' (Shih wei: ching liu kang tsen dwo, ta lu ying jieh bei), *World Journal* (18 November, 2005), p. A-3.

World Bank (1984) *China statistics* (Washington, DC: World Bank).

World Bank (1989) *China: Long-term Issues in Options for the Health Sector* (Washington, DC: World Bank).
Zeng, Y. *et al.* (1993) 'Causes and Implications of the Recent Increase in the Reported Sex Ratio in China', *Population and Development Review*, vol. 19, no. 2, pp. 283–302.
Zhang, W. (2006) Interview with Dr. Weizhang, 'China's hospital systems', Philadelphia.
Zhang, Y. Y. (19 April, 2004) 'Ageing threatens the future of China. Ageing population will be twice that of the young population by 2040' (Lao nien hwa wei hsieh wei lai chung kuo er ling shih ling lao nien ren ko we er tung liang bei), *China Industrial and Business Times*, Quoted from Beijing *Sina Net* (http://news.sina.com.tw/articles/11/88/93/11889301.html?/linkchina/).
Zheng, Zeguang (2005) 'China's Development and Sino–US Relations', Presentation at the Global Interdependence Center's 24th Annual Monetary and Trade Conference, 9 November 2005.

5. The World Trade Organization, Hospital Reform and Health Service Provision in China

China Economic Information Network (2003) *China's Pharmaceutical Industry in 2003*, China Industry Development Report (www1.cei.gov.cn/ce/e_report/hy/yy.htm).
China Population and Information Research Centre (2001) *Total population, CBR, CDR, NIR, and TFR of China (1949–2000)* (www.cpirc.org.cn).
'Competition for prescriptions in 2006 retail pharmaceuticals' (Er ling ling liu nien yao ping ling sho, tsen dwo tsu fan), *Chinapharm* (2006) (http://www.chinapharm.com.cn/html/scfx/11043520051226.html).
'Development of three ventures in a globalization framework' (Chiuen chiu hwa kwo tsen chung deh chung kuo yih yao shan tse chih yeh fah tsan shing shih fen shih), *Chinapharm* (6 March 2002) (http://www.chinapharm.com.cn/html/scfx/2002227144844.html).
'Digitalizing the pharmaceutical sector in China' (Yih yao han yeh de shu dze hw ashen tsuen), *Chinapharm* (14 September 2004) (http://www.chinapharm.com.cn/html/scfx/11032620040914.html).
'Features of China's current pharmaceutical market', *China Pharmaceuticals* (2002) 11(10), p. 32.
'Foreign investment shows fevered in pharmaceutical investment' (Kuo hwai dzih ben tsen hsien chih yao reh', *Chinapharm* (10 September 2003) (http://www.chinapharm.com.cn/html/scfx/200399234514.html).
'Foreign pharmaceuticals enterprises expand investment', *China Health Science News* (2002), Newsletter, vol. 3, no. 13 (http://beijing.lehmanlaw.com/newletter/pharma/20020612.htm).
'Generics are likely to account for 70 per cent of domestic market' (Fan dzih yao yu wan dzan jiu wei lai chih tsen shih tsan), *Chinapharm* (18 November 2005) (http://www.chinapharm.com.cn/html/scfx/10323720051118.html).
Gross, A. (1998) 'Regulatory Trends in China's Pharmaceuticals Market', *Pacific Bridge Reports* (December www.pacificbridgemedical.com).
'Issues related to OTC and prescriptions' (Tsai OTC tsan ping heh fei ying lin yao wu shang dzwo wen dzan), *Chinapharm* (13 August 2001) (www.chinapharm.com.cn/html/sefx/20010810165157.htm).
Jing, Feng Jieh (21 May 2005) 'Medical Reform Commission initiates another price cut on pharmaceuticals' (Shing fang ang nei wei you bieh ying zhen yih), *Sina News* (http://finance.sina.com.cn).

Kemani, F. and Findlay, G. (2000) *The pharmaceutical R&D Compendium*, CMR International (http://www.cmr.org).

KWA Pharmaceuticals Services (2006) (http://www.healthcare-in-china. com/services importeddrugs.htm, accessed January 1, 2006).

Lee, Shu-juan (2006) 'Lethal counterfeited drugs is a global challenge' (Wei lieh yao sha ren, chuan chiu mien lien kao yen), *World Journal* (16 September), p. E-8.

Liu, Z. L. (18 February 2006) 'Two strengths and one worry for Chinese herbal medicine exports' (Chung yao chu ko de liang ta liang ta liang tien han yih ta ying hwan), Quoted from *Chinese Management Newspaper* (http://news.sina.com.tw/articles/13/61/24/13612449.html?/linkchina/).

'New measures to reduce pharmaceutical costs starting in June 2005, affecting mainly antibiotics manufacturers' (Shih yi ren yao ping jian jian liu yue chih tung, kun shen shu chih yeh jian shout tson jih), *World Journal* (23 May 2005) (http:/finance.sina.com.cn).

'Pharmaceutical industry in China, 2004–2005', *Chinapharm* (13 June 2005) (www. okokok.com.cn/abroad/Abroad show.asp?ArticleID=110).

'Pharmaceutical companies strive for businesses related to health care reform' (Dzih yao jiu tou tsen chien chung kuo kai ge hsin jih), *Chinapharm* (9 December 2003) (http:/www.chinapharm.com.cn/html/scfx/200312915322.html).

'Pharmaceutical profit will concentrate in competitive manufacturers' (Yih yao han yeh shen tsan chih yeh li luen jian hsian you shih chih yeh jih chung), *Chinapharm* (12 February 2005) (http://www.chinapharm.com.cn/html/scfx/ 10291120050204. html).

'Pharmaceuticals are a rising industry' (Ban chiuen fen shih: Yih yao han yeh ban chiuen yung yuen deh tsao yan tsan yeh), *Chinapharm* (10 January 2005) (http://www.chinapharm.com.cn/html/scfx/16093420050110.html).

Rui, M. (2001) 'Discussion on the structure and system for the administration of pharmaceutical affairs in China', *Chinese Pharmaceutical Affairs*, 15(1), pp. 28–9.

'The derivatives of OTCs: a new competitive factor', *Sina News* (10 April 2001) (http://www.chinapharm.com.cn/html/scfx/20010410121959.htm).

'The IPR for Chinese herbal medicine needs to be reinforced' (Chung yao dzih shih tsan chuan bao hu chih tai jiah chian), *China News* (4 March 2005) (http://www. pharmtec.org.cn/allpage/newsall/content1.asp?id=1701000064).

'The Importance of Innovative R&D', *Business India* (2005), 10–23 October, p. 98.

'The internal and external environments facing the domestic pharmaceutical industry', *Industrial Profile*, Hong Kong Development Council (15 July 2002) (http://www.tdc-trade.com/report/indprof/indprof 20703.htm).

'The new trends for China's pharmaceutical economy', Chinese Medicine and Commerce Association, *Pharmaceutical Economic Information, China Pharmaceutical Information* (2003), 16 (6), pp. 8–9.

'The pharmaceutical market outlook to 2015: Implementing innovative, long-term strategies for sustainable future growth', *Business India* (May 2005) p. 131 (*See also* http://www.researchandmarkets.com/reportinfo.asp?report_id=302088).

'The status, problems, and solutions for Chinese herbal medicines IPR' (Chung yao dzih shih tsan chuan bao hu de hsien dwan, wen ti yu dwei tseh), *Chinapharm* (2001) (http://www.chinapharm.com.cn/html/scfx/200112139440.html).

Tufts Center for the Study of Drug Development (2002) *Outlook 2002* (http://csdd.tufts.edu).

Wang, J. (2005) *The internal and external environment facing the domestic pharmaceutical industry* (http://www.tdctrade,com/report/indprof/indprof_20703.htm).

Wang, M. L. (2005) 'Social determents of health', Lecture for Globalization and international Class University of the Science in Philadelphia.

'Who is in charge of regulating recalled drugs' (Fei fa hwei shou yao ping, she lai gwan), *Sina News* (24 May 2005) (http:/www.sina.com.cn/o/2005–05–24/05005968631s.shtml).
WTO (World Trade Organization) (2005) 'What are intellectual property rights?' (Accessed 1 May at http://www.wto.org/english/tratop_e/trips_e/intel1_e.htm).
'WTO hails China deal', BBC News (15 November 1999) (http://news.bbc. co.uk/1/hi/business/the_economy/521857.stm).
'WTO is no disaster for Chinese pharmaceutical industry' (WTO bu shih chung kuo dzih yao deh dzai nan), *Chinapharm* (7 November, 2001) (http:/www.chinapharm.com.cn/html/scfx/20011107152954.htm).
Zhang, Wei (20 January 2005) 'Commentary on China's Hospital System' (Philadelphia, Pa.: University of the Sciences).

6. The World Trade Organization, Challenges and Opportunities for China's Health Care System

'A commentary on the implementation of free mandatory education in rural villages' (Ping ren: nong tsuen yih wu jiao yuh deh luo shih shih yao yueh shu), *Sina News* (30 November 2005) (http://news.sina.com.tw/articles/13/39/96/13399668. html?linkchina/20051130.html).
'A Kwandzou discount drug chain traces pharmaceutical history of consumers' (Kwandzou ping jiah yao fan shou twei yao li, ji lu hsiau fei dzeh li zhe yon yoau chin kwan), *Sina News* (9 May 2005) (http://finance.sina.com.cn/chanjing/b/20050509/12141571253.shtml).
'A live lesson in the Harbin Hospital scandal for medical ethics' (Ping ruen: tian jiah yih yao shih jien shih yih ben yih the jiao yu deh hwo jiao tsai), *Sina News* (5 December 2005) (http://news.sina.com.tw/articles/13/41/55/13415576.html?/linkchina/20051205.html).
'A physician was stabbed to death by his patient in Fujou' (Fu jou bao shih yih shen, bei bing ren shih shih tao tung shih), *World Journal* (14 August 2005), p. A-13.
'Appointment scavengers sneak through the loopholes and cannot be stopped' (Hao fan dzih dzwan lo tung, yih yuen dzw bus hen dzwa), *World Journal* (14 August 2005), p. A-13.
'A review of the planning of the pharmaceutical sector in the Tenth Five-Year Plan' (Hwei gu: yih yao han yeh shih wu kwei hua), *Chinapharm* (1 July 2004) (http://www.chinapharm.com.cn/html/scfx/13450520040701.html).
'A scandal in Shih-tsua involves 128 individuals and more than $1 million in bribes' (Shih-tsuan jih kai yih yao go hsiao heh mu: yih er bah ren tse hwei ko jing chien wan), *Sina News* (16 January 2006) (http://news.sina.com.tw/articles/ 13/52/76/13527692.html?/linkchina/).
'According to the State Council's Anti-Poverty Office: The basic needs of the poor will be resolved by 2010' (Kwuo wu yuen fu ping ban: er ling yih ling jieh jiue ping kwen ren ko wen bao wen tih), *Sina News* (23 February 2006) (http://news.sina.com.tw/articles/13/62/81/13628110.html?/linkchina/20060223.html).
'Agricultural tax is eliminated' (Yen shiu lian chien liu bai nien deh nong yeh shuei jian chu Hsió), *Sina News* (30 December 2005) (http://news.sina.com.tw/articles/13/48/21/13482112.html?/linkchina/).
'All food categories have to examined and certified' (Wo kuo jian dwei shuo you shih pin jing shing dzih kian ren tsen), *Sina News* (19 January 2006) (http://news.sina.com.tw/articles/23/53/65/13536541.html?/linkchina/).
'An analysis of IPR' (Ban chiuen fen shih: Yih yao han yeh ban chiuen yung yuen deh tsao yan tsan yeh), *Chinapharm* (10 January 2005) (http://www.chinapharm.com.cn/html/scfx/16093420050110.html).

'An internet survey shows that two-thirds of Chinese children have suffered domestic violence' (Chung kuo wan lu tiao tsa fa hsien yu shan fen dzih er er tung tsen tsao shuo jia bao), *Central Daily News* (6 December 2004).

'Analysis of discount hospitals' (Ping jiah yih yuan), *Sina News* (23 January 2006) (http://news.sina.com.tw/articles/13/54/61/13546119.html?/linkchina/20060123.html/).

'Arranged marriage is the new way to find spouses for village youths' (Bao ban hwen yen, nong tsuen ching nien shing kwei shu), *World Journal* (11 December 2005), p. A-14.

'Beijing Children Hospital is overstretched' (Beijing er tung yih yuan, ren man we hwan), *World Journal* (11 November 2005), p. A-13.

'Beijing residents made 17,653 yuan, a narrower wealth gap in the city' (Beijing chu nien ren chiun sho rut a 17653 yuen, ping fu tsa jiu tung bi shuo hsiao), *Sina News* (8 February 2006) (http://news.sina.com.tw/articles/13/58/06/13580632.html?/linkchina/).

'Beijing will invest more than 100 billion yuan in the new Eleventh Five-Year Plan' (Beijing shih yih wu chien yih yuen jien sheh shing nong tsun), *Sina News* (23 January 2006) (http://news.sina.com.tw/articles/13/54/62/13546275.html?/linkchina/20060123.html).

Bian, Y. (2002) 'Chinese Social Stratification and Social Mobility', *Annual Review of Sociology*, vol. 28, no. 1, pp. 91–117.

Blumenthal, D. and Hsiao, W. (2005) 'Privatization and its discontents – the evolving Chinese health care system', *New England Journal of Medicine*, vol. 353, pp. 1165–70.

'Boys are preferred in reduced births among villagers' (Nong min shen yu shao, nan hai ren shih bao), *World Journal* (4 May 2005), p. A-14.

Brenner, M. (2001) 'Re-examining the Distribution of Wealth in Rural China', in Carl Riskin *et al.* (eds) *China's Retreat From Equality: Income Distribution and Economic Transition* (Armonk, NY: M.E. Sharpe), pp. 245–75.

'Canton engaged in serious attacks against illegal clinics and unlicensed physicians' (Canton yen tah heh tsen shuo, jia yih shen), *World Journal* (22 May 2005), p. A-13.

'Central Disciplinary Committee investigates the 5.5 million yuan medical cost in Harbin' (Chung ji wei jieh ru tiao chah bing ren hwa 550 wan yih yiao feih yiung), *Sina News* (30 November, 2005) (http://news.sina.com.tw/articles/13/39/96/13399669.html?/linkchina/20051140.html).

'Children of the floating population' (Nong ming kung dzh ti, tsen shih hsieh tsen), *World Journal* (6 February 2005), p. C-15.

'China and India have absorbed most FDI' (Chung kuo, lng du tsan hisen shih jing ta fah), *World Journal* (3 December 2005), p. C-3.

'China approved Wang's hospital in Hsiamen' (Hsiamen tsang ken yih yuan, chung kung pi dzuen), *Sina News* (29 May 2005) (http://news.sina.com.tw/articles/13/01/85/13018537.html??china/).

'China implements Nine Action Plans for villagers' (Wo kuo cheng shih chih tung shih shih nong yeh heh nong tsuen jing jih jiou ta shing tung), *Sina News* (29 December 2005) (http://news.sina.com.tw/articles/13/48/14/13481496.html?/linkchina/).

'China intensifies regulations on food safety', *People's Daily* (20 August 2002) English home edition (http://english.people.com.cn/200208/20/eng20020820 101744.shtml).

'China is ageing' (Chung juo lao deh kwei, chien dzih GDP tsen tsang), *World Journal* (16 February 2006), p. C-4.

'China is determined to contain avian influenza' (Wha shen twen yu bao: chung kuo tsen fu kan ching liu kan jiue shing jien ting), *Sina News* (23 November 2006) (http://news.sina.com.tw/articles/13/38/20/13382087.html?/linkchina/).

'China is popular with 5-speciality doctors' (Ta lu yih yuan shen shing wu kwan keh), *World Journal* (21 November 2004), p. 14.

'China issues human organ transplant regulations', *Xinhua News* (27 March 2006) (http://news.xinhuanet.com/english/2006-03/27/content_4352460.htm).

China National Statistics Bureau (March 2006) *2005 Economic and Social Development Statistical Reports in China*.

China Social Sciences Institute (2005) *Blue Paper on Social and Economic Conditions of China*.

China State Department (2005) *Policy Directives and Suggestions from PRC state Department*, (Kuo wu yuan bun kung ting kwan yu fu tse jia chin yeh fat sar ce ro kan yih jien).

'China to ban uncensored health food ads', *Xinhua News* (12 June 2005) (http://news.xinhuanet.com/english/2005-06/12/content 3075083.htm).

'China will become a major economic power' (Chung kuo jiang tsen wei chuien chiu ti shih ta jing jih tih), *World Journal* (14 December 2005), p. C-4.

'China's disease surveillance and monitoring system has made progress' (Chung kuo kung kung wei shen ti shih jien sheh jing tab u, yih ching shing shih wan ro jien chuan), *People's Daily* (15 May 2005) (http://cn.news.yahoo.com/050514/1019/2btn8.html).

'China's economic miracle sacrifices the poor labourers' (Chung kuo jing jih chi jih, lao kung shi shen ta), *World Journal* (10 December 2005), p. A-3.

'China's economic survey shows that 60 per cent are private enterprises' (Chung kuo shou tseh jing jih pu tsa liu tsen chih yeh wei shih ying), *Sina News* (7 December 2005) *Sina Net Beijing* (http://news.sina.com.tw/articles/13/41/88/13418832.html?/linkchina/20051207.html), Quoted from *Economics Daily*.

'China's seven major economic indicators ranked high among developing countries, according to the World Bank' (Shih han: Chung kuo chih tah ju yao fat san jih biao jiu fat san chung kuo jia chien lieh), *Sina News* (30 May 2005) (http://news.sin.com.tw/articles/20050530.html).

'Chinese lack willingness to donate to charities. Compared with Americans, the gap is 7,300 times less' (Tu lu ren jiuen kwan. Yu mei kuo ren tsa chih chien dwo bei), *Sina News* (2005) (http://news.sina.com.tw/articles/13/38/09/ 13380948.html?/linkchina/).

'Chinese villagers in Western provinces are losing their sight' (Kwan ming tsai liu shih, ta lu shih bu nong ming), *World Journal* (21 November 2004), p. 12.

'Chinese villagers' survey exposes the truth about village life' (Chung kuo nong min tiao pih lu nong tsuen tsen shih mien mao), *World Journal* (14 March 2004), p. 44.

'CIO Health information system conference in China, 2003' (Er ling ling shan chung kuo CIO nien hwei yih liao wei shen shing shih fen hua luen tan), *Sina News* (25 November 2003) (http://news.sina.com.tw/ articles/11/51/80/ 11518017.html?/linkchina/20031125.html).

Coale, A. and Banister, J. (1994) 'Five Decades of Missing Females in China', *Demography*, vol. 31, no. 3, pp. 459–86.

'Commentary from Hong Kong: wealth gap is a dangerous social problem' (Kang ping: chun gkuo ping fu chiuen shu wen ti yih ta wei hsien tsen tu), *Sina News* (21 February 2006) (http://news.sina.com.tw/articles/13/61/96/13619631.html?/china/20060221.html).

Communication with Xu Hua, Secretary General, China AIDS Foundation. (20 December 2005).

CPIRC, 'National Family Planning and Reproductive Health Survey, 2001' (Accessed on 24 March 2004 at www.cpirc.org.cn/en/enews20020710-1.htm).

'Diagnosis for the pharmaceutical sector: How to shake off the problem?' (Yih yao han yeh chiuen mien dzan dawn: tsen yan bai tuo han yeh jing ying kwen jing),

Chinapharm (18 August 2003) (http://www.chinapharm.com.cn/html/scfx/200381621440.html).

'Economists predict that China will experience high growth in the next thirty years' (Jing jih shueh jia lin yih fu: Chung kuo jing jih wei lai shan shih nien hsiu kao tsen dzan), *Sina News* (16 December 2003) (http://news.sina.com.tw/articles/11/57/12/11571245.html?/linkchina/).

'Environmental pollution is serious and is threatening the ecosystem in China' (Hwan jing wu ran yen dzong, shen tai sho wei hsieh), *Epoch Times* (28 October 2005), p. A-3.

'Fake milk in Henan' (Henan yeh tsa hsu jian tsuen nai hsing wei), *Sina News* (8 November 2005) (http://news.sina.com.tw/articles/13/33/78/13337836.html?/linkchina/).

'Fluid labour market challenges the rights protection of labourers' (Lau kung shih tsan liu tung shih jia tah jian tsong jih chung kuo chiuen li jieh go), *Sina News* (17 February 2006) (http://news.sina.com.tw/articles/13/60/92/13609241.html?/linkchina/20060217.html/).

'Food security: a commentary' (Shih ping an chuan), *World Journal* (28 January 2006), p. A-11.

'For ten years, the payment for carrying 500 kilos of coal was $.38 in China' (Yun mei chien jing tso lao san yuen, shih nien bu bien), *World Journal* (15 November 2005), p. A-13.

'Forty million people are overweight, a large market for Hong Kong businesses' (Chung kuo shih chien wan ren tsau tsong kang shan fen fen chian tsan pan tah shih shan), *Sina News* (19 January 2006) (http://news.sina.com.tw/articles/13/53/75/ 13537509.html?/linkchina/).

'Four major challenges in water resources and development' (Chung kuo shue dzih yuen mien lin shih tah wen tih. Shuei li fah dzan ren wu jien jiu), *Sina News* (19 February 2006) (http://news.sina.com.tw/articles/13/61/42/13614290.html?/linkchina/20060219.ht ml/).

Friedman, T. (11 November 2005) Commentary on NOW, PBS programme.

'GE increases its investment in China' (GE jia shu jing jiun chung kuo shih tsan), *World Journal* (10 December 2005), p. C-4.

'Global sex behaviour report' (Chuien chiu shing tiao tsa bao kao), *Sina News* (7 November, 2005) (http://eladies.sina.com.cn/z/2005sexreport/index.html).

Greenhalgh, S. (1990) 'The Evolution of the One-Child Policy in Shaanxi, 1979–88', *China Quarterly*, vol. 122, June, pp. 191–229.

Greenhalgh, S. and Winckler, E. (2001) 'Chinese State Birth Planning in the 1990s and Beyond' (Washington, DC: INS Resource Information Center).

'Half of Chinese cities suffer underground water pollution' (Chung kuo yih ban tsen shih ti hsia suei tsao wu ran), *Sina News* (1 December 2005) (http:// news.sina.com.tw/articles/13/40/33/13403375.html?/linkchina/).

'Health care access', *Sina News* (17 May 2003) (http://news.sina.com.tw/newsCenter/china/chinapress/2003/0517/604587.html).

'Health cost monitoring will expand to 50 cities in China' (Yih bao fei yung jien shih tien nien nei yao kwo ta tau shan shih tao wu shih keh tsen shih), *Sina News* (1 August 2003) (http://chinanews.sina.com.tw/market/2003–08–01/293108.shtml).

'Hospital pharmaceuticals are 63 times higher, severely hurting people's interests' (Yi yuan shou jia kao chu yao tien liu shih san bei, jau biau yao ping bai shing li yi ta shuei piao), *Sina News* (15 September 2002) (http://news, sina.com.tw/articles/13/41/49/13414930.html?/linkchina/).

'Hospital reimbursement and market system leads to costly health care after twenty years' reform' (Yih gai er shih nien yen bien: shig tsan hua dzih kan bing kwei, yih yuan but san tsen dzih ku), *Sina News* (8 March 2006) (http://news.sina.com.tw/articles/13/66/15/13661587.html?/linkchina/ 20060308.ht ml/).

Huang, Y. (2005) *Reform as Pandora's Box: China's Public Health Crisis* (Grand Valley State University) (Accessed in July 2005 at www.csis.org/china/020925huang.pdf).

'In Beijing, childbirth cost has increased more than 100 times' (Beijing shen yuh fe yung er shih nien shang dzan bai bei), Quoted from *Central Daily News, Sina News* (2005) (http://news.sina.com.tw/articles/12/49/69/12496973.html?/linkchina/).

'In 2008, rural health care will be completely covered' (Er ling ling bah chiuen mien shih hsing nong tsuen heh dzwo yih liao dzih tu), *Sina News* (9 March 2006) (http://news.sina.com.tw/articles/13/66/48/13664800.html?/linkchina/20060309.html).

'Income has increased for urban residents; consumption fluctuates; and disposable income has increased by 9 per cent' (Jiu ming shu ru tsen zhang, Hsiao fe dzih chu auo tung, shang ban nien jui ming ren jiun keh dzih pei shuo run tung bi tsen dzan 9 ge bai fen dien), *Sina News* (30 July 2003) (http://chinanews.sina.com.Tw/fnews/2003–07–30/290228.shtml).

'Internet users totalled more than 110 million, with more than 690,000 websites' (Wo kuo wan ming tsau kuo yih tien yih yih ren, wan tsan tsao kwo liu shih jiou wan keh), Remarks from the Deputy Director of the National Copyright Bureau, *Sina News* (10 February 2006) (http://news.sina.com.tw/articles/13/60/70/ 13607099.html?/linkchina/).

'Investigation into the financial situation in the Harbin Hospital scandal: unchecked power became bloated' (Ha yih tah erh yuan tsai wu dzwan kwan tiao tsa: chuan li wu jien tu but wan pong dzan), *Sina Net Beijing Sina News* (6 December 2005) (http://news.sina.com.tw/articles/13/41/60/13416043.html).

'It is difficult to see a doctor and it is expensive too' (Nanchang shih min fan ying chian lieh, kan bing nan kan bing kwei) *Sina News* (17 January 2006) (http://news.sina.com.tw/articles/13/53/16/13511641.html?/linkchina/).

Jackson, R. and Howe, N. (2004) *The Graying of the Middle Kingdom* (CSIS and Prudential Foundation) (http://www.csis.org/gai/GrayingKingdom.pdf); (http://www.csis.org/component/option,com_csis_pubs/task,view/id,887/); (tp://www.csis.org/index.php).

'Japanese tobacco maker is looking to the Chinese market.' (Reh ben jih yuh chung kuo yen tsao shih tsan), *World Journal* (14 August 2005), p. A-11.

Jiang, T. (31 March 2006) 'China attemps to slow down economic growth' (Chung kuo shih tu jien man jing jih tsen tsan shut du), *Duowei Times*, p. A-7.

Kennedy, Bruce (1999) 'Serving the People? China's Health Care System May Be Heading for a Crisis', *CNN News* (http://edition.cnn.com/SPECIALS/1999/china.50/dispatches/09.23.health/).

Kynge, J. (21 January 2004) 'China's GDP increased by 9.1 per cent in 2003' (http://news.sina.com.tw/articles/11/66/43/11664378.html?finance/20040121.html).

Lee, R. (10 May 2003) 'Lacking public health professionals in China' (Kung kung wei shan tih shih tu hsien ren tsai twan chue) (http://finance.sina.com.cn/roll/20030510/2218338923.shtml).

'Live man sent to a funeral home to be cremated due to his inability to pay the hospital' (Wu chien fu yih liao feh, hwo ren song bing yih kwan), *World Journal* (19 November 2005).

'Luxurious hospitals ignore the poor' (Hao Hwa kung li yih yuan, bei huh shih ping bing dzeh), *World Journal* (8 August 2005), p. A-13.

'Many problems with China's food safety' (Ta lu shih ping an chuan wen ti dwo), *World Journal* (24 April 2006), p. C-15 (http://news.sina.com.tw/articles/13/39/97/13399.735.html?/linkchina/20051130.html).

'Medical services receive check-up', *China Daily* (13 December 2001) (http://www.china.org.cn/english/23568.htm).
Men, L. (1993) 'Analysis of Social and Economic Factors Affecting Mortality in China', *Chinese Journal of Population Science*, vol. 5, no. 2, pp. 119–32.
'Minister Kao pointed out six reasons for high health care costs' (Wei shen bu dzan kao chien tsen liu ta yuen yin tao dzih kan bing nan), *Sina News* (19 February 2006) (http://news.sina.com.tw/articles/13/61/35/13613545.html?/linkchina/).
'More than 80% of residents believe that medical and pharmaceutical costs are too high' (Tiu cha hsien shih bah tsen shih min ren wei yi liao han yiao ping jiah geh kuo gao), *Sina News* (17 November 2005) (http://news.sina.com.tw/articles/13/36/42/1336/4215.html?/linkchina/20051117.html).
'More than 70 million need emergency aid this spring' (Jih tsun chung kuo you chih chien yu wan ren hsu jiu jih), *Sina News* (14 February 2006) (http://news.sina.com.tw/articles/13/59/97/13599717.html?/linkchina/20060214.html/).
'Most private firms in China exploit workers: government', Media Corp Press (29 December 2005) (http://www.todayonline.com/articles/92542.asp).
'New hospital concept introduced in China's capital', *People's Daily* (21 July 2003).
Overmyer, M. (2006) 'Year Four Status Check', *China Business Review*, vol. 23, no. 1, January–February.
Peng, X. (1989) 'Major Determinants of China's Fertility Transition', *China Quarterly*, vol. 117, March, pp. 1–38.
Pharmaceutical sales in China in the framework of the 2004 WHO report: Part II (Yih WHO pao kao kan chung kuo hsien dzwan II), *Chinapharm* (26 December 2005) (http://www.chinapharm.com.cn/html/scfx/09393220051226.html).
'Physical checkups show that 18 million are excessively overweight' (Jieh kan shih tseh, yi chien ba bai wan tsen nine ren tseh fei), *World Journal* (17 April 2005), p. A-10.
'Pig feed for human tufu' (Tung wan ha shing shan ren, dzu shih liao dzuo tu-fu), *World Journal* (22 May 2005), p. A-13.
'Poor Chinese children engage in illegal, hard labour day and night' (Chung kuo tung kung reh yeh tien tao ku kan hwo), *World Journal* (19 December 2004), p. C-17.
'Poor farmers cannot even afford a pack of cigarettes' (Ping nong ban nien shuo ru, mai bu chih yih tiao yen), *World Journal* (10 March 2006), p. A-14.
'Poor populations increase because of corruption' (Fu ping jih jing tsao lan jieh, ping kwen ren ko hwei shen), *World Journal*, (22 August 2004), p. A-13.
'Poor villager used a saw to cut frostbitten fingers' (Tung shang shih dzeh mei chien yih, yung kang jiu jien dawn), *World Journal* (3 July 2005), p. A-13.
Poston D. L., Jr. and Jia, Z. (1990) 'Socioeconomic Structure and Fertility in China: A County-Level Investigation', *Journal of Biosocial Science*, vol. 22, no. 4, pp. 507–15.
'Public health services barely pass the mark, according to a consulting firm' (Ling tien bau kao: kung dzong wei yih liao fu wu tah fen kang jih ge), *Sina News* (12 April 2006) (http://news.sina.com.tw/articles/13/75/93/13759315.html?/finance/20060412.html).
'Quality of care is uneven for breast enlargement' (Yih yuen lian shiou bu chih, rong ru ping fa tsen dwo), *World Journal* (14 August 2005), p. A-13.
'Report on the Nutrition and Health Status of the Chinese population', Chinese Ministry of Health (2006).
'Retired physician also suffered the slaughter of overpricing by hospitals' (Tuei shiu ren yuan dzih tien shing hwa sheh tsen yih shueh shih jia yeh deh ren yih tsai keh), *Sina News* (7 December 2005).

'Rural villagers wait for death at home because of inaffordability of health care' (Mei chien jiou yih, bah tsen nong min jiah chung ten shih), *World Journal* (7 November 2004), p. A-8.

'SARS inflicted nearly 2 billion dollars loss on Beijing tourism industry', *Xinhua News* (2003) (http://antisars.qianlong.com/8639/2003–6–17/208@902264htm).

'Security officer commited suicide because he could not afford hospital cost' (Bao an ching fei sho tsuan, fu bu chih kwei yao tiao lo), *World Journal* (August 14 2005), p. A-13.

'Severe Acute Respiratory Syndrome', *CDC Morbidity and Mortality Report*, Centre for Disease Control (2003) (http://www.cdc.gov/mmwr/mguide sars.html).

'Shanghai plans to control the population at under 9 million' (Hu chung shing tsen ren ko, kung zeh tsai jiu bai wan nei), *World Journal* (11 November 2005), p. C-4.

'Shangahi will be worth 400 billion yuan by 2010 in total worth of industries' (Er ling yih ling Shanghai tu shih tsan yeh dzong tsan dzih you wan ta tao shih chien yih), *Sina News* (16 January 2006) (http://news.sina.com.tw/articles/13/52/81/13528168.html?/linkchina/).

'Shocking loopholes in Harbin Hospital scandal' (Harbin tian jia yao fei shih jien pu lu yih liao jien tu kwan jin ren lo tung), *Sina News* (8 December 2005) (http://news.sina.com.tw/articles/13/42/20/13422046.html?/linkchina/20051208.html).

'Shonghua residents evacuated for fear of pollution' (Fan du hai, Song hua jian bien jiu ming tse li), *World Journal* (25 November 2005), p. A-11.

'Sixty per cent of married males reported overweight' (Beijing yih hwen nan shing liu tsen ti tsong tsau biao), *World Journal* (12 June 2005) from Central Daily News Services, p. A-5.

Solinger, D. (1999) *Contesting Citizenship in Urban China: Peasant Migrants, the State and the Logic of the Market* (Berkeley, Calif.: University of California Press).

'Spread of porcine flu in Shih Shuan Province' (Dzuwen dzai shih shuan buo jih jiou tsen shih), *World Journal* (31 July 2005), p. A-1.

'STD cases increase by 100 times in eighteen years.' (Shing bing hwan shih bah nien tsen yu bai bei), *World Journal* (12 June 2005), p. A-5.

'Strengthened control over health care by the central government is needed' (Yih liao tai yih lai ti fang dzih yih ching shu buo dwan jian jien yih chung kuo chien hua chung yan kwan li), *Sina News* (17 May 2003) (http://news.sina.com.tw/newsCenter/china/chinapress/2003/0517/604587.html).

'Taiwanese were the brokers in China's organ trade' (Chung kuo chih kwan, tsuan you Taiwan dzong jieh), *World Journal* (2005), p. A-11.

'The first case of a law suit by an HIV infected was closed. The plaintiff lost' (Beijing sho li ai dzih bing hwan dzeh kao yih yuan dzong shen, yuen kao bai shu), *Sina News* (30 December 2005) (http://news.sina.com.tw/articles/13/48/39/ 13483918.html?/linkchina/).

'The first internet pharmacy opens in China', *World Journal Weekly* (29 January 2006) p. 54.

'The government should improve the public health system. Delegates made three suggestions' (Cheng fu ying kai wan shan kung kung wei shen ti shih, tai biao ti chu shang ta jien yih), *Sina News* (10 February 2004) Quoted from *Southern City* newspaper (http://www.sina.com.cn/c/2004–02–10/10162818227.shtml).

'The hope for China's rural health: the Kanong Project' (Kang nong: Chung kuo nong tsuen yih liao deh 'shig wan king tsen), *Sina News* (29 December 2005) (http://news.sina.com.tw/articles/13/48/13/13481386.html?/linkchina/).

'The next fifteen years will see major changes in population structure' (Wei lai shih wu nien, ren ko jieh koh kwan jien chih), *World Journal* (17 July 2005), p. A-13.

'The rural–urban income gap is thirteen times greater for government employees' (Kung wu yuan shu ru tsen hsien tsa shih shan bei), *World Journal* (14 August 2005), p. A-11.

'The two-edged sword of low-cost China-made products' (Jing jih fa dzan deh Shwan ren jien lien jia deh chung kuo dzehdzau), *Sina News* (2 December 2005).

'There remain more than 100 million Chinese that do not have access to any health care' (Chung kuo san tsuen ta lian jian kang ping kwen wen ti jing yih yih ren mei you yih liao fu wu), *Sina News* (9 July 2003) (http://news.sina.tw/newsCenter/china/chinapress/2003/0709/6766188/html).

'Thirty per cent of HIV transmission in China' (Chung kuo ai dzeh bing yih mei nien bai fen shan shing shu du tsen dsan), *Sina News* (29 November 2003) (http://news.sina.com.tw/articles/11/53/16/11531609.html?/china/).

'Three major crises in China' (Wo kuo tan chien sheh whei mien ling shan ta fen hsien), *Sina News* (22 December 2005) (http://news,sina.com.tw/articles/13/45/89/13458999.html?linkchina/20051222.html).

'Top ten profit-making industries include health care and funerals' (Shih tah bao li han yeh, yih yao, bing tsan chiu shou), *World Journal* (8 February 2006), p. C-4.

'Total China–US trade was close to 200 billion US dollars in the first eleven months of 2005' (Chien shih yih yueh, chung mei mao yih jing 2000 yih mei yuan), *World Journal* (11 January 2006), p. D-4.

Tremblay, Jean-François (2005) 'Tempers Flare in China', *Chemical and Engineering News*, 26 September, pp. 21–8.

'Truth about HIV/AIDS in Shing Tai City of Hebei Province' (Hebei shing tai shih ai tse bing tsen hsian tiao tsa), *Sina News* (30 November 2005) (http://news.sina.com.tw/articles/13/39/99/13399961.html?/linkchina/).

'2005 health care reform general analysis' (2005 yih kai ta tung wu yen), *Sina News* (30 December 2005) (http://news.sina.com.tw/articles/13/48/17/13481766.html?/linkchina/20051230.html).

UNDP (2005) *2005 UNDP Human Development Report.*

'Urgent reform is needed behind the hospital cost scandal in Harbing' (Ping ruen: tien jia yau fei bai hou shing yih kai puo tsai mei jieh), *Sina News* (30 November 2005) (http://news.sina.com.tw/articles/13/39/96/13399670.html?/linkchina/ 20051130.html).

Verret, C. R. and Wang, M. L. (2005) 'Strategic Review and Analysis Paper on Social Exclusion and Health Inequity for WHO Commission of Social Determinants of Health' Unpublished paper for World Health Organization, Geneva, Switzerland.

'Wealth gap is a major social issue in China' (Chung juo ping fu hsiuen shu kwo ta tsen wei chu yao sheh hwei tih), *Sina News* (17 January 2006) (http://news.sina.com.tw/articles/13/53/11/13531106.html?/china?).

White, T. (1994) 'Two Kinds of Production: The Evolution of China's Family Planning Policy in the 1980s', *Population and Development Review*, vol. 20, suppl., pp. 137–58.

'Whose miracle? How China's workers are paying the price for its economic boom?', International Confederation of Free Trade Unions (9 December 2005) Report (www.workersvoiceatWTO.org/www/pdf/whosemiracle.ChinaReport.pdf).

World Health Organization (2003) 'Country Health Indicator: China', Statistical Information System (http://www3.who.int/whosis/country/indicators.cfm?country=chn).

World Trade Organization (2006) *2006 WTO Report*, 10 April.
Xu, B., Rimpela, A., Jarvelin, M. R. and Nieminen, M. (1994) 'Sex differences of infant and child mortality in China', *Scandinavian Journal of Social Medicine*, vol. 22, no. 4, December, pp. 242–8.
Yao, S. (1999) 'Economic Growth, Income Inequality, and Poverty in China Under Economic Reforms', *Journal of Development Studies*, vol. 35, no. 6, pp. 104–30.
'Young man abandoned by his father because of his inability to pay the hospital' (Jiao bu tsu yih feh, bing nan tsao fu yih chih yih yuan), *World Journal* (2 October 2005), p. A-13.
Zeng, Y. *et al.* (1993) 'Causes and Implications of the Recent Increase in the Reported Sex Ratio in China', *Population and Development Review*, vol. 19, no. 2, pp. 283–302.

Index

Note: **bold** = extended discussion or heading emphasized in main text.